6.82 Barnes & Noble 9-61 (Swearingen)

STRAFFORD IN IRELAND
1633–41

PLATE I

EARL OF STRAFFORD

from the portrait after Sir Anthony Vandyck
in the National Portrait Gallery, London

STRAFFORD IN IRELAND
1633 - 41

A Study in Absolutism

by

HUGH F. KEARNEY

Lecturer in History in University College, Dublin

MANCHESTER UNIVERSITY PRESS

© 1959
Reprinted 1961
Published by the University of Manchester at
THE UNIVERSITY PRESS
316-324, Oxford Road Manchester 13

To

MY PARENTS

Printed in Great Britain by Butler & Tanner Ltd., Frome and London

'Mind, none of us would feel exactly like this. What saves us is efficiency—the devotion to efficiency. But these chaps were not much account, really. They were no colonists; their administration was merely a squeeze and nothing more, I suspect. They were conquerors and for that you want only brute force. . . . The conquest of the earth, which mostly means the taking it away from those who have a different complexion or slightly flatter nose than ourselves is not a pretty thing when you look into it too much. What redeems it is the idea only. An idea at the back of it; not a sentimental pretence but an idea; and an unselfish belief in the idea—something you can set up and bow down before, and offer a sacrifice to. . . .'

Joseph Conrad,
Heart of Darkness

ACKNOWLEDGEMENTS

My thanks are due to the trustees of the Wentworth Wood-house estate for permission to quote from the Strafford papers. I am also very grateful to the staffs of the various libraries in which I have had occasion to work, especially Sheffield City Library, the National Library of Ireland, the libraries of Trinity College and University College, Dublin and particularly that of the Royal Irish Academy. The National University of Ireland made a very generous grant towards the cost of publishing this book and I wish to express my thanks to the authorities concerned. The President and Governing Body of University College, Dublin also assisted in its publication and I am grateful for their interest. Among those who helped me in various ways, I owe most to John Cooper, District Justice Liam Price, Brian Wormald, William O'Sullivan, Terence Ranger and Gerald Simms. Ann Ó Cléirigh and Gerald Simms very kindly helped me with the proofs. The maps and text figures were drawn by Mrs. Mary Davies. My greatest debt, however, is to my friend and colleague, R. Dudley Edwards, whose advice was given without stint on countless occasions. My friend, Terence Jones, secretary to Manchester University Press, has been very kind, patient and hospitable, not to say efficient.

H. F. KEARNEY

8 October 1958

PREFACE

THE name of Thomas Wentworth, earl of Strafford, is among the best known in modern English history, and the outline of his career is almost as familiar to students as that of his contemporary, Oliver Cromwell. For sheer ability and force of character, as well as a certain ruthlessness, his name may be coupled with Cromwell's, although he has never attracted a biographer of the capacity of Sir Charles Firth. Strafford stood out head and shoulders above the English politicians of the early Stuart period, but paradoxically he spent his most mature years in Ireland, and like Cromwell himself his name is bound up with the history of that country during the seventeenth century. Hence a study of the middle years of Strafford's career will be of necessity something of an excursion into Anglo-Irish history in which the historian attempts to maintain a slippery foothold on both sides of the Irish Sea.

Thomas Wentworth was born in 1593, eldest son of Sir William Wentworth, a leading member of the Yorkshire gentry, and his early career was typical of his fellows in almost every respect. He went up to Cambridge in 1608, he obtained a smattering of law in the Inner Temple, he married the Clifford heiress, he went on the Grand Tour, and in 1614 he was elected to parliament as a knight of the shire. The auguries could hardly have been more excellent.

However, the path to political power proved more difficult for Wentworth than they did for one who was almost the same age, George Villiers, duke of Buckingham. In 1627 his political future was unpromising; he, along with many others, was imprisoned for refusal to pay the Forced loan and he had lost the minor post of Custos Rotulorum for Yorkshire. However, in 1628 events moved more swiftly than he could have foreseen. Charles I was compelled to compromise over the Petition of Right in the agitation for which Wentworth played a leading role, and Buckingham's death in August 1628 created a new set of political circumstances, from which Wentworth was one of those who benefited. Late in 1628 he was appointed to the Presidency of the North, a key post in the administration of the Northern counties of England. Here Wentworth learned the practice of prerogative government of Tudor origins, which he was later to use in Ireland. This was indeed an English copy of the best continental model, arbitrary government in the interests of the monarchy, cutting right through any local opposition. In 1632, he was appointed to the most difficult post in the three kingdoms, the lord deputyship of Ireland, for which he was perhaps of all men the most unsuited. This period of office lasted until 1640. Late in 1640 he was impeached. When this failed a bill of attainder was brought against him and in May 1641, with the consent of a parliamentary majority, he was executed.

The Irish deputyship of Wentworth[1] has attracted far more attention, particularly from English historians, than any comparable period of Irish history before the Act of Union. We are normally asked to regard his period of office as the classical example of English administration in Ireland. At least, it is said, a lord deputy was appointed who was both efficient and incorruptible and who was determined to maintain the highest possible ideal of government, no matter how high the price. His economic policies have been compared by responsible historians like Unwin, Cunningham and Heckscher to those of Colbert and Frederick the Great; and so far as religion is concerned his attempt to restore the revenues of the Church has been described recently as a policy of 'heroic reaction'. Finally, 'nothing in his life became him like the leaving it'. His attainder and execution turned his life into a tragedy in which the Irish episode was the penultimate act before the final peripateia. The heroism with which he met his death made criticism appear ungracious and even petty.

Thus English historians have on the whole been favourable to Strafford's Irish policies; even those who criticised his abandoning the opposition to Buckingham in 1628 are nevertheless to be found to support him where Ireland is concerned. From the very beginning indeed there has existed a tradition of defending Strafford, going back to Edward Hyde, earl of Clarendon, who in his *Short View of the State and Condition of Ireland* (1719) wrote in adulatory terms of Strafford's deputyship.

[1] He became earl of Strafford in 1640, taking the title from the name of the hundred in which Wentworth Woodhouse was situated.

Clarendon rebuked the Irish rebels of 1641 for their part in Strafford's overthrow, in the following terms:

'They have now leisure enough, and I hope spirits better prepared to revolve the wonderful plenty, peace and security they enjoyed till the year 1641, when they wantonly and disdainfully flung those blessings from them; the increase of traffic, the improvement of land, the erection of buildings, and whatsoever else might be profitable and pleasant to a people.' . . . Taxes, tallages and contributions, Clarendon wrote, were things hardly known to them by their names: whatever their land, labour or industry produced was their own; being not only free from the fear of having it taken from them by the king, upon any pretence whatsoever, without their own consent but also secured against thieves and robbers . . . 'And yet', he went on, 'they childishly concurred with the greatest enemies their nation or religion had, in the conspiracy against the life of the earl of Strafford, lord lieutenant of that kingdom, by whose wisdom and government that Kingdom had reaped great advantages.'

To the influence of the greatest English historian of the seventeenth century was added that of one of the greatest of the eighteenth, Thomas Carte, who in his *Life of the Duke of Ormonde* (1735-6) took Strafford's side, as Ormonde himself had done. Four years after Carte's *Ormonde* appeared William Knowler's edition of Strafford's letters (1739). In both of these works a mass of original material was made available relating to Strafford's own version of his period of office. Knowler can be criticised for an occasional distortion and on the grounds of selection, but generally speaking historians have had little to complain of in Knowler's editorship. No other source of equal value existed for the history of the English administration in Ireland during these years. But the almost inevitable result was that Strafford's personal assessment of his deputyship came to be accepted at its face value. It is true that Rushworth's account of Strafford's trial, in which details of the charges against him are given, had been published in 1680, but on the whole the result of the publication of Knowler's two great volumes was that Strafford's case was heard and that of his critics and opponents went by default.

When the main lines of the history of the early Stuart period came to be laid down at the end of the nineteenth century, a further factor came into being which affected historians' view of Strafford —unrest in Ireland. During the Irish Land War, the figure of Strafford and his policy of repression took on a more immediate

significance. Thus we find Samuel Rawson Gardiner writing in
the years before 1884 taking a more favourable attitude towards
Strafford's policy in Ireland than one would have expected from a
Whig historian so critical of despotism in England. Gardiner
wrote[1] that 'the choice for Ireland in the seventeenth century
did not lie between absolutism and parliamentary control, but
between absolutism and anarchy'. He criticised Strafford's methods
of coercion, but his verdict was, on the whole, favourable—'[even]
if [Strafford] be taken at his worst, it is hardly possible to doubt
that Ireland would have been better off, if his sway had been
prolonged for twenty years longer than it was'.

The pendulum of English historical opinion was to swing no
further against Strafford. Gardiner, in fact, represented English
historians at their most critical, and from now on they were to
be increasingly favourable towards him. G. M. Trevelyan, for
example, whose father had been appointed chief secretary for
Ireland immediately after the Phoenix Park murders, came down
strongly on the side of Strafford in the few lines which he devoted
to his administration in *England under the Stuarts* (1904). In this,
he wrote (pp. 188–9):

In Ireland, though Pym never understood it, there was indeed some
use for the policy of 'thorough'. A society so backward and so distrac-
ted could be best ruled as India was afterwards ruled by its English
governors. Wentworth cleared his way through the opposition of self-
seeking officials such as Mountnorris and Loftus, crushing them by
methods akin to those used by Hastings against Nuncomar and Francis.
He saw the impracticability of a free jury system, where the English
never did justice to the natives and where the natives, in terror of their
chieftains' vendettas, would never do justice to each other. He often
made light of the law, where the law was an organised chicanery to
help the powerful in schemes of spoliation. At Council Board and in
Parliament he overrode all opposition by sheer force of his character
and will.

The attitude expressed in *England under the Stuarts* received
support from a remarkable source in 1923, when Hugh O'Grady's
Strafford and Ireland provided chapter and verse for Trevelyan's
generalisations. O'Grady threw himself whole-heartedly into the
defence of Strafford, in a book which is a strange mixture of
confused information, weird prejudice and chronological anarchy.
It nevertheless was accepted as an authoritative treatment of the

[1] *History of England, 1603–42*, viii. 197.

subject, and provided the basis upon which Lady Burghclere (1931) and Miss C. V. Wedgwood (1935) relied for their treatment of the Irish episodes in their lives of Strafford. In her recent volume, *The King's Peace* (1955), Miss Wedgwood showed herself as favourably disposed towards Strafford as she had been twenty years earlier and, using Knowler and O'Grady as her main sources, she has described Strafford's administration in an idealised form.

The paternal monarchy, which Strafford was taken as representing, was also admired elsewhere. R. H. Tawney, in his *Religion and the Rise of Capitalism,* implied that Strafford and Laud stood for a nobler, medieval ideal of society than their capitalistic opponents, while from more right-wing sources, such as Hilaire Belloc or David Mathew, Strafford received equally favourable treatment. Thus from many quarters of the English historical compass, Strafford's record in Ireland was viewed in a favourable light.

There was, however, another standpoint to the whole question. In particular, Irish historians have, on the whole, been critical of Strafford. In Ireland the typical view is that Strafford was despotic, unimaginative and crude in his treatment of the Irish problem. Lecky, for example, who wrote his great *History of Ireland in the Eighteenth Century,* partly as an answer to Froude, referred in it to Wentworth's refusal to grant the 'Graces' in 1634 as 'one of the most shameful passages in the history of the English government of Ireland'.[1] In Lecky's view 'the object of this great and wicked man was to establish a despotism in Ireland as a step towards despotism in England'. The English historian R. Dunlop, who contributed the chapters on modern Irish history to the *Cambridge Modern History,* wrote in 1913[2] that 'in our admiration of his strength of character and of his simple devotion to his sovereign and in pity at his untoward fate we are only too ready to forget that he was really a curse to Ireland ... there was nothing connected with the government of Ireland which he had not the misfortune to bungle. The fact is that he was not only disdainful of advice, but profoundly ignorant of the history of the country he had undertaken to rule.'[3]

[1] Lecky, *History of Ireland in the Eighteenth Century,* i. 31.
[2] R. Dunlop, *Ireland under the Commonwealth,* p. liii.
[3] See also P. Wilson's essay on Strafford in *Studies in Irish History 1603–49,* ed. R. Barry O'Brien.

Though this anti-Strafford tradition had no Clarendon or Carte, its roots were nevertheless well established in contemporary writers. In 1643, for example, a pamphlet was printed at Kilkenny entitled 'A Discourse between two Counsellors of State the one of England and the other of Ireland',[1] in which the Irish counsellor gave a résumé of Irish grievances during the first decades of the seventeenth century, before Strafford's arrival. These injustices of Strafford's predecessors, he said, even if 'all summed up together, would be but a peccadillo compared with the huge masse of oppressions and personal indignities layd upon the Nobility, Gentry and people by that Vizier Bashaw the Earle of Strafford who after the first yeare guided them with a rod of iron'. Strafford's journey into Connacht and his imprisonment of the Galway jury who did not find a title for the king were mentioned in particular as 'done like a Bashaw indeede'. This was a criticism made from the 'old English' side. Similar critical remarks were made by the 'new English' Richard Boyle, earl of Cork, in his Diary.[2]

Such conflicting interpretations are a commonplace of historical writing but once their existence is recognised the historian is no longer free to adopt the simplicity of one point of view alone. So far as Strafford's Irish deputyship is concerned, the historian must attempt to do justice to the attitudes of all the parties concerned, not merely that of the lord deputy. Thus the opening of the Wentworth Woodhouse archives in 1949, which presented a fresh opportunity to reassess Strafford's Irish deputyship, was a mixed blessing. Strafford's own version of events was now available in full, but this increased the temptation to ignore the other side of the picture. The value of the new material in the Strafford Papers is considerable, but since it expresses only the official outlook, it suffers from grave limitations. This study is an attempt to rewrite this episode in Anglo-Irish relations from a point of view which is not official, nor strictly English or Irish. The same historical problems, arising from a clash of sympathies, appear in the history of any colonial administration which attempts to go further than official history. The student of Spanish America, of British India, and of other empires will recognise the difficulties involved. Perhaps there is no answer to them.

[1] B. M. Egerton, MS. 917.
[2] A. B. Grosart (ed.), Lismore Papers, 1st series.

CONTENTS

		page
PREFACE	. . . .	vii
ABBREVIATIONS	. . . . .	xvii
1. ANGLO-IRISH RELATIONS	. . .	1
(i) The Sixteenth-Century Background	. . .	1
(ii) Politics, 1620–30	. . . . .	7
2. THE OLD ENGLISH IN IRELAND	. . .	15
3. THE APPOINTMENT OF WENTWORTH	. .	24
4. THE FINANCIAL BACKGROUND	. . .	32
5. PROLOGUE TO PARLIAMENT	. . . .	42
6. THE PARLIAMENT OF 1634–5	. . . .	45
7. THE POLITICS OF THE 1634 PARLIAMENT	.	53
8. THE INSTRUMENTS OF 'THOROUGH'	. .	69
9. THE PLANTATION OF CONNACHT	. .	85
10. CHURCH AND STATE	. . . .	104
11. WENTWORTH'S ECONOMIC POLICY	. .	130
(i) The Economic Background	. . .	130
(ii) The Irish Wool Trade	. . . .	137
(iii) Irish Linen	. . . . .	154
(iv) The Irish Customs Farm	. . .	159
(v) Summary	. . . . .	168
12. PERSONAL PROFIT	. . . . .	171
13. THE DOWNFALL OF WENTWORTH'S ADMINISTRATION		185
(i) Opposition in Ulster	. . .	185
(ii) Opposition in Parliament	. . .	189
(iii) The Parties in Parliament	. . .	192
14. THE IMPEACHMENT OF WENTWORTH	. .	199
15. AFTERMATH IN IRELAND	. . . .	209

		page
16. CONCLUSION		216
APPENDICES		223
I. The Membership of the 1634 Parliament .		223
II. List of Members of the Parliament of 1640 .		260
III. Commission for Defective Titles 1636		264
BIBLIOGRAPHICAL NOTE		269
BIBLIOGRAPHY		277
INDEX		287

LIST OF FIGURES

1. Fines for Liveries of Land, 1622–41	76
2. Pardons and Licences of Alienation, 1622–41 .	78
3. Exports of wool from Ireland, 1632–40 . .	152
4. Exports of Linen Yarn, 1635–40 . . .	158
5. Irish Customs duties, 1628–41 . . .	160

MAP

Ireland under Strafford, 1633–41 . . . . *end of book*

LIST OF PLATES

I. Earl of Strafford . . . . . *frontispiece*

[*from the portrait after Sir Anthony Vandyck in the National
Portrait Gallery, London*]

II. Cahir Castle, Co. Tipperary . . . *facing p.* 20
Dunsoghly Castle, Co. Dublin

[*Photographs, courtesy Commissioners of Public works, Republic
of Ireland*]

III. Portumna House, Co. Galway . . *facing p.* 48
Carrick-on-Suir, Co. Waterford

[*Photographs, courtesy Commissioners of Public works, Republic
of Ireland*]

IV. The Boyle Monument, St. Patrick's Cathedral,
Dublin . . . . . . *facing p.* 118

[*Photograph, courtesy Bord Failte Eireann*]

ABBREVIATIONS

Bagwell, *Stuarts* = R. Bagwell, *Ireland under the Stuarts* (3 vols., London, 1909–16).

B.M. = British Museum.

Burke, *Peerage* = *Dictionary of the peerage and baronetage*, ed. Sir Bernard Burke, (London, 1878).

Butler, *Confiscation* = W. F. T. Butler, *Confiscation in Irish history* (Dublin, 1917).

Cal. Carew MSS. = *Calendar of the Carew manuscripts preserved in the archiepiscopal library at Lambeth* (London, 1867–73).

Cal. S.P. dom. = *Calendar of State papers, domestic series* (London, 1856).

Cal. S.P. Ire. = *Calendar of the State papers relating to Ireland* (London, 1860–1911).

Cal. rot. pat. Hib. = *Rotulorum patentium et clausorum cancellariae Hiberniae calendarium* (Dublin, 1828).

Civil Survey = *The civil survey, A.D. 1654–6*, ed. R. C. Simington (Irish Manuscripts Commission, Dublin, 1931–54).

Commons jn. = *Journals of the house of commons.*

Commons jn. Ire. = *Journals of the house of commons of the Kingdom of Ireland* (Dublin, 1796–1800).

D.N.B. = *Dictionary of national biography.*

E.H.R. = *English historical review.*

G.E.C., *Peerage*, ed. Gibbs = G. E. Cokayne, *Complete peerage of England, Scotland, Ireland, Great Britain and the United Kingdom* (ed. Vicary Gibbs and others, London, 1910–).

Gilbert, *Ire. confed.* = J. T. Gilbert (ed.), *History of the Irish confederation and the war in Ireland, 1641 9* (7 vols., Dublin, 1882–91).

H.M.C. = Historical Manuscripts Commission.

I.H.S. = *Irish Historical Studies* (Dublin, 1938–).

Liber mun. pub. Hib. = Rowley Lascelles, *Liber munerum publicorum Hiberniae* (2 vols., London, 1852).

Lords' jn. Ire. = *Journals of the house of lords of Ireland* (Dublin, 1779–1800).

Louth Arch. Soc. Jn. = *Journal of the County Louth Archaeological Society* (Dundalk, 1904–).

N.L.I. = National Library of Ireland.

PP. List = *Return of members of parliament, ordered by the house of commons, to be printed. 1878* (part ii. 'Parliaments of Ireland' pp. 603–91).

P.R.O. = Public Record Office of England.

P.R.O.I. = Public Record Office of Ireland.

R.I.A. Proc. = *Proceedings of the Royal Irish Academy* (Dublin, 1836–).

R.S.I.A. Jn. = *Journal of the Royal Society of Antiquaries of Ireland* (Dublin, 1892–).

Rushworth, *Trial* = J. Rushworth, *The trial of Thomas, earl of Strafford* . . . (1680).

Steele, *Tudor & Stuart proclam.* = R. Steele (ed.), *Tudor and Stuart proclamations, 1485–1714* (2 vols., Oxford, 1910).

Strafford's letters = *The earle of Strafforde's letters and dispatches*, ed. W. Knowler (2 vols., 1739).

Strafford MSS. = Strafford manuscripts in Sheffield City Library (Part of the Wentworth Woodhouse collection).

Temple Newsam MSS. = Papers of Sir Arthur Ingram in Leeds City Library.

I

ANGLO-IRISH RELATIONS

(I) THE SIXTEENTH-CENTURY BACKGROUND

THE history of Ireland between the Reformation and the
1641 rebellion is normally interpreted in either religious or
racial terms or, on occasion, as a combination of both. It appears
as an endless series of bloody and bitter struggles between Catholics and Protestants, or between the English government and
'the Irish people'. There is a half truth in this view, but it is by no
means the whole story. For example, until 1641, there was no
one military struggle in Ireland, in which Catholics could not be
found in great numbers on the side of the English administration,
and this despite the deposition of Elizabeth by Pius V in the bull
'Regnans in Excelsis' (1570). It is true that several attempts were
made to invest with a religious aura, rebellions which might have
been justified on other grounds. Thus in 1579, James FitzMaurice
had Papal backing for his landing in Munster. In the same way,
during the Nine Years' War, Hugh O'Neill claimed that he was
fighting in the name of the Catholic Church, and called upon all
Catholics to follow him. But whereas Gregory XIII had supported
FitzMaurice, the anti-Spanish Clement VIII was much more cir-
cumspect in his attitude towards O'Neill, and his caution was
shared by the Catholic towns, the Catholic gentry of the Pale
counties, and such Catholic magnates as Clanrickarde, who fought
with the English administration alongside Protestant Englishmen.

Nor is it historically desirable to emphasise the racial character
of these wars and to describe them in terms of 'Saxon' and 'Celt'.
Men of 'old English' stock were by no means loyal of necessity
to the English Crown, nor were 'Gaelic Irish' lords always rebellious, against a government which could on occasion support
their interests. In 1579 the rising in Munster was led by men of
Anglo-Irish descent. In 1597 Hugh O'Neill's allies in the south

included the Anglo-Irish Butler nobles, Mountgarret and Cahir, and the Anglo-Irish earl of Desmond. In 1601 the Gaelic forces of Thomond and McCarthy Reagh fought on the English side at Kinsale, while elsewhere 'Gaelic Irish' and 'rebel' were by no means synonymous terms. Ireland later split as the wedge of early Stuart English administration was hammered home, but until 1641 the cleavages often followed the lines of traditional rivalries, in which religious and racial differences did not always play the decisive part.

The new factor in sixteenth-century Ireland was the expanding power of the English Crown. Its expansion did not take place however in a homogeneous society but amid an already existing system of alliances and factions. In 1530 the English administration based on Dublin was merely one among a number of centres of political power. It was confined to a comparatively small area around Dublin, and it depended in practice upon the support of the earl of Kildare, whose castle at Maynooth lay less than twenty miles from Dublin. The so-called 'Irish Parliament' drew its representatives from only nine counties and about a dozen towns, and English power declined in direct proportion to the distance from Dublin. Outside the Pale[1], ninety states of varying size enjoyed *de facto* sovereignty. The great palatinates of Ormonde and Desmond were, to all intents and purposes, independent principalities, while farther north the territories of O'Neill, O'Donnell and other Irish chiefs had never been incorporated within the English feudal structure, even at its period of greatest extent, and they maintained the freedom of sovereign states. On a smaller scale indeed, Ireland resembled the Holy Roman Empire with its shifting patterns of states, large and small. This was the situation under the early Tudors, and there was no reason to think it would change.

When change did come, it began with the disruption of the alliance between the Crown and the Geraldine house of Kildare. For one moment, the Geraldines seemed victorious, in 1534, when only Dublin and Waterford remained loyal to the Crown, but the military power of the Tudors prevailed largely as a result of a new weapon, artillery. By 1541, the foundations of a new policy had been laid, based upon alliance with Ormonde, the

---

[1] By 'the Pale' is meant that part of Ireland which accepted English administration, however vaguely.

ancient rival of the FitzGeralds,[1] and upon conciliation of the Gaelic princes. This was Henry VIII's method of 'sober ways, politic drifts and aimiable persuasions', and it was remarkably successful. It involved the alienation of the Geraldines of both Kildare and Desmond, however, and the results of this were to be seen in the Desmond rebellions of the second half of the century. Curiously enough, the Henrician reformation after 1540 did not disturb the government's relations with either Gaelic Irish or Anglo-Irish lords; and the local nobility continued to have the decisive voice in episcopal appointments, as they had always done. The Pope was repudiated by O'Neill, O'Donnell, McCarthy Mor, McCarthy Reagh and many others, and O'Neill's nominee to the bishopric of Clogher was not the only bishop to surrender his papal bulls when his lord renounced the Pope, and to continue his functions under a royal warrant. Monastic houses, however, often remained intact outside the areas of direct English control, despite the measures taken against them by the administration.

This policy of 'indirect rule' was not destined to last. Under Elizabeth, policies of more active centralisation and of more aggressive Protestantism began to move together. Against the background of war with Spain religious orthodoxy became the test of loyalty to the Crown, and of admission into the service of the Crown. It was increasingly unusual for a Catholic, even of English descent, to be allowed to enter the administration during the second half of the century, even though the Crown was dependent upon Catholic support in time of rebellion and war. But still the links of the towns and the Pale with the Crown proved stronger than were religious differences, and were even strengthened in the 1590's when the traditional enemies of the Pale, O'Neill and O'Donnell, joined forces against the Crown. The Ulster chiefs found their first experience of direct English control too strong for their liking, when in 1594 MacMahon's 'country', adjacent to their own, became a shire, open to the command of royal writs, which were enforceable by a Dublin-appointed sheriff; and the threat of losing their independence united the petty states of the north in a war which culminated at Kinsale in 1601. But though O'Neill attempted to make it into a war of religion, the

---

[1] Ormonde and the FitzGeralds of Desmond and Kildare who had taken opposite sides during the wars of the Roses continued their political rivalries into the 1560's.

Pale resisted the call. In 1600, Sir Edward FitzHarris, who was later to play his part in constitutional opposition to the lord deputy under the early Stuarts, made clear the outlook of the Pale in a colloquy with O'Neill's chaplain, Fr. James Archer. Archer demanded the restoration of Catholicism and of forfeited estates. FitzHarris then asked what would become of the old English, to whom Archer belonged by race. Archer's answer was that the old English were too strong to be dislodged by the Irish; besides, the conquest was many centuries old. FitzHarris then declared that he was loyal for these very reasons, and had no wish to see Tyrone as chief over the whole kingdom. Earlier, in 1599, the Anglo-Irish earl of Delvin informed O'Neill that 'all the inhabitants of the English Pale for the most part, and especially myself, are Catholics and were so when he was not thought to be one'. He maintained that O'Neill had no justification for rebellion against 'their anointed Christian prince'. In this exchange of opinions lay the crux of the matter—whether or not loyalty was still possible to a Protestant Crown, or still desirable when so many accepted liberties were being removed by an advancing and efficient, though often corrupt, administration.

The Pale chose to co-operate with the Crown. O'Neill and O'Donnell preferred armed resistance against an administration which they did not trust and there was indeed much to be said for their lack of confidence, in an era when the holding of administrative office offered so much opportunity for abuse, and perquisites and bribery were accepted as part of normal routine. Even so, their resort to arms was by no means inevitable. In 1596 the requests which O'Neill made from Elizabeth were for a free pardon, liberty of conscience for the inhabitants of Tyrone, and that no garrison or sheriff, except his own, be placed in Tyrone. It is clear from this that O'Neill was prepared to tolerate the *status quo* provided the administration proceeded no further in its advance. The requests of his ally, O'Donnell, were phrased in similar terms. It was only after these negotiations had broken down and O'Neill had achieved some military success that the war began to spread. O'Donnell's raids into North Connacht exposed the weakness of the administration in that area, and in 1598, O'Neill rubbed home the lesson with his victory at the Yellow Ford, the high-water mark of his military success. By 1602 the tide had turned; he was abandoned by one of his allies,

O'Cahan, and his northern flank was threatened by the English fleet. Spanish aid had provided the only hope but when it came it was almost too late and the outcome of the pitched battle fought at Kinsale by O'Neill and O'Donnell after a forced march of several hundred miles was disastrous. The war dragged on for two more years but in the end O'Neill was compelled to make the best terms he could. By 1603, Ulster was open to English administration for the first time in its history.

O'Neill found the transition from independence to vassalage too sudden and too drastic. The introduction of sheriffs and circuits of assize, the maintenance of garrisons at strategic points, the abolition of Irish land law in favour of English common law and the introduction of the State church, all emphasised the fact that the old order had suffered almost complete defeat. The personal ties which bound the Irish septs to their ruler were declared in 1605 to have no place in English law and the customs of tanistry and gavelkind suffered a similar fate in 1606-8. The final stage came in 1607 when O'Neill and O'Donnell took ship for Spain. This decision to escape seems to have taken the English administration by surprise but it was soon made the excuse for confiscation on a wide scale. By 1608, most of the land in the six counties of Donegal, Coleraine, Tyrone, Armagh, Fermanagh and Cavan had been declared forfeit to the Crown and the way was fully open for the entry of Scottish and English settlers. Geography favoured the Scots, who had already established themselves in parts of Antrim and Down and it was they, together with French emigrants from the Scottish lowlands, who took advantage of the opportunity.

In some ways the plantation of Ulster was a failure, particularly in the areas which were allotted to English undertakers. The rebellion of 1641 showed that thirty years of immigration had not completely destroyed the capacity of the Ulster Irish to wage a sustained military campaign. Nevertheless, though reservations must be made, the plantation in Ulster was too solidly established to be overthrown; a permanent problem was thus created. It was otherwise with the plantations made in other parts of Ireland which proved to be largely ephemeral growths. Only in Ulster did immigration take place on a scale which rivalled that to the New World, and for this reason it is difficult to exaggerate the importance of the plantation in seventeenth-century Ireland.

The results of the Flight of the Earls and of the Ulster plantation were fully reflected in the Irish parliament of 1613-15.
For the first time, Protestant members enjoyed a majority in the
house of commons, and though this was a gross distortion of the
relative strength of the two religions, it was nevertheless a sound
indication of the shift of political and administrative control which
had taken place since the last parliament was held in 1585. For
the first time all the counties were represented, but the increased
representation largely benefited the Protestants who in a house of
232 members enjoyed a majority of 32.

The course of this parliament showed that despite its new
accession of strength, the English administration was not to have
things all its own way. The lord deputy was forced to modify
drastically the legislative programme which he had prepared, in
the face of strong Catholic opposition. It was noticeable, however, that though any extension of the penal laws was fiercely
opposed, there was no opposition to the bills of attainder against
O'Neill and O'Donnell. The Catholic old English of the Pale were
still unwilling to regard the Ulster Irish as allies in a common
cause.

During the next twenty years Ireland continued to be a country
without unity. Political and economic factors intermingled with
religious factors in maintaining a permanent state of imbalance.
The clash of Reformation and Counter-Reformation, unrest in
Ulster, the plantation of other areas outside Ulster, the uncertainty
about land titles, together with the reaction against the expanding
administration, all helped to create instability. The only source of
unity in a country which had never been united came from the
external force of the English administration. It so happened,
however, that at almost the precise moment when centralised
government became possible, further causes of disunity, namely
religion and the confiscation of land, combined to make the task
more difficult than it had ever been. The moment produced a
great administrator in the person of Thomas Wentworth, but
it was almost in the nature of the case that administrative unity
should have to be imposed by force. There may have been another
choice open, but on the face of it force seemed the obvious
solution to a man of Wentworth's temperament. The term he
used to describe his policy in his correspondence with Laud was
'thorough', which implied driving 'through' or 'thorough' those

interests which lay in the way of fiscal, religious or administrative unity. It was in its essentials a policy of force, in which political concession and negotiation were regarded as signs of weakness. From a more general point of view, Wentworth was attempting to deal with problems which confronted all contemporary governments in their dealings with colonies. On the one hand they attempted to retain complete freedom of action, on the other they had to come to terms with the colonists themselves. Usually some kind of compromise was arrived at. In Wentworth's case, however, the English privy council was aiming at the restoration of complete freedom of action. This implied the removal of all the financial limitations which had hitherto curtailed the political power of the lord deputy. Complete freedom also implied an unwillingness to come to any understanding with existing bodies of opinion. A fresh departure was to be made by which policy decided in Whitehall was no longer to be modified by the facts of the situation in Ireland. As Wentworth himself put it in 1637, the King was to be 'as absolute here as any Prince in the whole world can be'.

Wentworth came to Ireland fresh from success as president of the Council of the North. There, his energetic and forthright methods of administration had achieved remarkable success and there was good reason to think that they would be not unsuccessful elsewhere. On the other hand it could be said that success in the limited field of northern England might prove a dangerous guide amid the complexities of Ireland. A country so divided could not be simply classified, as Laud and Wentworth tended to do, in terms of vested interests which it was their duty to destroy. In the short run it seemed possible that the policy of 'thorough' backed by the ability of a Wentworth might succeed, at any rate on the surface. In the long run, however, the odds were against it.

(II) POLITICS 1620–30

A description of Anglo-Irish politics in this period must take into account three main reservoirs of political power, the connections between each of them and the changing levels which occurred within them from time to time. These three were the English privy council, in particular its committee for Irish affairs;

the 'new English' administration in Ireland, in effect, the Irish privy council; and lastly the old English aristocracy, gentry and merchants who made their political influence felt through unofficial channels except on the rare occasions when a Parliament—as in 1613, 1634 or 1640—or a Great Council—as in 1627—was sitting.

Ireland in the early seventeenth century was not a self-contained political unit. The political initiative to a large extent lay across the channel with the particular group which happened to be in power within the English privy council. Decisions which had far-reaching consequences for Ireland, as well as ones less momentous, were taken at the English court, not at Dublin castle. Appointments to office in Ireland frequently depended upon the amount of influence which could be brought to bear in England; thus, for example, Sir Edward Villiers owed his appointment as lord president of Munster to his all-powerful half-brother, the Duke of Buckingham. High officials of the Irish administration found that they could maintain their position only by keeping in constant touch with the internal politics of the English privy council. Boyle, Loftus, Mountnorris and many another found to their cost that standing still in Dublin could involve running hard in Whitehall. The power exercised by the English privy council caused a constant shuttling to take place between the two countries, an activity pursued as much as anyone by the old English who sent agents to preach their cause at the English court as the occasion demanded—the agents who went over to negotiate the Graces late in 1627 were neither the first nor the last. Finally it followed that political changes within the English privy council could have direct repercussions in Ireland. To take one example, the appointment of Thomas Wentworth as lord deputy, which would have been most unlikely under Buckingham, became possible under Weston, the Duke's successor as chief minister to the king.

Despite this dependence upon England, however, Anglo-Irish politics were not English politics; they had their own peculiar flavour. The political game in Ireland was played until 1632 between two main groups—the new English planter class, well established in Ulster and in the administration, which covered the whole of Ireland for the first time, and the old English excluded in practice from the administration, but still in possession of the richest land in Ireland. (Gaelic Ireland, and especially Ulster, which had played such a large part in the politics of Ireland during the sixteenth century had ceased to count as a political force within the constitutional framework of the early seventeenth century, while the Ulster Scots had not yet begun to make their influence felt and looked to Scotland for political and religious leadership.) These political groups were divided, by religion, by tradition, and by material interests. Nevertheless, divisions within the new English group, that is, within the Irish privy council, could lead to situations in which Protestant new English would co-operate with Catholic old English if political advantage could be gained. Politics were not therefore in fact as simple as might be assumed *a priori*. In theory, Richard Boyle, earl of Cork, and Francis Annesley, lord Mountnorris, were closer to one another than to the Catholic old English peer, Richard Nugent, earl of Westmeath. In practice, however, each of them was capable of co-operating with him, if the political game seemed to require it. And vice versa, the old English were also used to this particular political gambit which they played for the last time in 1640, before circumstances finally, in 1641, forced them to throw in their lot with Gaelic Irish.

The new English were divided over the perquisites of power, but agreed about the foundations on which that power was based. It was difficult to imagine a situation in which they might feel that their interests were being attacked by the English privy council, since they were essentially the English interest in Ireland. It was they who ran the administration on general lines suggested from England. Many of them had been members of Elizabeth's armies in Ireland and looked upon the plantations in Ulster and elsewhere as the legitimate reward for their military endeavours. Most of them shared a common religious attitude, which was particularly hostile towards the Church of Rome, though this did not preclude friendships with individual members of the Catholic gentry. A policy of further plantation, and a stricter attitude towards the recusant majority were unquestioned by most of the new English and they were only held back by the changed attitude of the English privy council. To them the obvious solution for the financial difficulties of the administration lay in the collection of recusancy fines, and they could not understand why on grounds of foreign policy such a course might seem undesirable in England. Their emphasis upon religious differences was due essentially to the realisation that only in this way could they hope to maintain their grip upon the machinery of government. Their political future depended upon the failure to find an oath of allegiance acceptable to the Catholics.

Thus the new English formed a vested interest, which felt all the more insecure because it was only a generation old. Firmly entrenched in the Irish privy council in which no Catholic sat, they formed a strong barrier between the English privy council and the execution of any policy of which they did not approve. Such an attitude was not unique to Ireland. It was, and is, to be found in many colonial societies in which a newly established planter class has established itself by force of arms and has acquired land by widespread confiscation. The counterparts of the new English were to be found in many parts of the new and old worlds; in Ireland, however, the conquerors had to deal with a society in many respects similar to their own. This did not necessarily make for easier relations nor was it obviously the case that a more efficient, more legally advanced and more powerful society was more civilised than that which it replaced. What is surprising is that with such basic agreement on fundamental issues, there still should have existed violent political differences within the ranks of the new English.

Broadly speaking, in 1629, just before Falkland was recalled, there were two main political groupings within the Irish privy council. The first group, which co-operated with the lord deputy and hence enjoyed the benefits of the patronage which co-operation carried with it, was headed by Richard Boyle, earl of Cork, a man of great business ability.[1] Born in Kent in 1566, Boyle had made his way to Ireland in 1588 like many another with the hope of acquiring cheap land. In 1590 he became deputy-escheator and by 1595, after the use of dubious methods, he had become the proprietor of a large estate. To this he added in 1603 the Irish lands of Sir Walter Raleigh. By 1629 he enjoyed an income from rents alone of £20,000 a year. With him were associated a powerful group of officials. Sir William Parsons, nephew of Sir Geoffrey Fenton, who had been Boyle's patron, was master of the court of wards and liveries. Sir Charles Coote, who had fought at Kinsale

---

[1] Cf. T. O. Ranger, 'Richard Boyle and the making of an Irish fortune' in *I.H.S.*, x, 257-97 (Mar. 1957).

in 1601, was a planter in Cavan, vice-president of Connacht and a business associate of Boyle's. Roger Jones, Viscount Ranelagh, joint lord president of Connacht, was son of a former archbishop of Dublin and, perhaps more important, a son-in law of Richard Boyle. Richard Bolton, attorney of the court of wards and Sir Henry Docwra, treasurer at war and a planter in Ulster were also members of Boyle's group. Towards the end of Falkland's deputy-ship this group of new English, all of whom with the exception of Ranelagh had been born in England, were in power. Boyle's personal position, however, was none too secure and he had been forced to pay a protracted visit to England in order to defend himself and his estates against a series of attacks.

Within the Irish privy council, an opposition group had formed, of which the most prominent members were Adam Loftus,[1] Charles Wilmot and Francis Annesley, viscount Mountnorris. Loftus, first viscount Loftus of Ely, was nephew of Adam Loftus, archbishop of Dublin and Armagh (d. 1605), and in 1619 had been created lord chancellor of Ireland. Like many other officials he had acquired land in the various plantations and his essential interests were the same as Boyle's. Why there should have been antagonism between them it is difficult to say but there is no doubt that it existed. Wilmot had fought under Mountjoy, had been a member of the Irish privy council since 1607, and became president of Connacht in 1616. The third member of the triumvirate, Mountnorris, was also the youngest. He also had become a planter in Ulster and from 1618 to 1625 had been principal secretary of state for Ireland. In 1625 he was appointed vice-treasurer over the head of Ranelagh. These formed the nucleus of an opposition to the lord deputy. Loftus's relations were very bitter with both Falkland[2] and Richard Boyle,[3] and he had managed to keep his office of lord chancellor only with great difficulty.[4] At one period he had been forced to go to England in order to defend himself;[5] and his return to Ireland, unscathed, in August 1628 may be regarded as a defeat for the lord deputy's party.

---

[1] Not to be confused with Sir Adam Loftus of Rathfarnham who became vice-treasurer in 1636 as a nominee of Wentworth.

[2] *Cal. S.P. Ire., 1615–25*, p. 532.

[3] Ibid., *1625–32*, p. 223.

[4] Ibid., *1625–32*, pp. 121–2.

[5] In June 1627. *Lismore Papers*, ed. A. B. Grosart (1886), ii. 219. He returned in Aug. 1628. *Cal. S.P. Ire., 1625–32*, p. 373.

Loftus had been accused by them of supporting the lords of the pale in their opposition to the lord deputy during the financial negotiations of 1627, with how much truth it is difficult to say.[1]

The second member of the trio, Charles Wilmot, was appointed commander-in-chief in Ireland in August 1629, a sign that the star of the deputy's party was already on the wane. It was not surprising that he should have been found in the opposition camp to Falkland and Boyle since he had for years been under attack by a member of Boyle's party, Sir Charles Coote, who accused him of maladministration in Athlone.[2] The lord deputy himself expressed his resentment against both Wilmot and Annesley in March 1629.[3] Wilmot's behaviour, after Falkland's recall, fits clearly into the pattern of the opposition group. In June 1630, at a time when Falkland was doing his best to recover lost ground in England by bringing charges against Mountnorris and Sir Arthur Savage, Wilmot wrote to secretary Dorchester in their defence, claiming that they were the victims of Falkland's unjustified assaults.[4] At the same time, when Boyle's party in Ireland was co-operating with Falkland in this attack upon Mountnorris, Wilmot arrived at the Irish privy council in Mountnorris's company and defended him in a vigorous speech.[5]

Clearly, however, the key figure in the politics of the Irish privy council during the years before Wentworth's arrival, if we may judge by the attacks upon him, was Mountnorris himself. As vice-treasurer, he controlled the financial administration, and since he owed his post to the influence of Buckingham, he had been in a much stronger position *vis-à-vis* Falkland than had Loftus. Falkland might dislike him, but to criticise him implied criticism of his own patron. As late as May 1627, Mountnorris was still sure of the Duke's support even against Falkland. The following letter written by Buckingham on Mountnorris's behalf brings this out.[6]

---

[1] *Cal. S.P. Ire., 1625–32*, p. 241. The 'lords of the pale' were the leaders of the gentry of Co. Dublin, Co. Meath and other counties in which 'old English' stock predominated. See Appendix I.

[2] Ibid., *1615–25*, p. 436.

[3] Ibid., *1625–32*, p. 443.

[4] Ibid., *1625–32*, p. 545.

[5] Docwra's memorial touching lord Mountnorris 31 July 1630 (Boyle Letter book, Chatsworth MSS., f. 160). I am indebted to Mr. T. O. Ranger for drawing my attention to this document.

[6] B. M., Add. MS. 44919 N.

My lord,

I find there have been some mistakings betwixt your lordship and Sir Francis Annesley which I am desirous to reconcile for I would have my friends love one another. I have known him long and have observed his abilities and industry in his Majesty's service for which my late gratious Master and his Majesty that now is have taken special notice of him and have [shown] evident marks of their favour towards him as to their well deserving servant. I have also noted his sincere faithfullness in his particular professions unto those whom he had been obliged . . . and to myself he hath given such real testimonies of his gratitude and faithfulness for the courtesies I have done him that . . . I doe esteem him my thankfull and assured friend. With that valuation I recommend him to your lordships favour, praying you to receive him with good affection and the rather because I doe assure you he hath carried himself here fairely towards you and I know he is desirous to deserve your love and good opinion which I earnestly pray your lordship to afford unto him in such measure as he may not finde my recommendation unprofitable but that I may have cause to thanke you for your kindeness toward him whereof not doubting I rest.

Your lordships faithfull frend and servant
Buckingham

Annesley's elevation to the peerage in 1628 as lord Mountnorris fits into this general picture.[1]

The unexpected death of Buckingham, however, in August 1628 opened the door to fresh political developments both in England and Ireland and the wind began to blow hard against some of the Duke's former clients. Before a year had elapsed, Falkland knew that he was to be recalled.[2] On the other hand his political ally, Richard Boyle, who was in England at the time, made his peace with lord treasurer Weston at the cost of a loan of £15,000 and returned to Ireland as lord justice. Associated with him in office was Loftus, his former opponent.

During the years 1630 and 1631 the political situation was extremely confused. Falkland had returned to England but had not given up hopes of retaining the lord deputyship. He pinned a good deal of hope to a counter-attack against Mountnorris and others whom he claimed had slandered him.[3] Falkland's friends in Dublin, led by Boyle, came to his assistance by making charges

---

[1] D.N.B.

[2] The excuse for this was his mishandling of the plantation of the O'Byrne territory in Ranelagh, Co. Wicklow. Mountnorris used this as an opportunity to counter-attack.

[3] S. R. Gardiner, *Reports of cases in the courts of Star Chamber and High Commission*, Camden Soc. (1886), p. 1 ff.

of financial maladministration against Mountnorris, who in November 1630 was ordered to come to England to face a committee of enquiry,[1] consisting of Vane, Wentworth, Coke and Cottington.[2] During the whole of this period Falkland was in constant touch by letter with Cork, Parsons and especially Ranelagh.[3]

The threads were tangled but the ultimate object was clear enough. The prize for victory was political power under the next lord deputy. If Mountnorris were ruined, the future lay with Boyle's party. And early in 1631, it looked as if this might come about.

The links between Loftus, Wilmot and Mountnorris still, however, remained strong. Loftus co-operated with Boyle so far as official business was concerned, but otherwise drew no closer. In February 1631/2 Loftus wrote to the English privy council and specifically mentioned Ranelagh as his chief enemy;[4] and while this remained true, there was no possibility of political alliance between the two lords justices. Thus when Mountnorris took ship for England in February 1630/1, and his political prospects were at their bleakest, he was seen off at the seaside by his associates, Loftus and Wilmot.[5] A new year's party at which Mountnorris was present, had been held at Mellifont, the seat of Garret Moore, another member of the Irish privy council. The guests included the earl of Westmeath. As events later turned out, this may have been of political significance.[6]

Mountnorris's departure was a moment of some importance. If Falkland, Boyle and Ranelagh were successful in discrediting him, the next lord deputy might well have no choice but to carry on the same political alliance as his predecessor. So long as Falkland's successor had not been appointed, however, the future was very obscure.

---

[1] Acts of the privy council (P.R.O., PC 2/40, f. 194).
[2] Ibid., f. 488.
[3] Falkland Letter book *passim*. (P.R.O.I., MS. 2445 ff. 1a, 36, 37).
[4] *Cal. S.P. Ire., 1625–32*, p. 646. Cf. also Acts, privy council (P.R.O. PC 2/41, f. 453).
[5] Richard Boyle to Sir William Beecher, 13 Feb. 1630/1 (Boyle Letter book, Chatsworth MSS., f. 262).
[6] Richard Boyle to Sir William Beecher, 11 Jan. 1630/1 (ibid., f. 226).

2

THE OLD ENGLISH IN IRELAND

THE position of the old English in the years before the arrival of the new lord deputy now remains to be described. It provides a sharp contrast with that of the new English, whose links were largely with England and whose differences among themselves, though important to the immediate political situation, largely anticipate the narrowness of the next century, when personalities and the fight for office set the pattern for much of the political life of Ireland. By comparison, the old English—and the Gaelic Irish—belonged to a different world, a wider one, that of the Thirty Years War and the later phases of the Counter-Reformation. This was to emerge most clearly in the period after 1641, the years which saw the negotiations of the Confederation of Kilkenny with the Papacy, and the arrival of Archbishop Rinuccini; but the facts were already there in 1628. The filling of the see of Armagh in 1625, for example, engaged the rivalries of old English and Gaelic Irish, but it was not a merely domestic issue. It involved high politics at Rome, in which France and Spain were involved and a conflict between various religious orders.[1]

The term 'old English' is used throughout this book as a convenient shorthand to describe the political attitude of those who accepted the link of Ireland with the English crown and relied upon constitutional methods for the remedy of grievances. Most prominent of the old English was the acknowledged leader of the Connacht gentry, Richard de Burgh, earl of Clanrickarde, most of whose time was spent at the English court. With him were associated the 'lords of the Pale', Richard Nugent, earl of Westmeath, Luke Plunkett, earl of Fingal, and Nicholas Preston, Lord Gormanston. All three were prominent landowners with large estates north of Dublin and they were associated by blood or marriage with most of the gentry of Meath, Louth, and the adjacent areas. Farther south in Kilkenny, the Catholic

[1] B. Jennings (ed.), *Wadding Papers*, pp. 120–79.

leaders were junior members of the Butler family, Lords Cahir and Mountgarret. In Cork, David Roche, Viscount Fermoy, and Charles MacCarthy, Viscount Muskerry, and in Limerick, Sir Edward FitzHarris played the most active part in politics. Unfortunately, however, the historical evidence relating to these old English leaders is so scanty that we know nothing of the political differences which must have existed between them; the personality of Richard Boyle is much more of a reality than his counterpart among the Catholics. As time went on, certain changes did take place among the old English but their precise significance is elusive. Clanrickarde and Fermoy died in 1635; Fingall died in 1637 and Westmeath seems to have taken little part in politics after 1635–6. The initiative went to younger men who were less content than their elders with the existing state of affairs. For them the threat from Ulster was only a memory; the Dublin administration was the real danger.

The use of racial terms in political contexts is apt to be misleading. This is particularly true of Irish history at this date and the term old English must not be used to exclude completely those who were of Gaelic Irish stock. In the early seventeenth century it was as much a political label as anything else and this is the way in which it has been used throughout this book. The earl of Westmeath, for example, was of old English stock and his political attitude was based upon the belief that the king of England was also king of Ireland. He may be described as the spokesman for the old English when he went over to England in 1632 to negotiate concerning the Graces, and yet nearly half of those who supported him bore Gaelic Irish names, suggesting that Catholics who still enjoyed political power in the 1620's and 1630's were not exclusively old English by descent. On the other hand while it is true that most of those who were affected by the plantations were Gaelic Irish, the Franciscan Luke Wadding was of old English descent and his political sympathies were with Spain and the Ulster Irish. The terms old English and Gaelic Irish are too convenient to be thrown aside but they cannot be taken too literally. They represent two different political attitudes rather than two different racial strains. The axis of the old English groups was London–Dublin. The axis of the Gaelic Irish rested on Madrid and the Spanish Netherlands with the constant hope that the plantations would be overthrown.

The old English, however, also had links with the continent. One son might be studying at one of the Inns of Court in London while another was a member of the Irish college at Douai. The same families of the Pale who agitated in Chichester's parliament (1613–15) and Falkland's Great Council (1626–7) provided many of the members of the Capuchin mission to Ireland, which itself was established by a Palesman, Father Francis Nugent. Thus the old English, while conscious of their ties with England, were in constant touch with Counter-Reformation Europe and this link acted as a political yeast, preventing them from degeneration into an opposition of merely insular significance. The Catholic families of the Pale could hardly fail to be aware of horizons broader than those of a Boyle or a Loftus and their religious connections provided an unpredictable element in Irish politics during the first half of the seventeenth century.

Religious persecution, however, took place only spasmodically, and was not in itself sufficient to explain the peculiar problem which faced the old English. Religion in fact was closely associated with more mundane considerations. There was a glaring discrepancy between the economic strength of the old English and their political power. It is no exaggeration to say that the wealth of Ireland was largely in Catholic old English hands. The best land in Ireland, the rich counties of Meath, Dublin, Tipperary, Limerick, Kilkenny and Waterford, was held by old English proprietors. The English port books for Bristol, Chester and Liverpool give the names of old English merchants trading in wool, linen yarn and other commodities. All the economic importance of the old English, however, counted for very little when so much of the ordinary running of the country was out of their hands.

This exclusion of the old English from power took several different forms. In the first place, the higher administrative and legal posts which had been in their hands for much of the sixteenth century were now filled by Protestant new English. From the point of view of the English Crown this was an understandable development and merely marked another episode in the process of creating an administration of 'new' men, who would be more amenable to control. A simple comparison of names brings out clearly the difference between the old and the new.

In 1600 Adam Loftus, Protestant archbishop of Dublin, was lord chancellor and keeper of the privy seal; his predecessors in the recent past had included John Barnewall and Thomas Cusacke —both belonging to old-established families of the Pale.[1] These names disappear after 1555. In 1600 the Protestant Anthony St. Leger was Master of the Rolls; his predecessors since 1522 had included Thomas D'Arcy, Thomas Cusacke, Patrick Barnewall and Nicholas White.[2] In 1600 the chief Baron of the Exchequer was Sir Edmund Pelham; Bartholomew Dillon, Patrick Finglas and Lucas Dillon had been three of the five predecessors since 1513.[3] In the list of barons of the exchequer, the names of White, Cusacke, and Nugent have disappeared by the end of the century.[4] Delahyde, Cusacke and Dillon are numbered among the first four chancellors of the exchequer from 1532 onwards; after 1572 these old English names no longer occur. In the courts of King's bench and common pleas the families of the Pale had once occupied a dominating position;[5] by 1600 the recusant Sir John Everard, who was a justice of King's bench, was the exception, not the rule.

Exclusion from the administration might not have mattered so much, had the power and scope of the administration remained at its sixteenth-century level. But it now covered the whole of Ireland for the first time and was extending into new fields, of which a unified customs system and a rejuvenated court of wards provided two particular examples. New administrative families, Loftus, Ware, Domville, Bolton, Percival, Newcomen, Parsons and Dopping, appeared to take the place of the old. This development, however, was not merely an administrative one. At a time when office carried with it so many perquisites, exclusion from office could affect the fortunes of a particular class. Wardships, for example, found their way into the hands of the officials of the Court of Wards to the cost of many an old English family.[6] More than this, changes which could be represented as administrative improvements carried in their train far-reaching political

---

[1] *Liber mun. pub. Hib.*, pt. 2, p. 13.
[2] Ibid., p. 17.
[3] Ibid., pp. 49–50.
[4] Ibid., p. 51.
[5] *Liber mun. pub. Hib.*, pt. 2, pp. 30 ff.
[6] H. F. Kearney, 'The Court of Wards and Liveries in Ireland' in *R.I.A. Proc.*, lvii, sect. C, no. 2.

implications. The customs farm of 1613, for example, provided the Irish privy council with a source of revenue, which removed it further from dependence upon old English co-operation, even though it was largely drawn from the old English ports. Any improvement in the financial position of the administration weakened the bargaining power which the old English normally had at their command.

In times of financial crisis, the power of the old English appeared in its true light, but even then, the constitutional change which James I had brought about in 1612 by a stroke of the pen, took away its full force. During the second half of the sixteenth century, parliament was an institution dominated by an old English majority, which the lord deputy might woo but rarely overawe. The creation of forty new boroughs in 1612 and 1613 radically changed the character of parliament, which in the commons had now a small English majority.[1]

The year 1622 saw a further deterioration of the position of both old English and Gaelic Irish in the unplanted counties of Ireland, with the expansion of the Court of Wards.[2] So far, the Gaelic Irish areas had been the only ones to be planted and in some instances, for example, Longford in 1619, the old English had been represented on the plantation commission along with new English. This situation changed. The policy of the Court of Wards under its energetic master Sir William Parsons began to make increasingly difficult the sale of land or its inheritance by the old English. Fines were exacted for the alienation of crown land without permission, in a country where the crown could make out claims, which were largely unreal. Much was made by the court of the legal necessity imposed on all tenants by knight service *in capite* to take the oath of supremacy before they could sue out their livery. If the court were allowed to proceed in its activities unchecked, the old English were likely to lose control of their land piecemeal.

Open religious persecution was a further source of grievance, but in the years following the accession of Charles I, a policy of toleration by the state was evidence of the anxiety felt by the English privy council to keep Ireland peaceful during war with

---

[1] T. W. Moody, 'The Irish parliament under Elizabeth and James I' in R.I.A. Proc., xlv, sect. C, no. 6 (Dec. 1939), pp. 41–81.
[2] See below, Chap. 8, Sect. II.

Spain and France.[1] During the middle of the 1620's, therefore, the old English were presented with an opportunity, thanks to the distress of the administration, to seize the political initiative. The last time that this had been possible was ten years before, in 1615, when the increased anti-recusant legislation which Chichester had hoped to force through was dropped in order to obtain old English assent to the levying of a subsidy. During 1626 and the years following, therefore, the old English pressed for redress of grievances. Their attempts to have the concessions of the crown incorporated into statute were paralleled in England by the agitation for the Petition of Right.

In the 'Matters of Grace and Bounty' of 1626, the crown promised to remedy a comprehensive list of old English grievances. There were twenty-eight clauses, which can be reduced to six headings. Loyal subjects were not to be excluded from the administration and qualified Catholic lawyers were not to be excluded from practice, on grounds of religion; a simple oath of allegiance was to replace the oath of supremacy. The activities of the Court of Wards were to be curtailed. In Connacht, Thomond and Clare, tenants were to be given security against possible royal claims by surrendering their titles for enrolment to Chancery. The undertakers of Leitrim, Ossory and Longford were to be given until May 1628 to perform their obligations. Complaints against the administration, both military and civil, were to be heard. Finally a parliament was to be called.

The political background to this document is very obscure and in the absence of any evidence, which would throw light upon old English negotiations at this time, any discussion must of necessity be very speculative. It does not seem likely that a detailed change of policy, which this document represents, would have been adopted by the English privy council on its own initiative.

[1] R. Dudley Edwards, 'Church and State in the Ireland of Michael O Cleirigh' in Fr. Sylvester O'Brien (ed.), *Miscellany . . . in honour of Michael O Cleirigh*, pp. 1–20.

PLATE II (*a*). Cahir Castle, the home of a younger branch of the Butler family. Built fifteenth century, restored nineteenth century. Lord Cahir joined in the revolt of 1641 and took a prominent part in the Confederation of Kilkenny.

(*b*) Dunsoghly Castle. Built fifteenth century. Home of James Plunkett, member of the prominent 'old English' family. In 1641 the property was mortgaged to Sir Henry Tichbourne, a member of the administration.

(*a*) CAHIR CASTLE, Co. Tipperary

(*b*) DUNSOGHLY CASTLE, Co. Dublin

PLATE II

The old English character of 'Matters of Grace and Bounty' would indicate that the old English leaders had some contact with the English privy council. Hence came detailed knowledge of the kind of concessions which would lead the old English to make some contribution to the cost of the war. The later behaviour of Falkland and the Irish privy council made it clear that such negotiation had gone on behind their backs.

Richard Burke, earl of Clanrickarde, who was normally resident in England, may well have been a go-between in this affair. He kept in touch with Connacht, he was opposed to any plantation of Connacht and the reference to Connacht tenures in the 'Matters of Grace and Bounty' may well represent his influence. Another possibility is Richard Nugent, earl of Westmeath, who was noted by Falkland in 1624 as being particularly active in politics. Nugent belonged to a family which had a distinguished history and which in the fifteenth and early sixteenth centuries provided several vice-deputies of Ireland. He himself had been a member of the opposition to Chichester in the 1613 parliament. Another possibility is Sir John Bath, an old English proprietor of Co. Dublin.[1] What is certain, however, is that the 'Matters of Grace and Bounty' were not drawn up by the English privy council but rather represent the discontent which was felt within the old English counties of the Pale.

The 'Matters of Grace and Bounty' in September 1626 opened a two-year period of great political activity on the part of the old English. They were clearly determined to exploit their financial strength to the full. This was made clear in several different ways. In the first place, there was a marked difference between the 'Matters of Grace and Bounty' and the concessions which were granted in March 1628 and which were known as the Graces. The former consisted of twenty clauses, the latter of fifty, a fact which indicates a greater working out of detail. In the second place, the old English political leaders, namely lords Westmeath, Gormanston and Killeen (later Fingall) refused to give in to the pressure brought by the lord deputy before the concessions were granted. Falkland was forced to give way. He agreed that representatives of boroughs and counties should supplement the

<hr />

[1] Cf. H. O'Grady, *Strafford and Ireland*, i. 537; *Cal. S.P. Ire., 1625-60*, pp. 101; 308-10.

assembly of nobility and clergy which met in November 1626. And in 1627 when a Great Council met, including the elected representatives of the country as a whole, he capitulated to the old English insistence that they should be granted leave to send elected delegates to England. In the third place, the Graces of 1628 are a document of more than old English inspiration. Clauses referring to the Ulster plantation indicate that the old English were not alone in making a bargain with the Crown and when in December 1627, eight delegates were sent to England, they included two 'planters' from Ulster. The result of all this pressure was that in May 1628, Charles I, in exchange for payments amounting to £120,000, agreed to summon a parliament which would convert the Graces into statute.

Two comments may be made about all this. The first is that the old English were conscious of their political advantage during these years and made the utmost use of it. Falkland was unable to resist the pressure brought by their leaders. Secondly, the exigencies of Poynings' Law forced the old English into a new method of political procedure, namely, to establish direct contact with the English privy council concerning proposed legislation. The situation had changed since the sixteenth century when they were largely content with the *status quo* and used Poynings' Law as a bulwark against the attempts of the lord deputy to introduce legislative changes.[1] Now, the old English were anxious to change the *status quo* and had their own legislative programme to force through a parliament in the teeth of a hostile administration. The political tactic to which they had recourse during these years was to bypass the Irish privy council and to establish direct contact with Whitehall.

The success of the old English in 1628 has been underestimated. Though a parliament was postponed, some of the Graces did come into practice by power of the prerogative; there was a steep rise, for example, in the number of Catholic proprietors who sued out their livery. Charles I in 1632 was able to use the threat of withdrawing the Graces as an argument to induce the old English to consider granting further financial payments.[2] The withdrawal of Falkland in 1629, however, opened an interim period during

---

[1] See R. Dudley Edwards and T. W. Moody, 'The history of Poynings' Law, Part I, 1494–1615' in *Irish historical studies*, ii. 415–24 (Sept. 1941).

[2] *Strafford's letters*, i. 71.

which peace was made and the advantages enjoyed by the old English to some extent disappeared. Nevertheless, despite the anti-recusant measures indulged in by Boyle at Christmas 1630,[1] it was the new lord deputy who took the initiative in getting in touch with the Catholic leaders of the Pale in the second half of 1632.

[1] *Cal. S.P. Ire., 1625-32*, pp. 500-1; p. 504.

3

THE APPOINTMENT OF WENTWORTH

FALKLAND returned to England in October 1629 and the government of Ireland was left in the hands of the two lords justices. This arrangement could hardly have been intended to be permanent, however, and it was clearly only a matter of time before a new lord deputy should be chosen, or recommended, by the Irish committee of the English privy council. The correspondence of Sir William Beecher with Richard Boyle shows that no decision was taken before March 1630/1. Beecher, who was one of the clerks to the English privy council,[1] was in a position to know and he was able to tell Boyle, in July 1630, that Falkland was still hoping to be reappointed as deputy, though Beecher himself could see little chance of this so long as Loftus and Boyle remained united in the carrying out of official policy.[2] Falkland's optimism was shared by his former allies in the Irish privy council and he was still regarded by Boyle as the best hope for the future. When in January 1630/1 he wrote to Beecher in connection with the projected plantation of Ormonde,[3] and stressed the necessity for a lord deputy to carry the work out instead of 'us that hold a joynt government', he suggested Falkland as the best man.[4] At this date, therefore, well over a year after he had been recalled, Falkland was still regarded as the candidate of the Boyle group within the Irish privy council, and one whose return was still hoped for.

This picture began to change shortly after Mountnorris had arrived in England, in February 1630/1, to answer Falkland's charges in the Star Chamber. Beecher made it clear to Boyle that Falkland now stood no chance of returning as lord deputy and he

[1] *Cal. S.P. dom., 1629–31*, p. 41.
[2] Beecher to Boyle, 1 July 1630 (Boyle Letter book, Chatsworth MSS., f. 154).
[3] See Appendix I under 'Tipperary'.
[4] Boyle to Beecher, 11 Jan. 1630/1 (Boyle Letter book, Chatsworth MSS., f. 226). A month later Boyle wrote to Weston advising him to appoint 'an honourable and knowing deputie'. 11 Feb. 1630/1 (ibid., f. 244).

hinted that Boyle's own candidature had been discussed in high quarters. Boyle's reply to Beecher's letter was written on 2 March 1630/1 and in it he declared that he was willing to go forward provided he were assured of success. The letter is worth quoting because it provides evidence of Boyle's real ambitions at a time when he was protesting in other letters (e.g. to Secretary Dorchester)[1] his weariness of public life.[2] He wrote

... to express myselfe therein and faile would lay me open to endless envy and make the whole world untruly believe I ambitiously thirsted after government yett for that I am persuaded by the scope of your letters that this overture of yours hath his originall from some advice to taste my inclynations; iff you will vouchsafe to entrust me with the secretts whence this your proposition is derived I will not onely (when I shall truly know from what head it springs) enterteigne and hearken to your counsell and the authors thereof but also with your good directions propound for it in such manner as shall not onely in some degree lessen the King's present charge but alsoe show myself an [ardent] and hable servant to my master in entituling him to Ormond and the adiacent territories, as also of the counties of Roscommon, Mayo and Sligo in the Province of Connaught. ...

In a postcript Boyle asked to succeed Grandison, who had just died, as lord high treasurer of Ireland.

Boyle's prospects, however, faded almost as soon as they had appeared. He himself remained optimistic and regarded his appointment as lord high treasurer as reflecting victory over Mountnorris,[3] but his friend Falkland was more realistic. At the end of March he had written to Boyle warning him that he was out of favour with Weston for inefficiency over the transport of 10,000 quarters of wheat from Ireland to London.[4] In June, Falkland wrote to Ranelagh telling him that Boyle had also offended Cottington.[5] At the same time Mountnorris was successful in defending himself against the charges of both Falkland and Boyle.

The situation in the early months of 1631 was as follows; No lord deputy had as yet been appointed. The candidate of the Boyle party, within the Irish privy council, was first Falkland and then

---

[1] Boyle to Dorchester, 10 Mar. 1630/1 (ibid., f. 273).
[2] Boyle to Beecher, 2 Mar. 1630/1 (ibid., f. 269).
[3] Boyle to Weston, 20 April 1631 (Boyle Letter book, Chatsworth MSS., f. 293).
[4] Falkland to Boyle, 30 Mar. 1631 (P.R.O.I., MS. 2445, f. 198).
[5] Falkland to Ranelagh, 19 June 1631 (ibid., f. 215).

Boyle himself, but their hopes by now did not run high. The opposition party also seems to have had its candidate ready. This was Wilmot, if the letter which he wrote to Cottington some months later may be taken as evidence.[1] In that letter dated 10 January 1631/2 he expressed his disappointment.

I have seen it written by many Hands that my Lord Wentworth is designed by his Majesty for his service to govern this kingdom. My lord, it is true, that after so much expence of my Youth and my Blood in this Country, I should have thought myself honoured and happy to have attained to what Employment this Kingdom might have afforded me; but since it is our great Master's Will to make choice of a fitter instrument . . . I have learnt the rules of subordination. . . .

The tone of this letter shows that Wilmot had hopes of the deputy-ship, and viewed against the background of the political rivalries within the Irish privy council, it is more than likely that he was the candidate of the Loftus group. He was by no means a negligible figure. He had played a prominent part in the expedition to the Ile de Ré and was a member of the English privy council, which he attended when he was in England, as he was, for example, in the latter half of 1628.[2] Wilmot's chances of becoming lord deputy were not to be ignored.

There was another candidate in the field, namely Lord Danby (formerly Sir Henry Danvers), whose connection with Ireland lay in his having been lord president of Munster from 1607 to 1615.[3] The evidence for Danby's candidature is a letter which Beecher wrote to Cork in May 1630, stating the rumour, which he believed to be true, that Danby had made suit *again* for 'the imployment of Ireland'.[4]

During the first months of 1631 the issue was still open and there were at least three candidates in the field. By July, however, the choice had been made, though the news was not officially made known until six months later. A letter written by Laud to Wentworth dated 30 July 1631 implied that Wentworth had been

---

[1] *Strafford's letters*, i. 61. In Sept. 1631 Mountnorris himself boasted to Falkland that he would be deputy but by then the appointment had been made. Falkland to Ranelagh, 1 Sept. 1631 (P.R.O.I., MS. 2445, f. 229).

[2] P.R.O., PC 2/38, f. 345.

[3] Henry Danvers, earl of Danby (1573–1644). Lieutenant-general of the Horse in Ireland 1599. Governor of Armagh 1601. Lord President of Munster 1607–15. Created earl of Danby 1626. G.E.C. *Peerage*, ed. Gibbs.

[4] Beecher to Boyle, 4 May 1630 (Boyle Letter book, Chatsworth MSS., f. 149).

chosen as lord deputy of Ireland.[1] This is the first mention of the appointment, though the news soon began to leak out. Sir Arthur Ingram[2] heard the rumour for the first time at the end of August [3] and in September George Calvert wrote to Wentworth letting him know that the secret was out.[4] Falkland did not know until December[5] when he wrote to Ranelagh with the news, stating, correctly as it turned out, that Wentworth showed favour to Mountnorris and Loftus, not to the Boyle group.

The choice of Thomas Wentworth, lord president of the North and a man without any Irish connections, was an unusual one, which only becomes explicable when viewed against the background of English politics since 1624. The year 1624 had marked a decisive change in both domestic affairs and foreign policy. In that year, Lionel Cranfield, earl of Middlesex, was succeeded as chief minister by the duke of Buckingham, who was now pressing for war with Spain as the best way of recovering the Palatinate. This war policy was opposed by those who had no wish to see England drawn into a war with a country which was not only the strongest military power in Europe, but also the best market for English cloth, in the cause of the Palatinate. Thomas Wentworth was associated with those who opposed Buckingham on this point. They included members of the house of lords, the house of commons and the privy council itself. In November 1625,[6] Sir Arthur Ingram wrote to Wentworth to warn him that Buckingham, who was now in complete control of policy, knew who his opponents were in both upper and lower houses. 'In the higher house, it was my lords Grace of Canterbury,[7] my lord Keeper,[8] my lord Marshal[9] and my lord Chamberlain.[10] For them of the Lower

---

[1] *Strafford's letters*, i. 58.

[2] Sir Arthur Ingram (d. 1642). Comptroller of the customs of London for life 1607. Secretary of the council of the north 1612. Came into conflict with Wentworth over the collection of recusancy fines in Yorkshire. Prominent in many financial schemes of this period including the Irish customs farm. Built the great house of Temple Newsam near Leeds.

[3] Rober Cogan to Ingram, 13 Aug. 1631 (Strafford MSS., vol. 12, f. 240).

[4] Calvert to Wentworth, 7 Sept. 1631 (Strafford MSS., vol. 12, f. 249).

[5] Falkland to Ranelagh, 13 Dec. 1631 (P.R.O.I., MSS. 2445, f. 240).

[6] *Strafford's letters*, i. 28.

[7] George Abbot, archbishop of Canterbury 1611-33, who was later suspended for his opposition. *D.N.B.*

[8] John Williams, bishop of Lincoln 1621-41, later archbishop of York 1641-50. *D.N.B.*

[9] Thomas Howard, 2nd earl of Arundel 1586-1646. *D.N.B.*

[10] William Herbert, 3rd earl of Pembroke 1580-1630. *D.N.B.*

House he doth conceive there were many, who had their con-
ferences with these four Lords and Others that were depending
upon them; among which, you are not altogether free.'

Buckingham did not wait long to take measures against this
opposition. In November 1625, Williams was dismissed from
office, Arundel fell into disfavour, Cottington was forbidden to
appear at court and Calvert resigned his office of secretary of
state. Wentworth, too, lost his post of 'custos rotulorum' of
Yorkshire and was effectively excluded from the parliament of
1626 by being 'pricked' as sheriff. The only two politicians to
emerge unscathed from these drastic changes were Pembroke,
who was too powerful to be attacked, and Weston who was
sufficiently pliable to be able to adjust himself to the alterations
of Buckingham's mind.

The group to which Wentworth belonged was separated from
Buckingham by no difference of principle. Once Buckingham had
decided to compromise, therefore, there was no particular
reason why they should remain out of office. After the first session
of the 1628 parliament, Buckingham yielded on the main point,
so far as they were concerned—namely the war with Spain.[1] The
war with France was to go on, but peace negotiations were to be
entered into with Spain. Arundel rejoined the privy council;
Sir James Ley lost the treasurership and Weston took his place,
and, as his share in the proceedings, Thomas Wentworth was
given a peerage.

This is sometimes looked upon as the moment of Wentworth's
great betrayal, when he abandoned the cause of 'the Commons' in
its battle against the prerogative and its fight for liberty. To do
this, however, is to misconceive the nature of Wentworth's
opposition. His refusal to pay the 'Forced Loan' and his opposition generally were not ends but means. The religious wars on
the continent provide the background to his outlook and that
of others with him. He objected in 1625, as he did later in 1638,
to England's being dragged into the bitter religious conflicts
which are known to history as the 'Thirty Years War'. Once some
move towards peace had been made, and his group, or some of it,
were conciliated, there was no reason why he should have remained in opposition. A priori also there was no reason why the
Eliot group should not have been brought into the administration,

[1] S. R. Gardiner, History of England 1603–42, vi. 334–5.

but the price which they asked included religious change, which
the King's conscience would not permit.

Arundel's friends were thus brought into the administration
while the 'Eliot' group remained in opposition, harping on religious
and 'constitutional' grievances. There was no startling change
on Wentworth's part. His joining the administration has been
over-dramatised largely because the early seventeenth century
itself has been over-dramatised, as the crucial period of the fight
for England's liberty. He did not betray the 'Commons', any more
than Arundel who suffered imprisonment in 1627, betrayed the
'Lords'. Both of them were members of a group which by determined opposition had forced the administration to a drastic
modification of policy.

The death of Buckingham in August 1628 was an unexpected
event which increased the power of the pro-Spanish[1] party by
removing the one man who could dominate the king. Once
Buckingham had gone, the way was clear for politics of a more
normal nature. Power was more equally distributed. No one
individual succeeded to the position of Buckingham. The privy
council became much more a group of men, each with a certain
amount of influence, and less like a 'cabinet' dominated by a
single minister, though Richard Weston, as lord treasurer, was
very powerful.

By the end of 1629, the shape of politics had become clearer.
Cottington, who had been in disgrace since 1624, returned to the
privy council, and took an active part in making peace with Spain.
He and Weston counted for a great deal. So also did William Laud,
bishop of London, who, like Weston, owed his rise to the influence of Buckingham. Arundel, who had strong views on foreign
policy, was another prominent member of the inner circle sur-
rounding the king. Thomas Wentworth, who was only made a
privy councillor late in 1629, was, by comparison with the rest,
a minor figure.

Even if there were no positive evidence for it, one would not
unnaturally seek the explanation for Wentworth's appointment
as lord deputy in his close association with members of this
group. There is some evidence, however, which points to
Weston and Cottington as those who put Wentworth forward for
Ireland. In his letter to Wentworth of 30 July 1631, Laud made

[1] More truly, those who opposed war with Spain.

some enigmatic references to Cassius and Brutus. 'You may find
more danger in a ship to Ireland than over the Thames in a
skuller. Did ever Brutus, or Cassius do thus or thus at Tiber?'[1]
Laud had made a previous reference in this letter to having had
some information from Cassius, so that his comparisons were not
merely literary ones. Presumably the assassinated Buckingham
was Caesar. If so, were Weston and Cottington, who had profited
from the tragedy, Brutus and Cassius, the first a friend of the
Duke, the second a friend who had become a critic?[2]

The real evidence for the part played by Weston and Cottington, however, is contained in a letter written to Wentworth, in
September 1632, by a relation by marriage, Sir Edward Stanhope,
to dissuade him from accepting the appointment.[3]

Stanhope's argument was that Weston and Cottington were
trying to get rid of Wentworth for their own ends. He took it
for granted that the post had not been sought for by Wentworth,
but had been tendered him by his apparent friends. He attributed
the worst possible motives to Cottington whom he regarded as
looking forward to the treasurership when Weston died. He then
went on to argue about the various difficulties which Ireland
presented—'this great burthen, too heavy for the shoulders of
Atlas'. He asked Wentworth whether 'in avoyding an English
Silla [he did] endanger to split [his] bark on an Irish Caribdis and
[doe] suffer shipwreck in those fatall seas'. He also referred to the
example of Essex, whose friends had urged him to his ruin in
order to profit from it. (A bare summary like this does not give a
true picture of this long, rambling but sincere letter which makes
its points over and over again.)

In his reply, dated 25 October 1631[4] Wentworth did not deny
that Weston and Cottington had offered him the post, but he took
a more charitable view of their motives than did his kinsman by
marriage, which Stanhope was. 'I cannot believe so ill of the
propounders,' Wentworth wrote, 'both because in my own

[1] *Strafford's letters*, i. 58.

[2] On Dec. 15 1630, Cottington wrote to Charles from Spain, 'I have had
information that in the King's house in Cartagena, there were two rare heads
of Brutus and Cassius, both of white marble: so I begged them of the King'.
Clarendon State papers (1767), i. 49.

[3] Sir Edward Stanhope to Viscount Wentworth, 23 Oct. 1631 (Sheffield
City Library, Strafford MSS., vol. 21, f. 79). I am indebted to Mr. John
Cooper, Trinity College, Oxford, for a transcript of this letter.

[4] *Strafford's letters*, i. 60.

Nature I am the man least suspicious alive and that my heart tells me, I never deserved but well of them, indeed passing well. It is impossible it should be plotted for my ruin. . . .' Thus Wentworth did not deny that Weston and Cottington, whatever their motives, were behind his appointment.

The decision formally lay with the Irish committee of the English privy council, of which both Weston and Cottington were members at the crucial period in March 1631. Wentworth was also a member at this date, though it is not clear when he was actually made one. Laud too was a member. (Not until early in 1634 was its membership reduced to six, consisting of Weston, Laud, Arundel, Cottington, Coke and Windebank.) Certainly, Weston had his own reasons for wanting a deputy who would be amenable to his wishes. The soap monopoly, with which Weston was closely connected, hoped to use Irish tallow in the manufacture of English soap, and during the first year of his deputyship, Wentworth received numerous letters on the subject, from Weston, urging him to restrain the export of Irish tallow for the benefit of the monopolists. Wentworth's refusal to do so, however lost him the goodwill of the lord treasurer.

The role played by Laud and Arundel in Wentworth's appointment is not clear. Laud's letter of July 1631 was frank in hinting at the dangers which confronted the new lord deputy, and to judge by this, it is most unlikely that he took the initiative in suggesting Wentworth as the best man for Ireland. There is no evidence one way or the other for Arundel's attitude. Certainly he had no good reason for opposing a man who was both a neighbour and a political associate. His letters to Wentworth show that he was on good terms with him, and in fact he may have hoped for more favours from Wentworth than the latter was prepared to give. This is the probable explanation of Arundel's visit to Ireland in 1634, which had as its object, to lay claim to lands which his ancestors had once held as part of the medieval lordship of Carlow. It would appear then that of the four most prominent members of the English privy council, Weston and Cottington actually took the initiative in putting Wentworth's name forward, while Laud and Arundel remained passive, but well-disposed towards him.

D

4

THE FINANCIAL BACKGROUND

THE result was the introduction to Ireland of something more than a successor to Falkland. The significance and the originality of Thomas Wentworth have perhaps been overstressed, but there is no doubt that his personality and character were a new and all-important element in the Irish situation. Wentworth came as a successful president of the north. He seems to have been a man without many doubts, with a gift for simplifying, indeed over-simplifying, a situation and for acting ruthlessly in accordance with his diagnosis. He had the capacity to overawe most opposition, on the other hand he could indulge in measures of conciliation, particularly in his early years. It was perhaps his early successes which led him to over-confidence and to place too much reliance upon force against all opposition. As a man, he was, in himself, a power to be reckoned with, quite apart from his political position. In conjunction, the two helped to raise the temperature of Irish politics to a point which makes the 1641 rebellion more intelligible. In any assessment of this deputyship, the personality of Wentworth cannot be left out of account, difficult though it is for the historian to reach precision in these matters.

The new lord deputy had to face the same financial problem as his predecessor, which had its origins in the need to provide a standing army in Ireland during time of war. Before war had broken out with Spain in 1625, the Irish administration had been able, on the whole, to make ends meet without calling upon England for help. This improved state of affairs had existed since the great financial reorganisation which followed the report of the commission set up in Ireland in 1611.[1] The gap between income and expenditure, which had been £25,000 in 1611, had been reduced to £2,000 by 1619. The establishment of a customs farm on the English model took place in 1613. This was followed in

---

[1] *Cal. Carew MSS., 1603-24*, pp. 96-115.

1615 by the voting of a subsidy by the Irish parliament, which was to be levied according to the English method, of 2s. 8d. in the £ on goods and 4s. in the £ on land. It was expected to bring in £30,000 once the necessary assessments had been made in each county. Finally a commission of wards and liveries was set up in Ireland in 1616, designed to exploit the position of the Crown as universal landowner by levying fines upon proprietors who had alienated Crown land without permission and by exacting payment for suit of livery. Thus the improvement in the financial situation during Grandison's deputyship (1616–22) was due in part to improved fiscal methods.

It was also due, however, to the long period of peace which ensued in Ireland, once the disturbed atmosphere which followed the flight of the earls and the Ulster plantation had died down. The last ten years of James I's reign were on the whole tranquil. But with the declaration of war against Spain in 1625 and subsequent fears of invasion Ireland was expected to provide for a greatly increased army out of her own resources. The military establishment was raised to 5,000 foot and 500 horse. Even though ordinary income was double what it had been in 1611 and was now £40,000 it was still insufficient to make ends meet. There was a gap between revenue and expenditure of £50,000 per annum. So great a deficit could only be met by extraordinary measures, and it was this which provided the background for the attempt made by the English privy council to meet Irish grievances in return for three payments of £40,000 per annum. In return for the Graces, the old English gentry and merchants took the initiative in promising these three annual subsidies. Even so there was still a deficit of £10,000 per annum besides a debt which amounted to £60,000 in March 1628. The negotiations for peace, however, in 1629 brought about a speedy reduction of the army to 1,250 foot and 400 horse. This brought revenue and expenditure closer together, but there was still a gap to be filled.

The immediate background to the financial situation, as Wentworth found it, was as follows. From 3 March 1628 to 30 September 1629, the subsidies had been paid at the agreed rate of £10,000 a quarter (£40,000 a year). This meant that half of the £120,000 had been paid by 30 September 1629, leaving £60,000 still due to be collected. The coming of peace and the consequent reduction of the size of the army made possible a reduction of the rate, at

which the £60,000 was drawn upon by the administration. The
payment of the money from the subsidies into the exchequer was
therefore reduced from £10,000 a quarter to £5,000 a quarter.
From September 1629[1] to September 1630, £20,000 was paid; from
September 1630 to September 1631, £20,000 was paid; a further
£10,000 was paid by 31 March 1632, leaving only £10,000 (or the
equivalent of two quarterly payments) to the credit of the administration. Thus at the time of Wentworth's official appointment,
the financial state of Ireland was as follows. There was a gross
debt of £76,000.[2] Ordinary income was roughly worth £40,000
per annum, but ordinary expenditure, both civil and military was
£60,000 per annum. The gap was filled by an extraordinary levy,
voted in 1628 and being paid at the rate of £20,000 a year; but only
£10,000 from this source was left to be drawn upon. Upon his
appointment therefore Wentworth had to take immediate action
and to enter into negotiations for a continuation of the financial
aid which had been granted originally from 31 March 1628
onwards.

Wentworth's task was to persuade all parties in Ireland to
accept the burden of the payments for another year, without
sacrificing too much the freedom of manœuvre which he enjoyed
as a new lord deputy. The solution of the financial problem
involved delicate and important political decisions, and it was to
some extent the actions which he took in 1632 that decided the
political pattern of Wentworth's deputyship. He had to make up
his mind what attitude he was to adopt towards Richard Boyle and
his party, towards Mountnorris who was being criticised so
strongly by Boyle, and towards the Catholic old English who
represented so much of the economic strength of the country,
both in trade and in land.

He remained in England for over eighteen months after his
appointment had been made in January 1631/2. By doing so he
remained to some extent aloof from Irish politics, a decision which
may or may not have been intentional. The death of his second
wife in October 1631 certainly caused him great unhappiness and
may have played a part in holding him back in England. As well

¹ *Cal. S.P. Ire.*, *1625–32*, pp. 656–7.
² £94,000 Irish. *Strafford's letters*, i. 183. In 1636 Wentworth claimed to
have paid off nearly £100,000 (misprinted by Knowler as £1,000,000). Ibid. ii.
17. Other references to this debt, ibid., i. 273, 264.

as this, however, Falkland informed Parsons in December 1631 that the new lord deputy would not leave for Ireland till the King had returned from Scotland.[1] The delay in Charles I's visit to Scotland which did not take place till May 1633, may therefore explain in part, Wentworth's own delay. There was also the fact that Wentworth needed time to settle his affairs in the north, both public and private. Finally, he may in fact have thought that by remaining in England until a financial agreement with the various Irish groups was reached, he could retain a certain freedom of movement.

The financial problem did not become really acute until the beginning of 1632, when by March 31 only £10,000, the equivalent of two quarterly payments, remained to come in, of the grant of £120,000 which had been made in 1628. The first months of 1632 therefore saw Wentworth moving towards some kind of decision about future policy. He could choose to associate himself with either Boyle or Mountnorris. In the event, he decided upon Mountnorris. In March 1632, the committee of enquiry which had been set up to enquire into Boyle's charges of peculation against Mountnorris, and of which Wentworth and Cottington were the most important members, reported favourably on Mountnorris and declared that Boyle's charges were unworthy of serious consideration.[2] In June 1632 Mountnorris's post of vice-treasurer was combined with that of treasurer-at-wars.[3]

Wentworth's support of Mountnorris, however, did not imply an open breach with Boyle. On the contrary, though Wentworth, newly-bereaved, refused to accept Boyle's offer of a marriage alliance with his daughter, he suggested as an alternative, the marriage of Boyle's second son, Dungarvan, to the daughter of his own kinsman, by his former marriage, Henry, Baron Clifford, son and heir of the 4th earl of Cumberland.[4] (This marriage took place and led ultimately to Dungarvan being member for Appleby in the Long Parliament of 1641, during Wentworth's impeachment.) In a letter to Wentworth, Mountnorris complained that the prospect of this marriage had increased Boyle's prestige in Dublin and made his own task more difficult.[5] Boyle also tried to please

---

[1] Falkland to Parsons, 17 Dec. 1631 (P.R.O.I., MS. 2445, f. 241).
[2] Cal. S.P. Ire., 1625–32, p. 657.
[3] Ibid., p. 668. A routine step now that peace had been signed with Spain.
[4] Wentworth to Ranelagh, 16 July 1632 (Strafford MSS., vol. 1, f. 55).
[5] Mountnorris to Wentworth, 23 Aug. 1632 (ibid., ff. 60–2).

the deputy and was careful to suggest to him that George Rad-cliffe, who was his former secretary as president of the north and who had preceded him into Ireland, was the best candidate for the office of Master of the Rolls, left vacant by Aungier's death.[1]

A clash with Boyle, however, could not be long delayed, as Wentworth, in preferring Mountnorris, had made a choice not merely between two personalities and two parties, but also between two distinct policies.

Of the two, Boyle's policy was the clearer, and had a Puritan administration been in power in England, it might well have been put into practice. He took the long-term view that the cost of a standing army in Ireland should be placed upon the shoulders of those who were primarily responsible for it being in existence—namely the Catholics, whose recusancy he equated with dis-loyalty. In Boyle's view the enforcement of the recusancy fines would both relieve the planter class of a financial burden which they could ill afford and by the same means bring pressure upon the recusants to accept the new religion. It was a plausible principle and one which, in the court of wards, had found a con-crete application.

Boyle first put forward this policy in January 1631/2,[2] though he had hinted in a letter to Beecher earlier in the year that he had a scheme which would solve his majesty's financial difficulties in Ireland.[3] In December 1631 the advice of the Irish privy council, which Boyle largely controlled at this date, was that a decision on the recusancy fines should be postponed until the remainder of the subsidies had been paid. The scheme was considered reasonable, but the timing unsuitable as it might cause discontent among the recusants. Boyle's view was that he could see no way of raising money to pay the army except by extending the recusancy fines. Nine months later, he was still pressing the scheme;[4] he cannot have known that by then Wentworth had definitely decided upon an alternative policy.

Perhaps under the influence of Mountnorris, and perhaps owing to his own unfortunate experience of collecting recusancy fines

---

[1] Cork to Wentworth, 9 Oct. 1632 (Chatsworth MSS., Boyle Letter book, f. 472).

[2] Boyle to Dorchester, 2 Jan. 1631/2 (Chatsworth MSS., Boyle Letter book, f. 381).

[3] Boyle to Beecher, 2 Mar. 1630/1 (ibid., f. 269).

[4] Boyle to lord keeper, 5 Oct. 1632 (ibid., f. 499).

as a source of revenue[1] Wentworth decided against Boyle's proposition and chose as an alternative long-term policy, the better administration of the customs. Customs administration loomed larger, therefore, during the seven years of Wentworth's period of office than under his predecessors. The new farm of the customs at an increased rate in March 1632 coincided with the favourable decision on Mountnorris by the committee of enquiry. George Radcliffe and Mountnorris were associated in the farm along with Arthur Ingram and Robert Cogan. The rates of duty upon the most prominent Irish export commodities were increased in the new Book of Rates which was issued at the same moment. Mountnorris returned to Ireland later in the year and he made a personal tour of customs officials. All this, and also the amount of attention which the lord deputy and Radcliffe devoted to the customs administration after their arrival in Ireland, point to the conclusion that Wentworth hoped to find the solution for the long-term financial difficulties of the crown in an increased customs revenue. It was an obvious way of increasing the revenue and Sir Edward Stanhope, in his letter of September 1631, had referred to the Irish customs as 'one of the most probable meanes' by which Ireland could be made profitable for the King. He was more aware than Wentworth of the dangers involved and asked him 'to consider . . . what an error itt is to pull frute whylst it is in rypeninge, before it comes to perfect maturyte . . . nothing is gaind by such unseasonable covetousness . . . were it not more just to stay till there were both meanes of subsistence and a reasonable overplus, of which there is yet neither?' [2]

In 1632, however, Wentworth's decision over the customs was a policy for the future which could not solve the present financial shortage, when the 1628 payments ran out. In 1632, his immediate object was the straightforward task of negotiating for an extension of the payments for one year, at the rate of £20,000 a year, in order to cover the gap between revenue and expenditure. This was not an easy matter. The old English would show no enthusiasm to extend a bargain which had brought them no advantage, though they had been promised much, while some of

---

[1] While he was president of the north. He may also have suspected the existence of a link between Boyle and Sir Arthur Ingram, with whom he had recently quarrelled on the very subject of recusancy fines. Cf. J. Cooper, 'The Fortune of Strafford' in *Econ. Hist. Rev.* (1958).

[2] See above, p. 30.

the planters, as their later behaviour showed, were willing to go into active opposition on the point. It was in order to strengthen his hand in bargaining with the old English that Wentworth kept up as much as possible his links with Richard Boyle during the middle of 1632. Boyle's recusancy fine policy was to be used as a bogey with which to frighten the old English into Wentworth's arms.

In July 1632, Wentworth informed Mountnorris, but not the lords justices, that he had sent over a papist agent named Michael Hopwood to try to get some agreement among the Catholic gentry to extend the contributions for another year.[1] The agent was to use the argument that the new lord deputy had no wish to enforce the recusancy fines but he might have no alternative, should no financial aid be forthcoming. Hopwood met with some difficulty. He got in touch with Westmeath, Antrim and Netterville and reported that none of them were unwilling to give satisfaction, but they did not wish to send agents, owing to the way in which their last agents had been treated. This objection was mysterious but the real difficulty was presumably that the Graces had been promised and then largely disregarded. Mountnorris arrived in Ireland on September 2; he joined forces with Hopwood and conferred 'daily with some principal men of the recusant party such as Ormond, Westmeath, Gormanstown and Netterville'.[2]

Wentworth became impatient and declared that if they did not reach a decision soon, his majesty would be forced to levy the recusancy fines in order to pay for the army. As a concession he promised to look into the question of the Graces on his arrival.[3]

Matters now began to reach a climax. The point at issue in November 1632, when the negotiations of Wentworth with the old English were at a critical stage, was a letter which the lords justices had received in April 1632 from the English privy council.[4] This letter led to remarkable scenes at the Irish privy council on the 17 and 19 November, which were described by

[1] Strafford MSS., vol. 1., f. 53. 'Hopwood' may have been a pseudonym.
[2] Mountnorris to Wentworth, 28 Sept. 1632 (ibid., ff. 67v–71v).
[3] 'they complain they have not the benefit of the Graces . . . I will promesse . . . to look into it at my coming.' Wentworth to Hopwood, 19 Oct. 1632 (ibid., f. 80).
[4] *Strafford's letters*, i. 71–2.

Mountnorris in a letter to Wentworth.[1] A great number of recusants came to the privy council on Saturday, 17 November, and asked to see the letter of April 1632. Mountnorris moved that it should be published, but Boyle refused to give way. On Monday, 19 November, however, when the Catholic nobility and gentry again presented themselves, Boyle gave way to the extent of having the letter read out. Mountnorris reported that Coote, Bolton and Parsons 'all birds of a feather and of the Earl of Corke's partie' declared that the Protestants would not consent to contribute further to the army. The importance of this incident in deciding the attitude of the Catholic gentry was shown by the fact that Westmeath left almost immediately for London with a list of signatures agreeing to make a further contribution.

Why should this letter of April 1632 have been thought so important? The answer seems to be that during the months following April, Boyle had been actively pursuing an anti-recusant policy. In August 1632 Mountnorris had written to Wentworth, informing him that the lords justices had fined the jurors in Dublin who refused to present 'notorious recusants'.[2] Boyle's policy was therefore meeting with resistance. It was not clear, however, to the old English whether he was carrying out a policy of his own or the decision of the English privy council. For all they knew, the new lord deputy had decided upon a policy of levying recusancy fines, as he had been accustomed to do as president of the north, and Boyle was merely carrying out his orders.

The full text of the letter of 14 April would have made the position clear. It ordered Boyle to go ahead with preparing for the levying of recusancy fines, but more as a threat than anything else. The English privy council clearly hoped that there would be voluntary extension of the contributions. In March Boyle had stressed the dark side of the picture and the reaction of the English privy council, speaking through the mouth of the king, was to say that since 'there is so much difficulty in the settlement of the Payments and considering the small hopes you mention in your letters of further improvement there, we must be constrained, *if they be*

---

[1] Mountnorris to Wentworth, 21 Nov. 1632 (Strafford MSS., vol. 1, ff. 83v–85v).
[2] Mountnorris to Wentworth, 23 Aug. 1632 (Strafford MSS., vol. 1, ff. 60–2).

not freely and thankfully continued' . . . to put into execution the statute concerning the Recusants' fines.

Boyle and the Protestant planter party had everything to gain from not making available the full text of this letter. Their object was to keep silent on the qualifications made concerning full prosecution of the anti-recusant policy and to carry on presenting recusants in the hope, presumably, that by the time the lord deputy arrived the situation would have gone too far to be remedied and for him to withdraw, without injuring the future of his whole period of office.

Wentworth was willing, as we have seen to play this game, but only up to a point.[1] On 28 September 1632 Mountnorris informed him that the King's letter was still sealed up in the council book and its contents unknown to the old English.[2] On 15 October Wentworth wrote to the lords justices (which really meant Boyle) ordering them to enter and publish the letter as they had been commanded.[3] A week later he wrote to Cottington, informing him that Boyle had concealed the King's letter of 14 April, with the object of throwing the blame for the recusancy presentments on the lord deputy.

The incidents of 17 and 19 November 1632 at the Irish privy council were thus a trial of strength, with Boyle and the 'Protestant party' resisting, so far as possible, the alliance of lord deputy, Mountnorris and Catholic old English. The Protestants went into opposition and were dealt with by Wentworth as vigorously as he later dealt with the opposition of the Galway jury. Sir William Cole and other prominent planters in Fermanagh were imprisoned in Dublin castle in May 1633 for their refusal to co-operate with the deputy.[4]

Meanwhile the negotiations with the Catholic gentry proceeded smoothly enough. The earl of Westmeath went over to England with a letter signed by fifty-four prominent Catholic proprietors from Munster, Leinster and Connacht, in which they declared themselves to be 'among the forwardest of his majesty's subjects of this realm to pay our parts of twenty thousand pounds in an equal contribution'.[5] Wentworth's first intervention in Ireland

---

[1] I.e. as a threat to make the old English more amenable.
[2] Strafford MSS., vol. i., f. 70v.
[3] *Strafford's letters*, i. 77–8.
[4] Cole to Ingram (*H.M.C.*, *Var. Coll.*, viii. 37).
[5] *H.M.C.*, *Cowper MSS.*, i. 481–2.

thus ended successfully. The Protestants were brought round in their turn by the threat of force. The gap of £20,000 in the revenue was filled for another year, until December 1633. Against the opposition of Richard Boyle, the alliance of Wentworth, Mountnorris and the Catholic earl of Westmeath had proved itself an efficient, if unlikely political combination. It remained to see how long this understanding between the lord deputy and the Catholics, against the planters, would last.

5

PROLOGUE TO PARLIAMENT

WHEN the new lord deputy arrived in Ireland in July 1633 the political situation was much as it had been six months earlier. Mountnorris was in favour; Boyle's party was out of favour. The Catholics were optimistic for the future, now that the attempt to enforce the recusancy fines had been dropped. The leaders of overt Protestant opposition in Fermanagh were still imprisoned in Dublin Castle. The payment of £20,000 which had been negotiated between the earl of Westmeath and Wentworth in December 1632 had six months to run. Altogether it looked as if the pattern of future politics under Wentworth had taken definite shape, with the deputy, the Catholics and a group of the privy council on one side and Boyle's party and the main body of planters on the other.

Wentworth held two meetings of the Irish privy council almost as soon as he arrived.[1] At the first, he stated clearly the financial problem, stressing the deficit of £20,000 a year in the revenue, and the general debt of £80,000. He asked that suggestions as to how the additional revenue might be raised should be brought forward at the next meeting, a few days later. Wentworth's account of the second session makes it clear that those privy councillors upon whom he could rely were lord chancellor Loftus, vice-treasurer Mountnorris and Sir Adam Loftus. Sir William Parsons showed a marked lack of enthusiasm while, during the early part of the meeting, when Wentworth asked for proposals, Boyle remained silent. The crux of discussion was whether the payment of £20,000 should be renewed for another year. Wentworth clearly thought that it should, and in this he was supported by the Loftus-Mountnorris group, but the general attitude of the council seems to have been against it. Boyle and Parsons thus were not alone in their passive opposition. Not until the deputy proposed a parliament, did Boyle speak and say that he was in favour of the contribution being levied for another year, as a temporary solution,

[1] *Strafford's letters*, i. 98.

provided that a parliament met in the meantime to discuss some permanent arrangement. The tactics of Boyle's group were not direct opposition to the wishes of the deputy, but a marked disinclination to be helpful. They may have hoped that the summoning of a parliament would weaken his position to such an extent that he would be forced to make concessions in the direction of the Boyle group. They agreed, however, that steps should be taken towards the temporary solution of the deputy's financial difficulties, by negotiation with the Catholics and the planters, which resulted, as they had done six months earlier, in a grant of £20,000. The financial gap was now closed till December 1634.

Wentworth met with no serious opposition in the English privy council for his suggestion that a parliament should be summoned and in January 1634 he put forward his plans for it in a well-known letter to the king.[1] He suggested that two sessions should be held, in the first of which finance would be dealt with, while in the second, redress of grievances would be discussed.

His experience over the financial negotiations of December 1632 and August 1633 seems to have convinced him that his best plan was to create a deputy's party which would hold a balance between the two main groups, 'papist' and 'protestant'. He proposed to use his influence in the elections to secure the return of a number of 'official' candidates[2] since he anticipated that he would meet with difficulties on both sides. On the one hand, the Catholic old English, who since 1628 had been enjoying the benefit of many of the Graces, would be anxious for them to be passed into statute law. Wentworth foresaw that he would not be able to meet some of their most important demands; in particular the settling of land titles in Connacht and the substitution of an oath of allegiance for an oath of supremacy as a test for office and legal practice would make the proposed plantation of Connacht[3] impossible and bring about the disappearance of Protestant lawyers from the courts. On the other hand, he foresaw that the planters would resist any attempt to tighten up the regulations concerning the plantations. The deputy's problem, therefore, was to hold some kind of balance between these two groups and to prevent them from forming an alliance against him. 'The Truth

[1] *Strafford's letters*, i. 183 ff. [2] See below, p. 46 ff.
[3] See below, p. 85 ff.

is', he wrote to Secretary Coke, 'we must there [i.e. in the forth-coming parliament] bow and govern the Native by the Planter and the Planter by the Native.' [1]

It was now only a matter of time before the good relations which existed between the deputy and the old English gentry changed for the worse. The actual break did not come till November 1634 in the second session of the parliament but it was fore-shadowed in Wentworth's interview with Fingall in May. The earl of Fingall, next to the earl of Westmeath, was the most prominent of the old English proprietors of the Pale. It was not unnatural that he should represent them in a visit to the deputy to discover what they might expect in the parliament. Fingall called upon the deputy, where 'very gravely and in a kind of electorate way, he told [him] that the report went there would be a parliament and that their Lordships of the Pale had been accustomed to be consulted with before those meetings to assemble and take advice together, what to propound for the good of the people and therefore desired to be ascertained therein to the intent they might prepare themselves accordingly'. Fingall's approach was a reasonable one; he had the precedents of Chichester and Falkland to go upon and the support of lord chancellor Loftus. [2] Wentworth denounced him, however, in the most grandiloquent terms, telling him that 'his Majesty would reject with Scorn and Disdain all such Foreign Instructors or Moderators betwixt him and his People'. Whatever the reasons he gave Fingall, however, the real one could not be mentioned, namely that the legislation proposed by the administration did not include all the Graces. Had Wentworth acceded to Fingall's request, he would have found it very difficult to keep his plans for the parliament secret, and once the cat was out of the bag, the old English might well have indulged in the same kind of open opposition to the financial demands of the deputy, which had brought Falkland to his knees in 1627. Two months before parliament met, the clash of Wentworth with Fingall showed that the honeymoon of the Catholic party and the new lord deputy, which had begun in December 1632, was coming to an end. The forthcoming parliament would show whether in time of peace they were still in a position effectively to bring pressure to bear upon the administration. Much depended on the outcome of the elections which were about to take place.

[1] 31 Jan. 1633/4. *Strafford's letters*, i. 199.   [2] *Strafford's letters*, i. 246.

6

THE PARLIAMENT OF 1634-5

THE results of the 1634 elections followed in general the pattern of those of 1613. Catholic members were returned by the counties and boroughs which were still in old English hands, while the planted counties, the newly created boroughs and the garrison towns returned Protestants.[1] Thus the old English counties of Louth, Meath, Kilkenny, Kildare and Tipperary all returned Catholics and the planted counties of Ulster as well as King's and Queen's County returned Protestants. In some areas, such as Wexford, Carlow, Waterford and Limerick, the division which existed between planted and unplanted parts of the same county was reflected in the election of members. Thus north Co. Wexford, a Gaelic Irish territory which had been recently planted, returned new English members, while south Co. Wexford, still under old English control, returned Catholics. In these circumstances, it was almost certain that the Irish house of commons, as in 1613, would contain a substantial Protestant majority. This, in fact, was what happened. Out of a house numbering 256, at least 143 were Protestant of whom about fifty were office holders. This result was a wholly misleading reflection of Catholic numbers and wealth but it did indicate the political power enjoyed by the class of new officials. A large proportion of the new English members were officeholders whose connection with the area which they represented was merely an official one. Elections in the normal sense of the word were few and in most cases were a formal registering of a decision which had been arrived at by less formal means.

A Protestant majority in the house of commons was not necessarily a deputy's majority, as Wentworth himself saw clearly. The split within the Irish privy council was bound to reveal itself in parliament also and even officials might owe their first allegiance to a local magnate like the earl of Cork rather than to the lord

[1] For a fuller discussion of the membership of the parliament see Appendix I.

45

deputy. Wentworth took definite steps, therefore, to ensure the election of a group of members upon whose loyalty he could fully rely and who in certain circumstances might well hold a balance of power between old English and new English.

The amount of evidence, however, upon which to base any conclusions as to the practical effect of the lords deputy's influence is very scanty. First may be mentioned a letter which Wentworth wrote to St. Leger, lord president of Munster in April 1634, nearly three months before the election was due to take place. In it he asked St. Leger to 'keepe the towns under your government from factious and tumultary labouring for places beforehand . . . and to keep them free without engagement and to send me a list of some twenty of the most leading men of the province which you conceive to be well affected and fitt to be sent to the meeting as also your advise how upon recommendations hence to the towns wee may gett such others chosen as shall be named unto them . . .'[1] From the evidence of this letter it may be concluded that much of the responsibility for the choice of candidates in Munster and probably elsewhere in the new English boroughs lay directly with the administration, and it is not, therefore, surprising that so many of the candidates should have had official, and yet local, ties.

In Dublin, the influence of the lord deputy was exercised directly in favour of his own candidates Barry and Catelin, and the corporation was forcibly prevented from electing candidates of whom Wentworth did not approve; elsewhere, however, his influence could be felt only at a distance. It is known that he sent out a hundred letters recommending the election of certain chosen candidates. The letters probably followed the formula of that which was sent to Trinity College, Dublin, in support of Sir James Ware and James Donnellan.

To our very loving friends the provost and fellows of Trinity College near Dublin[2]

After our hearty commendations. Whereas there are two Burgesses to be elected for the University of Dublin to serve at this ensuing parliament appointed to begin on the 14th July next. And forasmuch as we are desirous that Sir James Ware Knight and James Donnellan Esquire may be nominated for the said burgesses; we have therefore thought good to recommend them to you for that employment, that by your good means and assistance, they may be chosen accordingly who we

[1] Strafford MSS., vol. 8, f. 105.
[2] Printed in J. W. Stubbs, History of the university of Dublin, p. 68.

rest assured will well and honestly perform the trust reposed in them and that without any charge to you or the University. And so leaving unto your care what may more conduce to the furtherance of this service, we bid you heartily farewell.

From his Majesty's castle of Dublin, the 30th May 1634

Your assured loving friend

Wentworth

Another piece of evidence is to be found in the diary of the earl of Cork. Richard Boyle, earl of Cork, received six letters on 30 May 1634, presumably written in the same vein, commanding him to see that members chosen by the deputy were elected.[1] The boroughs concerned were Bandon, Tallagh, Clonakilty and Lismore, in which Boyle clearly would be able to exercise great influence, and Askeaton and Dingle in which the role which Wentworth expected him to play does not seem to be so obvious. Three of the letters achieved results. Sir George Wentworth, youngest brother of the deputy, was elected for Bandon; Maurice Williams, Wentworth's physician, was elected for Askeaton; Philip Mainwaring, Wentworth's confidant and secretary, was elected for Clonakilty. For whatever reason, there was no success in the other boroughs. Roger Mainwaring and Thomas Little, 'my lord deputy's secretary' who had been recommended for Dingle and Lismore, were elected for Lifford and Cashel respectively. Bartholomew Pesely, who was keeper of the writs for the Court of Common Pleas, does not seem to have been elected to the 1634 parliament; he had been recommended for Tallagh, a borough which Boyle seems to have kept for his own candidates, one of whom was his brother-in-law, Sir William Fenton.

A further piece of evidence is provided by the memoirs of a traveller in Ireland in the year following the election.[2] In July 1635, Sir William Brereton, an Englishman, arrived at Dundalk. During his short stay he noted that the inhabitants were 'popishly affected' and went to mass openly. He also learnt that Sir Faithful Fortescue, who garrisoned the town with a company of fifty soldiers, was rejected at the last election, along with Sir Arthur Terringham, although they were commended to the borough by the lord deputy. 'A couple of recusants' were elected instead.[3] In

[1] A. B. Grosart (ed.), *Lismore Papers* (1886), series I, iv. 30.
[2] E. Hawkins (ed.), 'Brereton's Travels in Holland, the United Provinces, England, Scotland and Ireland', *Chetham Soc.*, vol. i.
[3] Peter Clinton and Oliver Cashell. See Appendix I.

this case at least the lord deputy's advice seems to have been ignored.

No general conclusion can be drawn from these twelve examples, but they do suggest that the influence of the lord deputy was by no means successful in every case. In Dublin his four candidates were elected. In Cork, only three of six names which he put forward were returned, while in Dundalk both of his nominees were rejected. Wentworth thus met with resistance from the Protestant earl of Cork as well as the Catholic burgesses of Dundalk. Nevertheless the large number of officials in the 1634 parliament implies that the letters sent out by Wentworth did bear fruit in many cases.

It is even more difficult to indicate the successes in 1634 of the anti-Wentworth group within the Irish privy council. In the second session the 'Catholic party' enjoyed a majority for some days, which implies that about thirty Protestant members were absent for one reason or another. In view of the fact that Ranelagh was to be found agitating for the Graces in the first session with the Catholic Fingall, the suggestion may be made that in the second session, certain Protestant members abstained from voting. This would suggest that the anti-Wentworth group, led by Boyle and Ranelagh, could count on the support in the commons of between twenty and thirty members. Had it been more, they would have held the balance of power and had the deputy at their mercy. Piers Crosby, member of the Irish privy council and formerly commander of the Irish regiment at the Ile of Ré, was not content with passive resistance and took an active part against the lord deputy. Sir William Cole, member for Co. Fermanagh, was hardly likely to be an uncritical supporter of the deputy, after his imprisonment at Wentworth's order in mid-1633. In the absence of direct evidence, however, too much speculation about the cross-currents among the Protestant members would be dangerous; we can only be certain that there was some Protestant opposition to the deputy, which was expressed to some extent in the elections of 1634.

So far as the Irish house of lords was concerned, the lord

PLATE III (a) Portumna House, seat of the earl of Clanrickarde. Built early seventeenth century.

(b) Carrick-on-Suir. Built late sixteenth or early seventeenth century. One of the seats of the earl of Ormonde.

(*a*) PORTUMNA HOUSE, Co. Galway

(*b*) CARRICK-ON-SUIR, Co. Waterford

PLATE III

deputy was on much surer ground than any of his predecessors had been. Since the last parliament, there had been a radical change in the composition of the peerage of Ireland which was without doubt of great benefit to the government. The obvious reason for this was the great increase in the numbers of Protestant peers. In 1613 the house had been composed of twenty lords spiritual and twenty-five lords temporal. Of the latter, seventeen were Catholic and five were Protestant while three were minors. The total membership of the house at this date was forty-five. In 1634, owing to the creation of new peers, membership of the house had trebled and was now one hundred and twenty-three, made up of twenty-four lords spiritual and ninety-nine lords temporal, most of whom were Protestant.

The creation of new peerages had indeed been one of the most striking features of crown policy during the last years of James I's reign and the early years of Charles I's. Of the forty barons who had the right to sit in the 1634 house all but fourteen had been ennobled since 1617. James Hamilton, Lord Strabane, was the first of these; Francis Annesley, who had been made Lord Mountnorris in 1629, was the latest. Only two of the new barons were Catholic; Cecil Calvert, Lord Baltimore, and Theobald Bourke, Lord Bourke of Brittas. Of the forty-three viscounts, all were recent with the exception of the Catholic Lords Mount-garret, Fermoy and Gormanston. Like the baronages, the new viscounties begin in 1617 and end in 1629; the first was Richard Wingfield, Viscount Powerscourt, and the last Terence Dempsey, Viscount Clanmalier. Of the new creations, five were Catholic; John Taaffe, Viscount Taaffe; Pierce Butler, Viscount Ikerrin; Thomas Fitzwilliam, Viscount FitzWilliam of Merrion; Charles MacCarthy, Viscount Carty of Muskerry; and Nicholas Netter-ville, Viscount Netterville of Dowth. The overwhelming majority were, however, Protestant. Finally, of the third and last division of the Irish peerage, the sixteen earldoms, all but four, Clanrick-arde, Thomond, Ormonde and Kildare, were of recent creation. Four of the new earldoms were Catholic; Fingall, Westmeath, Antrim and Castlehaven, with Clanrickarde, made five Catholic earls in all. The first of the recent creations dated from 1616; the latest, from 1628, when William Pope was made earl of Down. In short, within the space of little more than a decade, the whole character of the Irish peerage had been transformed.

The results of all this were twofold. In the first place the Anglo-Irish nobility who had previously formed a majority of the lords temporal were now completely outnumbered. In 1613, the administration had had to consider various expedients by which the Protestant majority in the lords might be fortified. In 1634 this problem had disappeared; the very possibility of the Catholic lords being able to defeat the government seemed to have been ruled out completely. The vast majority of the new creations were in fact Protestant. Many of them belong to the new English planter class, as might have been expected; Others, like Montgomery and Claneboy, were Scottish in origin; others, like Thomas Dillon, Viscount Dillon of Costello-Gallen, were Anglo-Irish by blood, even if they were not Catholic. Their shades of protestantism might vary and lead to internal dissension, but as against the Catholics the government could depend upon a solid Protestant majority. Wentworth could, without immediate inconvenience, ignore the old English nobility in a way in which even Chichester could not. Whatever the reason behind the creation of these new peerages—and with the early Stuarts it may have been primarily a financial rather than a political expedient and a cheap method of rewarding services rendered—the results upon the Irish house of lords were even more devastating than the conscious decision of James I to create forty new boroughs upon the Irish house of commons. In the commons the possibility still remained that the Catholics, given favourable circumstances, could defeat or delay the aims of the administration; so far as the house of lords was concerned even this had gone.

The second major result of the wholesale creation of peerages was probably unforeseen. In 1634, the position of the lord deputy in the house of lords was greatly strengthened because of the number of non-resident lords, which meant that a large number of proxies were put at his disposal. In the first session of the 1634 parliament not all the absentee peers made arrangement for proxies but even so the lord deputy was able to share thirty-five votes in blocks of four or five among eight 'government' peers—Moore, Baltinglass, Stewart, Conway, Ormonde, Esmond, Loftus and Claneboy. There was thus a strong nucleus upon which, together with the majority of the bishops, the lord deputy could rely and which enabled him to hold the balance of power in the house of lords. Except in the contingency of an alliance between the Catholic Anglo-Irish and the Protestant planters the lord deputy was assured of a majority without the necessity of going to any manœuvring. That Wentworth was conscious of all this is clear from his correspondence. In January 1634 he wrote to Charles: 'In the higher House, your Majesty will have, I trust, the Bishops wholly for you. The titular Lords rather than come over themselves will put their proxies into such safe hands as may be thought of on this Side.' [1] Not that he anticipated much difficulty in the house, for he went on: 'And in the rest, your Majesty hath such interest, what out of Duty to the Crown and Obnoxiousness[2] in themselves, as I do not apprehend much, any difficulty amongst them.'

The fact that non-resident peers did have a say in the voting of taxes, which they would not have to pay, does seem to have given rise to dissatisfaction. On this point there was possibly some fellow feeling between Catholic and Protestant if the proposal to make non-resident peers buy land in Ireland can be taken as evidence. A petition was submitted to the deputy requesting that non-resident Irish peers be obliged to purchase lands to the value of £300, £250, or £200 per annum according as they were earls, viscounts or barons; they were otherwise to have no voice in affairs. If this petition had become law much of the newly-acquired 'reserve' power of the deputy would no doubt have disappeared. A bill does seem to have been prepared along these lines, only to be condemned by Wentworth at the end of the first session, when he made it clear that he stood by Poynings' Law, by which the initiative, so far as the actual framing of legislation to meet grievances, rested with the lord deputy and the Irish privy council. An act was passed in the third session, 'whereby certain of the nobility of this kingdom of Ireland dwelling within England or elsewhere out of this realm are made liable unto certain charges within this kingdom'. It is doubtful, however, whether this act affected the real issue, since taxation in Ireland would still fall only on those who owned property of one kind or another in Ireland.

The large number of absentees in 1634 meant that the difference in numbers between the 1613 house and that of 1634 was not as

---

[1] Cf. also Wentworth to Coke 13 May 1634. *Strafford's letters*, i. 246: '. . . if I were to chuse, had rather have their Proxies than their company'.
[2] Sc. dependence.

great in actual practice as seemed possible in theory. Of the twenty-four lords spiritual and ninety-nine lords temporal, there were at the opening of the first session, twenty-two and forty-three respectively. The latter consisted of ten earls, sixteen viscounts and seven barons. For the second session the numbers dropped slightly to seventeen lords spiritual and thirty-nine lords temporal; and for the third session much lower to eight and twenty-four respectively.

It is perhaps useful to indicate the religious proportions of the house, though the combination of the Catholic Fingall with the Protestant Ranelagh in debate showed that religious differences were not a sure sign of political antagonism. During the first two sessions Catholics formed about a quarter of the house; in the third the general drop in numbers brought the Catholic proportion up to nearly a third. Thus what had taken place in 1612 for the house of commons, was followed by 1634 in the house of lords.

A mere counting of heads, however, is insufficient without some indication of the relative authority of the various peerages in the country as a whole. There had been a time when the Fitz-Geralds of Kildare and of Desmond had been the most powerful families in Ireland. For the time being, however, the earl of Kildare counted for little; he was an irresponsible young man whose chief claim to importance was as son-in-law to Richard Boyle, earl of Cork. Far more important were the three great landowners, Thomond, Clanrickarde and Ormonde. Of these only Ormonde threw in his lot with the lord deputy, and whereas Clanrickarde put all his influence against any extension of the plantations further into Connacht, Ormonde, who had been brought up a Protestant, thanks to the Court of Wards, was a whole-hearted supporter of Wentworth's plantation policy. Thus the old English in the central and richest part of Ireland were left without a leader. The prestige of the house of Ormonde was a factor of great value for the lord deputy, not only in the house of lords but also in much of the central and southern areas of the country.

7

THE POLITICS OF THE 1634 PARLIAMENT

PARLIAMENT met on 14 July and the first session lasted until 2 August, that is for slightly less than three weeks. There was then an interval of three months until the second session began. During the second session opposition grew against the lord deputy to such a pitch that certain officially sponsored measures were rejected. This opposition was kept up during the third session which lasted, apart from a short interval, from the end of January to the third week of April.

As is the case with so many other topics, there is remarkably little evidence upon which to base an account of this parliament. No diaries have survived, nor any division lists, if indeed they ever existed. The historian must perforce rely upon the prejudiced and highly coloured letters of the lord deputy and the uncommunicative pages of the journals of the house of commons and house of lords. Since Wentworth was not seeking to present an exact and impartial report but rather to justify his own sometimes violent proceedings, it is only possible very rarely to catch a glimpse of the other side of the picture.

The first session went comparatively quietly. At this stage the old English party were hoping that their demands for the Graces would be fully met in return for financial aid, while for his part, the lord deputy was unwilling to take any step which would suggest that all the Graces were not to be granted. There was one episode, at the beginning of the session, which recalled some of the violence of the 1613 parliament, but it failed to create prolonged antagonism. The old English party in the commons challenged the validity of the election of members who were not resident in the boroughs which they represented. Had this challenge been successful, the old English would have achieved a majority at the expense of the lord deputy's 'official' members. Two divisions took place. The first, on 17 July, was to decide the composition of the committee of privileges. On this question, the old English took the view that the committee should be made up of members selected one from each county. This, from their point of view, would have been better than a committee selected by the house as a whole, since, though it would not have given the old English a majority, it would have ensured the representation of counties which were dominated by old English and given them a powerful minority on the committee. The old English motion was, however, defeated by eight votes.[1]

The second division took place on the next day, 18 July. The question was 'long and very much debated' whether the house should examine the legality of elections before proceeding to the reading of bills. Here again, the old English were defeated by 129 votes to 101.[2]

Neither of these two divisions was in theory for or against the administration, though had the voting gone with the old English, the position of the lord deputy would certainly have been weakened. The fact that the subsidies were voted *unanimously* on 19 July showed that the old English had no desire to declare open war on the policy of the administration. Again, the number of subsidies was six, which was very large and in view of financial history since 1626 could easily have given rise to trouble,[3] but as things turned out the £120,000 voted in 1634 caused much less fuss than the same sum six years earlier. Wentworth's calculations were proved correct and neither old English nor new English dared give the impression of hostility for fear the deputy would throw his weight upon the opposite side.

The bill for the confirmation of defective titles, which in other circumstances would have been hotly debated since it involved the possibility of increasing rents for those crown tenants, whose titles were confirmed, was read three times and passed for the royal signature. This, however, apart from the bill for the subsidies, was the only important measure to be passed during the first session. Such time as was left was occupied with uncontentious legislation (including a bill against unnatural vice which probably had reference to the recent scandal of Lord Castlehaven). In his report to Coke, Wentworth described this as a deliberate manœuvre: 'The rest of the session', he wrote, 'we have enter-

---

[1] *Commons jn. Ire.*, p. 64.
[2] Ibid., loc. cit.
[3] The 1613 parliament was asked to vote one subsidy only.

tained and spun them out in discourses but nevertheless kept them from concluding anything'.[1]

There were indications, however, which suggested that the lord deputy in less favourable circumstances might meet with considerable opposition. Hints from Wentworth's letters point to the existence of a political alliance between Boyle's party and the old English party. Wentworth found Ranelagh and Parsons wanting in enthusiasm for a rapid moving of supply[2] and he suspected that Ranelagh was in touch with 'some leading men amongst the commons', though none of these were mentioned by name. It was also significant that Ranelagh was mentioned as having pressed, along with Fingall, for the Graces 'at every turn' during the session. Thus, Wentworth linked together specifically the most active member of Boyle's party and one of the leaders of the 'lords of the pale'. The wheel had come full circle since the days of 1632 when the lord deputy and the earl of Westmeath had been in alliance against the political dominance of Boyle's party in the Irish privy council. Such evidence as this, slight though it is, suggests a parliamentary alliance between the old English and Boyle's party, the former anxious for the Graces, the latter using the pressure of this discontent as a weapon for their own benefit and as a method of forcing their way back into the inner circles of the administration. It was an alliance which anticipated the successful attack upon Wentworth in 1640, when once again new English and old English were united in the impeachment of the lord deputy. It was, however, an alliance which was essentially brittle. The plantation of Connacht divided the material interests of Boyle's party and the old English party in the years after 1635. Ranelagh and company were willing to co-operate with the lord deputy in this enterprise at the expense of the old English Clanrickarde and the Galway gentry.

The pressure exerted by Ranelagh and Fingall gave rise to an incident concerning Poynings' Law, which illustrates how its interpretation had changed since the late sixteenth century. Poynings' Law in the 1585 parliament had been the bulwark of the old English, protecting them from the too hasty action of the Irish administration; it was a well-tried method of spinning out the time of a parliament in order to prevent, for example, the

[1] *Strafford's letters*, i. 278.
[2] St. Leger was also mentioned. *Strafford's letters*, i. 277.

introduction of more severe penal laws. The old English had then been by and large satisfied with the *status quo*, while the deputy was seeking to change it.

In 1634, however, the situation had radically changed. It was now the opposition party who were pressing for legislative action, while the lord deputy held on to the ambiguities of a *status quo* which left him greater freedom to prosecute his land policy. Had the Graces become law, the plantation of Connacht and the commission of defective titles would have been legally impossible and in other ways the prerogative of the deputy would have been hedged about with restrictions.

Wentworth was therefore quick to scent danger in an attempt made by the committee of grievances in the house of lords to initiate legislation. The committee had given orders for the drawing up of several bills, the most important of which concerned the limitation of royal title to land to not more than sixty years. (In other words, the officials of the crown would not press home claims which rested on far-fetched titles several centuries old.) This bill had it become law would have made the commission for defective titles a dead letter, since it would have cut down considerably the numbers of those who felt their titles endangered. Wentworth's plan to increase the rents of crown tenants would have been stifled at birth. In addition, the plantation of Connacht, the legal basis of which rested on old and, to the Connacht gentry, unreal, crown titles, would have been impossible.

There is little doubt that this attempt to initiate legislation was made by Ranelagh and Fingall, though Wentworth in his later report spoke in general terms of 'the house of lords', without mentioning particular names. He met the danger by appealing to the letter of Poynings' Law which placed the power to frame or draw up legislation in the hands of lord deputy and council. The house of lords as such had the right only to draw the attention of lord deputy and council, by petition or remonstrance, to such matters as pertained to the public good.[1]

In actual fact, Wentworth's control of the proxy votes of absentee lords made his position in the lords impregnable. But during this first session he was anxious to avoid a direct display of power. The appeal to Poynings' Law served its purpose. Fingall and Ranelagh were defeated for the moment.

[1] *Strafford's letters*, i. 291–2.

On 27 November Wentworth gave a detailed reply on the Graces.[1] On the day following, the storm burst. On 28 November, according to the account which Wentworth wrote a fortnight later, 'the Popish party' rejected the bill against bigamy, the laws for correction houses, against fraudulent conveyances and for the bailments. The journal of the house of commons states also that the bill for the explanation of the statute of murders was rejected. The situation was serious. Wentworth admitted in a frank letter to Laud that he had lost control of affairs for five or six days and that by the 'extreme perversity' of the Papist party the parliament was 'in great danger to have been lost in a storm'.

The crisis did not end until 3 December, when it became clear that the lord deputy was once again in control of the house. He told secretary Coke that he had brought pressure to bear upon the lords and had asked the council to see that their friends attended the house with more regularity during the next ten days.[2] The political realities which lay behind this description of the methods resorted to by the lord deputy must remain obscure, but one may suggest, without evidence, that Boyle's party in the commons may deliberately have abstained in order to embarrass the administration. On 2 December the old English member for Clonmel, Geoffrey Barron, who was a confederate after 1641, was accused of an unspecified offence, but the house declared itself satisfied with his explanation. On the next day, however, *under pressure from the lord deputy*,[3] the house ordered that he be expelled and committed to the castle on the grounds of 'his misinformation made yesterday to the House'. On the day following it was clear that the opposition had been crushed when the marriage bill which had been defeated on 17 November, received three readings in one day and was passed by the house. On 6 December it was thought safe to bring in the important bill of uses for its third reading: it passed the house two days later.[4] At this time also the right of the old English boroughs, Fore, Bannow and Clonmynes, to send members to the commons was challenged: this may be taken also as evidence of Wentworth's intention to weaken the opposition and of his confidence in his own majority.

---

[1] See below, p. 61 ff.
[2] Wentworth to Coke, 16 Dec. 1634. *Strafford's letters*, i. 350.
[3] *Strafford's letters*, i. 351. The vote was carried by a majority of sixteen.
[4] *Commons jn. Ire.*, p. 88.

There is one feature of Wentworth's letters describing these events which may be commented upon. They all show a startling lack of appreciation of the causes of the old English opposition. Wentworth may have been aware that it was the land question which went to the heart of the agitation against him, but he refers to it as 'a strange and insolent forwardness, refusing and rejecting all which came from the state'. His constant reference to 'the Popish party' served to cloud the issue by appealing to religious bitterness—the Popish party were ill to please, they 'lost all temper', they 'broke forth into such a forward sullenness as was strange'. He blamed the fact that 'this people should be so obstinately set against their own good', [upon the influence of] 'the Friars and the Jesuits'. 'Indeed I see plainly that so long as this kingdom continues Popish, they are not a people for the Crown of England to be confident of.'[1] Eighteen months in Ireland seem to have brought him less not more understanding of the problems of that country, though there is no evidence that enforcement of the penal laws became more intense during his deputyship.

We must now consider the specific decisions which Wentworth took upon the Graces.

The clash between the lord deputy and the old English which became open conflict in the middle of the second session arose. largely because of their different expectations from parliament. For Wentworth, the summoning of parliament was primarily a financial expedient, and once the subsidies had been granted, it was the duty of a loyal administration to preserve its freedom of action as much as possible. In his speech[2] at the opening of the first session, the main tenor was upon finance, 'for it is far below my great Master to come at every year's end, with his hat in his hand, to intreat that you would be pleased to preserve yourselves'. But even if a financial settlement was arrived at, he did not actually promise that all grievances would be settled in the second session; the King's interests had still to come first—'I dare assume that if you fail not in this former, his majesty . . . you can think will go along with you in this later session, through all the expressions of a wise and gracious king: but still according to the order of good manners, Reason and Nature, himself first, his people afterwards.'[3] For the old English party, however, redress of grievances came

---

[1] *Strafford's letters*, i. 350-1.   [2] Ibid., i. 286-90.
[3] Ibid., op. cit.

first, and their expectations can be summed up under two headings. In the first place, they demanded that all the Graces should
come into force. In 1628 Charles I had agreed to all the Graces
but, in fact, some of the major concessions seem to have remained
in abeyance. In the second place, they asked that specified Graces,
and this included most of the fifty clauses, should become statute
law. By this means they hoped to provide a constitutional limit to
the action of the royal administration in Ireland. This, perhaps,
was the major point at issue. In 1628, the old English had received
half of the whole loaf which they had been promised. Events since
1632 seemed to point to complete victory being within their
grasp. The lord deputy had wooed them successfully and though
the outlook was now less promising, a good deal of hope still
must have remained. The explosion of the second session must be
attributed to the contrast between the expectations of the old
English since 1632 and what they were given in November 1634.
Not all the Graces, however, were equally important in their eyes.
Those, to which attention was drawn particularly in the 1634
prologue to the Grace, concerned land titles and the methods suggested to improve trade. The 'uncertainty of estates' was their
great grievance, the remedy for which was in their eyes the
application to Ireland of the English statute (21 Jac. I) allowing the
validity of a sixty years' title to land. The preamble to the Graces
returns to this point in its last sentences, though one of the reasons
why the statute was asked for could not be mentioned explicitly
—namely fear that the Crown itself would be the one to benefit
from the investigation of titles, with the consequent extension of
the system of plantation and further decrease in the influence of
the old English.

With this in mind, we must examine the specific decisions
which Wentworth took about the Graces,[1] and which, as an-
nounced on 27 November, proved so obnoxious as to arouse prolonged opposition during the next few days.[2] In the first place, he
proposed that only ten of the Graces should be translated into
law. Of these the most important were numbers 26 and 27, confirming the title of the undertakers in Ulster, and allowing more

[1] *Lords jn. Ire.*, p. 36.
[2] Cf. Butler, *Confiscation*, p. 105, in which it is implied that the Graces were
not confirmed and that parliament was dissolved before a Sixty Years' Act
could be brought in. Most of the Graces were confirmed: the point was that
they were not made law.

time to the planters in Leitrim, Longford and Ossory, King's County, Queen's County and Westmeath. Wentworth thus made these concessions mainly to the new English elements in parliament, though the old English, who were involved in the Leinster plantations, also stood to gain. There was no reason why the titles in Connacht should not have been confirmed in the same way, apart from the fact that plantation would be made very difficult for the future and 'if the plantations be hindered, then a principal means of civilising the people and planting religion will be taken away'.[1] The granting of Graces 26 and 27 while refusing 24 and 25 was a clear indication that Wentworth had decided to go ahead with the plantation of Connacht, whatever the opposition.[2] It was also necessary to placate Ulster in some way if Wentworth were to go ahead with the 'Laudian policy' which is implied in Grace 41, which was another one of the ten proposed as legislation. Grace 41 proposed an examination of the number of rectories and impropriations which were in laymen's hands. The quarrels which arose with Richard Boyle showed how dangerous it was to raise the issue of church property, but with the concessions made in Graces 26 and 27, the 'new English' could hardly object to Grace 41, even if might affect them adversely for the future. Piers Crosby's antagonism to Wentworth may perhaps be explained partly on these grounds, since the Crosbies stood to lose church property in the diocese of Ardfert if Grace 41 became law.[3]

The remainder of these ten Graces were of minor importance.[4] They dealt with such matters as the licensing of Aqua Vitae, wine, ale and beer, the changing of the penalty for using the short plough, the assignment of places for the tanning of leather, a general pardon, assessment for robberies and the denization of Scottish undertakers.

The next group concerned those Graces which were to be continued at his Majesty's good pleasure. They were, in short, to continue as 'before', though the whole point of summoning a parliament had been the hope that many matters now lying within the jurisdiction of the prerogative, which for Ireland meant the

---

[1] *Strafford's letters*, i. 320.

[2] Cf. also his remarks on Grace 24, ibid., i. 320.

[3] Cf. 'The case of Sir Piers Crosby baronet', in *Kerry Arch. Mag.*, iv. 1–15 (Oct. 1916).

[4] Nos. 5–6, 8–8, 34, 36 and 40.

administration, should become law, much in the way that the Petition of Right in England had restricted what was considered to be the excessive freedom of action enjoyed by Buckingham. Three[1] of these Graces proposed important economic concessions, namely freedom of trade in staple articles of trade, without any restriction other than customs duties; but perhaps the most important of this group concerned the grant of liveries[2] and admittance to the practice of law, upon the taking of a simple oath of allegiance. The fact that it remained merely a grace meant that it would be revoked at any time at the pleasure of the administration. Other minor financial grievances were dealt with in this way.

So far as these clauses were concerned, the fears of the opposition that they would remain paper concessions only were largely justified. Export licences were in fact demanded from 1635 onwards for the export of wool, linen yarn and pipestaves, and these had to be paid for in addition to the normal customs duties.[3] These Graces, therefore, despite Wentworth's promises, remained a dead letter. On the other hand, Grace 15 was at least partly observed and Catholic proprietors did seem to be able to obtain livery of their land without being obliged to take the oath of supremacy. In addition Catholic lawyers were allowed to practise, provided they did not come into collision with the lord deputy, as Patrick Darcy did in 1636.[4]

A further group of sixteen articles, dealing with such matters as the court of wards, was 'referred to the care and integrity of his majesty's judges', a decision which might have meant everything or nothing.[5] Other articles were left to the discretion of the deputy.[6] A commission was to be set up to deal with fees, which had been the subject of Grace 23. Other Graces were to be granted temporarily.[7] Grace 2 was settled by proclamation; Grace 35, concerning pluralities, was to be handed over to the discretion of the archbishops and bishops; creation money was to be paid to the nobility.

Superficially, Wentworth had agreed to take action upon all the Graces except two. Appearances were deceptive, however. In the first place, the articles which were regarded by Wentworth 'for

---

[1] Nos. 10, 11 and 12.
[2] No. 15.
[3] See Graphs 1 and 2
[4] See below, p. 92.
[5] Nos. 16–22, 29–32, 38, 43, 46.
[6] Nos. 1, 3, 33, 43.
[7] Nos. 28, 45 and 44.

F

great and weighty reasons of State', as 'not expedient', were precisely the two articles to which the old English attached most
importance. In the second place, though none of the Graces
except two were refused, only ten were to be converted into
statute. Matters thus remained where they had been before 1634,
and the old English could feel with justice that they had been
misled. The main object of the agitation for the Graces from 1627
onwards was to take power away from the administration and by
new legislation, to set bounds to the process of gradual wearing
away, to which old English political power had been exposed
since the closing decades of the sixteenth century. While, therefore, it is untrue to suggest that all the Graces were refused, they
did not become law, and while they remained at the mercy of any
administration, the old English could not feel secure. They did not
express their discontent in an unconstitutional way. The opposition of the second session—and third session—was as far as
they went.

*　　　*　　　*

It remains now to consider the third session of the parliament:
from 26 January 1634/5 to 18 April, with a short break from
21 March to 24 March. The journal is even more uncommunicative about this session than the previous two, and were it not for
a long letter of Wentworth to Coke, there would be no way of
knowing what happened. The journal provides information about
the bills which were passed, most of which concerned Graces, and
the subsidy arrangements, but throws no light upon the attitude
of the Anglo-Irish party and gives no hint that any measures were
opposed by them. In March, however, Wentworth wrote a letter[1]
to Coke, in which he remarked *en passant* that 'the Parliament hath
passed most of the Lawes, albeit we find the Popish partye in the
same temper wee left them the last session, by no other arguments
to be persuaded into any reason but plurality of voyces'.

Later in May, when the parliament had been dissolved, he was
able to give a more detailed picture:[2]

. . . the Popish party was as peevish towards the conclusion of the
sessions as formerly: soe I wished the Howse to send some of their
members unto me being desirous to speak unto them, which accordingly

[1] Wentworth to Coke, 2 Mar. 1634/5. Strafford MSS., vol. 5, f. 190.
[2] Ibid., 19 May 1635. Strafford MSS., vol. 9, f. 30.

they did, where I recommended unto them the Lawes of Powder,[1] for the Churche and for setting up howses of correction, which wrought very little effect. For the next day they cast out the Bill for the first and were against the Engrossing of the rest.[2] Soe I was inforced roundly to sett forth the proclamation for Powder and openly to declare a great dislike of their proceedings. Some two days before the Parliament ended, there came a Committee of both houses to putt into my hands the Petition and Articles delivered against Sir Vincent Gookin.[3] And to desire that I would take care there might be a prosecution against him. My answere was that I should not faile to serve them according to their desires. And willed my Lord Dillon[4] to tell the Howse of Commons I would take revenge of them for shewing soe little regard of all things recommended unto them by me, giving all the respect I possibly could to everything that came to me from them. This his Lordship delivered to the Howse accordingly which, whether that or something else wrought amongst them I know not: but the very morning the Parliament was to end, upon a sudden when wee least expected it, They called for the two bills, concerning the Churche and that for the Howses of Correction, passed them one after another with as much chearfulness as might be.[5] And I am persuaded would have done the like for the Powder had they not absolutely rejected it upon the third reading.

These two letters supply the only evidence to show that the old English opposition continued into the third session. They do not mention, however, the discontent which seems to have been felt over the levying of the subsidies. Wentworth was not content with the way of collecting subsidies, which had been established in 1615 and which laid down no definite sum to be paid by each county. Wentworth insisted that each county be assessed according to its wealth, and much of the time of the third session was taken up in deciding how the burden of £40,000 should be allotted.[6] In the event, Leinster was to pay £13,000, Ulster £10,000, Connaught £6,800 and Munster £11,200. It was clear from the assessment that the 'Anglo-Irish counties', which contained the richest

---

[1] To restrain the importation of gunpowder. *Commons' jn. Ire.*, p. 113.
[2] There is no trace of this in the Journal.
[3] He was accused of writing a pamphlet which slandered Ireland. Bagwell, *Stuarts*, i. 223–5.
[4] The delegation consisted of Lord Dillon, Sir Wm. Sarsfield, Sir John Borlase, Sir Charles Coote, Sir Wm. St. Leger, Sir Piers Crosby, Sir William Parsons and Sir George Radcliffe.
[5] This is borne out by the Journal, p. 119, 18 April 1635. The powder bill was introduced on 1 April, when it received first and second reading. There is no mention of it after that date.
[6] Excluding the contribution of the members of the house of lords.

land, bore the brunt. Not until the 1640 parliament met, however, does evidence become available to show how this was felt as a grievance, when the demand was made by the opposition in the commons that the four subsidies which had been voted should be levied 'in a moderate parliamentary way'.[1] Wentworth does mention the reluctance to accept his new method of levying subsidies but gives no hint as to how much discontent it must have led to.

The parliament was dissolved on 18 April in accordance with the wishes of the king. On 19 May, however, a letter[2] from Wentworth to Coke, showed how Charles had once again changed his mind. Wentworth noted how 'With this Paquett came the Commission for continuing the Parliament which was absolutely dissolved before'. Wentworth recalled how he had advised against dissolution on the ground that it would be difficult to summon so favourable a parliament again, in which 'the Protestants should be the greater number'. The parliament, however, had been dissolved and had gone out of legal existence.

Wentworth now had a suggestion to make for the future which may be regarded as the counterpart of the action of James I in creating new boroughs returning members favourable to the crown. Wentworth proposed to disfranchise some of those old boroughs which returned Catholic members, as a method of ensuring that 'the Popish party' would not be so strong again in the future. Again he was relying upon political mechanics of the kind which Charles I had used in 1626 when he picked as sheriffs those members who had given trouble in the first parliament of the reign. It is ironical to find Wentworth hoping by the same methods to remove future opposition.

There are a great many of the old Corporations within this Kingdom that claim right and accordingly sent Burgesses to this Parliament, whose charters if they were legally questioned by the Attorney would certainly appear to warrant noe such power. And upon this point wee might well overthrow at least twenty of these old corporations who all sent, and soe will still, meare Irish and Papists, the most obstinate senseless creatures I am persuaded of the world, who had noe more witte nor will then to doe just as their Jesuits and friers appointed them. . . .

And if these feathers were handsomely and gently taken out of their

[1] See below, p. 190.
[2] Strafford MSS., vol. 9, f. 35. 19 May 1635.

wing, by degrees one after another, as if it were *aliud agens*, it would not be much observed and yet by this meanes, if his Majesty had occasion to call another Parliament hee should not only lessen the number of the Howse and soe find them much more easy to be governed. But a very facile way opened to have the Protestants always in far greater number and by them to establish the English Government and Laws on this side, even as many as pleased yourselves to have, of both which I should be utterly hopeless if a Parliament was now to be summoned again.

On 6 July, he mentioned that he was going to take action in the matter.[1] 'There shall a speedy course now be taken by the Attorney to call in the Old Corporations by Quo warranto which I will trust be a means to cast at least twenty of them and much facilitate the Kings affairs in a Parliamentary way were there occasion for it.'

Events in the 1640 parliament showed that several boroughs were in fact disfranchised between 1635 and 1640.[2] They were, Ardee, Newcastle, Naas, Fore, Bannow, Taghmon, and Clonmynes. Cross Tipperary was also not represented as a county in the 1640 parliament. Newcastle had been newly incorporated in 1613; in 1634 however it had returned two old English members and this may have been the reason why it was picked out for this treatment. The borough of Naas had received a writ for the parliament of 1560 and had sent two members ever since that date. The only reason for its being disfranchised seems to lie in the fact that Wentworth could not tolerate an old English borough within half a mile of the palace which he was building for himself at Jigginstown. The rights of the remaining four boroughs were much more open to question and it was not so surprising that they should have not been sent writs in 1640. During the second half of 1640 these deprivations played their part in causing friction between the house of commons and the lord deputy, though Wentworth did not go as far as to disfranchise the twenty boroughs mentioned in his original letter.

There was now open conflict between the old English and the lord deputy, which was to become even more acute as he pressed ahead with his plan for the plantation of Connacht. Not for the first time the opposition began to be led by a peer normally

---

[1] Wentworth to Coke, 6 July 1635. Strafford MSS., vol. 9, f. 54.
[2] See below, p. 190. I cannot offer any suggestion why Ardee should have been excluded.

resident in England, Richard de Burgh, Viscount St. Albans, and 4th earl of Clanrickarde. It remained to be seen whether his influence at court would bring about a check to Wentworth's policy of 'thorough'.

8

THE INSTRUMENTS OF 'THOROUGH'

I

From Wentworth's point of view the parliament of 1634 had been an almost unqualified success. The subsidies which it had granted relieved the financial pressure upon the lord deputy and enabled him to escape from the necessity of making political concessions for the future. The parliament also passed legislation upon which Wentworth's policy was to be based and in the light of this it was clear that during the next few years a policy of resumption, in both church and state, was to be attempted on a large scale. Alienated rectories and impropriations were to be restored to the church, while at the same time the revenues from Crown lands were to be increased by several methods, including the plantation of new areas, the increasing of rents upon the discovery of Crown titles and the raising of the incomes which the Crown derived from its exploitation of feudal incidents. During the course of the parliament the unpopularity of such a course had been revealed and there was little doubt that its enforcement would be a matter of great difficulty, since at almost every turn Wentworth was bound to come up against the inertia or active opposition of an established interest. Wentworth came to rely therefore upon the activities of four executive tribunals, the Irish Star Chamber, usually known as the Court of Castle Chamber, the Court of High Commission, the Court of Wards and Liveries and the Commission for Defective Titles. Of these, none were strictly Wentworth's creation but during his deputyship they were used for the first time as co-ordinated instruments of policy.

The Court of Castle Chamber, founded under Henry VIII, had been revived in 1581, and its patent was renewed at the beginning of the reigns of James I and Charles I.[1] Like the English Star Chamber, on which its procedure was modelled, its competence extended to cases of riot, conspiracy, perjury, extortion, forgery,

[1] H. Wood, 'The Court of Castle Chamber' in *R.I.A. Proc.*, 32, C 152–70.

the receiving of popish books and pictures and charges of a similar character.[1] It could not sentence to death but it could inflict heavy fines, imprisonment and corporal punishment, such as the pillory, ear-nailing, etc. Unlike the common law courts the defendant was questioned as a matter of course, sometimes by the process known as *ore tenus*, in private. It has been described as a system more suitable for catching the guilty than saving the innocent[2] and certainly it is hard to deny its inquisitorial character.

In Ireland the court was clearly under the control of the executive. The quorum consisted of the lord deputy, the lord chancellor, the treasurer and the vice-treasurer. Other legal officers of the Crown, the lords chief justice of common pleas and king's bench, the lord chief baron of the exchequer and the master of the rolls, were entitled to sit but their presence was not essential. Thus in 1629 the quorum of the court consisted of Falkland, lord chancellor Loftus, lord treasurer Boyle and vice-treasurer Mountnorris. In their hands the executive character of the court was clearly predominant; it was also unlikely that the powers of the court would be used to support policies of which Boyle, Loftus and Mountnorris disapproved. Recently indeed the court had directed its attention against the recusants[3] and it was hard to imagine a time when not only would it be used against Protestants but Richard Boyle himself would suffer from its close attentions.

The new lord deputy was determined to ensure that so useful and powerful a weapon should be completely under his own control. A new patent was issued in 1634,[4] presumably with the object of excluding the lord treasurer from the court, in view of the fact that within a matter of days after the new patent had been received Boyle was summoned before the court. He was required to answer charges concerning illegal acquisition of church property and ultimately in 1636 was heavily fined.

From one point of view this attack upon Boyle can be regarded as Mountnorris's revenge for Boyle's political assault upon himself in 1629. Within a short time, however, Mountnorris was to

---

[1] For examples of the cases dealt with before the deputyship of Wentworth see T.C.D. MS. G.3.1, ff. 74–99.

[2] Tanner, *Tudor Constitutional Documents*, p. 256.

[3] *Cal. S.P. Ire., 1625–32*, p. 445.

[4] *Strafford's letters*, i. 330. The terms of the patent allowed Wentworth to issue a new commission with such alterations as he should think fit. *Liber mun. pub. Hib.*, ii. 180.

lose the confidence of the lord deputy and with it, his political offices, including his seat in Castle Chamber. The break between the two men led to a struggle for power in the course of which Wentworth obtained complete control of Castle Chamber. Already in 1633 his cousin Christopher Wandesford had been created Master of the Rolls with a seat on the court.[1] The new chief justice of common pleas, Sir Gerald Lowther, appointed in 1633, was also trusted by the lord deputy.[2] As neither the lord chancellor, Viscount Loftus, or the Master of the Court of Wards, Sir William Parsons, showed any desire to support him in opposition, Mountnorris found himself an increasingly isolated figure. By April 1635, Wentworth had decided to get rid of him and wrote to Secretary Coke,[3] complaining that Mountnorris was 'an Officer of no great nor quick endeavours in his Majesty's Service, a person, held by us all that hear him, to be most impertinent and troublesome in the Debate of all Businesses'. He recommended that Sir Adam Loftus should succeed Mountnorris as vice-treasurer.

The clash between Mountnorris and the lord deputy was almost inevitable, since the post of vice-treasurer was the key to the administration. Mountnorris controlled the balances which in 1635 amounted to £55,000 and which were to increase further.[4] He was also a member of the customs farm in which he held a quarter share of the profits which by 1635 had reached the unprecedented sum of £20,000 a year. Finally, he was a member of the quorum of the Court of Castle Chamber. It was, however, easier to protest against him than to remove him and six months later Mountnorris was not only still in office he was also negotiating behind the deputy's back for a new arrangement of the customs farm.[5] Nor, in view of Wentworth's enemies at court and Mountnorris's friends, was his fall from power certain. The position of apparent stalemate seems to have driven Wentworth to desperate measures and he seized upon some words of criticism which Mountnorris was said to have uttered, after his brother who was a member of the deputy's troop of horse had been reprimanded.[6] In his capacity as a captain in the army, Mountnorris was summoned before the Council of War, charged with offences against the

[1] *Liber mun. pub. Hib.*, ii. 19.   [2] *Strafford's letters*, i. 392.
[3] Ibid., i. 403.   [4] *Lismore Papers*, 1st ser., iv. 155.
[5] *Cal. Clarendon Papers*, i. 361.   [6] *Strafford's letters*, i. 499–500.

articles of war and on 12 December 1635 sentenced to death, though Wentworth asked that the sentence should not be carried out. This incident has often been regarded as a purely personal matter between the two men in which Wentworth's gout played a decisive part. In fact, however, it was merely the excuse for driving Mountnorris from his threefold grip upon the administration, in the exchequer, the customs farm and not least, in the Court of Castle Chamber. On 3 January 1635/6, three weeks after the court martial, Wentworth sent to London a copy of the charges against Mountnorris in connection with his office as vice-treasurer. He was accused of 'sundry corruptions and misdemeanors' by a commission set up under the great seal and composed of Wentworth's supporters in the administration, Lord Dillon, Sir William Parsons, Sir Gerald Lowther and Sir Richard Bolton.[1] The result was a foregone conclusion. By the end of January, nine months after Wentworth's original request, Mountnorris was replaced as vice-treasurer by Sir Adam Loftus, cousin of the lord chancellor.[2]

By the beginning of 1636, therefore, Wentworth was in complete control of the Court of Castle Chamber, the members of which were either his own nominees like Wandesford and Loftus or men who had thrown in their lot with him like Lowther, lord chief justice of common pleas. The only exception to this was the lord chancellor, Viscount Loftus. It was not until 1638, that a split occurred between the lord deputy and himself, the cause being an apparently minor incident over a dowry. Wentworth complained that the chancellor's attitude threatened to 'distemper the whole government . . . and set all loose again to faction and party'.[3] In April 1638, Loftus was sequestered from the privy council and ordered to refrain from exercising any power as chancellor.[4] He was replaced by the chief baron of the exchequer, Sir Richard Bolton, who was also attorney general of the Court of Wards. The fall of Loftus from power however did not mark the complete disappearance of the groups which had made all the political running in the decade before Wentworth's arrival. Coote and Ranelagh remained, and with them Sir William Parsons, who managed to hold on to the lucrative position of master of the Court of Wards despite his links with the discredited

---

[1] *Strafford's letters*, i. 505.   [2] Ibid., 512–13.   [3] Ibid., ii. 163.
[4] Ibid., ii. 160.

Richard Boyle, earl of Cork. In November 1639, when Wentworth had left the country, he was even made a member of the
Court of Castle Chamber, along with Sir Robert Meredith,
chancellor of the exchequer.[1]

Without control of the Court of Castle Chamber it is very
doubtful whether Wentworth would have been able to force
through his policies so effectively and so swiftly. He depended on
it to deal with any tendency towards opposition which he found
in important quarters. Resistance to the plantation of Galway was
crushed by the imposition of heavy fines and the imprisonment of
the Galway jury on the grounds of conspiracy. Here indeed was
the classic example of the way in which reluctance to carry out
the wishes of the administration could be regarded by the lord
deputy as falling under the heading of those crimes which Castle
Chamber was competent to deal with. Since he himself controlled
the court the verdict could be predicted in advance.

Although no detailed records of the court have survived, there
is sufficient evidence to show that it did not operate rarely or
spasmodically. It was used to enforce proclamations[2] as well as to
punish offence of 'conspiracy' and one of the objects of the 1634
patent was to enable the court to meet more than twice a week.
Among those who were threatened by its action were Sir Vincent
Gookin, who incurred the lord deputy's displeasure during the
parliament,[3] and Viscount Wilmot, former vice-president of Connacht who was charged with alienating Crown lands worth £500
a year.[4] Other references in the State papers[5] provide examples of
heavy fines and imprisonment being inflicted. Perhaps the most
important intervention of the court in Wentworth's later years
was in Ulster where it inflicted heavy fines and life imprisonment
upon a group which refused to take an oath denouncing the
Scottish National League and Covenant.[6]

The Court of Castle Chamber was thus only a court in theory;
in practice it was an instrument at the full disposal of the lord
deputy, particularly after the fall of Mountnorris in 1635. It ceased

[1] Cal. S.P. Ire., 1633–47, p. 228.
[2] Steele, Tudor & Stuart proclam., ii, no. 309, etc. from April 1635.
[3] Strafford's letters, i. 349.　　　　　[4] Ibid., i. 401; ii. 10.
[5] E.g. the Sexton case in 1639, when heavy fines were imposed upon a
recusant family for attempted conversion of the husband. Cal. S.P. Ire.,
1633–47, p. 304.
[6] In 1639. Cal S.P. Ire., 1633–47, pp. 222–3.

to be used against the recusants as a body and was in the main directed at those who ventured to oppose in any way the policies of the lord deputy. The resentment which it aroused was concealed until after Wentworth's fall from power, but even then it was difficult to attack the legal position of the court directly and the opposition groups in the 1640 parliament had to content themselves with asking by what law were jurors sentenced to great fines, pillories, loss of ears, being bored through the tongue, branding and similar punishments.[1]

The Court of Castle Chamber lay at the heart of Wentworth's administration, making the rule of 'thorough' possible. It became the instrument of a despotism as severe as that of Richelieu in providing an arbitrary sanction for every act and organ of the administration.

II

Problems of government and finance were rarely completely separated during Wentworth's administration and even the Court of Castle Chamber made a small contribution to the Exchequer, estimated in 1640 at £800 per annum.[2] Unlike the Court of Wards and Liveries and the Commission for Defective Titles, however, it was not primarily a financial instrument. By contrast the Court of Wards and Liveries and the Commission for Defective Titles were legal in name but not in spirit; their main *raison d'être* was to use the existing land law as a method of increasing Crown revenue.

The Court of Wards, like the Court of Castle Chamber, had existed on paper in Ireland since Henry VIII's reign,[3] with the object of turning into money payments, the king's feudal rights to wardship and marriage, primer seisin, relief and licence to alienate.[4] What had long been polite fictions were now to have a definite cash value for the Crown. By comparison with its English counterpart, however, the Irish Court of Wards languished, since its activities were largely confined to a small part of the country. It was in fact not an institution with officials and records of its own but a committee of judges who met from time to time, plus

---

[1] 'The Queries', no. 16. *Cal. S.P. Ire., 1633–47*, p. 334.
[2] *Cal. S.P. Ire., 1647–60*, p. 234.   [3] *Liber mun. pub. Hib.*, pt. 2, p. 176.
[4] For a table showing the principal tenures of the Crown and the obligations of each see H. E. Bell, *An introduction to the History and Records of the Court of Wards and Liveries*, p. 75, footnote.

one permanent official. However, the extension of English control over the whole country led to the creation of more officials in the early seventeenth century and whereas one escheator had been sufficient in the sixteenth century, in 1605 four escheators were created, one for each province.[1] They differed from escheators in England in that they were appointed not annually, but under patent, during good behaviour; they thus bore some resemblance to the feodary, the permanent official of the English Court of Wards, though they were still attached to the exchequer.

The first phase in the reorganisation of the Court of Wards took place during the period 1615–22. The background to this and other financial measures was the financial crisis in England, which made it essential to reduce the continual drain which Ireland made upon the royal treasury. In England, the rise of the royal debt, the excess of expenditure over revenue by £200,000, and the failure of the 'Addled parliament' of 1614 brought James I to the most difficult years of his reign and it was inevitable that further attempts should be made to make the Irish administration solvent and help indirectly to improve the financial position in England. The solution of the problem was seen to be in the introduction of fiscal methods which had already proved their worth in England. Of these the Court of Wards and Liveries was one.

In December 1615, the English privy council authorised a committee to investigate the possibility of setting up a Court of Wards in Ireland.[2] After some consideration, it was decided to establish a commission as a temporary measure. In October 1616, Richard Percival, an official of the English Court of Wards, was appointed clerk to the Irish commission.[3] This temporary phase came to an end in 1622, when a permanent court was created by Sir William Parsons as master.

Thus the Court of Wards had already been fully in existence ten years when Wentworth was appointed lord deputy. Its financial yield in 1628 was said to have been £7,000[4] Irish in a total public revenue of £50,000.[5] At the same date the English Court of Wards was bringing in £49,000.

[1] *Liber mun. pub. Hib.*, pt. 2, pp. 57–8.
[2] *Acts privy council 1615–16*, p. 346.
[3] He was chief remembrancer. H. E. Bell, *Court of Wards*, p. 31.
[4] *Cal. S.P. Ire., 1625–32*, p. 419.
[5] Ibid., pp. 418–19. It ranked fourth as a source of revenue. Crown rents brought in £20,470, customs duties £11,451, and composition money £7,229.

The most important event in the history of the court before Wentworth's arrival occurred in connection with the Graces. This may be best illustrated pictorially. If the number of fines for livery of land is plotted on a graph, the following picture results.

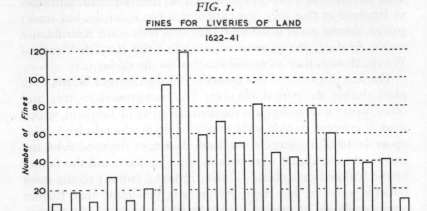

FIG. 1.

FINES FOR LIVERIES OF LAND

1622-41

From this it appears that there was a startling increase in 1628 in the number of proprietors who were allowed to sue out their livery. All of these proprietors had old English or Gaelic Irish names. The flood of liveries began in December 1628, only seven being granted in the months before. From this evidence it is difficult to resist the conclusion that the astonishing change was due to the coming into force of the Graces of 1628 and represents the accumulated backlog of proprietors wanting to sue livery but unable to do so during the years before owing to the insistence upon their taking out the oath of supremacy. If this is correct, it is one of the few pieces of evidence available to gauge how far the Graces came into actual practice.

It is commonly assumed that Charles I failed to implement his share of the bargain of 1628, and that though the Catholic gentry paid their share of the £120,000 granted to the king, the Graces never in fact came into force. The conclusion to be drawn from this graph is that at least one of the most important of the Graces did come into force and remained in force until 1641. This conclusion is strengthened by the fact that Charles I, as part of his attempt to bring pressure to bear on the Anglo-Irish, did threaten to withdraw the Graces, a threat which would hardly have been made if they had not partially come into force.[1] Wentworth also declared in 1634 that the king had lost £6,000 a year in the Court of Wards owing to this particular Grace.[2] Not all Catholic proprietors found it possible to sue out their livery,[3] but considerably more did so from 1628 onwards than did not. Nor were all those who failed to do so Gaelic Irish proprietors; on the contrary, numbers were equally divided between them and the Anglo-Irish. The graph also shows that even during Wentworth's deputyship, Catholic proprietors were allowed to sue out their livery without hindrance. As a consequence, it followed that the amount of land available to be leased out by the court declined considerably, a fact which must have caused the revenue derived from the court to drop also. The question therefore arises as to where the Court of Wards derived its income while Wentworth was lord deputy. Part of it was derived from the fines for liveries, part also from the fines which were collected from those proprietors who had been accused of alienating crown land without due livery. Graph no. 2 shows a great increase in the number of cases of this character, and on the whole the level was maintained during Wentworth's deputyship, though there was a drop from 1633 to 1635; this may represent the policy of appeasement towards the Catholics which Wentworth adopted during the negotiations for the continuation of the £20,000 per annum, before the 1634 parliament and during the first session.

Under Wentworth the most important event in the history of the court was the passing of the Statute of Uses in 1634.[4] Until then, it had been possible to evade the burden of livery and feudal incidents by granting lands to use. The administration therefore put through the parliament of 1634 a statute of uses, which had an object similar to that of the English act of Henry VIII's reign —namely to make those who had the use of land liable for feudal incidents just as much as if they had full seisin. Wentworth hoped that this measure would lead to an increased revenue of £4,000 from the Court of Wards.[5]

In addition to this, Wentworth, shortly after his arrival in Dublin, had criticised 'base tenures in socage' and expressed his

---

[1] *Strafford's letters*, i. 71. [2] Ibid., i. 317.
[3] Cf. T.C.D. MS. F.1.12.
[4] *Stat. Ire.* ii. 21–8. 10. Car. I, cap. 2, also concerned wardships (ibid., pp. 28–40).
[5] *Strafford's letters*, ii. 8.

belief that 'reserving tenures *in capite* was the greatest means of drawing the subjects to depend upon his majesty, which, as in all Kingdoms, so in this, is most principally to be attended and laboured for'.[1] This was an expression of his policy of increasing the effectiveness of the court of wards, and he attempted to put it into practice in Ulster by changing the tenure of the planters from common socage to tenancy-in-chief.[2] As a result not merely were rents increased, in itself an unpopular change, but in addition the tenants were made liable to the payment of feudal incidents from which their socage tenure had spared them hitherto.

FIG. 2.

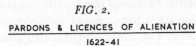

PARDONS & LICENCES OF ALIENATION

1622-41

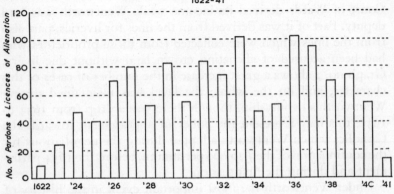

This new development under Wentworth led to grave discontent among the planters, whose support of the administration had on the whole been unquestioned. There was, however, one feature of the court's activities which passed them by; this was its searching into the past for Crown land which had been 'alienated' without permission, a simple task in Ireland. It was the Anglo-Irish who were particularly exposed to this form of investigation from which only a sixty years' title statute would have relieved them.

The following table provides an analysis of the fines for alienation, county by county. This shows how during the years 1625–41 the planted counties in Ulster,[3] Armagh, Cavan, Donegal, Fermanagh, Londonderry and Tyrone, were hardly affected at all by

[1] Wentworth to Coke, 23 Oct. 1633 (ibid., i. 132).
[2] *Cal. S.P. Ire., 1633–47*, p. 272.
[3] A similar conclusion emerges from analysis of T.C.D. MS. F.1.12.

PARDONS AND LICENCES OF ALIENATION

County	1625	1626	1627	1628	1629	1630	1631	1632	1633	1634	1635	1636	1637	1638	1639	1640	1641	Total
Antrim				1	1	1	1	1	3	2	3	3	5	1	3	5		30
Armagh																1	1	2
Carlow		3		2	3	1	1		7	2	2	1	4	2	5			35
Cavan								1										1
Clare		2	8	2	2	3	2	2	2	3	2	3	1					32
Cork		7	11	8	11	7	15	20	6	4	8	11	10	14	13	6	2	154
Donegal																	1	1
Down			2		1		6	3	5		4	8	5	2	2	2		40
Dublin		9	6	7	6	5	6	2	3	3	3	6	8	1	1	1	3	70
Fermanagh		1										1						2
Galway		3		1														20
Kerry	1	2	2	2	2	3	2	5	5	2	1	3	3	2	5	3	1	43
Kildare		1	3	5	2	6	2	4	6	1	2	2	4	6	2	1		46
Kilkenny		1	2	3	2	1	2	2	3	1	4	7	5	2	3			41
King's Co.			2	1	4	2		1	2	3	3	2	2	3	2			21
Leitrim							1											1
Londonderry																		2
Longford					3			1	3	1		1			1			5
Louth	2	8	2	5	7	1	1	5	2		2	7	1	2				28
Limerick	3	9	8	4	13	9	2	1	9	9	3	12	1	10	8	4	3	101
Mayo		4		4	1		4					2	4	5	4	4		11
Meath		1	7	1		6	9	2	7		5	1	6	1	1	2		100
Monaghan		6	3		2		5	1					9	4	2	4		18
Queen's Co.		3	1		2		3	3	9		1		3					23
Roscommon		2		4	8	3	2	1	2	3	3		2			2		34
Sligo					2		8	8	9	1								15
Tipperary		3	6	3	6					2		18	9	6	9	6	1	106
Tyrone																	1	1
Waterford		2					8		3	3	4	7	3	2	4	3		39
Westmeath			2		2	2	3	4	7	5	1	4	7	2	6	5		66
Wexford		5	8	3		5		4	4	1	1	3	4	4	1	6	1	52
Wicklow						3		1		1		1	1	1	1	1	1	11
Annual Totals	6	72	80	56	85	58	86	75	103	52	56	103	97	70	75	56	15	1,151

G

this activity of the court nor were Longford, the northern baronies of Wexford and Leitrim which had also been planted under James I. It also shows how that plantation, by introducing common socage tenure, in practice diminished the geographical areas open to the full action of the court. This also seems to have been the effect of the plantation in Connacht, since Sligo and Mayo disappear from this record after 1634, and Roscommon after 1635. The resistance of the Galway jury is reflected in Galway remaining till 1636. The effect of the plantation of Clare is seen when Clare disappears after 1638. Elsewhere, in partially planted areas of Leinster and Munster, 'planters' seem to have been hardly affected by the court, if we may go by the small number of new English names which occur. In other words the main burden of the Court of Wards was felt by those counties in which the old English and Gaelic Irish were still strong, in particular Cork, Limerick, Meath and Tipperary. Resentment among the Catholics must have been increased by the fact that a high proportion of the wardships and confiscated lands were leased out to the actual officials of the court of wards. One of the spoils of office was the opportunity given to make money in this way. It is true that leases and wardships were granted to some Catholics, but they formed only a small proportion of the whole.

The total income derived from the court during the years 1630–40 was stated officially to have been £69,370.[1] This was an average of £7,000 a year, which was no considerable increase on the previous decade.[2] The manner in which the revenue was collected, however, was a major political irritant which ultimately affected Protestant as well as Catholic proprietors. The discontent which the court aroused was disproportionate to its importance as a source of revenue and must be taken into consideration in attempting to assess the cause of the downfall of Wentworth's administration.

The court was thus a confused mixture of finance, politics and religion, which for over twenty years figured as a major political grievance in the eyes of the Catholic gentry. If anything it was more unpopular in Ireland than its counterpart was in England, since the novelty of English land law in many parts of the country and the *de facto* religious discrimination made its activities seem

---

[1] Carte MSS. (Bodleian). I, f. 321.
[2] In 1640 it was £10,000 a year. *Cal. S.P. Ire., 1647–60*, p. 234.

the more obnoxious. Under Wentworth the court did not change its character. Sir William Parsons remained in control and the only difference of policy between this and the previous deputyship lay in the dropping of the oath of supremacy and in the attempt to extend the range of the court into Ulster. As as instrument of the policy of 'thorough' the Court of Wards and Liveries was already made to Wentworth's purposes before he ever arrived in Ireland; it was the only organ of the administration which did not incur the charge of inefficiency and which Wentworth himself made no attempt to adapt.

III

The third of Wentworth's executive courts, the Commission for Defective Titles, was no more of his own creation than the Court of Castle Chamber and the Court of Wards.[1] Its activities were closely linked with these and most of its members were common to both. What was new about it was its increased efficiency under Wentworth. In 1636, Sir Adam Loftus, Sir Gerald Lowther and Sir Richard Bolton were all members, though other senior members of the administration were all entitled to sit. Links with the Court of Wards were provided by the presence of Bolton and from time to time by that of William Parsons himself.[2]

The Commission had been set up in June 1634 by royal patent,[3] though it was also to be confirmed by statute during the first session of the 1634 parliament.[4] The fiction behind it was that it existed to supply a firm title to those who requested it to do so. Thus in principle it was the answer of the Crown to the Grace demanding that a sixty-year title provable in law should be sufficient against all comers. Wentworth had opposed this Grace on the grounds that at one stroke it would cut off the Crown from 'discovering' alienated land and from raising rents when defective titles were enrolled.[5] In his view the Commission for Defective Titles would provide an effective remedy for those proprietors

---

[1] 'There has nothing stood soe much in our way as the patents past upon a former Commission granted for that purpose in the tymes of the Lords Chichester and Grandison.' Wentworth to Coke, 21 Feb. 1636/7. Strafford MSS., vol. 9, f. 209.

[2] T.C.D. MS. F.3.15 ff. 533, 535. 19 Feb. 1639.

[3] *Cal. S.P. Ire., 1633–47*, pp. 56–7.   [4] *Stat. Ire.*, ii. 93.

[5] *Strafford's letters*, i. 320.

who felt that their titles were liable to be threatened while at the same time Crown revenues would benefit. This was the view which prevailed and by 1636 the Commission was estimated to be bringing in £500 a year, which was eventually expected to reach £5,000.[1]

The Commission supplemented the activity of the Court of Wards, by creating new tenants *in capite* who were liable to feudal incidents and by discovering old feudal tenures which had previously been concealed. When, for example, the Ulster planters were pressed to change their tenure from socage to capite, the procedure which was envisaged was that the Commission for Defective Titles should pass two-thirds of their land *in capite*, which would immediately bring them under the jurisdiction of the Court of Wards, with all the financial and religious drawbacks that that entailed.[2] Thus at every turn the administration held trump cards. The existing insecurity of land titles forced proprietors into seeking some measure of protection from the administration, but once they had taken the step the remedy often proved worse than the disease. Wentworth may have felt that he was merely recovering the rights of the Crown and restoring it to its proper place, and he wrote proudly in 1636 of the contentment of the ancient English colonists 'their Possessions now being most graciously secured by the Commission of Defective Titles'. But the attitude of those affected was revealed as something different in 1640 when the opposition groups in parliament demanded that 'those who have been terrorised into passing their estates on the Defective Titles Commission at higher rates shall be allowed to surrender them and pass them at rates secured under the Graces'.[3] Later on, in 1643, the Anglo-Irish, in their statement of grievances, specifically mentioned Parsons, Lowther and Bolton as having 'voided 150 letters patent' in the course of a morning's work. For all Wentworth's estimate of its utility for proprietors there is no doubt that the Commission for Defective

---

[1] *Strafford's letters*, ii. 90.
[2] *Cal. S.P. Ire., 1633–47*, p. 272. After 1640 they were allowed to return to socage tenure at the new rents, ibid., p. 327. See also Strafford MSS., vol. 9, f. 209. 'We have now begunn to call before us at that Commission the Planters, Natives and Servitors within the Province of Ulster, where the King hath not soe much as one tenure in Knight's service'. Wentworth to Coke, 21 Feb. 1636/7.
[3] *Cal. S.P. Ire., 1647–60*, p. 240.

Titles was regarded with resentment by those who were most exposed to its operations, namely the old English and Gaelic Irish proprietors in those areas which were still unaffected by plantation. It was significant that Bolton and Lowther, the two most prominent members of the commission, should be two of the four officials impeached by the Irish parliament in 1641.

The membership of the Commission was in practice the same as that of Castle Chamber. In April 1636 it underwent a similar reorganisation, when Mountnorris was removed. Its active membership then consisted of Sir Adam Loftus, Lord Dillon, Sir Robert Meredith, chancellor of the exchequer, and Sir James Ware.[1] All its monies were to be paid into the exchequer and it was not to encroach upon the activities of the Court of Wards by dealing with tenures *in capite*. It could, however, deal with former monastic lands and it was probably in this sphere that much of its work was done. In order to encourage the two legal officers concerned, from early in 1636 they were paid 4*s.* in the £ of the first year's rent in each case.[2]

Few of the records of the Commission have survived, but some indication of its financial nature may be gained from a list of rent increases, which is to be found among the Strafford papers.[3] Dated 4 May 1636 and headed 'Compositions made upon His Majesty's Commission of Grace for remedy of Defective Titles', this document shows that rents were increased by £417 over the old rate of £738. In addition new rents to the value of £138 were imposed. Over a hundred proprietors were involved, of whom only about a quarter were Catholics. As a high proportion of these were O'Farrells, it seems probable that the Commission was operating a good deal at this date in Farrell's Country (County Longford). The large number of officials involved include Sir William Parsons, Sir George Radcliffe, Matthew Derenzi and Sir Charles Coote. Clearly the Commission did not apply merely to the old English and Gaelic Irish, but it may well be that the officials, as they did in the Court of Wards, used their privileged position to obtain land on cheap terms, and that this threat, as much as increased rents, was one of the real causes of

---

[1] Ibid., *1633–47*, pp. 56–7.
[2] Strafford MSS. vol. 9, f. 151.
[3] See Appendix III and *Guide to the Manuscript Collections in Sheffield City Libraries*, p. 12, under heading 'Official papers'.

the unpopularity of the commissions. So many legal fictions were involved that at this date it is almost impossible to discover the exact truth.

IV

Together with the Court of High Commission, these three interconnected prerogative institutions lay at the heart of Wentworth's administration. Members of these courts formed a close oligarchy dominating the legal as well as the administrative machinery. Under the lord deputy's eye they worked hard and long hours. As Wentworth wrote to Coke, 'the misery is most of them on this side waxe weary of the paines and toyle, their sittings . . . continually almost, forenoon amd afternoon . . . so many things are there to be put in order both in Church, State, Plantations, Revenew and Trade, as might well affright a man from beginning any of them, considering the slender and short thread of life and the greatness and extent of the Worke'.[1] For the first time Ireland was controlled by a lord deputy, who was not only in the closest contact with the English government but also had an almost unchallengeable grip upon the machinery of Irish government. The circle of control was completed by a proclamation issued larly in 1635 forbidding anyone to leave Ireland without the permission of the lord deputy.[2] This was ostensibly aimed at meeting the abuse of absentee landownership; in practice, however, Wentworth intended to prevent the sending of agents to England, as had happened under Falkland. Wentworth condemned these 'Agencyes' as 'a kind of Treatyes which have more in them of the Republick than consists with the Indepedency and Prerogative of a Monarch'.[3] From 1635, therefore, there was no appeal from the rule of the Court of Castle Chamber and the other organs of Wentworth's government.

The odds against successful opposition to the lord deputy were very slender indeed, yet it was attempted, both by old English, new English and Ulster Scots. In all three instances grievances over land and religion were closely associated. Wentworth was to find that the plantation of Connacht would meet with as determined resistance among the old English as his religious policy among the Protestant groups of both English and Scottish descent.

[1] Strafford MSS., vol. 9, f. 151.   [2] *Strafford's letters*, i. 362.
[3] Strafford MSS., vol. 9, f. 105.

9

THE PLANTATION OF CONNACHT

THE attempt to plant Connacht was one of the most important episodes of Wentworth's administration, but, like so many other things, the plan did not originate with him. From the strategic point of view it was obvious enough: the plantations of Leitrim and Longford in 1615 and the years following[1] marked the extension of new English influence to the line of the Shannon and the proposed plantation of the territory of Ormonde would have continued this control down to Limerick. To the eyes of the English administration the plantation of Connacht might well appear to follow on logically from the plantations in Ulster and elsewhere. Connacht indeed was the only province in which recent English settlement had not taken place.

The strategic argument could be reinforced by a financial one. In 1611 the commission which had been set up to put forward suggestions for the improvement of crown revenues in Ireland had included Connacht in its recommendations.[2] The composition of Connacht, which had been agreed upon in 1585 and which in 1611 was worth £3,000 to the crown was viewed by the commissioners as capable of increase.[3] They also considered that the many insecure titles to land, if investigated, would give the opportunity for the levying of good fines and increased rents. In short, Connacht was an obvious target for the administration.

The problem, however, was not as simple as it appeared at first sight. Strategic and financial simplicities concealed political complications. Connacht was not Ulster, and Clanrickarde was not Hugh O'Neill. During the Nine Years War, Connacht, under Clanrickarde and Thomond, had been loyal to the English connection against its traditional enemy from the north and at the battle of Kinsale, the men of Connacht had fought on the side of Mountjoy against O'Neill and O'Donnell. The overwhelming

---

[1] Cf. Butler, *Confiscation*, pp. 79 ff.
[2] *Cal. Carew MSS., 1603–24*, p. 101: 105.　　　[3] Ibid., p. 130.

victory of Kinsale which was followed six years later by the Flight of the Earls, gave the English government the opportunity to plant Ulster, an opportunity which though it may have come about accidentally,[1] was nevertheless seized with both hands. The success of the plantation and the apparent removal of what had been the greatest threat to the English administration in Ireland brought as its consequence a lowering of the value of Connacht as an ally, in the eyes of the administration. With Ulster subdued, there was no longer the same necessity to placate the traditional allies of the English in Ireland, whether the Anglo-Irish towns, the gentry of the pale or Clanrickarde in Connacht. The centralisation of the customs system in 1613 undermined the independence of the Anglo-Irish ports and the establishment of the court of wards in 1616 brought the Catholic landowners increasingly within the purview of the administration; it was clearly only a matter of time before something was done about Connacht, in which the influence of Clanrickarde and Thomond very much resembled the palatine jurisdictions of England in the later middle ages, which had disappeared there in the sixteenth century, but lingered on in Ireland.

In the last session of the 1613 parliament, under the promptings of the old English party, a bill had been forwarded to England,[2] which would have stabilised the composition of Connacht and hence made a plantation much more difficult. This bill came to nothing, because parliament did not meet again and during the years following the plantations of Leitrim (Connacht) and Longford (Leinster) took place. In July, 1623, however, the commissioners who had been sent from England to report upon the state of Ireland advised against further plantation.[3] They considered that discontent aroused by previous plantations, added to the fact 'that works of that nature had been much perverted by the private aims of many particular persons to get only large scopes of land into their hands for their own profit without any care of settling them for the strength and safety of the country' made it unseasonable to think of further plantation for the present.

---

[1] T. W. Moody, *The Londonderry Plantation*, p. 29.
[2] *Commons jn. Ire.*, p. 56.
[3] *Cal. S.P. Ire.*, *1615-25*, pp. 427-8. Wicklow was the particular area in view at the moment.

There is no evidence that the plantations of Leitrim and Longford (and *a fortiori* the plantation in Ulster ten years before) had given rise to any criticism of the administration by the old English. On the contrary, the earl of Westmeath, who in a few years time, was to lead the old English party in the agitation for the Graces, received one of the largest grants in the plantation of Longford.[1] These plantations were, however, concerned with Gaelic Irish territories, those of the O'Rourkes and the O'Farrells, with whom the Burkes of Clanrickarde and the Nugents and other old English families of Westmeath certainly had long standing traditions of hostility. It was otherwise with the proposed plantation of the main area of Connacht itself.

By June 1624, the old English began to show open opposition for the first time to further plantation. The first article of the 'Grievances of the Landholders of the Pale' stated that 'the late plantations adjoining the English Pale and the dispossessing thereby of many who, time out of mind, did quietly enjoy their lands, does much affright the inhabitants of the English Pale'[2] This document did not specifically mention a proposed plantation of Connacht, though the sixth article complains of the insecurity of titles in Connacht. The first direct evidence that something definite for Connacht was in the wind was contained in a letter written by Clanrickarde himself to Sir Henry Lynch in March 1623/4. 'I doe understand', he wrote, 'by som that are lately come over[3] that at Dublin they hearde about the plantation of Conaght and that ther are many wayes of persuasion and motives used to draive many to submit themselves and that amonge other thinges it has been sayde and written that I had a hand therein, a most abominable wicked invention, I should rather [put] my hand in the fier first.' At this stage, however, it was not intended to include Co. Galway in this plantation. This was a tactic by which presumably the administration hoped to circumvent Clanrickarde's opposition.

During the next few years, Clanrickarde's optimism that the plantation would not take place was justified. War with Spain in 1625 and with France in 1626 created a difficult situation for the Irish administration, in which the old English opposition to the plantation of Connacht was pressed home. This opposition

---

[1] Butler, *Confiscation*, p. 82. [2] *Cal. S.P. Ire., 1615–25*, pp. 506–8.
[3] N.L.I. Clanrickarde MSS. (N.L.I. MS. 3111).

found expression in articles 24 and 25 of the Graces. Grace 24 concerned the limitation of royal title to sixty years; Grace 25 would have made possible the registration of Connacht land titles in chancery. Had these Graces become statute law then the plantation of Connacht would have become legally impossible. The crown gave way and for the moment, the old English were successful, but full victory was prevented by the fact that a parliament did not meet in 1629 as was anticipated.

After Falkland's recall to England[1] and the making of peace with France and Spain, the movement for plantation began to make headway once more. The Boyle party within the Irish privy council was behind it. In April 1631 Boyle sent a letter to Portland by Sir Charles Coote, in which he stated that a plantation of Connacht *excluding Co. Galway* (where most of Clanrickarde's land lay) had now become possible.[2] Agents were sent over to England and in June 1631 Falkland writing in England informed Ranelagh that the plan was proceeding slowly but surely.[3] In August, however, the scheme came to a halt, for reasons which are not clear,[4] but which were probably connected with the appointment of Thomas Wentworth as lord deputy in the middle of 1631.

It is clear from Falkland's letters that a branch of the Dillon family in Co. Roscommon was very much concerned in pressing for the plantation. Sir Lucas Dillon,[5] Sir James Dillon[6] and Lord Dillon of Kilkenny West all belonged to a group, which though old English by name and tradition had thrown in their lot with the 'new religion'. One would like to know the economic position of this group[7] and whether or not they were hard-pressed financially, but it is very doubtful whether the question will ever be answered.

---

[1] See above, p. 13.
[2] Boyle to Weston, 17 April 1631. Boyle Letter book (Chatsworth MSS.), f. 286.
[3] 19 June 1631, Falkland Letter book (P.R.O.I. MS. 2445), f. 215.
[4] 12 Aug. 1631 (ibid., f. 223).
[5] Falkland to Sir Lucas Dillon, 12 Aug. 1631 (ibid., f. 223).
[6] Falkland to Sir James Dillon, 17 Dec. 1631 (ibid., f. 241).
[7] I.e. whether they can be seen against a background of 'rising' or 'declining' gentry and whether the generalisations of R. H. Tawney or H. Trevor-Roper have any relevance to early seventeenth-century Ireland. Cf. R. H. Tawney 'The rise of the gentry' in *Economic History Review*, 1941; H. Trevor-Roper, 'The gentry 1540–1640' (*Economic History Review Supplement*, no. 1); and R. H. Tawney's rejoinder in *Economic History Review*, 1954.

In May 1632 Falkland wrote to Coote informing him that the plantation had been made the responsibility of the new lord deputy.[1] Clearly Wentworth at this stage had to move very carefully, since he was trying to conciliate the old English party in order to obtain a renewal of the £20,000 subsidy. It was not surprising, therefore, at this date that the plantation scheme should hang fire. Early in January 1632/3 Falkland wrote to Sir James Dillon telling him of the success of the earl of Westmeath's mission. He added that there was 'noe doubt' of Westmeath's opposition to the Connacht plantation.[2] Thus the plantation of Connacht formed part of the background of the financial negotiations between the new lord deputy and the old English party at the end of the year 1632.[3] Part of the price which Wentworth had to pay was at any rate to give the appearance of dropping the plans put forward by Cork, Falkland, and the Dillons. He also said that he would consider the Graces.

From the end of 1632 to November 1634 no action was taken about the plantation of Connacht. But six months before the 1634 parliament met, Wentworth clearly had it in mind. In writing to the King to advise the summoning of the parliament he had said that one of the two main objections to his advice was the danger lest parliament would prejudice the plantations of Connacht and Ormonde.[4] Later in the same month he wrote to Portland of his hope that 'forth of the Plantations of Ormonde and Connaght, there will be settled a revenue in the Crown of five thousand pounds per annum, and more, if the Quantity of Acres be such as they report them to be'.[5] It followed as a consequence that Grace 25 could not be allowed to come into practice, until the plantation had been settled. Thus very early in 1634 and well before the parliament Wentworth had taken his stand upon this question. It was not, however, until the second session of the parliament that Wentworth showed his determination to refuse the two 'darling articles' of the old English party.

In April 1635, a month after Portland's death[6] and with parliament drawing to a close, Wentworth began to take more active steps. There was however a most important difference between the

---

[1] 30 May 1632. Falkland Letter book (P.R.O.I.), f. 263.
[2] 2 Jan. 1632/3 (ibid., f. 279).   [3] See above, pp. 46 ff.
[4] 22 Jan. 1633/4. *Strafford's letters*, i. 184.
[5] 31 Jan. 1633/4 (ibid., i. 191).
[6] There had been a danger that Portland might interfere.

plantation he envisaged and that which had been originally planned while Richard Boyle was lord justice. Whereas Boyle had excluded Galway from his plans Wentworth proposed to include it, Clanrickarde's county, within his general scheme. It was this step which gave rise to so much bitterness. The county of Galway could be regarded as old English as much as the Pale itself. Clanrickarde's influence at court and the unprecedented nature of the plantation inevitably caused a long struggle to take place. Part of the explanation for the rising of the old English in rebellion in 1641 must be attributed to Wentworth's decision to proceed with the plantation of Galway at all costs and to the ruthless manner in which he crushed all opposition. The whole Connacht episode reveals the political limitations of Wentworth. He created unnecessary trouble for himself by including Galway in the plantation of Connacht. He met with no opposition whatever in the other three counties, but he refused to be satisfied with this partial success and he reaped the fruits of the policy of 'thorough' in 1640 when the old English lent their aid to his impeachment.

Parliament was dissolved on 18 April 1635 and Wentworth wasted no time in taking measures for the plantation. By June the commission and instructions which he had sent over to England for consideration had been returned and a month later on 13 July, Wentworth was able to write from Boyle that his Majesty's title had been found for Co. Roscommon. Sir Lucas Dillon who had been involved in the scheme four years before was praised by the deputy for his skill as foreman of the jury which found for the King.[1] Mayo and Sligo followed suit. It now remained to deal with Galway.

As had been foreseen, Galway proved to be a great stumbling block and for the next year the lord deputy, Clanrickarde and the gentry of Galway were engaged in a struggle which was fought bitterly on both sides of the Irish sea. The struggle coincided with Wentworth's struggle for power with Mountnorris,[2] and for a time during 1636 it seemed as if the lord deputy might be defeated; he was forced to go to England for six months during that year in order to defend himself. The Mountnorris and Galway crises coincided with a crisis in England largely caused by the political vacuum left by Portland's death in April 1635. The treasurership was not filled immediately and it was only in March

---

[1] *Strafford's letters*, i. 444.   [2] See above, p. 71.

1636 that Juxon, bishop of London and political associate of Laud, was appointed to replace the Commissioners who had succeeded Portland. Clanrickarde's resistance came at an awkward moment for Wentworth and had Laud lost the king's confidence in England, he might well have suffered a fate similar to that of Falkland—to be recalled because of political changes within the English privy council.

The desperation of Clanrickarde was matched, therefore, on the deputy's side, by a realisation that his political future was at stake. Both sides were equally determined to go on to the end. Both sides also fought as much in England as in Ireland, a sign, once more, of the way in which the key to political power in Ireland lay outside the country.[1]

In his report to Coke, dated 25 August 1635, Wentworth described the opposition which he had met as conspiracy; conspiracy engineered by the family of Clanrickarde, the recusants and the 'natives'. He appeared to regard recusancy as sufficient reason in itself to explain opposition to his Majesty. 'The Counsellors at Law,' he wrote[2] 'being all of them recusants showed themselves over busy, even to faction, in this service against the King and by whose advice we find reason to believe, the jury were very much guided'. The personal ambition of Clanrickarde was also stressed as a reason and the power which he exercised as governor of the town and county making it 'in Nature little less than a County Palatine'.[3] Inevitably, there was no attempt made to put the other side of the case, of those who regarded the Crown as doing on a large scale what 'beagles' were doing on a smaller, choosing juries 'to return a verdict for the King upon indifferent evidence' and finding a title upon 'some nice points or motheaten record'.[4] There was no mention of the composition of Connacht or of the reasons which led the gentry of Connacht to believe that Wentworth was perpetrating a grave injustice.

Neither side in fact could see the other's point of view. Wentworth looked upon the opposition which he met with in Galway, or at least represented it in his reports as mere obstruction, continued in another sphere, by the same kind of men as he had

---

[1] See above, chapter 1. [2] *Strafford's letters*, i. 451. [3] Ibid., 452.
[4] 'A discourse between two Counsellors of State the one of England, the other of Ireland', printed at Kilkenny, Dec. 1642 (B. M. Egerton MS. 917). Cf. E. R. McClintock Dix, 'Printing in the city of Kilkenny in the seventeenth century', in *R.I.A. Proc.*, sect. c, xxxii, no. 7, 125–37.

met with in the 1634 parliament. This comes out clearly in the
letter of 13 October 1635 informing Coke that Sir Roger
O'Shaghnessy, Patrick Darcy and Richard Martin had been
sent over to England as agents for Galway.[1] 'Before I goe further
to the matter', he wrote, 'it will be fitt I certifie you of the condition of these three agents they imploy. Sir Roger O'Shaghness
of as much power in those parts of a thousand pounds a yeare
landes all subject to plantation as I take it. A person that in the
parliament went with temper indeed, but with as much constant
stiffness against the King as any amongst them. A person on whom
the Romish clergie hath a great dependence as he on them. A
person that cunningly wrought himself off the jury whereon he
was returned by practising the Sheriff not to give him summons as
was by us all conjectured being upon the place.' Darcy was
described in more friendly terms as 'a Lawyer and in as great
practise as any other of his profession. Earnest in the way of his
owne religion, but yet to speak truly of the man, that in divers
particulars carried himself very well this last parliament, driven
into this business I am persuaded either by Mr. Martin his brother
in law or by some greater persons, for which in truth I am sorry'!
The third agent was Richard Martin[2] who in Wentworth's view
was also an able lawyer 'in great practise', but 'one that carried
himself very obstinately and indeed malevolently all the parliament, one that for certain hath been a cheefe . . . contriver in all
that hath past in this business as well before as since our meeting
upon the commission at Portumna'; one whom Wentworth
thought fit 'to have made a defendant in the Castle Chamber with
the rest of the jury to have tendered him the oath of supremacy
and thereupon to have prohibited him his practise'. This latter
evidence brings out how Wentworth was prepared to use religious
weapons in a political struggle (or rather, perhaps, how religion
and politics were so interconnected in his own mind, that he
could see nothing extraordinary in such tactics). According to
Wentworth the opposition were very confident of their chances
and openly boasted about the money levied among them to support the venture, 'as if their coyne was the price of all things'.[3]

---

[1] Strafford MSS., vol. 9, f. 100.
[2] Darcy and Martin acted as Richard Boyle's lawyers in the Castle Chamber
case 1634-6.
[3] Strafford MSS., vol. 9, f. 101.

Again, however, it must be noted that all the evidence is on one side and none seems to have survived to throw light upon the attitude of Clanrickarde and the Galway gentry or upon the measures which they proposed to take in England.

The delegates arrived in England in late October or early November 1635. They suffered a stroke of bad luck almost immediately in the death of Clanrickarde, who died within a few days of the agents' delivery of their petition to the king.[1] In other circumstances this might have been of benefit to their cause. Laud was conscious that there was some feeling against Wentworth for his prosecution of 'persons of quality' like Clanrickarde and Mountnorris, who were supported 'by some on the Queen's side'. He advised Wentworth to tread more warily.[2] The earl of Danby, who had been a candidate for the deputyship in 1630, was more open than Laud in his criticism. On 27 November 1635 he wrote to Wentworth:[3] 'I came very lately from my lord of St. Albans Funerall who died in the 72 yeare of his Age full of honour and Dayes according to David. And yet his People report that the apprehension of your Lordships discourtesyes and misrespect hastened his end, whereof my Lord his sonne seems very sensible. And is allsoe possesst with many other causes of complaint under your government, wherein I presume he means in person to crave redresse from your Lordships owne hand, soe soone as the season and some English occasions will permitt his journey into Ireland. In the meanetyme, give me leave I humbly beseech you to remember the extraordinary merits of that nobleman deceased, farre above any of his Nation in our tymes. . . .'

Wentworth was unsatisfied with verbal reassurance of royal support. He was anxious for some tangible sign of royal confidence such as the return of 'these Agents of Galway in the condition of prisoners',[4] their fate being left to his own discretion and the Irish Privy Council. In a letter of 12 January 1635/6, Coke made it clear that the game was won and that the agents would be ordered to return.[5] They showed an understandable reluctance to leave England and eventually, early in February, Martin had to be accompanied[6] over to Dublin by a special messenger.

---

[1] Coke to Wentworth, 16 Nov. 1635 (Strafford MSS., vol. 15, f. 260.).
[2] Laud to Wentworth, 16 Nov. 1635 (*Strafford's letters*, i. 479).
[3] Strafford MSS., vol. 15, f. 279.   [4] *Strafford's letters*, i. 493.
[5] Coke to Wentworth, 12 Jan. 1635/6 (Strafford MSS., vol. 15, f. 321).
[6] Ibid., 8 Feb. 1635/6, f. 345.

Another correspondent described how he had been apprehended in Fetter Lane 'in a place obscure enough'.[1]

In a letter of 7 March 1635/6,[2] Wentworth wrote to Coke expressing his relief that the agents were on their way back. They still had not returned, however, and this in his view was delaying the plantation still further. He had decided not to prosecute the jury until the agents had returned. Part of the letter sounds an unexpected note. Wentworth made out the commissioners of the plantation had proved less enthusiastic than might have been expected. The commissioners, it appeared, were hardly yet 'confident but something may be procured to alter the course advised from Portumna, which makes them more cunctative, disputing every step forwards and leave me single still, to presse on the business as well I may, albeit there is noe possibility for me to doe it all myselfe'. The reluctance of the commissioners, who included Coote and Ranelagh, possibly had its roots in a suspicion that Wentworth might be recalled, in which case they would have no wish to be committed too far in support of his policy.

Less than a week later Wentworth reported that O'Shagnessy and Martin had returned to Dublin and after a preliminary examination, had been committed to prison.[3] Patrick Darcy did not return however. He remained in England where he had become involved in negotiations to increase the Irish customs farm by £11,000 per annum.[4] He begged to be allowed to remain in England.[5] This strange episode may have some connection with Mountnorris, who by now had fallen into disfavour with Wentworth and had made similar offers to increase the customs farm.[6] Darcy failed to make any impression on the English privy council and in May he also was on his way back to Ireland.[7]

The confidence which Wentworth must have felt that all would now be well was revealed in the scheme which he drew up in April to show the various sources of income upon which the Crown could now draw. It was noticeable in this, that the amount he expected from the plantation of Connacht had greatly increased:

[1] Coke to Wentworth, 9 Feb. 1635/6.
[2] Strafford MSS., vol. 9, f. 146. Wentworth to Coke, 7 Mar. 1635/6.
[3] 12 Mar. 1635/6. *Strafford's letters*, i. 521.
[4] Windebank to the king. 13 Jan, 1635-6. *Cal. S.P. dom.*, *1635-6*, p. 179.
[5] Ibid., p. 180.
[6] Mountnorris to the king. 26 Nov. 1635. *Cal. Clarendon MSS.*, i. 361.
[7] *Cal. S.P. dom. 1635-6*, p. 405.

a year earlier, he had criticised Portland for giving £15,000 as a figure which could be expected and had complained that it was unrealistic by comparison with his own figure of £6,000. By April 1636, however, his own estimate had soared to £20,000, part of the reason being no doubt to strengthen his arguments against the opponents of the plantation. On 9 April 1636, he informed Coke that he had appointed a dozen surveyors to survey the three counties in which his Majesty's title had already been found.[1] He hoped that they would have completed their task by Christmas. Presumably, he expected that the Galway jury would find for the king within a short time and that the survey for this county also would be undertaken within a short time.

The Galway jury, however, proved more stubborn than might have been expected. They were probably given hope that they might benefit eventually from the difficulties which Wentworth had to face elsewhere.[2] There were rumours that he was going to pay a sudden visit to England in March 1635/6.[3] There could be little other reason for such a visit except the conviction that only his presence in England could counteract the unpopularity which his policy in Ireland had created. It was, in the event, not till June that Wentworth left for England.[4] So far as the plantation of Connacht was concerned, he left at a very awkward moment and it is hardly likely that he would have done so had he not considered that it was necessary for him to visit England. The feeling that Wentworth might be withdrawn must have played its part in persuading the Galway jury to withstand the pressure of the lord deputy.

Their cross-examination took place before he left,[5] on 27 May 1636 and the day following. From the rough notes which are still extant, it appears that the same questions as at Galway concerning the king's title were again put to the members individually. The opinion[6] of the judge was that 'the chardge against these gentlemen is for a wilful refusall to fynde the title of his Majesty to the whole county of Galloway contrary to their

[1] Wentworth to Coke. Strafford MSS., vol. 9, f. 161.
[2] E.g. the customs farm. See below, Chap. 11.
[3] Garrard to Wentworth, 15 Mar. 1635/6. *Strafford's letters*, i. 523.
[4] He wrote from Dublin on 7 June and from London on 30 June and must have travelled between those dates. *Strafford's letters*, ii. 7–8.
[5] Carte MSS. (Bodleian) i, ff. 139–52.
[6] Ibid., ff. 148–52.

H

evydence . . .' and that 'All we have to do (as I conceave) will be to consider whether the evydence proved here to have been given to this jury at Portumna was suffycyant in our judgements to have convinced the understanding of a rationall and indifferent jury'. The jury persisted in its refusal and was fined £4,000 each man and imprisonment, a heavy punishment. It is worth noting that a number of the jury possessed Irish names—O'Madden, O'Connor, O'Bryan and O'Machermurrough: clearly one can stress too much the old English part in the Connacht resistance to Wentworth.

Wentworth left matters in the hands of Wandesford when he left for London. Early in June, the sheriff, who had chosen the Galway jury, died in prison.[1] Wentworth was conscious of the embarrassment which this might cause him, but, characteristically, asked Wandesford to make sure that the king should not lose his fine. It was inhumanity such as this which helps to explain the hatred of Wentworth among men of completely different views.

While Wentworth was in London, there came news that the jury continued to resist.[2] He argued in a letter to Coke that 'it is conveycd from thence that some vaine hopes are given them from this side or else they could have no such cause of confidence'. He went on to add, presumably again to impress Coke with the importance of the issue, that 'not only those Galway men are thus transported but the whole county in generall (as I am informed) doe provide some hope unto themselves to be releeved from this intended plantation'. If Wentworth's statement is to be taken as evidence, it would appear that his return to England, during the second half of 1636, was regarded in Ireland as ground for hope that he would be dismissed. Wentworth's request[3] for a further mark of royal favour in August 1636, shows his awareness that in some quarters he was regarded more as 'a Basha of Buda than the minister of a pious and Christian king'. Charles' refusal showed that he was not prepared to commit himself to unqualified approval of his lord deputy's policy, without hope of withdrawal.[4]

---

[1] *Lismore Papers*, iv. 190.
[2] Strafford MSS., vol. 9, f. 173. 26 July 1636, Wentworth to Coke.
[3] In a letter to Charles from Wentworth Woodhouse, 23 Aug. 1636. *Strafford's letters*, ii. 27.
[4] *Strafford's letters*, ii. 32.

The next trial of strength between Clanrickarde[1] and Wentworth went once again in favour of Wentworth. Clanrickarde made an attempt to have John Donnellan, a member of the jury, now in prison, brought over to help him with urgent business, connected with his father's estate. On 24 July 1636 Wentworth[2] had received a letter from Windebank, 'signifying that it was his Majestie's pleasure that Mr. Donelan (one of the jury of Galway) should have licence to come into England upon the pretence of service to be by him done for the Earl of St. Albans'. After agreeing to it, Wentworth appears to have thought that it would be taken in Ireland as a sign of encouragement for the jury and he felt strong enough to countermand the royal order.

It may have been this which finally decided Clanrickarde that his best hope now was to capitulate. He seems to have been in financial straits.[3] In March 1636 he had complained to Wentworth about his debts; 'I have soe greate a burthen of debt upon me to discharge and my creditors importunate in calling there moneys in, that necessity compells me to make speedy preparation for the sale of land or mortgage to give them satisfaction.[4] And in a letter to Wentworth later in the year he made out that his own and his father's debts amounted to about £25,000 'besides the large proportion I have and am to pay for his Majestie's subsidyes there and the suing of my livery, all which would sinke a farre better estate than mine without some timely remedy'.[5] A year later he still complained that he had no way to discharge himself from a great debt 'but by raising of fines or mortgage of land'.

If Clanrickarde's financial position was so bad, there was little point in continuing the struggle, once it had become clear that Wentworth was likely to remain in Ireland as lord deputy. In August Clanrickarde came to Coke and showed him the submission made by the gentlemen of Galway,[6] which they had sent him to present to the king. This did not satisfy Wentworth and

[1] Ulick Bourke, 5th earl of Clanrickarde, only son and heir. 1604–57. Cf. G.E.C. *Peerage*, ed. Gibbs, under 'Clanrickarde'.
[2] Strafford MSS., vol. 9, f. 174. Wentworth to Coke. Windebank's letter is to be found in ibid., vol. 16. 23 July 1636, f. 40.
[3] Clanrickarde to Wentworth, 4 Oct. 1636. Strafford MSS., vol. 16, f. 70.
[4] 2 Mar. 1636/7, Strafford MSS., vol. 16, f. 143.
[5] 18 July 1637. Strafford MSS., vol. 17, f. 125.
[6] Coke to Wentworth, 30 Aug. 1636. *Strafford's letters*, ii. 31.

he refused to accept it, apparently on the ground that it had not been shown to him first, and that it implied that the county gentry were yielding to force and not to justice. In his reply to Wentworth's letter of 2 September,[1] Clanrickarde went to great pains to stress the completeness of the Galway surrender, though the jury would not admit that there had been perjury. He thought that there was now a great opportunity for Wentworth 'to gain thanks from many persons in Fear and Trouble, by mediating to his Majesty to accept of this free and unanimous resignation of their Estates without further dispute and your Lordship and the State to receive the Jury's humble acknowledgement of your justice and their error of judgement, the rather in regard they have laboured to redeem this first offence by persuading the rest of the county to this general surrender'. This submission was said to have been signed by 175 persons of the best quality of the county.

Clearly the victory lay with Wentworth and he was not the man to waste the opportunity, and he proposed to punish the recalcitrance of Galway by planting half the forfeited land instead of the proposed third or fourth.[2]

Wentworth returned to Dublin on 23 November 1636. He was able to inform Coke within a couple of days that Roscommon, Sligo, and Mayo had been surveyed.[3] Then on 9 December he wrote to Coke to tell him that the jury of Galway had at last submitted.[4] By 31 December, they had been set at liberty, after acknowledging the clearness of the King's title.[5] In February he was able to report that the 'prime gentlemen of Galway had presented a petition that a commission goe down to find for the King'. Finally, on 19 April 1637, he wrote that two inquisitions had been held at Galway to find his Majesty's title to the county at large and the city.[6] Thirty surveyors were sent down and it was hoped to finish the work by the summer.

Wentworth had achieved a complete victory but in a sense a pointless one. The loyalty shown to Charles I by Clanrickarde after 1641 showed that the plantation was unnecessary, it had been justified on the grounds that Connacht was the most insecure

---

[1] Clanrickarde to Wentworth, 27 Sept. 1636. *Strafford's letters*, ii. 35.
[2] Wentworth to the king, 10 Sept. 1636. Ibid, ii. 34.
[3] Wentworth to Coke, 25 Nov. 1636. Strafford MSS., vol. 9, f. 186.
[4] Ibid., f. 191. 9 Dec. 1636.
[5] Ibid., f. 208. 21 Feb. 1636/7.   [6] Ibid., f. 220.

province left in Ireland. In fact, however, there was every reason to think that the best policy from the English point of view was not plantation but simply to bolster up the influence of Clanrickarde. Wentworth persisted in a policy which antagonised Clanrickarde who was as English as Ormonde in his outlook. It was a policy which confirmed the great anxieties of the Pale itself. As Wentworth himself wrote to Coke in November 1635, 'they within the Pale beginn now to find his Majestie hath the same title to a great part of Meath which he hath to Conaght and that many other places amongst them alsoe are upon other faire and just claims subject to plantation'.[1] The old English proprietors might well feel after Galway that they would be next. Indeed at this particular time, the earl marshal, who was a member of the committee of the privy council for Irish Causes, was pressing hard for land in South Leinster, which he claimed had belonged to his ancestors. Wentworth thought that these could be taken 'to contain all the landes of the five counties of Wexford, Kilkenny, Carlow, Ossory, Kildare and most of the province of Leinster'.[2] In a letter of 8 December 1636, however, he opposed the whole scheme. But the possibility was always there.

In fact, however, even the plantation of Connacht itself was not put into full effect. In March 1637 almost at the moment when the royal title to Galway had at last been discovered, there came news that war threatened. This was the first event which played its part in preventing Wentworth from reaping the full fruit of his victory over Clanrickarde.[3] He submitted a memorandum— 'Considerations upon the great Question, whether his Majesty should declare a war against the House of Austria': and in this one of the points made, was the fact that war would endanger the plantation of Connacht. Even the rumour of war, apparently, was having disastrous consequences and the plantation he wrote 'which was in a sort settled totters again and great ado there is to keep the undertakers to their first propositions so much do they apprehend a distraction through war with Spain'. On 19 April 1637 he wrote to Coke: 'Surely were it not soe commonly reported and believed on this side that his Majestie is going into a warr with Spaine, there had never been such a time to have gone on roundly with all the other plantations as now.'[4] In May 1637, Coke tried

[1] Strafford MSS., vol. 9, f. 105. [2] Ibid., vol. 9, f. 107.
[3] *Strafford's letters*, ii. p. 60. [4] Strafford MSS., vol. 9, f. 220.

to assure the lord deputy that the war was only a rumour,[1] but in August Wentworth still believed that it was possible, for he wrote to Cottington in strong terms, opposing the idea of war with the House of Austria 'whilest we on this side with mighty thought and labour have eased the revenew here some thirty thousand pounds a yeare, it seems wondrous to us that there should be amongst you [some] that with equal, diligence endeavour to ingage his Majestie in actions which will cost the Crown millions'.

Rumours of war did not prevent Wentworth from going ahead however with finding the king's title for Ormonde and Thomond. In August 1637, he wrote from Clonmel[2] to announce that the king's note to Ormond had been acknowledged and less than a fortnight later on 28 August that it had been found without trouble in Clare. The stage was at least completely set for the vast scheme of plantation which Wentworth had envisaged five years before.

If five years had been necessary in the preparation however, it was clear that a similar length of time at least would be necessary for consolidation. That time was not to be given. Only a year elapsed between the final acknowledgement of the king's title to Galway in April 1637 and the beginning of the Scottish crisis in the middle of 1638, and even during that time as is clear, the strong rumours of war with Austria, handicapped Wentworth's attempt to translate administrative policy into economic reality. The plantation of Connacht existed on paper but hardly at all in fact. Even after the Scottish crisis had broken, the titles to Galway were still in the process of being enrolled and it was only in November 1638 that Philip Percival[3] could report from Lough Reagh, that the task for which he and other members of the Commission had spent 'eight Sundays' in the town was complete. By that time, however, it must have been clear that the plantation would have to be postponed. Some land in the other three counties did change hands. The Books of Survey and Distribution drawn up after the Restoration of Charles II throw only dubious light upon the extent to which it had done so by 1641.

Wentworth's own survey has not survived and there was no civil survey for Connacht. In any case, however, the actual settle-

[1] Coke to Wentworth, 3 May 1637. *Strafford's letters*, ii. 76.
[2] Ibid., ii. 90.   [3] H.M.C. *Egmont MSS.* I, pt. i, 105–6.

ment of Connacht by the English can hardly have gone far enough by 1641 for any significant changes in the occupation of the land to have taken place. The appointment of undertakers of itself did not of necessity bring settlers in its wake, as the history of previous plantations had shown. In April 1638[1] Wentworth had written to Laud complaining of the shortage of men; in his reply Laud commiserated[2] with Wentworth that he 'should want men in Ireland and that the while, there should be here such an universal running to New England and God knows whither'. This lack of settlers was not surprising: during the thirties the main motive for emigration seems to have been the desire to escape from religious persecution. A puritan fleeing from what he considered the tyranny of Laud in the province of Canterbury would be unlikely to emigrate to Connacht to endure the more efficient control of Wentworth. The second great source of settlers was Scotland, but as appears clearly in his letters, Wentworth was adamant in his policy of excluding the Scots from Connacht. Once religious refugees and Scottish emigrants had been ruled out, it would have taken more than a year's administrative action, however violent and energetic, to bring in English settlers on a sufficiently grand scale.

From the Books of Survey and Distribution, it is clear that Mayo was hardly affected at all by increased new English penetration. Ormonde, Cork and Sir Henry Bingham held land there in 1641, but all three of them had done so before 1635.[3] In Sligo and Roscommon, however, the process of plantation may have gone further. There, Sir George Radcliffe, Edward and William Crofton, Sir Robert King and Sir Roger Jones were large proprietors in 1641, probably as planters, though the O'Connors, the Nolands, the Bourkes and other Irish proprietors still remained in possession of much land. In Roscommon the Croftons and Sir Robert King were again found, along with Sir Charles Coote, Lord Ranelagh and Alderman Parkhurst of the city of London. Native Irish like proprietors O'Connor Don, Flynn and Hanley and old English like Clanrickarde, the earl of Westmeath and Sir Thomas Nugent were still to be found.

---

[1] Wentworth to Laud, 10 April 1638. *Strafford's letters.* ii. 157.
[2] Laud to Wentworth, 14 May 1638. Ibid., ii. 169.
[3] O'Sullivan (W.) ed. *Strafford Inquisition of Co. Mayo*, pp. 23, 152, 74.

The Books of Survey and Distribution also show that Galway was not affected at all by the plantation. This was partly due to the delaying tactics which had held up Wentworth for nearly two years, but also to the good fortune of Clanrickarde, who, possibly through the influence of the earl of Holland and the 'Queen's Party' was able, during the early months of 1639 to escape from the partial confiscation which Wentworth had hoped to inflict upon him. The Scottish crisis indeed strengthened the hand of anyone who 'like Clanrickarde', could be relied upon to keep Ireland quiet. In July 1639[1] Wentworth wrote to the king to say that he had obeyed the letter of 20 June, ordering him to grant Clanrickarde all his lands, though he argued bitterly that this would make the plantation of Connacht impossible. On the same day[2] he wrote to Coke explaining in detail how the five best baronies of Galway would be lost to the Crown as a result of his Majesty's action, 'yet shall this Earl not only lose nothing for his opposition but he now put into far better condition than those that have done his Majesty most effectual service'. In August,[3] he wrote that 'all the rest of the nobility and prime gentry' of Connacht proposed to petition his Majesty for the same relief as Clanrickarde had obtained. In short the whole question was to be reopened again. By this time, however, the Scottish crisis had begun more and more to occupy Wentworth's attention. In September 1639[4] he was withdrawn to England to advise the king and the history of the plantation did not begin again till the meeting of the Irish parliament in March 1640.[5]

The significance of the plantation of Connacht lay in the fear which it created. It formed part of the same story as the court of wards and the commission of defective titles in the way in which it threatened to cause large-scale changes in the ownership of land. For the first time, old English proprietors and those Gaelic Irish who had come to terms with the English government during Elizabeth's reign were faced with the threat of plantation. The determined attempt which the old English made, successfully, in 1640–1, to have the plantation reversed shows that the downfall of Wentworth was regarded by them as only a means to an

[1] Wentworth to the king, 9 July 1639. *Strafford's letters*, ii. 365.
[2] Wentworth to Coke, 9 July 1639. *Strafford's letters*, ii. 366.
[3] Wentworth to the king, 13 Aug. 1639. *Strafford's letters*, ii. 381.
[4] Wentworth to earl of Northumberland, 2 Sept. 1639. Ibid., ii. 384.
[5] See below, pp. 190 ff.

end. After Wentworth's death, the agents of the old English remained in England for some months in order to make sure by legislative action that the plantation would not take place. It was by his insistence upon the plantation that Wentworth wrecked the possibility of a political alliance between himself and the Catholic old English proprietors and drove them for a time into the arms of the planter class, with whom for political and religious reasons, they had fundamentally little in common.

CHURCH AND STATE

WENTWORTH'S land policy created bitterness between himself and the old English. By contrast, it was his religious policy which alienated the new English (and the 'new Scots') who in the normal course of events would have supported any extension of the system of plantations. The establishment of a Court of High Commmission was a novel departure, in that it was the instrument of a religious policy which for the first time in recent Irish history was to be directed at Protestants rather than Catholics. For seven years members of the established church were to be subjected to increasing pressure from the administration while the recusants escaped comparatively free. Wentworth's deputy-ship witnessed not only an attempt to restore its lands to the Church of Ireland but also to set up what appeared to most Protestants as a new standard of orthodoxy, not far removed in important respects from that of Rome itself. In order to appreciate the full novelty of this situation, some attempt must be made to sketch the state of religion, both of Reformation and Counter-Reformation, in the decades before Wentworth's arrival.

I

By 1630, despite or perhaps because of its backing from the English administration, the Reformation had made little progress among the general run of the population, old English as well as Gaelic Irish. This fact emerges clearly in the survey of his diocese which was made by the Protestant archbishop of Dublin, Lancelot Bulkeley, in that year.[1] Of every parish almost he was compelled to report with disconcerting regularity that 'most of the parishioners' were papists, who attended Mass in local houses. In most instances he even knew the name of the 'mass-priest' who served

[1] *Archivium Hibernicum*, viii. 56 ff.

the parish. If this was the situation in the capital, it was similar outside the immediate control of the central government. Bedell, who was appointed bishop of Kilmore in the planted area of Cavan, found that here the Ulster plantation had made little difference to the number of Protestants and that most of his flock were recusants who had their own bishop resident within the diocese. Throughout Ireland indeed membership of the established church was largely confined to recent settlers of Scottish as well as English origin and, though there were cases of Irish-speaking priests who were converted to the new faith, in general they were few. A man like James Ussher who was of old English descent and had many Catholic relatives was an unusual member of the Protestant episcopate. Similarly, the Protestant sympathies of the earls of Ormonde and Thomond were exceptional among the older nobility and gentry.

Generally speaking, the influence of the Church of Ireland depended on the proximity of military garrisons, administrative centres or plantation settlements. Only in Ulster can it be said to have taken root in any numbers and this was largely due to the influx of immigrants from the Scottish lowlands, which took place before as well as during the plantation of Ulster. Their religious views with some exceptions[1] were largely Calvinist in origin but at this date there was no clash between them and the theological outlook of a Puritan-minded episcopate or of a lord deputy like Chichester who had Puritan sympathies. Even refugee ministers from the Scottish episcopacy found it comparatively easy to come to terms with the bishops of the Church of Ireland. For example, John Livingston who was silenced by Archbishop Spottiswood in 1627 gave the following account of his reception in Ireland in 1630.

And because it was needful that I should be ordained to the ministry and the bishop of Down, in whose diocese [my living] was . . . would require some engagement, therefore my Lord Clanniboy sent some with me and wrote to Mr. Andrew Knox, bishop of Rapho; who when I came and had delivered the letter from my lord Clanniboy . . . told me that he knew my errand; that I came to him because I had scruples against episcopacy and ceremonies according as Mr. Josias Welsh and

[1] For example the Hamiltons who became planters near Strabane and introduced Catholic tenants. *Cal. S.P. Ire., 1625-32,* pp. 509-10. This family did not become Protestant until after 1690. Cf. Simms, *The Williamite Confiscation,* p. 89.

some others had done before; and that he thought his old age was prolonged for little purpose but to do such offices; that if I scrupled to
call him 'my lord' he cared not much for it; all he would desire of me,
because they got there but few sermons, [was] that I would preach at
Ramallen the first Sabbath and . . . he would send for Mr. William
Cunningham and two or three neighbouring ministers to be present who
after sermon should give me imposition of hands; but although they
performed the work, he behoved to be present; and although he
durst not answer it to the State, he gave me the book of ordination and
desired that anything I scrupled at, I should draw a line over it on the
margin and that Mr. Cunningham should not read it. But I found that
it had been so marked by some others before that I needed not to mark
anything. . . .[1]

Not all the bishops were as obliging as Bishop Knox (a distant
relative of John Knox), but in general they were sympathetic
towards Calvinism. Puritan influence was strong at Trinity
College, which had Walter Travers the prominent English puritan
as its second provost, and James Fullerton and James Hamilton,
pupils of Andrew Melville, among its first fellows. James Ussher's
theological outlook was also nearer on certain points to Geneva
than to Canterbury. At this date, indeed, though the organisation
of the Church of Ireland was episcopal, its doctrine as expressed
in the Articles of 1615 was Calvinist in its emphasis. The Articles
made no mention of episcopacy and in them were to be found
typical Calvinist views on predestination, original sin and the
Scriptures. It was stated that 'God hath predestinated some unto
life and reprobated some unto death; of both which there is
a certaine number, knowen only to God, which can neither be
increased nor diminished'. Man was said to have no power to do
good works without the grace of God since he had been deprived
of original righteousness by Adam's sin and deserved God's
wrath and damnation. 'We are accounted righteous before God,
onely for the merit of our Lord and Saviour Jesus Christ, applied
by faith and not for our own workes or merits.' Mankind is
damned by divine justice though the elect are saved in order to
show forth his mercy. On these and on other points the articles
provided a Calvinist interpretation of Christian doctrine. So far
as church government was concerned, however, the articles
omitted any mention of synods and a general Assembly. They
accepted the Royal Supremacy of the Church, professing that 'the

[1] Reid, *History of the Presbyterian church in Ireland*, i. 116–18.

supreame government of all estates within the said Realmes and Dominions, in all causes, as well Ecclesiastical as Temporall, doth of right appertaine to the Kings highnes'.[1]

Though the doctrine of the Church of Ireland was at this date Calvinist in its inspiration, it had taken over the structure of the pre-Reformation church. The boundaries of the ancient dioceses were left unaltered and the whole system of livings and tithes was accepted as the norm. Some of the sees indeed had only recently been taken over. In Ulster, the dioceses of Raphoe, Clogher and Derry, had remained, so to say, 'in partibus infidelium' until the Flight of the Earls and the plantation of Ulster. Elsewhere, in areas of old English influence and control, the power of the bishops remained largely nominal. In Meath diocese, for example, the patronage of nearly half of its 200 livings was in the hands of Catholic landowners such as the earl of Westmeath and viscount Netterville. In Galway, the authority of the Catholic earl of Clanrickarde counted for more than that of the archbishop of Tuam. A situation had developed in which the local population no longer felt any responsibility for the upkeep of the local parish church with the result that the great majority of the churches were in a state of ruin, or at best disrepair, while the houses of the local gentry became religious centres for Catholics. In such circumstances, the local landowners both Catholic and Protestant profited. Tithes were farmed out and large-scale alienation of church lands took place. Landowners such as Richard Boyle acquired former monasteries not merely for the lands but also for the impropriate rectories attached to them. In the archdiocese of Dublin the Crown had leased out its impropriate tithes to local Catholic gentry.[2] In the diocese of Killaloe, the earl of Thomond, most powerful magnate in the area, possessed a dozen of its sixty livings.[3] In the diocese of Cloyne Sir John Jephson, a new English planter farmed the endowments of a score of livings.[4] In the diocese of Ross the long list of livings which were impropriated to the College of Youghal went to swell the rent rolls of Richard Boyle.[5] All this was almost inevitable in a church which appealed to only a small minority of the population. Its endowments were bound

---

[1] The full text of the 1615 articles is to be found in Elrington, *Life of Ussher*, pp. xxxiii–l.

[2] *Archivium Hibernicum*, viii. 57.   [3] Ibid., iii. 211 ff.

[4] Ibid., ii 195.   [5] Ibid., ii. 211 ff.

in large measure to be taken over for their own profit by the local gentry.

A situation in which many livings were non-resident and most bishoprics were impoverished was one which appealed to Catholic and Calvinist alike. The Catholics had no wish to pay tithes twice over, as often happened in districts served by both parson and priest.[1] The Puritans, whether of English descent like Richard Boyle or of Scottish descent like Lord Claneboy, had no wish to overendow an episcopate. Those who wished to change matters were in fact in a small minority and but for the accession of William Laud to power in England their voices would without much doubt have gone unheard. There seemed little to prevent the Church of Ireland from remaining poor, but comprehensive enough to include within its fold those who fled from episcopal government in Scotland. For Ussher, as for many other the main enemy seemed to be Rome not Geneva and he saw no irony in recommending Richard Boyle and Adam Loftus to Laud as true friends of the church.[2]

II

If the Reformation had made little headway in Ireland outside Ulster, the same cannot be said for the Counter-Reformation. The progress of this latter movement, however, was much slower than is often supposed and did not reach its most active and fruitful stage until over half a century after the end of the Council of Trent in 1563. The expedition of FitzMaurice in 1579 and Hugh O'Neill's war, culminating in the battle of Kinsale in 1601 were episodes in which political considerations were paramount and can hardly be regarded as evidence for a general religious revival. The struggle against the extension of the power of the English administration was only incidentally a fight against Protestantism even though in the course of it 200 priests and religious were executed. Politics continued to overshadow the Irish Counter-Reformation during the first half of the seventeenth century, particularly in Ulster after the plantation, but in most parts of the country a condition of *de facto* religious toleration

[1] Cf. Bishop Ram's report in Mant, *History of the Church of Ireland from the Reformation to the Revolution*, p. 370.
[2] *Cal. S.P. Ire., 1633–47*, p. 6.

from about 1618 onwards made possible, particularly in the towns, a general revival of full religious practice. Despite the official reaction to Gunpowder Plot the administration failed either to enforce attendance at Protestant services or to extend the penal laws on the English model in the Parliament of 1613.

From 1618 onwards a policy of toleration was officially sponsored by the English Privy Council for reasons of foreign policy and once begun the government found itself compelled by circumstances to continue this policy. War with Spain in 1625 and with France in 1626 made the government dependent upon Catholic financial aid and upon Catholic loyalty in the face of an expected Spanish invasion. Even after peace was made, toleration continued, although there was a short outbreak of persecution in Dublin. Wentworth also showed himself more anti-puritan than anti-Catholic.

This long period of toleration provided the forces of counter-reformation with freedom and opportunities which had not existed since Mary's reign and of which the results were to be seen in the Confederation period (1642-9). By then a bare toleration was unacceptable to the clergy, and the return of churches and ecclesiastical endowments was demanded as a matter of course. A purely political settlement between the Crown and the Confederation of Kilkenny was condemned in 1646 by the Papal Nuncio, Archbishop Rinuccini. While this attitude seemed impolitic and impractical to many, particularly after 1647, the fact that such demands could be confidently insisted upon is decisive evidence for the strides which the Counter-Reformation made in Ireland during the quarter of a century before 1642.

The driving force behind the movement came from the continent. Douai in the Spanish Netherlands, and Salamanca in Spain were the main Irish seminaries abroad, but there were several others, at Lille, Bordeaux, Paris, and Alcala.[1] In 1626, the Irish Franciscans established the college of St. Isidore at Rome. From these centres, a small stream of missionaries flowed into Ireland. Most numerous were the Franciscans, but the Jesuits from 1596 and the Capuchins from 1615 also made their appearance. In 1623, it was estimated that there were 200 Observant Franciscans, 40 Jesuits and 20 Dominicans in Ireland, plus numbers of Cistercians, Augustinians and Capuchins. At the same date, there were

[1] For a full list, see Kenney, *Sources for the ecclesiastical history of Ireland*, i. 29,

800 secular priests. There was thus no shortage of Catholic clergy, though there was a marked difference of standard between the seculars ordained at home and the regulars trained in continental seminaries.

The main centres of religious activity were the ports, and it was here that the clergy congregated. In 1630, for example, Comerford, bishop of Waterford and Lismore, reported that he had forty secular clergy and thirty regulars in his diocese, but he complained that they kept to the towns. There was loss and gain in this. Most of the ports had direct trading links with the continent, and it was comparatively easy for young men to make their way to the seminaries abroad. In 1600, the Irish College, Douai was reported to contain sixty young men, the sons of gentry and merchants. A further consequence followed from the fact that the majority of families in the towns were old English, in that much of the first impetus of the Counter-Reformation came from the old English. Peter Lombard, Luke Wadding, Francis Nugent, David Rothe and many other prominent figures came from old English stock, though their views on politics were not identical.

One feature of the Counter-Reformation in Ireland which is in marked contrast to England, was the reappearance of a resident Catholic hierarchy. Between 1590 and 1620, most of the Catholic bishoprics remained vacant, and the archbishops of Armagh, Tuam, Cashel and Dublin remained abroad. Peter Lombard, archbishop of Armagh 1601–25, for example, did not set foot in Ireland during his episcopate. However there was a marked change of Papal policy on this question during the 1620's, and as a result, by 1629 most of the dioceses had a resident bishop. This reinforcement of the hierarchy undoubtedly played its part in providing a strong ecclesiastical framework, the full effects of which were to be seen during the Confederation of Kilkenny (1642–49); but it also led to sharp clashes with the regular clergy who had grown used to freedom from episcopal intervention. Another feature of these years was the holding of provincial synods in which the decrees of the Council of Trent were published at least in part.

But no religious movement in the seventeenth century was ever free from political overtones, and Ireland was certainly no exception. There was a strong body of ecclesiastical opinion in favour of military intervention by Spain as the best hope for Catholicism.

The Irish colleges in Spain and the Spanish Netherlands were an obvious link here, but equally important were the descendants of the exiled Ulster earls, whose only hope since 1607 lay in a Spanish invasion. The earl of Tyrone, backed by the King of Spain, had an important say in the appointments to Irish sees made during the 1620's and 1630's. The Observant Franciscans were also pro-Spanish, and it was of some political significance that three out of four archbishoprics in 1625 were in Franciscan hands, while the fourth was appointed because of Franciscan influence. These political manœuvrings did not go unopposed, however. In 1625 for example, during the war with Spain, the archbishopric of Armagh fell vacant. Its previous occupant, Peter Lombard, had by O'Neill's death, came to favour a rapprochement with the English crown in the hope of achieving some measure of toleration and his death in 1625 was the signal for an intense period of ecclesiastical politics. The old English candidate was David Rothe, bishop of Ossory. The pro-Spanish candidate, backed by Luke Wadding, Florence Conry and the earl of Tyrone, was the Ulster Franciscan, Hugh McCaughwell, who was eventually appointed. On his death in 1626, the whole episode was repeated with the appointment of Hugh O'Reilly, bishop of Kilmore, who was also from one of the planted counties of Ulster.

Thus a major theme of early seventeenth century Ireland, and one whose importance is frequently underestimated by English historians was the spread of post-Tridentine Catholicism. Many of the ordinary laity still remained ignorant of the rudiments of their religion, particularly in the countryside; but the gentry and the merchants, from whose ranks so many of the regular clergy were drawn, were unquestionably influenced by this religious movement. As a result, secular pressure upon Catholics was more than counter-balanced by increased religious awareness. Exclusion from office, from political power, and from easy livery of land, did not result in Catholic landowners conforming to the established Church, as many did in the eighteenth century, but on the contrary, created a growing sense of irritation. Twenty years religious toleration from 1618 onwards gave the Counter-Reformation an opportunity to put down permanent roots, the results of which were to be seen after 1641.

I

III

Thus before Wentworth's arrival in Ireland, the religious situation was comparatively a simple one. The two rival systems of Catholicism and Calvinism existed side by side, providing in Ireland a local variant of the state of affairs which prevailed in many parts of Europe. Neither side was sufficiently strong to attempt to eject the other and the result was in most areas a state of uneasy toleration. In 1622 Ussher, then bishop of Meath, denounced the Papists in strong terms but for this he was immediately reprimanded by his ecclesiastical superior, Hampton, archbishop of Armagh.[1] Four years later, in 1626, thirteen bishops of the Church of Ireland, led by Ussher, who was now primate, condemned the proposal to grant toleration to Papists in return for a financial contribution, but the government's economic needs defeated them.[2] In 1629, the lords justices were responsible for closing the Franciscan oratory in Dublin,[3] but protests were made in England[4] and by 1630 though public mass houses remained closed, in private, things went on as before.[5] All this did not prevent Ussher from remaining on friendly terms with David Rothe, Catholic bishop of Ossory and other Catholic scholars.[6] From 1633, however, the Puritan party within the Church of Ireland, and this included the main weight of important opinion, clerical and lay, was placed on the defensive. It was now their turn to be subjected to a sustained attack, which had the backing of the lord deputy.

The change was already implicit in the coming to power in England of William Laud. From 1628 as bishop of London and then from 1633 as archbishop of Canterbury, Laud pressed hard for what he regarded as a modicum of discipline within the Church of England and for financial improvements, without which a preaching clergy could not be maintained. The Court of High Commission was at one and the same time an instrument for disciplining those who regarded bishops as 'the spawn of Papists' and for recovering the full economic value of lands and

---

[1] Elrington, *Life of Ussher*, pp. 59–60.
[2] Mant, *History of the Church of Ireland*, p. 423.
[3] Jennings, *Wadding Papers*, p. 341.   [4] Ibid.
[5] *Archivium Hibernicum*, viii. 57 ff.
[6] W. O'Sullivan, 'Ussher as collector of manuscripts' in *Hermathena*, lxxxviii. 54–5.

impropriate tithes.[1] Laud's struggle was partly against the full tide of Puritanism within the church of England and partly against the results of the rise in prices which had so greatly reduced in value those church lands which had escaped the attention of speculators, courtiers and local gentry. His views were shared, ironically by those Puritans, who bought up impropriations in an attempt to support their own preaching clergy.[2] He thus had to contend with idealism and self interest. It was an impossible task.

In Ireland the Laudian movement came nearer to apparent success than it did in either England or Scotland. For this the energy and determination of Wentworth were largely responsible, though there is no evidence that his views on doctrine and ritual were distinctively Laudian.[3] His dislike of Puritans sprang from his belief that they were the enemies of lawful authority rather than distaste for any particular doctrine. His treatment of several Irish bishops on the other hand showed that he had little reverence for the episcopal state as such. He told one bishop that he deserved to have his rochet pulled over his ears.[4] Whatever his real views, however, Wentworth's methods were Erastian. For the first time, and the last, the royal supremacy exercised by the king's deputy, was made into a reality in Ireland.

Apart from Wentworth the main instrument of Laud's policy in Ireland was John Bramhall, who came over in 1633 as chaplain to the lord deputy. Bramhall's appointment to the see of Derry in 1634 was a foretaste of the changes which were to occur within practically the whole episcopate during the next five years. Bramhall succeeded George Downham a Puritan whose treatise on Grace had incurred Laud's criticisms when it was published in 1631. Here the lord deputy's nominee replaced that of the planters. It was a pattern to be repeated many times and during the course of the next few years most of the sees which fell vacant

---

[1] The best recent discussion of the economic side of the Laudian movement is C. Hill, *Economic problems of the Church*. It contains a full and clear exposition of those complex matters, tithes and impropriations.

[2] I. M. Calder, *Activities of the Puritan Faction of the Church of England*. Cf. also Hill, *Economic problems of the Church*, chap xi.

[3] However Richard Boyle noted in his diary that on Whitsunday 1635 in Christchurch that the dean knelt 'all the time he was speaking the words both at the delivery first of the sacramental bread, so lykewise of the wyne'. The lord deputy received the sacrament on this occasion. *Lismore Papers*. 1st ser. iv. 105.

[4] *Strafford's letters*, i. 171.

were filled with men newly arrived from England. Doctrine apart, this was not a practice which appealed to those members of the Protestant clergy whose families had been resident for some time in Ireland. The new English found their influence slipping away to a group of completely new men in much the same way as they themselves had replaced the old English in the second half of the sixteenth century. In 1634 on the death of the bishop of Limerick George Webb, a Laudian and chaplain to Charles I was appointed to succeed him. In 1635, Henry Leslie, a Scot of Arminian views, succeeded Robert Echlin, bishop of Down and Connor. In the same year the death of Michael Boyle, relative of Richard Boyle, left the see of Waterford and Lismore vacant; he was succeeded by John Atherton,[1] who had received rapid promotion in the church since Wentworth's arrival. In 1638, the united sees of Cork, Cloyne and Ross were split and the more valuable half of Cork and Ross went in commendam to the Laudian, William Chappell, provost of Trinity. Wentworth's nominees, Robert Sibthorp and Henry Tilson were appointed to Kilfenora and Elphin respectively in 1638 and 1639. Finally, the bishop of Killala, who had incurred the displeasure of the lord deputy for his ambivalent attitude towards Puritanism, was removed from his see, fined and imprisoned. He was replaced by John Maxwell, who had been forced to flee from his own see of Ross in Scotland and whom Charles I had originally recommended for Elphin.[2]

By 1640, the episcopate of the church of Ireland had almost completely changed its character. Men such as George Andrews who with Ussher's backing might have obtained a well-endowed see found themselves relegated to small and poor dioceses like Ferns, almost as a punishment.[3] Ussher though he was primate found that real power had passed to Bramhall and the lord deputy. He had no real voice in the appointment of bishops or indeed of deans. It was the lord deputy who appointed the dean of Armagh and who also introduced new men from England as deans into Christchurch, Dromore and other cathedrals.[4] Thus even where the bishop was not a Laudian the lord deputy had his representative on the spot. Equally important was the attempt to transform Trinity College, Dublin from being a centre of Puritan teaching,

[1] Rushworth, *Trial*, p. 123.   [2] *Strafford's letters*, ii. 369.
[3] Ibid., i. 344.
[4] Rushworth, *Trial*, p. 124. cf. also Strafford MSS., vol 6, ff. 125, 164-5, 180.

which, in Laud's words was 'as ill governed as any in Christendom or worse' into 'a good seminary for that church'.[1] The existing provost Robert Ussher, a relative of James Ussher was replaced by Wentworth's nominee William Chappell and eventually was appointed to the very poor see of Kildare. William Laud himself became chancellor of the college and in alliance with the lord deputy and the new provost tried to make Trinity into a Laudian seminary. By 1636 an open quarrel had developed between archbishop Ussher and Chappell, which was still in existence in 1638 and had led to strained relations with Laud.[2]

These changes in the personnel of the higher clergy were accompanied by similar changes in doctrine and discipline. Here again the decisive voice was that of the lord deputy. In 1634, Convocation was summoned to meet at the same time as Parliament, the upper house consisting of bishops and the lower house of representatives of the provincial synods. In the upper house the lord deputy's representative was Bramhall, and in the lower his own chaplain, Croxton. Their function was to keep a watching brief while the lord deputy was engaged in managing parliament. Convocation was to be the instrument by which the Thirty-Nine Articles were to be introduced into the church of Ireland. At a later session it was hoped to have the English canons of 1604 passed. Both of these measures involved a radical break with the recent past. Whereas the Irish Articles of 1615 had been of unmistakably Calvinist inspiration, the English articles had been left deliberately vague at disputed points and were therefore open as much to an Arminian as a Puritan interpretation. On the other hand the Canons of 1604 had been passed while the anti-Puritan Bancroft was archbishop of Canterbury and had been designed as a clear rejection of the Puritans' demands made in the Millenary Petition. The attempt to introduce these into the church of Ireland was plainly a declaration of war against those who, like Ussher, had been tolerant of Puritanism in doctrine.

Some opposition was met with in the lower house of Convocation when the Thirty-Nine Articles were introduced there. It was led by George Andrews, dean of Limerick, whom Wentworth suspected, not without reason, of having Ussher's support. A committee with Andrews at its head attempted to debate which of the English articles should be accepted and at the same time

[1] *Strafford's letters*, ii. 36.   [2] Ibid., ii. 263.

to impose an obligation on all clergy to accept the 1615 articles under pain of excommunication.[1] As soon as he heard of this, Wentworth summoned Andrews before him and told him that 'certainly not a Dean of Limerick but an Ananias had sate in the Chair of that Committee' and 'all the Fraternities and Conventicles of Amsterdam'.[2] Next day he told the whole Committee that he would not tolerate the spirit of 'Brownism' which he detected in their deliberations. After this harangue there was no further difficulty with Convocation. The English articles were passed and the authority of the 1615 articles was left purposely vague. When the 1604 canons came before Convocation, however some minor concessions were made. In deference to Ussher's objections, no specific obligation to bow at the name of Jesus appeared in the text, but the canon referring to kneeling at communion was retained. As Wentworth remarked to Laud, 'as for boweing at the name of Jesus it will not downe with them yet. They have noe more joints in their knees for that than an Elephant.'[3] This was bound to lead to trouble with the Puritans, particularly in Ulster. The general result of the Convocation was to create a new minimum of doctrine and of discipline which was now to be enforced upon a largely unwilling church.

The instruments of the new policy were Bramhall and Leslie, who found ample scope at first within their own dioceses of Derry and Down and Connor. Both of these sees were within heavily planted areas of Ulster and Bramhall had reported of Down and Connor in December 1634 that 'it would trouble a man to find twelve Common Prayer Books in all their churches'. He also mentioned the absence of altars, in place of which there stood tables 'where they sit and receive the Sacrament together like good fellows'.[4] But, unsupported, episcopal authority was insufficient to deal with the problem of enforcing the Canons and the use of the Book of Common Prayer. For this something with more formidable powers than an episcopal court was needed. Falkland had already, in 1629, pressed for the establishment in Ireland of a Court of High Commission but he intended it to be used primarily to enforce the collection of recusancy fines.[5]

---

[1] *Strafford's letters*, i. 343.   [2] Ibid., op. cit.
[3] Strafford MSS., vol. 6, f. 164.
[4] Shirley, *Papers relating to the Church of Ireland*, p. 41.
[5] *Cal. S.P. Ire., 1625–32*, p. 446.

Nothing came of this proposal for the moment and when it was suggested again it was clearly with the Puritans not the Catholics in mind. This time Ussher opposed its establishment.[1] In the event on Wentworth's advice[2] it was not set up until after parliament had been dissolved in 1635. As in England, the court consisted of a group of bishops with power to initiate proceedings and to summon witnesses before them. It was significant that Ussher specifically requested that his presence as primate should not be necessary for a quorum.[3] From 1635 to 1640 the Court sat regularly, with power to inflict punishments either of fine or imprisonment.

With the Court of High Commission at their back from 1635, the Laudian bishops were in a much stronger position, and in August 1636 Bramhall and Leslie held a visitation followed by a meeting at which certain Puritan ministers of the diocese of Down and Connor were required to accept publicly the Canons of 1634, particularly that which referred to kneeling at communion. The discussion, which hinged largely upon the implications of kneeling at communion, followed the lines of a formal medieval disputation. James Hamilton, nephew of Lord Claneboy, was the spokesman for the five ministers who refused to subscribe to the canons.[4]

. . . Hamilton: That which makes us without a warrant to serve our God as idolaters serve their gods, cannot abide the trial of the rule of God's word to wit Deut. xii. 4, 30, 31. The Book of Common Prayer presses some constitutions which make us without any warrant to serve our God as idolaters serve their gods, ergo . . .
Bishop Leslie: Prove your minor.
Hamilton: That which presses a constitution to kneel before the elements of the sacrament or to kneel at the receiving of the sacrament makes us without warrant to serve our God as idolaters serve their gods; the Book of Common Prayer makes us to kneel before the elements at the sacrament or at the receiving of the sacrament; ergo. . . .
Bishop Leslie: I deny your minor.
Hamilton: The Papists kneel before the elements in serving their breaden god in the sacrament; and we kneeling before the elements serve our God; therefore we serve our God as idolaters serve their god.
Bishop Leslie: That cannot be a right syllogism. . . .[5]

[1] Ibid., 1633–47, p. 6.   [2] Strafford's letters, i. 188.
[3] H.M.C. Hastings MSS., iv. 70.
[4] There were about forty ministers in the diocese of Down and Connor at this date. For a list in 1622, cf. Reid, History of the Presbyterian Church, pp. 519–22.
[5] Reid, p. 523. Appendix IV.

After the conference had finished, the five ministers were deprived of their livings and ordered to refrain from preaching, and ultimately were compelled to take refuge in Scotland.

A doctrinal clash of a similar kind had already taken place in Dublin in 1633 and 1634, when the protagonists had been Wentworth and Richard Boyle, earl of Cork. Its occasion was the monument which Boyle had recently erected to his wife's memory in St. Patrick's cathedral, Dublin. Neither Ussher nor Bulkeley, archbishop of Dublin had raised any objection[1] to its being placed at the east end; Laud, however criticised it on the grounds that it stood 'where the High Altar stood and where the Communion Table ought to stand'. A struggle followed between Boyle and the lord deputy, which both of them regarded as a trial of political strength as much as a quarrel over the theological implications of the siting of the tomb. In 1634 Wentworth expressed the view to Laud that 'if the Earl can by any meanes (and every stone he will stir before we remove one of his tombs) master this business, it will, I fear deterr all men from complaining. But if it come in against him, it opens every floodgate.' On his side Boyle appealed to the English lord treasurer, Richard Weston, who was Wentworth's chief critic in the English privy council.[2] Victory went to the lord deputy and by 1635 the tomb had been pulled down and placed in its present position on the south side.

The clash of Laudianism and Puritanism also took place on a less dramatic plane in other quarters, notably with Ussher. More and more Ussher found that his views were ignored. On the collection of recusancy fines, on the Thirty-Nine Articles and the Canons of 1634, on the very organisation of his archdiocese, Ussher experienced defeat. He openly clashed with Chappell whom Wentworth had nominated as Provost of Trinity College. By 1636 it was clear that he was merely a figurehead without effective influence. Laud wrote of him at this time that he had long known 'that no man can easily be found more unfit for government than the Primate'.[3] When the lord deputy visited Ussher in 1638 he noticed a silent commentary upon his Laudian policy in the fact

[1] Ussher, *Works*, xv. 572; *Strafford's letters*, i. 211.
[2] *Strafford's letters*, i. 411.   [3] *Laud's works*, vii. 387.

PLATE IV. The Boyle Monument, originally erected in the chancel, it was moved soon after Strafford's arrival to its present position near the south door.

PLATE IV
THE BOYLE MONUMENT, ST. PATRICK'S CATHEDRAL
DUBLIN

that there was no altar in the archbishop's own chapel.[1] Though
his opposition was not as open as that of Boyle and the Ulster
ministers, there can be little doubt that Ussher disapproved of
most aspects of Wentworth's religious policy. Ussher retired from
Dublin to his palace at Drogheda early in 1636, ostensibly for
financial reasons but Wentworth suspected that disapproval of
official religious policy was the real cause.[2]

What made Laudianism harder to bear was the lord deputy's
willingness to allow the Catholics *de facto* toleration. This was
to be one of the charges brought against him at his impeachment
though it was never actually pressed.[3] Though this toleration
seemed to many to be based upon a sympathy towards Popery, it
was in fact grounded by Wentworth upon reasons of state pure
and simple. In July 1636, for example, he advised against enforcing anti-recusant measures, stating that though 'till we be brought
all under one form of Divine Service, the Crown is never safe on
this side, but yet the time and circumstances may very well be
discoursed and sure I do not hold this a fit season to disquiet or
sting them in this. . . .'[4] This view was one which he put forward
several times during the following years and it fitted in well with
his opposition to a war with the Hapsburgs. He dreaded a breach
with Spain because of the support which the Spaniards could give
to the Ulster exiles such as Owen Roe O'Neill.[5] His attitude
towards the Irish Catholics and towards his Most Catholic Majesty
was based upon what he believed to be strict political realities. He did
not foresee, that more trouble would come in the short run not from
the Catholics but the Ulster Puritans. His own attitude, however,
was to be justified in 1641, with the rising of Sir Phelim O'Neill.

IV

Laudian policy, in England as well as Ireland, was not confined
to doctrine and discipline; it also attempted to solve, as questions
of great urgency, the financial problems facing the Church. It had
long been apparent in England that many of the defects for which
the Church was criticised were due in large measure to its poverty,
and that the shortage of an adequately educated clergy, pluralities
and non-residence and many undesirable practices could be traced
to this one cause. In themselves the endowments of the Church

---

[1] *Strafford's letters*, ii. 249.   [2] Strafford MSS., vol. 6, f. 296.
[3] Rushworth, *Trial*, p. 69.   [4] *Strafford's letters*, ii. 39.   [5] Ibid., ii. 111.

would have proved more than sufficient, were it not for the fact
that much of this wealth was syphoned off into lay hands by a
system of impropriations. An impropriate rectory was one in
which the rector was either a monastic corporation or a layman,
such as the king; the rector drew the income from the living, while
granting a portion of it to a vicar. This practice had been well
established before the Reformation[1] but the result of the dissolution of the monasteries had been to place the great majority of
impropriate rectories in the hands of laymen. One third of the
9,000 odd livings in England were estimated to be impropriate in
1603 and of these five-sixths were declared by the bishops to be in
lay hands.[2] For example, in the dioceses of York, Norwich,
Rochester and Lincoln, laymen controlled 1,987 of the 2,323
benefices.[3] Any attempt to deal with the problem on a large scale
was clearly bound to come up against the opposition of powerful
vested interests.

Two factors, however, were responsible for growing discontent with the existing state of affairs; they were in the first place
the steady rise in prices which took place from the third quarter of
the sixteenth century onwards, and secondly, the religious revival,
of which the Puritan movement and its counterparts in more
traditional circles were the mainstay. The rise in prices lowered
the real value of benefices at a time when higher standards of
education were being demanded from the ordinary clergy. Thus
in this respect religious and economic movements were running
counter to one another. The diagnosis of the problem was clear
enough to contemporaries, Puritan and non-Puritan alike, and the
remedies suggested all stressed the need to deal with the problem
of impropriations. Laud would have found little to disagree with
in the blame which the Puritans Penry and Crashaw laid at the
door of impropriations.[4] However, so long as impropriate
rectories remained pieces of property protected by the common
law there was little hope of a direct attack upon the system. Laud
could only hope to persuade like-minded laymen to return their
rectories to the Church or else to buy them back by the establishment of a fund for purchase. In this, however, he was far less
successful than a group of Puritan laymen, the Feoffees for

---

[1] See R. Hartridge, *A history of vicarages in the middle ages.*
[2] Hill, *Economic problems of the Church*, p, 144.
[3] Ibid., p. 145.   [4] Ibid., p. 146.

Impropriations who, between the years 1625 and 1633 succeeded in raising over £6,000 by voluntary contribution.[1] This money was devoted to the augmentation of livings or the establishment of 'lecturers'. The disbanding of the Feoffees in 1633, when they fell foul of the ecclesiastical authorities marked the end of the only organised attempt to deal with the problem of impropriations,[2] at any rate in England. Laud himself did not reach the target which he aimed at of buying in two impropriations each year.[3]

In Ireland similar problems confronted the established church. Large-scale alienation of church lands or leasing at low rents for very long periods had taken place, during Elizabeth's reign, particularly in Armagh under Primate John Long, in Ferns under Bishop Allen and in Leighlin under Bishop Cavenagh. In the diocese of Meath, in 1622, out of 243 rectories, over half were impropriate to the Crown and farmed out to laymen. No less than half of these were in the hands of Catholic landowners like the earl of Westmeath and Viscount Netterville.[4] In other dioceses members of the Irish Privy Council, such as Richard Boyle and Adam Loftus, were among those who drew a share of the rich harvest. Adam Loftus, though a layman, was archdeacon of Glendalough[5] and Richard Boyle, thanks to the fact that two of his kinsmen were bishops of Waterford and Cork respectively, was very well placed to make profitable leases. The situation was such that in many dioceses the bishop came to depend for most of his income upon recusancy fines and mortuary fees.[6] If the bishops were badly off, so also were the incumbents of most livings and the Commissioners of 1622, sent over from England to report upon the state of Ireland made it their first recommendation that proprietors of impropriate churches should be compelled to provide adequately for the vicar.[7]

To the eyes of a Laud or a Wentworth the state of affairs in Ireland appeared almost beyond reform, and many historians have taken their despondency for descriptive fact.[8] The established church, however, commanded the loyalties of only a fraction of

---

[1] Ibid., p. 254.
[2] Cf. I. M. Calder, *Activities of the Puritan Faction of the Church of England.*
[3] Hill, op. cit., p. 319.   [4] Elrington, *Life of Ussher*, App. V.
[5] *Cal. S.P. Ire.*, *1633–47*, p. 189.
[6] John Roche, Catholic bishop of Ferns noted this fact in 1630. Cf. Jennings, *Wadding Papers*, p. 370.
[7] *Cal. S.P. Ire.*, *1615–25*, p. 416.   [8] Even Hill, *Economic problems*, p. 334.

the population of Ireland as a whole, and even within its ranks there were many Puritans who saw little to object to in a powerless, impoverished episcopate and a lower clergy dependent for their income upon the offerings of the congregation. During these years the Catholic church was flourishing and to some observers there seemed almost too many clergy. Patrick Comerford, Catholic bishop of Waterford, complained to Luke Wadding that 'our countrie is soe furnished with clergiemen that ere it be long we are like to have one against every house . . . a man can not sitt at table to a raffe of tripes but presentlie one or two clergie menn will come in. . . .'[1] It is true that Comerford criticised the standard of many of the regular clergy but this was a symptom in itself of a new critical outlook. These were the years of the Counter-Reformation in Ireland the effects of which were not to be measured entirely by an increasing volume of complaints against the usurpations of the Papists in the State Papers. The yardstick of Bramhall was not the only, or perhaps the most appropriate criterion for the state of religion among Papists or Puritans. What seemed a matter for lament to the Laudians was not infrequently a reason for rejoicing to the Catholic Bishops or the Calvinist ministers of Ireland.

It was, however, the Laudian party which controlled the administration from 1633 onwards and which initiated a financial policy of which an attack upon impropriate rectories was a prominent feature. In Ireland, the Crown itself seems to have held most of the impropriations, though most of them were farmed out to laymen. Laud's plan was for the Crown to make a grant of these leases to vicars perpetual who would continue to pay the old rent to the Crown.[2] As soon as a lease fell in, it was to be granted to the vicar concerned, without power to alienate, but while he paid the old rent to the Crown he could exact improved rents from his own tenants. In this way it was hoped eventually that over £3,000 would be raised to endow a 'rural and resident clergy'. The main obstacle in the way of success was the existing farmers, many of whom held their rectories on long leases. It was estimated in 1635 that over three-quarters of these leases were for periods ranging from sixteen to eighty years.[3] On the surface therefore the

[1] Jennings, *Wadding papers*, p. 609.
[2] For its details, cf. *Strafford's letters*, i. 383–6.
[3] In August 1635. *Cal. S.P. Ire., 1633–47*, p. 97.

plan was a long term one; in fact, however Laud hoped for speedy
results. As soon as the Crown had agreed to the 'great business
of the Impropriations' Laud wrote to Wentworth, urging him to
settle the business with 'all the speed you can; for if they die in
your hands, I will never hope to see them again. . . .'[1]

The second part of the plan therefore was to buy out the
farmers as soon as possible. Laud and Bramhall followed the
example here of the Feoffees for Impropriations. There was however no hope of raising the large sums necessary by voluntary
subscription and Bramhall seems to have relied mainly upon increased rents from diocesan lands. In the diocese of Armagh, for
example the episcopal revenues, which in 1629, stood at £1,800,
had been raised by 1639 to £3,500.[2] In 1634 Bramhall reported
to Laud that he had been in contact with 'the greatest farmer of
the King's impropriations, £400 a year very easily rented and
sixteen years in being'. The price which the farmer asked was six
years purchase.[3] In April 1636, he stated that the appropriations in
Meath had been passed and that the other dioceses were expected
to follow suit. But it was inevitable that the business should drag
on. In 1639 he was still negotiating with the earl of Westmeath
about eleven impropriations in the diocese of Kilmore.[4] Nevertheless a good deal had been accomplished by 1640. In the archdiocese of Armagh as a whole Bramhall was able to report an
increase of £14,600 of which half went to the lower clergy. In his
own diocese of Derry the rents of rectories and tithes were raised
by over £1,000 per annum and he was able to boast to Laud that
'all the appropriated tithes in this diocese are not worth above
fifty or sixty pounds per annum. And I doubt nott butt to have
them within a yeare . . . which I think can be said of few Bishop-
rickes in Europe.'[5] In Down and Connor the improvement in
rectorial incomes amounted by 1639 to £2,600 per annum which
included the recovery of 'usurped' rectories as well as purchases of
leases.[6] In Armagh the patronage of eight rectories was bought

[1] *Laud's Works*, vii. 175.

[2] Shirley, *Documents relating to the Church of Ireland*, p. 7.

[3] *H.M.C. Hastings MSS.*, iv. 60. The Feoffees bought at or under twelve
years' valuation. Hill, *Economic problems*, p. 254.

[4] Shirley, *Documents relating to the Church of Ireland*, p. 23.

[5] Ibid., pp. 11–12.

[6] Ibid., pp. 14–15. Nine rectories were purchased in this diocese from the
recusant Christopher Barnewall and his wife.

back. In Clogher, improved income for rectories amounted to £750, in Raphoe to £153, and in Ardagh to £370.[1]

Measured in financial terms Bramhall's achievement was a considerable one, on a scale comparable to that of the Feoffees for Impropriations and certainly much greater than anything Laud was able to accomplish in England. It was however, open to the criticism that it was largely concentrated in only one province and that in which, to judge from Ussher's estimates of 1629 the Church was already well provided for. The dioceses of Derry, Clogher, Raphoe and Armagh had indeed benefited from the fact that they had only been effectively brought within the Church of Ireland since 1605, and along with Meath they were by far the best-endowed sees in the four ecclesiastical provinces, richer than even the archiepiscopal see of Dublin. Ussher himself regarded Derry as 'absolutely the best in this kingdom'. Moreover, they were also sees which contained a much greater proportion of Protestants than any others. In the light of this, the comment may be made that Bramhall's success was achieved in an area where it was easiest and also where it was least needed. The main result of his work was to create an enduring discontent, eventually to be expressed in the petition presented to the Long Parliament in 1641 'on behalf of some Protestant inhabitants of . . . the Province of Ulster'. The petitioners complained that in addition to religious persecution 'the prelates with their faction have been injurious . . . to the temporal estates of most men; for under the colour of church lands they have injuriously seized into their hands much oft he best lands in every county, so that there is scarce a gentleman of any worth whom they have not bereaved of some part of his inheritance, few daring to oppose their unjust demands'.[2]

Some indication of the contrast between the financial state of the archdiocese of Armagh and the remaining three provinces may be gained by examining the lists provided by Ussher and Bramhall respectively in 1629 and 1639. From this it is clear that the richest parts of Ireland, the dioceses which lay in the fertile areas of the South were worth comparatively little, while those in the poorer North were worth much more even in 1629. The burden of episcopacy was greatest where it could be least afforded and where

---

[1] Bramhall's full report in 1639 is to be found in Shirley pp. 5 ff.
[2] Reid, *History of the Presbyterian Church in Ireland*, i. 283 ff.

it was least desired. The same causes which led to the outbreak of the Bishops' Wars in Scotland existed also in Ulster and it was surprising that open resistance did not spread there. As it was, the opposition to Bramhall did not express itself until it was safe to do so, when in February 1640/1, after the fall of Wentworth from power, he was impeached by the Irish Commons.

DIOCESAN REVENUES

1629[1]	£ per annum	1639	
Archdiocese of Armagh			
Armagh	1,800	3,500	(Shirley, *Documents of Church of Ireland*, p. 5 ff.)
Meath	700	?	
Clogher	800	1,300	(Ibid.)
Derry	800	1,900	(Ibid.)
Raphoe	650	1,000	(Ibid.)
Kilmore &	(350)	800	
Ardagh	(100)	650	(Ibid.)
Dromore	400	?	
Down & Connor	300	1,000	(Ibid.)
Archdiocese of Cashel			
Cashel & Emly	260		
Waterford & Lismore	100	1,000	(*Cal. S.P. Ire., 1633–47*, p. 166)
Limerick	126		
Cork, Cloyne & Ross	200		
Killaloe	—		
Ardfert	—		
Archdiocese of Dublin			
Dublin	450[2]	(1,000)	
Kildare	60		
Ossory	—		
Ferns	130		
Leighlin	40		
Archdiocese of Tuam			
Tuam	131		
Elphin	300	1,340	(Shirley, *Documents*, p. 56)
Clonfert	54		
Kilmacduagh	25		
Killala	—		
Achonry	—		
Kilfenora	32		

[1] Ussher provided these figures for Laud, 11 Sept. 1629. *Cal. S.P. Ire., 1625–32*, p. 481.
[2] Cf. *Cal. S.P. Ire., 1633–47*, pp. 165–6.

V

While Bramhall was waging his financial crusade in Ulster, Wentworth was engaged in a similar task in the dioceses of Lismore and Cloyne. Richard Boyle, earl of Cork, was the most important proprietor in this area of South-West Waterford and East Cork, which had originally been planted after the Desmond rebellion of 1580. Sir Walter Raleigh had been one of the original planters and it was from Raleigh that Boyle in 1603 had bought this vast estate.[1] The purchase included questionable but nonetheless effective control of the episcopal lands of the diocese of Lismore. Richard Boyle lived in the Bishop's Palace at Lismore and successfully resisted the attempt made by Bishop Lancaster to restore the 'minuted estate' of his bishopric by a bill of resumption in the 1613 parliament.[2] Further down the Blackwater, in the neighbouring diocese of Cloyne, Boyle had acquired in fee farm the lands and impropriate rectories of the collegiate church of Youghal which had been founded by the earl of Desmond in 1464 and generously endowed. By 1630 Boyle seemed to have little to fear. His namesake and kinsman was bishop of Cork, Cloyne and Ross and another relative Michael Boyle was bishop of Waterford and Lismore. Of Youghal it could be said that 'the whole College was bedded down and slept her last under the safeguard of three Boyles, a Patron, a Warden and a Fellow, the Earl, the Bishop of Cork and the Bishop of Waterford'.[3] Richard Boyle was indeed the most outstanding example in Ireland of a layman who appropriated for his own profit not merely the revenues of rectories but also those of bishoprics.

Almost as soon as Wentworth arrived in Ireland he began his attack upon Boyle. Early in 1634 the bishop of Waterford and Lismore complained to Laud that the earl of Cork held illegally diocesan lands to the value of £900 per annum and was about to swallow finally the College of Youghal with its £700 per annum endowment. The bishop, who was Michael Boyle, kinsman of the earl's, stated that although the temporalities of the see were about £1,600, his own income was only £50. He went on to claim to be

---

[1] See T. O. Ranger, 'Richard Boyle and the making of an Irish fortune', in *I.H.S.* x. 282.
[2] *Cal. S.P. Ire., 1608–10*, pp. 439–40; *Lismore papers*, 1st ser., i. 54.
[3] Quoted in Burghclere, *Strafford*, i. 251.

an old college friend of Laud's.[1] The full story behind this letter is not clear, but Bramhall claimed the credit for having brought pressure to bear on his fellow bishop.[2] Richard Boyle thus found himself facing the prospect of losing property which he had controlled for thirty years.

The attack began in October 1634, when Boyle was summoned to appear before the Court of Castle Chamber to justify his possession of the College of Youghal.[3] The formal hearing began in March 1635 and dragged on for over a year. In addition to his ordinary legal defence, which was conducted by the Catholic lawyers, Darcy and Martin, Boyle tried two other methods. The first of these was to have the case heard in England where he hoped that his friendships in high places would stand him in good stead.[4] The second was to trade upon Wentworth's personal feelings by using the Youghal lands as a marriage portion for his son Lord Dungarvan, who was to marry into the Clifford family. Wentworth's first wife had been a Clifford and Boyle gambled on this relationship. Both stratagems failed, however. Wentworth's protests against the prospect of the case being transferred were listened to in England and his reaction to a visit from Boyle and Lord Clifford was to strengthen his determination to go ahead in a very unpleasant business.[5]

In April 1636 matters reached a climax. Wentworth was attacked on several sides at this time and as he was about to leave for England in the near future he had no wish to leave the case to drag on. He summoned Boyle before him and threatened him with the prospect of a public hearing and a fine of £30,000.[6] Boyle's compromise figure of £15,000 was accepted, to be paid in three instalments of £5,000 each. For his part of the bargain, the lord deputy ordered the records of the case to be removed from the files of the court and promised that while he was in England he would procure from the king a new grant of the college and its lands though not of the impropriate rectories.[7] Boyle paid the last

---

[1] Cal. S.P. Ire., 1633-47, p. 44.
[2] H.M.C. Hastings MSS., iv. 56.
[3] The case was whether or not Boyle could prove the consent of the Warden and the Fellows to the fee farm.
[4] Cottington informed Wentworth that Cork's friends at court 'especially the Lord Chamberlain and Lord Salisbury' had pressed the King hard on his behalf. Strafford's letters, i. 449.
[5] Ibid., i. 459.
[6] Lismore papers, 1st ser., iv. 182.　　　　[7] Ibid., 1st ser., iv. 185.

K

instalment of the fine on Midsummer day 1638.[1] It was the
equivalent of rents of £500 per annum over a period of thirty
years and in view of the fact that he retained some of the property
it was not too bad a bargain.

Agreement between Boyle and the Bishop of Waterford and
Lismore over the question of the diocesan palace and lands was
not reached until July 1637. A compromise settlement was agreed
upon by which Boyle surrendered the manor of Ardmore and
paid £500 in gold for the new bishop,[2] Atherton, to build himself
a house. He himself retained the manor of Lismore and certain
other lands at a total rent of £33 6s. 8d. As a result of this and
other compositions Bramhall expected that the income of the see
would be raised to £1,000 per annum.[3] Boyle's own feelings may
be gauged from the fact that on 2 August he left for England to
settle in his newly purchased manor of Stallbridge.[4]

The conflict between Wentworth and Boyle has been frequently
told in terms of a dramatic quarrel between two different types of
men. It was this but it was also something more. Lismore and
Youghal were episodes in a story which was taking place in other
countries as well as Ireland. In Germany Ferdinand's attempt to
enforce the restitution of church lands inevitably came up against
the opposition of vested interests, as did Wentworth's. In Scotland
the Act of Revocation (1625) attempted to restore to the church
lands which had been under lay control since 1542 and here as in
Germany the reaction of the possessors was violent. In Ireland
Wentworth's forceful not to say autocratic methods made resistance for a time unprofitable but the time eventually came when he
needed support and found that he had alienated almost every
Protestant group in Ireland. Much of the explanation for the
short-lived alliance in 1640 between Catholic and Protestant
political groups must be attributed to Wentworth's religious
policy.

There were, however, long term as well as short term effects.
After the Restoration in 1660 the policy of Wentworth and Bramhall triumphed over that of Ussher. Comprehension wide enough
to include those of Presbyterian sympathies was abandoned finally

[1] Lismore papers, 1st ser., v. 25.
[2] Cal. S.P. Ire., 1633–47, p. 166–7. Michael Boyle died in 1635.
[3] Ibid., op. cit.
[4] Lismore papers, 1st ser., v. 57.

then, but its roots went back to the years of Wentworth's deputy-ship. The splitting of the Protestants in Ireland into two distinct groups of Establishment and Dissent can be traced back to 1633 when Laudianism supplanted the wide Puritanism of Ussher. In 1661 Bramhall succeeded to Ussher's see of Armagh, after a five-year interval. This was ironical enough but an even greater irony occurred when Michael Boyle, nephew of the former bishop of Lismore, himself became archbishop of Armagh in 1679. Per-haps indeed the final victory went to the Boyles.

WENTWORTH'S ECONOMIC POLICY

(I) THE ECONOMIC BACKGROUND

THE general features of the economy of Ireland in the time of Wentworth are comparatively clear. The staple articles of Irish trade—livestock, pastoral by-products like hides, butter and tallow, and fish, timber and iron—these clearly derived from a society in which tillage was of secondary importance. It is true that quantities of wheat were exported to Scotland from the ports of Ulster[1] and a county like Wexford produced a good deal of barley, oats and wheat.[2] Lord treasurer Weston could expect Irish wheat to supplement the normal supply to London in times of scarcity.[3] But production beyond self sufficiency rested upon pastoral farming, fishing, timber and the spinning of flax. When in 1632 customs duties in Ireland were increased,[4] the commodities involved were all of a mainly pastoral character—cattle, wool, hides, tallow and butter, together with herrings, pilchards, linen yarn and rugs. Clearly these were the articles from which the administration anticipated the greatest increase in revenue. They were the staple Irish exports. The duties upon imports were left unchanged with the exception of those upon salt and wine.

But if it is safe to accept this general picture of Ireland as a country whose wealth lay largely in livestock, fish and timber, a good deal of difficulty arises when more precise and detailed information is required. Trade routes, the relative importance of each European country in the general picture of Irish trading, the extent of sheep or cattle farming in particular regions of Ireland —all these and other questions are far from being answered and since it is impossible to deal with them adequately without a

[1] Cf. Port Book for Lecale, Strangford and Down. Jan. 1613–Nov. 1614 (Temple Newsam MSS.).
[2] *Civil Survey; Wexford, passim.*
[3] See above, p. 25.
[4] *Cal. S.P. Ire., 1625–32*, p. 648.

detailed examination of the available commercial archives in England and Europe generally, all that is attempted here is a tentative sketch, stressing the point that direct Anglo-Irish trade is not the only aspect of the Irish economy worth serious consideration.

Ireland depended upon Europe for many important commodities, such as wine and hops and above all salt, without which Irish herrings, butter and beef could not have been preserved for export. Figures for salt and hops are not available but an examination of the Irish wine trade 1614–15[1] may be undertaken to show the pattern of trade in one commodity. Wine was mainly imported, not via England but directly from the continent, chiefly from France and in particular the ports of St. Malo, Bordeaux and La Rochelle. Not all of this was necessarily French wine; a good deal of it was described as sack, which may have been Spanish wine, re-exported through French ports. A good deal of wine was also imported from Middleburg in Zeeland. The official figures for the year 1614–15 show that a total of c. 380,000 gallons (1,511 tuns) was imported, slightly more than a third in English ships, slightly less than a third in Irish ships. So far as the wine trade was concerned the Dutch came a poor fifth to the Scots and the French. The large Irish share, however, was mainly due to the ships of Waterford. The wine trade of Cork was carried in English ships and that of Limerick in French and English ships. Only one of nine ships bringing wine into Galway was Irish, though it carried a greater cargo than all the rest put together. The ports of Cork, Limerick, Galway, Dublin and Waterford accounted for more than three quarters of the wine trade in this particular year.[2] A good deal of the trade was of Cork and Limerick with St. Malo. Dublin, on the other hand, traded with Dutch and English ports. The Ulster ports naturally were closely connected with Scotland especially the ports of the Clyde. Direct trading links also existed between Ireland and St. Lucar, Malaga, Cadiz and the Canaries.

The total number of ships involved was 143, about a third of which had ports of registry in England and the Channel Isles. The number of Irish and Scots ships were equal at 31 each, while the French and Dutch came very low down with 8 and 6 respectively. In the wine trade at least the number of Dutch ships was very low

---

[1] Based on P.R.O., E122/196/14. Cf. H. F. Kearney, 'The Irish wine trade, 1614–15' in *Irish Historical Studies*, ix. 400–42 (Sept. 1955).

[2] Cork 20%; Limerick 17%; Galway 16·5%; Dublin 12%; Waterford 11%.

and offers a sharp contradiction to what is usually thought to have been the place of Dutch merchant shipping in the early seventeenth century.

This analysis of the wine trade, however, may be misleading in some respects. In the first place it makes no allowance for the considerable amount of smuggling which must be presumed to have gone on. In the second place, the document on which it is based is the return submitted by the officials of the wine monopoly. They were interested only in levying a duty on the wine carried by a particular ship; the remainder of a general cargo was dealt with by the officers of the main customs farm whose records have mostly perished. The survival of a few port books for Ulster,[1] however, enables us to show how a ship might bring wine as part of a general cargo. In 1613, for example, the *Speedwell* of Liverpool brought to Coleraine a cargo of sea coal, bay salt, vinegar and French wines.[2] In 1615 the *Cathren* of Carlingford brought a cargo of bay salt, wines and vinegar from France,[3] to Coleraine. Such mixed cargoes must have been typical of many of the ships recorded in the 1614–15 wine document.

One general conclusion, however, may be drawn from the existence of direct trade in wine with the continent, namely that exports were required to pay for it. Direct imports imply direct exports. A few scraps of evidence[4] suffice to show the nature of these exports. In 1614 the *Greyhound* of Londonderry was outward bound for France with a cargo which included hides, tallow, butter, wool, candles and stagskins.[5] In 1623 James Bath, an Irish merchant, was trading with France in hides and tallow.[6] In 1627 a Dutch ship took a cargo of Irish pilchards from Crookhaven to Marseilles.[7] Some years earlier, in 1611, St. Malo was said to be the main port for Irish hides.[8]

Similar scraps of evidence are available to throw a little light upon the obscurity of Irish trade with Spain. In 1611 hides were said to be exported to Seville and the Canaries, and occasionally to Lisbon.[9] In 1614 a group of Galway merchants freighted two ships belonging to Lubeck and Calais for a voyage to Spain, with

---

[1] Preserved in Sir Arthur Ingram's papers (Temple Newsam MSS.).
[2] Coleraine Port Book, 1612–13 (Temple Newsam MSS.).
[3] Ibid., 1615.   [4] Besides continental archives.
[5] Derry Port Book, 1614–15 (Temple Newsam MSS.).
[6] *Cal. S.P. Ire., 1615–25*, p. 423.   [7] Ibid., *1625–32*, p. 421.
[8] Ibid., *1611–14*, p. 200.   [9] Ibid.

a cargo said to have been worth over £3,000. It is typical of the scarcity of evidence, however, that something is known of this venture only because the ship fell into the hands of pirates and the grievances of the merchants concerned ultimately came before the Privy Council.[1] In 1625 five merchants from Waterford were imprisoned in Spain when war broke out with England.[2] In 1614 pipestaves were exported from Coleraine to Spain[3] and twenty years later it seems to have been a common practice for English ships trading with Spain to call at an Irish port on their way out to collect pipestaves, which had to be supplied in Spain before wine could be exported.[4] Fish was another article of export from Ireland; in 1613 the *Grace of God* sailed from Coleraine to Spain with a cargo of thirty tons of salmon.[5] There are hints of a more complex trading pattern in the voyage of the *Mary* of Wexford which sailed from Bristol on 20 August 1625 for the Canaries with a cargo of English cloth.[6]

During the war with Spain, 1625–30, a ban on trade with the enemy was imposed by the lord deputy.[7] There is no evidence to show whether or not licences were granted. In 1634 Captain Plumleigh in a letter to lord treasurer Portland went out of his way to note the presence of a Spanish ship in Galway, the first that he had seen there for trading purposes.[8] All this would bear out the implications of Wentworth's correspondence with John Taylor, an English agent in Spain, that Irish trade with Spain had fallen away to nothing. On the other hand, Wentworth may have been seeking an excuse to indulge in trade on his own account and it was not uncharacteristic of the time to justify a private venture on the grounds of public benefit. His agent Joshua Carpenter took steps to fit out a ship which was to sail from Dingle in 1634.[9] The cargo was to consist of hides, butter, tallow, salt beef, bacon, salmon, fish, friezes and wheat. In August 1633 John Taylor, English agent in Spain, provided Wentworth with a detailed list of the cargoes which would be suitable for the various Spanish ports,[10] and the corresponding imports which included wine, fruit,

---

[1] *Acts P.C., 1613–14*, p. 430.   [2] *Cal. S.P. Ire., 1615–25*, p. 566.
[3] Coleraine Port Book, 1613–14 (Temple Newsam MSS.).
[4] *Cal. S.P. dom., 1631–33*, p. 221.
[5] Coleraine Port Book, 1612–13 (Temple Newsam MSS.).
[6] P.R.O., E190/1135/5.   [7] *Cal. S.P. Ire., 1625–32*, p. 81.
[8] *Cal. S.P. Ire., 1633–47*, p. 68.   [9] *Strafford's letters*, i. 110.
[10] Ibid., i. 104–5.

spices, tobacco, sugar and oils. The actual state of trade between Spain and Ireland during these years, however, is a question which depends for its answer upon the analysis of commercial archives in Spain itself. Until that is done it is difficult to make even the most tentative statements.

Trade with Holland undoubtedly existed but as the 1614 wine trade showed, it is easy to exaggerate its importance. In 1633, Wentworth said that 'all the trade within this channel, save that of coals, is wholly carried in Dutch bottoms', but no general statement like this can be accepted without evidence in confirmation.[1] There are signs that the Dutch merchants in Dublin were an important colony and some of them like Westenra, Vandeleur and others later became prominent in Irish life. The Dutch were the general carriers of Europe during the seventeenth century, and it would have been surprising had they not had a great hold upon Irish trade, but the evidence of the 1614 wine list makes us pause in going too far, since it shows that the Dutch share in the wine trade was much smaller than would have been expected. Scraps of evidence suggest a more general picture. In 1614 hops were brought from Amsterdam to Carrickfergus; in the same year beef, oats, tallow and butter were exported in the reverse direction.[2] In 1613 the *Cathren* of Ayr brought from the Low Countries a cargo of tar, pitch, tilestones, hops, earthen pots, iron pots, salt, vinegar, soap, sugar and small wares.[3] Richard Boyle exported iron from his forges in Co. Cork to Amsterdam.[4] In 1616 three Drogheda merchants were engaged in trade with Middleburg; their return cargo consisted of wine, hops, alum, madder, etc.[5] These commercial links with Holland were presumably of a similar character twenty years later, though little direct evidence is available. The archives at Middleburg were destroyed during the second world war. Those at Rotterdam contain very little information. The notarial archives show 200 tons of meat exported from Dublin to Rotterdam in June 1640.[6] Irish cloth was also exported to Holland.[7] The archives of Amsterdam are more

[1] *Strafford's letters*, i. 106.
[2] Carrickfergus Port Book, 1614–15 (Temple Newsam MSS.).
[3] Coleraine Port Book, 1612–13 (Temple Newsam MSS.).
[4] A. B. Grosart (ed.), *Lismore Papers*, series 1, ii. 53.
[5] *Cal. S.P. Ire., 1615–25*, p. 124.   [6] Delphius, *Miscellanea*, p. 272.
[7] N. W. Posthumus, *Bronnon tot de Geschiedenis van de Leidsche Textielnykereid 1611–50*, iv. 356.

promising. They illustrate at least one distinct trade route which followed the pattern Holland—Norway—Ireland—Spain. Timber was brought from Norway to Ireland. Pipestaves were then taken from Ireland to Spain where they were exchanged for wine, which was sometimes brought back to Ireland and on other occasions shipped direct to Holland. George Radcliffe mentioned in 1634 that many Dutch merchants were engaged in trade in tallow.[1]

Trade between Ireland and Scotland cannot be left out of account. It existed mainly between the Ulster ports of Coleraine, Londonderry and Carrickfergus and the Clyde ports of Renfrew, Dumbarton, Greenock and Glasgow. A good proportion of the trade of a port like Coleraine was with Scotland though it had also strong links with London, Barnstaple and Chester.[2] Coal, iron and linen cloth were imported from Scotland, in return for hides, cows, beef, oats, cheese and sheepskins. Scottish merchants also brought French salt and wines into Coleraine,[3] taking advantage of their particularly favourable position in France, where they were exempt from all alien customs, a privilege confirmed by Henry IV in 1599.[4] Spanish salt, tobacco and silk were imported into Derry by the *Daniel* of Leith in 1615.[5] One rather odd cargo was Scots whisky brought by the *Kathren* of Glasgow to Coleraine in 1613.[6]

When all is said, however, it is difficult to resist the conclusion that Anglo-Irish trade was the most important single item in Irish commerce. Trade between the two countries was based largely upon the export of Irish cattle, foodstuffs and raw material in exchange for English manufactured goods, especially cloth. The ports of north-east Ireland, and in particular Drogheda and Dundalk, supplied linen yarn and wool for the fustian manufacture of Lancashire through the ports of Liverpool[7] and Chester. Trade in live cattle was very important and from June to October 1634 almost every ship entered in the Chester Port Book carried live cattle, especially from Dublin.[8] The average cargo was twenty

[1] Radcliffe to Ingram. 28 Oct. 1634. *H.M.C. Var. Coll.*, viii. 44.
[2] Coleraine Port Book, 1612–13 (Temple Newsam MSS.).
[3] Ibid., 1614–15 (Temple Newsam MSS.).
[4] Theodora Keith, *Commercial relations of England and Scotland 1603–1707*, p. 4.
[5] Derry Port Book, 1615 (Temple Newsam MSS.).
[6] Coleraine Port Book, 1612–13 (Temple Newsam MSS.).
[7] P.R.O., E190/1334/25: 1335/12. They were the staple ports for linen yarn.
[8] E190/1335/11.

cows. Sheep and hogs were also exported and the return cargoes usually consisted of coal and cloth. In June 1613 for example the *Bride* of Hilbre[1] brought to Coleraine a cargo of silk, perpetuanoes, fustian, broadcloth, serge, calico, hollands and canvas, together with spices, tobacco and hops.[2]

Further south, the pattern of trade was slightly different. The Wexford herring fisheries drew ships from most ports on the west and south-west coasts of England and Wales. During the busiest month, November, when the herrings shoaled, the official figures alone[3] for the year 1614 show the export of over 10,000 barrels of salted herring. For the other months the figures were much less, 1,230 barrels in December, 730 in January and 920 in February. During the period July to November 1614, in preparation for the busy period, over 6,000 barrels of salt were imported, most of them during September and October. A good deal of beer— nearly 600 barrels during September and October—was imported at the same time possibly to cope with the thirst of the increased population of Wexford during the salting season.

The cloth manufacturers of Devon drew upon southern Ireland for wool to supplement home supplies. Youghal, in particular, was important as a staple port for the wool trade to Minehead, Barnstaple and the ports of North Devon.[4] The predominance of Youghal is borne out by figures provided by Adam Loftus in 1641.[5] Butter and tallow were also shipped to Minehead. In return, the most usual cargoes were cloth, sempiternums, kerseys and broadcloth, as well as haberdashery, woollen stockings, hats and other articles.[6]

Irish trade formed a large part of the trade of Bristol. During the year 1638, for example, ships from almost every port in the east coast of Ireland found their way there, including Wexford, Ross, Drogheda, Derry, Youghal, Dublin, Cork and Waterford.[7] Exports to Bristol consisted of wool, herrings, hides, salmon, butter, linen, yarn, tallow and beef. In return, Irish merchants frequently brought unspecified parcels of 'wares'. On 31 March

---

[1] An outport of Chester at the mouth of the Dee.
[2] Coleraine Port Book, 1612–13 (Temple Newsam MSS.).
[3] Wexford Port Book, 1614–15 (Temple Newsam MSS.).
[4] P.R.O., E190/1088/12. Cf. also W.G. Hoskins, *Industry, trade, and people in Exeter 1688–1800.*
[5] Cf. Graph No. 1.
[6] P.R.O., E190/1088/12.　　　　　　　　　　[7] Ibid., E190/1136/10.

1637 the *Anne* of Milford brought 160 lb. Virginia tobacco, 10 score tobacco pipes and 35 cwt. Spanish iron.[1] Hops and cloth were other common cargoes.

There is also some evidence of direct Irish trade in cattle with Virginia in return for tobacco[2] and it is significant that there was so large an amount of tobacco stored in the 'magazines' of the tobacco monopoly, which Wentworth had set up, that it could be used as payment in kind for parliamentary troops in Cork and elsewhere, after the rising of 1641.[3]

In conclusion, it may be suggested that Irish trade was more important and more varied than is usually thought to have been the case. Merchants were a prominent and powerful element in Ireland, a fact which had political consequences. The merchants of the ports of Limerick, Cork, Waterford and Galway were almost exclusively Catholic and old English. They may be regarded as forming the commercial, urban counterpart of the old English gentry, though the distinction between town and country must not be overstressed, since trade in pastoral commodities provided a strong economic link between merchants and gentry, while many merchants owned land. The wine-list of 1615 shows that the majority of merchants in the wine trade possessed old English names—the Lynches, Frenches and Browns of Galway, the Flemings, Cashells, Chillams and Peppers of Drogheda, the Roches, Terrys and Meads of Cork and the Whites and Dobbins of Waterford. It would appear from this that just as the old English held the best land in Ireland, they also had a lion's share of the trade. The appearance of commercial clauses in the Graces becomes more intelligible, in view of the importance of the old English merchants. The struggle between Wentworth and the old English was so bitter and so prolonged because of the economic resources at their command and it was for this reason also that they were ultimately successful in their resistance to him.

(II) THE IRISH WOOL TRADE

In a well-known passage, George Unwin compared Wentworth to Colbert and Frederick the Great and claimed that nothing short

[1] P.R.O., E190/1136/8.
[2] Cf. A. Gwynn S.J., 'The Irish in the West Indies', *Analecta Hibernica*, no. 4, 160–1.
[3] Strafford MSS., vol. 41.

of the full mercantilist dream was the object of his policy.[1] The 'full mercantilist dream', however, seems to have been a concept clearer to latter-day historians than to politicians of the seventeenth century. 'Mercantilism', in the sense of the full-blooded pursuit of a long-term economic policy, conceived in the light of certain general principles, is a historical term, which has failed to stand up to the test of detailed examination.[2]

A recent article has shown that Thomas Mun's *England's Treasure of Forraign Trade* is to be seen as the product of the crisis of the early 1620's and of the concomitant economic discussion,[3] and in general it would appear that historians have exaggerated the amount of choice which government had in following an economic policy and have underestimated the effects of contemporary economic problems. In other words, the conduct of seventeenth-century politicians was not governed as much by long-term considerations of 'mercantilism' as historians once liked to think. The pressing problems of the day—and above all finance—were sufficient preoccupation for any government, though they might like to feel sometimes that principle or policy guided their actions. If Wentworth had an economic policy, it was largely dictated by the practical necessity of relieving the English administration of the financial burdens of Ireland; he had to succeed where Falkland failed.

Trade could be left to find its own channels provided it made its due contribution to the Irish Exchequer; only one commodity raised questions which involved long term economic considerations—wool. The dominant position of the cloth industry in England made it impossible for the English privy council to look upon the export of Irish wool as a matter of indifference. In good times, Irish wool was needed as a marginal source of supply of raw material. In bad times, Irish wool could not be allowed to find a market with England's own competitors. In both cases, it was to England's economic interest to supervise and control the export of Irish wool. This was an unsatisfactory position from the Irish point of view, as during years in which the English cloth

---

[1] G. Unwin, *Industrial organisation in the sixteenth and seventeenth centuries*, p. 172.

[2] Cf., for example, A. V. Judges, 'The idea of a mercantile state' in *Trans. R. Hist. Soc.*, 4th ser., xxi. 41–70.

[3] B. E. Supple, 'Thomas Mun and the commercial crisis, 1623' in *Bulletin of the Institute of Historical Research*, XXVI, no. 75 (May 1954), 91–4.

industry did not prosper and their market declined, they were prevented from seeking compensation elsewhere, in France or the Netherlands. A clash of interest existed between Irish wool producers and the English cloth industry on this point. The attitude of the English privy council was consistent over a number of years and perhaps therefore merits the description 'mercantilist'. The economic situation itself and the policy of the English privy council however left the lord deputy with little initiative in this particular instance and it would have been very surprising had Wentworth been able to introduce any radical changes. In fact he followed the policy laid down for his predecessors. Some account of what this was may now be given in a little more detail.[1]

The English economic attitude towards Ireland during the Elizabethan period has been described[2] as a 'systematic war . . . waged against Irish trade', but such a description rests upon an over-estimate of the importance of Ireland as a competitor to England. In the late sixteenth century, whatever may be said of the late seventeenth, Ireland and England were hardly economic competitors. The staple Irish exports of cattle, beef, hides, tallow and associated products did not compete with the staple export of England—cloth. The explanation of the statutes passed by the Irish parliament in 1569 and 1571,[3] by which prohibitive duties were placed upon the exportation of the staple Irish commodities including wool, may therefore be sought elsewhere. Nor is it necessary to accept the preambles of the acts at their face value, describing the aim of English policy as the creation in Ireland of a rival to the English manufacture of cloth. The explanation for these acts is to be found neither in English malevolence nor benevolence, but in the economic situation of the years following 1569. It was in that year that Alva prohibited the import of English cloth into the Netherlands, as a measure of retaliation against Elizabeth's detaining the Spanish silver on its way to pay his troops.[4] The Irish acts of 1569 and 1571 fall into place as part of

---

[1] Wentworth did resist an attempt to confine the export of Irish tallow to England in the interests of the English soap monopoly. In this case he may be described as having acted in a 'non-mercantilist' fashion as the ostensible object of the soap monopoly was to free England from dependence upon foreign soap.

[2] G. O'Brien, *The economic history of Ireland in the seventeenth century*, p. 57.

[3] *Irish Statutes* (ed. 1765), i. 349–54; 376–87.

[4] *Cal. S.P. Foreign, 1569–71*, p. 5.

Elizabeth's own measure of retaliation, not against Ireland but against an enemy unmentioned in the acts themselves—the Spanish government in the Netherlands. The economic war between Elizabeth and Alva did not end until 1573, when Alva climbed down and once more admitted English cloth.

The acts themselves remained on the statute book but it can hardly be doubted that by the beginning of the seventeenth century, they were not enforced for their original purpose. Instead they had become a source of revenue. Licences to export wool[1] were freely granted by the lord deputy, upon payment of a fee, which seems to have been regarded as a perquisite of the office.[2] The circumstances which had brought the acts into existence had for the moment vanished; from being instruments of economic retaliation they had become merely a minor and indirect source of revenue. The chaotic state of the Irish customs administration gives reason to think that wool was often exported without a licence.[3]

This state of affairs continued until 1611 when among a list of proposals drawn up for consideration in the forthcoming parliament, the suggestion was made that licences should be abolished and that all merchandise, including the 'prohibited commodities' should be exported freely provided customs duties were paid.[4] The background to this change of front lay in the proposed reorganisation of the Irish customs system[5] and it reflected the natural anxiety of the customs farmers to ensure conditions as favourable for their venture as possible. The abolition of the licences would encourage trade and make smuggling less profitable. In June 1614 a decisive victory for the customs farmers seemed to have been achieved when James I directed Chichester to publish a proclamation, making it lawful for any person to transport out of Ireland all wares and merchandise, except linen yarn, without licence.[6] Wool was included in the general liberty

---

[1] For an example, cf. A. Longfield, *Anglo-Irish trade in the sixteenth century*, p. 80.

[2] Wentworth to Coke, 31 Jan. 1633/4 (*Strafford's letters*, i. 202). In 1612 it was estimated that licences for the export of prohibited commodities would bring in £1,000 per annum. *Cal. S.P. Ire., 1611–14*, p. 314.

[3] Cf. the 1611 report on the Irish customs. *Cal. Carew MSS., 1603–24*, pp. 175 ff. Cf. also ibid., pp. 97–8.

[4] *Cal. Carew MSS., 1603–24*, p. 160.

[5] See below, p. 159, for an account of this.

[6] *Cal. S.P. Ire., 1611–14*, p. 486.

of trade, which followed within a year of the setting up of the Irish customs farm.

This liberty, however, did not last long. In September[1] it was revoked 'for reasons of state' unspecified, and in December, came a further vacillation. On 18 December, James I wrote to Chichester that he understood some prejudice had been caused to the customs and some breach of contract with the customs farmers by his recall of the free liberty of export. Under this pressure from the customs farmers, he ordered Chichester to renew the proclamation for liberty of exportation without any further licence or charges. This time however he made the significant exemption of unwrought wool and woollen yarn, as well as linen yarn, giving as his reason 'because under that liberty much unwrought wool was exported to the great prejudice of clothing in Ireland and of the drapery in England.'[2]

The reasons for this vacillation of policy in the second half of 1614 and the sudden decision of James I to prohibit the export of Irish wool except under licence are not far to seek. The conditions of the years 1569–73 had returned in a new form, and the prohibition of December 1614 was a defensive measure similar to that of those years, not an unprovoked attack upon an infant Irish industry which threatened to become a serious rival to the cloth trade of England. Anglo-Dutch commercial rivalry in the Baltic came to a head during the first decade of the seventeenth century. The Eastland merchants had complained some time before that undressed English cloth, finished in Holland, was underselling English dressed cloth.[3] No steps, however, were taken to remedy this state of affairs until a further blow befell the cloth trade in 1612. In April 1612 a movement to restore the lost prosperity of the Flemish cloth trade had come to a head when the Archduke refused to renew the licence of a Dunkirk merchant for the importation of English cloth into the Spanish Netherlands.[4] Lionel Cranfield wrote a report in August of the same year suggesting that the ban would do Flanders more harm than good and that Antwerp would continue to provide a means of entry for undressed English cloth.[5] In December William Trumbull, the English representative in Brussels, reported that the Flemings

---

[1] *Cal. S.P. Ire., 1611–14*, p. 502.   [2] Ibid., *1611–14*, pp. 534–5.
[3] A. Friis, *Alderman Cockayne's project and the cloth trade*, pp. 230–1.
[4] *H.M.C. Sackville (Knole) MSS.*, p. 273.   [5] Ibid., p. 276.

were much encouraged by the great abundance of smuggled wool which they were able to obtain owing to the selfishness of his majesty's evil-affected subjects.[1]

This period of economic rivalry, taken in conjunction with James I's chronic shortage of money and the unpopularity of the Merchant Adventurers, provided the background for a scheme which aimed at exploiting to the full the dominant position held by England in the cloth-trade. The object of Alderman Cockayne's[2] project was to export only dyed and dressed cloth from England.[3] A new company was to be formed to replace the Old Merchant Adventurers: and from its estimated income of £600,000 to £700,000 a year, the Crown was to receive £300,000 in return for granting a monopoly.[4] The opposition in the 'Addled Parliament' in the first half of 1614[5] did not deter James I, and in a proclamation of 23 July it was made known that after 2 November no undyed or undressed cloths were to be carried out of the country.[6] The old Merchant Adventurers voluntarily surrendered their charter in February 1615.[7] A determined attempt was now to be made to bring the cloth industries in the Netherlands to a standstill.

All this helps to explain James I's decision in September 1614 to revoke, for 'reasons of state best known to himself' the freedom of exportation granted to Irish merchants in June. The decision had nothing to do with antagonism to the Irish wool trade as such. As in 1569 Ireland was a pawn in the game; the real enemy was regarded as lying elsewhere.

The position in 1614, however, was not precisely what it had been in 1569. In the interval the 'new draperies' in England had become much more important, and it was here that Irish wool found a growing market. However much Irish friezes may have been imported into England in the early sixteenth century, it is clear by the last decades that raw wool had become a major Irish export.[8] Yorkshire makers of cheap cloths supplemented their supplies of cheap wool by drawing upon the cheaper grades from

---

[1] *H.M.C. Sackville (Knole) MSS.*, p. 282.
[2] He was a member of the Eastland Co. Friis, *Cockayne's project*, p. 235.
[3] Friis, p. 236.   [4] W. R. Scott, *Joint Stock Companies to 1720*, i. 141 ff.
[5] Friis, pp. 254–5.   [6] Ibid., p. 267.
[7] Ibid., p. 271.
[8] Cf. A. Longfield, *Anglo-Irish trade in the sixteenth century*, p. 86, for figures in 1588 and 1590.

Ireland and elsewhere.[1] Considerable quantities of Irish wool were imported into Chester[2] and Liverpool.[3] In 1627-8 it was reported that most of the new draperies in Lancashire were made 'of low rates and prices, and of course wool, and a great part of Irish wool'.[4] Norwich also specialised in the cheaper fustians and was said to have bought £100,000 worth of Irish yarn.[5] The main market, however, for Irish wool was in south-west England, where Minehead, Bideford and Bristol were the main ports of entry.[6] Coarse Irish wool was used to supplement home supplies of raw wool in the production of the cheaper kind of 'new drapery'. In short, it would appear that changes in the English cloth industry since 1570 had been to the benefit of the Irish wool trade.

Until 1614 it seems to have been possible to export Irish wool to countries other than England,[7] provided a licence was obtained from the lord deputy.[8] The circumstances of 1614, however, and the determination of James I to support Cockayne's project created a situation in which it was regarded as necessary to control strictly the exportation of Irish wool and to prevent it from reaching Flanders or the Seven United Provinces. But the absolute ban of December 1614 could hardly be expected to last, and in 1615 there was at least one example of it being waived in favour of a merchant who gave a definite undertaking to export his wool to England.[9] The farmers of the Irish customs were scarcely prepared to acquiesce in a complete ban on the wool trade, and it was not surprising that they should be represented on the committee which met to discuss ways and means of regulating the export of wool.[10] There could be no objection in principle to the transportation of wool to England: the difficulty was to prevent smuggling

[1] H. Heaton, *The Yorkshire woollen and worsted industries*, p. 205.
[2] Cf. Port Book for 1620, E190/1332/1.
[3] Cf. Port Book for 1632, E190/1334/25.
[4] A. P. Wadsworth and J. de L. Mann, *The Cotton trade and Industrial Lancashire*, p. 13.
[5] G. O'Brien (ed.), *Advertisements for Ireland R.S.A.I.*, 1923, p. 8.
[6] Cf. W. G. Hoskins, *Industry, Trade and People in Exeter 1688-1800*.
[7] O'Brien, *Advertisements*, p. 8. Spain, France and the Low Countries are mentioned.
[8] A licence granted in 1595 allowed Nicholas Weston to export wool to any port beyond the seas. Longfield, op. cit., p. 80.
[9] *Cal. S.P. Ire., 1615-25*, p. 64.
[10] George Lowe and Lionel Cranfield were members: so was Cockayne himself. *Cal. Carew MSS., 1603-24*, p. 329.

L

to the continent on a large scale. Revival of the old system of
staple ports appeared to be the most practicable solution of the
problem: the wool trade was to be canalised and wool merchants
compelled to account at both ends, England and Ireland, for the
wool which they were exporting. A receipt brought back to Ireland
from the English staple port would prove that the wool had in
fact been delivered. In July 1616 the Lord Chancellor reported to
the Privy Council favourably upon the scheme drawn up by the
committee.[1]

The failure of Cockayne's project and the restoration of the
Old Merchant Adventurers brought no change in English commercial policy towards Ireland. The depression in the English
cloth trade which began in 1615, continued during the years following[2] and from the English point of view it was more necessary
than ever to keep a strict watch upon the export of Irish wool.
Despite its unpopularity with Irish wool growers and merchants,
and even with the Irish administration, the staple port system was
favoured by the English privy council. The original scheme, as
sketched by the committee, envisaged the staple towns as follows;
in Ireland, Dublin, Drogheda, Waterford, Cork, Limerick, Galway, Carrickfergus and Londonderry; in England, London,
Bristol, Barnstaple, Chester or Liverpool, and Workington.[3] In
February 1617 Sir James Ley and Richard Hadsor reported from
Ireland upon certain details of the working of the organisation of
the staple.[4] But by January 1620 the only Munster staple port in
action was Youghal.[5] The establishment of this, however, had
been sufficient to arouse the protests of the lord president and
Council of Munster, supported by the lord deputy and the Irish
privy council: they complained about the effect of the staple upon
the English plantations and the revenue from customs duties, and
they claimed that smuggling had greatly increased.[6]

[1] *Cal. Carew MSS., 1603–24*, p. 329–30.
[2] *Cal. S.P. dom., 1611–18*, pp. 389, 410.
[3] *Cal. Carew MSS., 1603–24*, p. 334.
[4] *Cal. S.P. Ire., 1615–25*, p. 150. Ley was later lord treasurer in England,
1624–8.
[5] In April 1618 a list drawn up by the customer at Drogheda illustrates
the working of the bond system in that port. Drogheda merchants, most of
whom had Anglo-Irish names, took out bonds ranging from £60 to £5 to
export their wool to England. SP/63/234/f. 156 (*Cal. S.P. Ire., 1615–25* p. 189).
[6] Ibid., pp. 252–3. The reply of the staplers was made in Jan. 1620, ibid.,
p. 273.

In the existing state of the English cloth trade, however, it was impossible to expect any concessions. In the parliament of 1621 the depression was debated, and Sir Edwin Sandys was not alone in his feeling that 'all the grievances of the Kingdom are trifles in comparison with the decay of trade'. Unemployment in Wiltshire, Gloucestershire and Worcestershire was blamed upon the stealthy exportation of English, Scottish and Irish wools to Middleburg.[1] Cranfield, in the report he made in June 1621, included among his suggested remedies for the decay of trade effective measures to prevent the exportation from England, Scotland and Ireland of wool and yarn.[2]

In this atmosphere the staple system in Ireland was unlikely to be modified to permit a greater freedom in the wool trade. The appointment early in 1622 of commissioners to enquire, amongst other things, into the reasons for the decay of trade in Ireland[3] coincided with most distressing reports from the justices of the peace in Suffolk, Oxfordshire and Gloucestershire[4] on the state of the clothing industry. In September 1622 the committee of twelve which had been appointed to confer with English merchants about the decay of trade, was asked to investigate the methods required *inter alia* to secure the import of Scotch and Irish wools into England instead of to other countries.[5] It was thus small wonder that the commissioners sent over to Ireland did not recommend a relaxation of the staple, but contented themselves with suggestions, for establishing cloth manufacture in Ireland. These suggestions came to nothing: the English Privy Council refused to permit the free exportation of fullers earth to Ireland. It is difficult, however, to see how it would have brought itself to do otherwise: the creation of a further rival to English cloth provided no solution of the problem of unemployment and declining trade. Until trade began to revive little would be done. Thus the three Irish representatives, Sir Christopher Plunkett, Sir Hugh Clotworthy and Sir John Tristeene, who visited England in June 1623 to put the Irish case 'concerning wool and matter of Trade'[6] —and it was significant that an Ulster undertaker as well as a

[1] Friis, p. 320.   [2] Ibid., p. 418.
[3] *Cal. S.P. Ire.*, *1615–25*, pp. 346–7.
[4] *Cal. S.P. dom.*, *1619–23*, pp. 359, 362, 401.   [5] Ibid., p. 450.
[6] The commissioners of 1622 did, however, refer to a 'goodly clothing work' set up by Sir Thomas Roper near Dublin, where all the processes of cloth manufacture were said to be carried out. *Cal. S.P. Ire.*, *1615–25*, p. 361.

representative of the Pale was a member of this small committee
—obtained no reward for their trouble. The economic crisis
afflicting England's chief manufacture dictated an economic policy
towards Ireland which it seemed impossible to change until conditions improved. In 1624 therefore the landholders of the Pale
seem to have accepted this fact, and the grievances which they
presented to the Crown in that year made no mention of wool,
the wool staples and licences.

This was the remoter background of Wentworth's attitude
towards the Irish wool trade. Attention may now be turned to the
period of the Graces and the years following.

The matters of Grace and Bounty which were drawn up in
September 1626 did not propose any change in the existing
regulations. Wool was still to be exported from the Irish to the
English staple towns, according to the Staplers' Charter, paying
only existing impositions.[1] By 1628, however, the bargaining position of the discontented in Ireland had improved[2] and therefore
in the list of 'humble requests' presented in the first months of the
year, the request for freedom to export wool, implied in its silence,
the abolition of licensing and of the staple system, though accepting apparently without question the obligation to export it to
England alone,[3] paying ordinary customs and duties. In general,
the other economic clauses of the Graces look back to the concessions which had been hoped for in the parliament of 1613–15:
there was the same attempt in 1628 to have the restrictive statutes
of 11 Eliz. and 13 Eliz. repealed and free trade in the prohibited
commodities restored. It was requested for example in 1628 that
corn merchants should need no export licence for exporting corn
into the king's dominions and countries maintaining friendly
relations with the English Crown, when it was not above ten
shillings a barrel in price. In comparison with the concessions
which were demanded for the other 'prohibited commodities'
that concerning wool made a modest demand. Irish discontent did
not go so far as to demand the exportation of wool to foreign
countries, though the abolition of the staple system would have
removed what was perhaps the only practicable method of
preventing smuggling on a large scale.

During the years 1627–8 there does not seem to have been the

---

[1] *Cal. S.P. Ire., 1625–32*, p. 157.   [2] See above, pp. 21 ff.
[3] *Cal. S.P. Ire., 1625–32*, p. 331.

openly-expressed discontent in the English cloth trade as in previous years[1] and this may have made possible a more liberal attitude towards the Irish wool trade on the part of the English privy council. But the improvement was only temporary. In April 1629 a petition said to be signed by 200 persons complained of unemployment in Essex and intimated that over 30,000 persons were likely 'to partake of that misery'.[2] In July 1629 the clothiers of Suffolk complained of the decay in trade.[3] In December 1630 there were reports of great distress among the Surrey clothiers and in Norwich. Such reports continued to reach the privy council during the three years following. In such circumstances, the privy council looked with disfavour upon suggestions to do away with restrictive measures upon the transportation of Irish wool. In 1630 the drapers of the City of London presented a petition on behalf of the drapers of England, setting forth the reasons for the great decay of the cloth trade and blaming, amongst other reasons, the export of wools 'whereby the stranger's wheel is set going'.[4] In April 1630 a proclamation was once more issued to prevent the exportation of wool. There was now little chance that the Grace doing away with both the staples and the need for licences would come into force. During the period of the lords justices, indeed, the restrictions seem to have become greater than before, and in June 1631 it was reported that even the staple towns were forbidden to sell wool to England, and that nobody was able to transport it without special warrant from the lords justices.[5] The restrictions were taken so seriously that even Wentworth, on 8 September 1633, a few months after his arrival, felt himself obliged to write to Coke asking for a warrant to enable him to grant licences for the transportation of wool.[6]

Coke's reply to the letter[7] makes clear that the lord deputy enjoyed little or no freedom of action in this field. Coke explained that there had been so many petitions presented against the exporting into foreign parts of English, Irish and Scottish wools that 'a general restraint thereof is agreed upon as a matter much importing the Cloth Trade and specially the Manufactures

---

[1] There is no mention in *Cal. S.P. dom.* for these years, of unemployment in the cloth trade.
[2] *Cal. S.P. dom., 1628–9*, p. 521. [3] Ibid., *1629–31*, p. 8.
[4] Ibid., *1629–31*, pp. 446–7.
[5] Esmond to Dorchester, 20 June 1631. *Cal. S.P. Ire., 1625–32*, p. 616.
[6] *Strafford's letters*, i. 202. [7] 24 Oct. 1633, ibid., i. 137.

which run an hazard of being banished out of France and the Low Countries by their ordinary working them of our own wools'. He saw no difficulty, however, in granting Wentworth's request provided it stretched no further than the exporting of Irish wool to England and his Majesty's dominions.

So little freedom did the lord deputy enjoy, that, during the period before Wentworth received his warrant, it would appear that no wool at all was being legally exported. In his reply to Coke's letter,[1] Wentworth assured Coke that he had given strict orders to the ports that the law restricting the exportation of wool should be enforced, and he added that he had imprisoned two people for failing to observe it. Sir Roger Jones, governor of Sligo, was also charged with transporting wool without licence.[2]

A month later, Wentworth explained his own attitude in more detail. In his letter to Coke of 31 January 1633/4, he poured scorn upon the idea of staple towns: he considered it 'a remedy worse than the disease'.[3] He put forward two arguments why the exportation of Irish wool to England should be allowed: the first was for the bettering of the customs, since wool which was first exported as raw material and then imported, paid customs duties four times 'if it be indraped and spent within the Kingdom': the second argument made out that the wool would be left on the hands of the growers unless exportation was granted and it could not be 'left at large without great prejudice to the clothing of England'. Wentworth was thus in favour of a system of licensing by the lord deputy which would keep the initiative in his own hands, and against a staple system which he considered to be inefficient and corrupt. He concluded this section of the letter with a reference to 'the clamour of such as press me daily for licenses in that kind'. Six weeks later George Wentworth reported that 'the King had agreed to grant the lord deputy a warrant to give licences for the transportation of wool into England'.[4]

Wentworth had written to Portland on the same day that he had written to Coke.[5] The views which he expressed in this letter have

[1] 8 Nov. 1633, Wentworth to Coke. *Strafford's letters*, i. 152.
[2] Strafford MSS., vol. 5, f. 90.
[3] *Strafford's letters*, i. 202.
[4] 13 Mar. 1633/4. *Strafford's letters*, i. 220.
[5] I.e. 31 Jan. 1633/4. Ibid., i. 193.

been taken as a classic statement of his policy towards Ireland. He wrote that he was 'of the opinion that all Wisdom advises to keep this Kingdom as much subordinate and dependent upon England as is possible and holding them from the Manufacture of Wool (which unless otherwise directed, I shall by all means discourage) and then inforcing them to fetch their clothing from thence and to take their salt from the King[1] (being that which preserves and gives value to all their native staple Commodities) how can they depart from us without nakedness and beggary?' There was nothing, however, in this letter which was new: the manufacture of cloth in Ireland had been made impossible by the decision of the privy council to prohibit the export of fuller's earth to Ireland, thus nullifying the recommendations of the commissioners of 1622-3.[2] Wentworth was in fact recommending the creation of a state of affairs which already existed: the two countries, so far as wool was concerned, were bound by strong economic ties as long as Ireland was a source of raw material for English manufacturers. Both countries were interdependent, though Ireland was in the weaker position when English trade declined, since England could prevent the Irish wool growers from seeking new markets.

Under Wentworth the only change so far as wool exports were concerned was the introduction of a system of licensing, though this was combined with the use of staple towns, of which Youghal and Dublin were the most prominent (see Fig. 3 p. 152). Licences gave the lord deputy yet another opportunity of increasing revenue.

The next step was taken at the end of the year. On 17 November 1634 Wentworth gave his decision concerning the Graces. Grace 10 asking that wool should be transported to England without restraint or licence and paying only the ordinary customs and duties, was included among those which were not to be made law, but merely continued at his Majesty's good pleasure. The improved state of the English cloth trade may have made possible

[1] A reference to a proposed salt monopoly.

[2] This prohibition was repeated in July 1636 expressly to prevent cloth manufacture in Ireland. *Cal. S.P. Ire., 1633-47*, p. 136. It is not clear whether or not Roper's manufacture was still in existence in Wentworth's deputyship. The English port books bear witness to large imports of English cloth in almost every ship, so that it is doubtful whether Roper's works can have supplied the Irish domestic market to any appreciable extent.

this lip service to a more liberal policy. From 1634 onwards there does not seem to have been as heavy pressure upon the English privy council to take action against unemployment. The clothiers of Devon and Kent complained not of the lack of a market for their cloth, but of the monopolistic policy of the Merchant Adventurers, who were blamed for restricting trade to a few of their own members.[1] In January 1634/5 the clothiers of Essex and Suffolk made similar complaints.[2] In April 1636 there was evidence of increasing demand and of revival of trade in the complaint of the Suffolk clothiers that wool was too dear.[3] In July 1637 the justices of the peace in Bolton, Lancs., reported how the great trading in fustians and woollen cloth at Bury had given the inhabitants continual employment for their children. Finally, in 1638 the Merchant Adventurers, making a case for the banning of interlopers in the cloth trade, declared that there was 'no want of ready men among the Adventurers to buy up more cloth than could be made in the kingdom', i.e. they did not press for an enforcement of their monopoly on grounds that there was not enough trade to go round.

In actual fact, however, the Irish wool trade was no more free after 1634 than before it. The figures provided by Sir Adam Loftus for the years 1632–40 show that wool exporters paid both customs duty at 8s. a great stone and licence duty at 4s. a great stone throughout the whole of Wentworth's deputyship. This improvement in the English cloth industry created once more a demand for Irish wool, a point which was made clear by Coke in a letter written to Wentworth in May 1635.[4] He complained, not that the smuggling of Irish wool abroad was leading to the decay of the cloth trade, but rather that it was depriving England of a raw material which was much in demand. 'The frequent transportation of the wools of Ireland into foreign parts', he wrote, 'is as notorious as prejudicial unto both Kingdoms, carrying away the Manufactures with the Materials: *especially at this time when we are able to convert into cloth all the wools we can get*'. He then went on to insist that the control of the Irish wool trade must be tightened up, and to recommend the reintroduction

[1] *Cal. S.P. dom., 1634–5*, p. 390.
[2] Ibid., p. 487.
[3] Ibid., *1635–6*, p. 383.
[4] 25 May 1635. *Strafford's letters*, i. 423–4.

of the staple system in a modified form, despite the criticism which Wentworth had made of it in January 1634. Staple ports were not to be re-established in the full sense, whereby the export of wool was put in the hands of a staplers' company; but all Irish wool exporters were to take out bonds that they would deliver the wool at one of the appointed English ports, which would be named in documents carried by the ship. The English ports were selected as follows: Chester for supplying all the northern parts, including presumably Manchester, Yorkshire and Norwich; Bristol, Minehead, and Barnstaple for the hinterland of the Severn; and Exeter and Weymouth for the western shires. Coke requested the lord deputy and the Irish council to prohibit by act of state the landing of wool in other ports, and to order that the bonds should not be discharged until an official certificate was brought back from England and sealed by the customers and farmers, or their collectors, and testifying that the wools had been landed at the specified port. He also stressed the importance of making sure that, once the wool had been landed, it should not be permitted 'to be waterborne towards the sea, but only towards the land'. Finally, in order to avoid the return of forged certificates, Coke pointed out the need for a good working arrangement between the farmers of the customs in England and Ireland, so 'that every half year, they send certificates each to other, what wools have been exported out of Ireland and what received here in every Port, specifying the quantities, the ships and the masters' names, that by comparing these returns, every default may appear and be question in due time'.

From this letter it seems clear that the initiative in the sphere of wool lay with the secretary of state in England rather than the lord deputy in Ireland. During the previous two decades, the economic situation in England dictated this policy towards Ireland, and, during the years of Wentworth's deputyship, the same pattern emerges. The importance of the cloth trade in England involved the paradox that the years of its prosperity and decline did not make possible a radical change of economic policy. In years of decline, the object of regulating the trade in Irish wool was to prevent it falling into the hands of foreign manufacturers, so making the crisis worse: in years of plenty, the object namely to ensure a constant supply of raw material for the new draperies in England might be different, but the methods of supervision

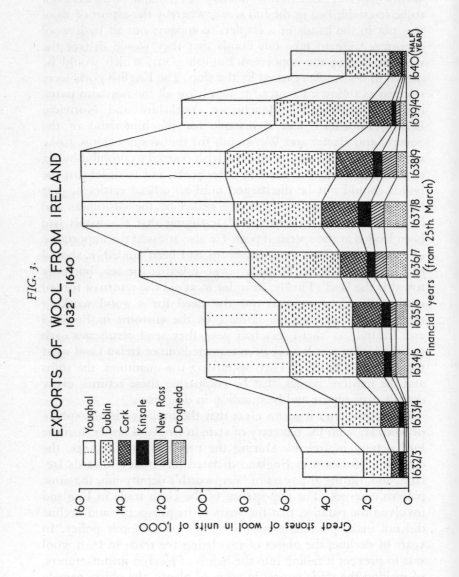

FIG. 3.

EXPORTS OF WOOL FROM IRELAND
1632 – 1640

Youghal
Dublin
Cork
Kinsale
New Ross
Drogheda

Great stones of wool in units of 1,000

Financial years (from 25th. March)

1632/3 1633/4 1634/5 1635/6 1636/7 1637/8 1638/9 1639/40 1640 (HALF YEAR)

remained the same. In August 1638 the same policy was being carried out.[1]

The Port Books for this period reveal that nearly every ship between Youghal and Minehead carried Irish wool.[2] During 1636, for example, the *Frances* of Minehead plied regularly once a month between these two ports carrying wool or cattle from Ireland and bringing in exchange hops, cloth and haberdashery. The *Lyon* of Youghal followed a similar trade. These were years of peace and it was not surprising that the customs figures should reveal a great increase in the export of wool from Ireland.[3]

The fall of Strafford from power in November 1640 made it possible once more for Irish discontent to express itself on this point in a manner which had been impossible since the Graces of 1628. As in 1628, however, it seems to have been taken for granted that complete freedom for the wool trade was out of the question. What the Irish objected to in 1640 were the increased customs duties and the need to pay for export licences.[4] Charles I's reply came in July 1641 when he agreed to the reduction of the duties upon wool etc. and to the repeal of the statutes forbidding the export of wool.[5] The point of this latter concession was not to allow the Irish merchants to export wool abroad, but to remove the legal basis for any future lord deputy to charge for issuing licences. The merchants demanded not liberty of trade but liberty from what they regarded as excessive duties, which were particularly burdensome in years of declining trade.

To sum up, the part played by Wentworth in the history of the Irish woollen trade was far from being dramatic. The main change lay in the enforcement of a licensing system, largely for financial reasons. He did not indulge in any grandiose mercantilist scheme as far as the Irish woollen trade was concerned. He carried on in the same way that his predecessors Chichester, Grandison and Falkland had done, creating nothing but destroying nothing. The initiative for such creation and destruction lay outside his hands—in the English privy council.

[1] Wentworth to Coke, 11 Aug. 1638. *Strafford's letters*, ii. 205.
[2] Cf. P.R.O., E190/1088/12, Minehead Port Book for 1635.
[3] See Fig. 3.
[4] *Commons jn. Ire.*, 30 Jan. 1640/1, p. 167.
[5] 16 July 1641, *Cal. S.P. Ire.*, *1633–47*, p. 317.

(III) IRISH LINEN

Some words must now be said about the Irish linen industry and Wentworth's policy towards it. Stated in mercantilist terms, this episode appears as an attempt by Wentworth to establish an industry in Ireland which would not seriously compete with any English manufacture. Woollen cloth manufacture was ruled out as a possibility, though it is sometimes made out that a native Irish cloth industry could have arisen in Ireland. The absence of the necessary capital, skill and the raw materials made this most unlikely. For the manufacture of cloth of an English quality, more was required than coarse wool, and a somewhat similar development to that which took place in iron-smelting, where skilled labour, capital, raw material and machinery were first brought from England, would have been necessary.[1] The slump in the English cloth trade during the two decades before Wentworth's arrival in Ireland plus the ban upon the export of English fuller's earth, combined to prevent the export of capital to establish a woollen cloth industry in Ireland. It is true that Irish friezes were imported into England[2] during this period but the quantities involved were not great enough to arouse opposition from English cloth manufacturers nor did the loosely woven Irish material really compete with the 'new draperies'.

If woollen cloth was ruled out of account, the main alternative was to work up Irish linen yarn into linen cloth. Superficially, the conditions were favourable for the establishment of a linen weaving industry. In the sixteenth century, linen yarn was an important export to England,[3] where its main market was the linen manufacturing area around Manchester. During the first half of the seventeenth century this economic link between Eastern Ulster and Lancashire continued to be of importance and Irish linen yarn was exported in great quantities from Drogheda, Dundalk, Derry, Coleraine, Carrickfergus to Chester and Liverpool.[4] Even at this

[1] See H. F. Kearney, 'Richard Boyle, Ironmaster' *J.R.S.A.I.*, LXXXIII, 1953, 156–62.

[2] See, for example, the Port Book for Minehead 1635–6 (E190/1088/12). 200 yards of Irish friezes were imported in the *Lyon* of Youghal, 8 Feb. 1635/6.

[3] A. Longfield, 'Anglo-Irish Trade in the sixteenth century', *Proc. R.I.A.*, 36, sect. c., p. 325.

[4] See Liverpool Port Book for 1610–11 (E190/1329/15) and for 1631–2 (E190/1334/25); Chester Port Book for 1633–4 (E190/1335/1).

date the spinning of linen yarn for export was largely concentrated in north-east Ireland and by comparison with yarn exports from here, those from other parts of the country were negligible. The growth of flax was an economic proposition on the smallest of holdings[1] and its spinning into yarn was a domestic skill which was normally undertaken by the women at home. Payment of rent to the Ulster planters may have been made in linen yarn before it was eventually exported from the ports of Ulster.

The question arises should not this spinning industry have developed naturally into weaving also, especially as there was a good market for linen in England, where most linen was imported from abroad. Linen, however, was a term of wide application covering all cloth made from hemp or flax and including calicoes, canvas, tabling, damask, lawns and buckram. The same conditions were in fact necessary for linen manufacture as for cloth manufacture—skilled labour and capital on a large scale. Neither of these was forthcoming in Ireland during the early seventeenth century. It was more profitable to export Irish linen yarn to Manchester than to attempt to work it up into cloth at home. Later on, of course, conditions changed. Manchester turned more and more to cotton goods which fulfilled many of the purposes for which linen had been used earlier and, with the appearance of skilled labour in Ireland, thanks, among other things to the Revocation of the Edict of Nantes,[2] the way was open for the development of successful linen manufacture. The dropping out of Manchester as a market for yarn and as a manufacturing rival and the immigration of skilled linen weavers must be counted among the conditions which favoured the growth of a linen industry in Ireland but they did not exist in the early seventeenth century.

While Wentworth was on his way to Ireland in 1633, he wrote from Chester about his project to 'increase the Growth and set up the Manufactury of Hemp and Flax in that your Kingdom'.[3] His words may be taken as an example of what can be called a mercantilist attitude.

I will hope to leave your subjects there in a much happier condition that I found them without the least Prejudice to your Subjects here:

---

[1] C. Gill, *The Irish Linen Industry*, p. 10.
[2] See E. R. R. Green, *The Lagan Valley, 1800–50* pp. 57–8.
[3] *Strafford's letters*, i. 93–4, 16 July 1633.

for this is a Ground I take with me that to serve your Majesty compleatly well in Ireland, we must not only endeavour to enrich *them*, butt make sure still to hold them dependant upon the Crown and not able to subsist without *us*: which will be effected, by wholly laying aside the Manufacture of Wools into Cloth or Stuff there and by furnishing them from this Kingdom and then making your Majesty sole Merchant of all Salts on that Side: for thus shall they not only have their cloathing, the Improvement of all their native Commodities (which are principally preserved by Salt) and their victual itself from hence: (strong Ties and Enforcements upon their Allegiance and Obedience to your Majesty) but a Means found, I trust, much to advance your Majesty's Revenue upon Salt and to improve your Customs: the Wools there grown and the Cloths there worn thus paying double Duties to your Crown in both Kingdoms; and the Salt outward here, both inward and outward there.

All this sounded very ambitious but it was written before Wentworth had set foot in Ireland and the reality, both political and economic, was different from what he expected.

In July 1636,[1] three years later, he wrote a similar letter to Wandesford, explaining his report to the privy council. He had described how there was little or no manufacture among the Irish and how he had discouraged what small beginnings there were towards a clothing trade. 'In Reason of State, so long as they did not undrape their own Wools, they must of Necessity fetch their clothing from us.' This was a simplification of the position, looking at it from an administrator's point of view. The merchant of Dublin or Youghal or Drogheda exporting wool to England depended on the English market for his livelihood and would hardly have welcomed the setting up of a cloth industry in Ireland. That this was so was made clear with linen yarn.

In the same letter to Wandesford, Wentworth described the steps which he had taken to encourage linen manufacture in Ireland. He had sent for a superior kind of flax seed from Holland and claimed to have sown a thousand pounds' worth of it and to have set up six or seven looms with workmen from the Low Countries and France. He hoped to undersell the linen cloths of Holland and France by at least twenty per cent. Here was a typical project similar to that of Cockaygne and a hundred others by which manufactures were to be set up to free the commonwealth from dependence upon other countries and to relieve unemployment. If government measures and good will alone had

[1] 25 July 1636. From London. *Strafford's letters*, ii. 19–20.

been sufficient, Wentworth's project would have been successful. Before his visit to England in July 1636 he had taken measures to assist his enterprise. In June 1635 he imposed a ban upon such linen cloth as was made in Ireland upon the ground that it was too narrow.[1] On 31 May 1636 he issued a proclamation regulating the production of linen yarn and preventing its sale when it did not fulfil the requirements laid down in the proclamation.[2] Wentworth's agent later bore witness that some of the confiscated yarn found its way to the lord deputy's looms.[3]

The object of this second proclamation was ostensibly to improve the standard of linen yarn and thereby to promote the manufacture of finer linens. Export figures for the years 1635–9 suggest, however, that its effect was only short-lived.[4]

Total in packs:	1635	1636	1637	1638	1639
	1,415	1,307	823	1,553	1,177

There was, according to these statistics, which were provided by Adam Loftus for the English privy council in 1641,[5] a sharp drop during the year 25 March 1636–24 March 1637. Nearly all of this yarn was exported through the port of Drogheda, which accounted for 655 out of 800 packs.[6]

Drogheda	829	700	655	858	666
Dundalk	282	265	—	366	164
Dublin	37	32	23	79	69
Derry	147	111	16	107	147
Coleraine	43	69	—	36	45
Carrickfergus	45	80	—	52	52
Bangor	9	8	—	—	—

If these figures are taken at their face value, they suggest that Wentworth's mercantilist intervention into the linen trade was short and unsuccessful. This conclusion is reinforced even if they are not fully accepted. It is probable that a good deal of unlicensed yarn was smuggled out of those ports which registered no exports. If this was the case, Wentworth's prohibition was even less

[1] Steele, Tudor & Stuart proclam., ii. 35, no. 310. (See also M. D. O'Sullivan, Old Galway, p. 402; 411n.)

[2] Ibid., 36, no. 313.　　　　　[3] Rushworth, Trial, p. 417.

[4] The proclamation was relaxed on 23 Feb. 1637/8. Steele, Tudor & Stuart proclam., ii. 37, no. 325.

[5] 1 July 1641. Sir Adam Loftus to Secretary Vane (S.P. 63/259/f. 219. Cal. S.P. Ire., 1633–47, pp. 311–12); i.e. after Wentworth's death.

[6] 1 pack = 4 cwt. 1 cwt. = 120 lb. Cf. 'Thomas Cave's instructions for customs officers . . .' T.C.D. MS., F.3.17, f. 128.

successful than appears at first sight. On either hypothesis, however, the linen episode in Wentworth's deputyship seems to have
been exaggerated out of all proportion to its real significance.

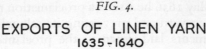

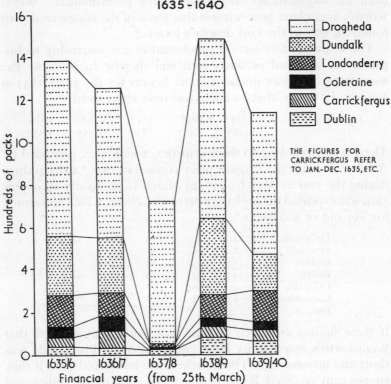

EXPORTS OF LINEN YARN
1635-1640

Wentworth's own manufacturing scheme proved as ill-fated as
his excursion into cannon-founding. At his trial, he claimed to
have lost £3,000 in his linen venture.[1] The appearance of this
linen episode among the charges against him at the trial, was, however, a sign of the discontent which it had aroused. Economically
well meant, Wentworth's linen policy had disastrous political
effects. Since yarn production was concentrated in the planted
area of Ulster his actions affected the prosperity not only of the

[1] Rushworth, *Trial*, p. 422.

planters, but also of the Gaelic Irish tenantry and the Anglo-Irish merchants of Dundalk and Drogheda.[1] Each of these sections of society in Ireland had other reasons for discontent against Wentworth and this added one more. The episode brings out clearly, however, how the economic interests of the English planter and his Gaelic Irish tenant could coincide. Clotworthy and his father-in-law Ranelagh were witnesses against Wentworth on this issue and Richard Fitzgerald, member of parliament for Strabane, bore witness to the distress which had been caused among the Irish natives, who had been particularly affected by the proclamation, since they concentrated upon the growing of flax. The economic discontent among the planters which found its outlet at the trial of Wentworth in 1641 may have had its parallel therefore among the Gaelic Irish in the rebellion of 1641 especially as linen yarn exports declined again after the high-water mark of 1638. From Wentworth's point of view the episode was of minor significance and he denied that his looms were important: at the trial he said the value of the cloth which they produced was only £1,600 to £1,700 a year.[2] But the figures for yarn exports suggest that administrative decisions taken and enforced upon mercantilist grounds (even leaving aside suspicion of personal profit)[3] could cause great economic distress and discontent in a most sensitive part of Ireland. Here as in other matters Wentworth cannot be cleared from the charge of political short-sightedness.

(IV) THE IRISH CUSTOMS FARM

One of the best-known features of Wentworth's deputyship, as familiar to historians as the woollen and linen episodes, was the remarkable increase which took place in the yield from Irish customs duties.[4] This is worth attention not only for the light it throws upon Wentworth's administrative ability and the greater efficiency which he introduced into this branch of the Irish fiscal system, but also for the struggle which took place between Wentworth and his associate in the administration, vice-treasurer Mountnorris, for the financial fruits of political power. The whole

---

[1] The two main ports for the export of linen yarn.
[2] Rushworth, *Trial*, p. 422.
[3] And there seems no doubt that Wentworth hoped to reap a financial reward from his capital investment.
[4] See Fig. 5.

M

business also illustrates the difficulty, perhaps the impossibility, of isolating economic matters from the general history of the period.

The Irish customs farm was not established by Wentworth himself. Its foundation went back to the first decade of the century. During the early seventeenth century, Ireland was drawn into an increasingly close economic relationship with England. This process was seen at its most dramatic in the plantation in Ulster,

FIG. 5.

IRISH CUSTOMS DUTIES

1628-41

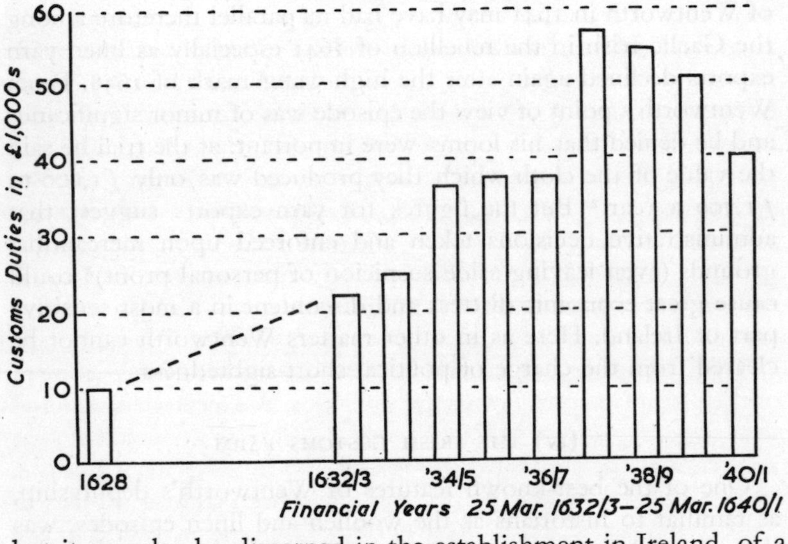
Customs Duties in £1,000 s
60
50
40
30
20
10
0
1628
1632/3
'34/5
'36/7
'38/9
'40/1
Financial Years 25 Mar. 1632/3–25 Mar. 1640/1

but it can also be discerned in the establishment in Ireland, of a customs system similar to that which had recently been set up in England. There, during the last decade of the sixteenth century, it had become clear that direct administration of the customs, to which the Crown had resorted after 1589, was in practice less profitable than farming the customs out.[1] In 1604, therefore, after much negotiation, the right of collection of customs and subsidy was farmed out to a group of wealthy London merchants who agreed to pay £112,000, increased in 1607 to £120,000.[2] It

[1] A. P. Newton, 'The establishment of the Great Farm of the English customs' in *Trans. R. Hist. Soc.*, 4th ser., i. 147.

[2] Ibid., p. 152.

was natural that a similar kind of reorganisation should be attempted in Ireland, now that the authority of the English Crown extended for the first time in practice over the country.

In England, the medieval customs system which had remained largely unchanged since the days of Edward III[1] had been re-formed in 1564, when a much greater degree of centralisation was introduced, symbolised by the Port Book—a uniform register issued by the Exchequer to the various ports and filled up accord-ing to recognised rules of entry.[2] The Great Farm of 1604 did not introduce an administrative revolution comparable to that of 1564, rather it was a return to the farms of the middle years of Elizabeth's reign, with the difference that London and the outports were included within the one great farm. By comparison with England however the customs in Ireland in 1604 were in a state, similar to that which prevailed in England before Winchester's reforms of 1564. There was indeed no unified customs system in Ireland, when James I came to the throne. The most important ports, Dublin, Waterford, Drogheda and Galway, enjoyed exemption from the basic duty of poundage[3] and figures[4] provided in 1607, lead to the conclusion that as a source of royal revenue in Ireland, the customs were of small importance; during the two years preceding 1607, the revenue from the Irish customs amounted to little more than £700 per annum.

There was no great interval of time between the establishment of the Great Customs Farm in England on 25 December 1604 and the reorganisation of the Irish customs. It was no accident that Arthur Ingram, Controller of the Customs in the Port of London and agent for Lord Cranborne, who had been a prime mover in the negotiations for the Great Farm,[5] should be involved in the Irish scheme also. In 1607 James I informed Chichester, the lord deputy, that he proposed to introduce a uniform customs system into Ireland.[6] Robert Cogan, kinsman of Ingram,[7] was commissioned to carry out an enquiry into the state of the Irish

---

[1] W. A. Morris and J. R. Strayer, *English Government at Work, 1327–1336*.
[2] N. Lewis, *Welsh Port Books.*
[3] 5% duty or 1s. in the pound, assessed according to the Book of Rates.
[4] *Cal. Carew MSS., 1603–24*, pp. 85–6.
[5] A. P. Newton, 'The establishment of the Great Farm of the English customs' in *Trans. R. Hist. Soc.*, 4th ser., i. 149.
[6] *Cal. S.P. Ire., 1606–8*, p. 105.
[7] *H.M.C. Var. Coll.*, viii. 35.

customs and in March 1610 he was appointed first surveyor-general of the customs in Ireland,[1] at a fee of £100 per annum. The lists of Irish customs officials[2] bear witness to the reorganisation introduced by him. In every considerable Irish port, a customer, a comptroller of the great and small customs and a searcher were introduced, though for the purposes of administration some of the ports were linked together.

Meanwhile, the freemen of the cities of Waterford, Dublin, Drogheda and Galway had successfully defended their rights to exemption from paying poundage; they took their case to England, where at the end of a legal examination, 'it was resolved (and so certified to the King) that the said 12d. in the pound was due unto the King by all men trading in that kingdom saving only the freemen of Waterford, Dublin, and Drogheda', who were exempt by the Act of Parliament and of Galway, who were (in their own port) free by their charter.[3] The king evaded this difficulty by ordering the lord deputy to introduce an imposition of 12d. in the pound into these four ports, in order to bring them into conformity with the rest of the Irish ports.[4]

By July 1613, thanks to Cogan's reorganisation and the new imposition upon the trade of the most important ports in the kingdom, the Irish customs were regarded as a commercial proposition sufficiently attractive for the farm to be undertaken by a London group, consisting of Arthur Ingram, Martin Freeman, Richard Cowthorpe and George Low for nine and a half years at £6,000 a year.[5]

This arrangement lasted until 1618 when the Irish customs were farmed out to Buckingham for ten years at the same rent:[6] any profit over this sum was to be equally divided between the king and himself. In 1623 this grant was renewed for a further seven years at the same farm.[7] Buckingham, in his turn handed the farm

---

[1] *Liber. mun. pub. Hib.*, pt. 2, p. 137.

[2] See ibid., p. 146 ff. The patents of these new officers in every case dated from 1612 to 1613. One wonders how many of them were veterans of the Nine Years War, rewarded by the Crown. Cf. *Cal. S.P. dom., 1611–18*, p. 131.

[3] *Cal. Carew MSS., 1603–24*, p. 171.

[4] Ibid., p. 172.

[5] *Cal. S.P. dom., 1611–18*, p. 195. Cf. also Sir John Bingley to Arthur Ingram, 20 Feb. 1637/8, *H.M.C. Var. Coll.*, viii, pp. 49–50.

[6] Rushworth, *Trial*, p. 242. *Cal. S.P. Ire., 1615–25*, p. 254.

[7] *Cal. S.P. Ire., 1615–25*, p. 431.

over to a business group, consisting of Weston, Cranfield, Falkland, Chichester, Claneboy, Ranelagh and Caulfield.[1]

In the last years of Falkland's deputyship, the war hit the customs farmers hard and at least one of them, Ranelagh, complained how 'in these declinying tymes of Trade [we] suffer great losse by our bargayne'.[2] On 25 March 1629 the existing customs farm was due to come to an end and Sir Edward Bagshawe, comptroller of the customs in Dublin,[3] went to England to confer with the executors of the Duke of Buckingham and to decide what was to be done.[4] From 1629 to 1631 the Duchess of Buckingham kept up the same arrangement as had been enjoyed by her deceased husband. She paid £6,000 for the farm and half the remaining profits.[5] The actual running of the farm in Ireland presumably remained in the hands of much the same group, of whom Ranelagh was one, though there is no definite evidence on this point.[6]

The appointment of Wentworth, however, as new lord deputy coincided with an attempt to raise the terms of the farm, which the increased Book of Rates of April 1632 did something to make more attractive.[7] New farmers were appointed, Sir Arthur Ingram and Robert Cogan representing the old, Mountnorris and Sir George Radcliffe the new. The connection of Ingram and Cogan went back to the very beginning of the Irish farm, while Mountnorris and Radcliffe were clearly the representatives of the new lord deputy, whom they preceded into Ireland.[8]

These changes were reflected in the greatly increased customs farm, which now stood at £15,000 per annum with an £8,000 entry fine in addition.[9] Despite this, under the improved administration, inspired by the new lord deputy, the farmers made a total profit

---

[1] Ibid., *1633–47*, p. 101.

[2] Ibid., *1625–32*, p. 433 (S.P. 63/248/f. 10), 22 Feb. 1628/9.

[3] *Liber. mun. pub. Hib.*, pt. 2, p. 147.

[4] Thomas Cave to Endymion Porter, 17 Feb. 1629 (S.P. 63/249/f. 199). *Cal. S.P. Ire., 1625–32*, p. 431.

[5] *Cal. S.P. Ire., 1647–60*, p. 237; *Cal. S.P. Ire., 1625–32*, p. 655.

[6] Some of its members were dead or in disgrace.

[7] Steele, *Tudor & Stuart proclam.*, ii. 33, no. 295; *Cal. S.P. Ire., 1625–32*, p. 648. Poundage was a duty of 5% levied according to the value of the commodities assessed in the Book of Rates of 1604 (E122/173/3). This still remained at 5% in 1632 but the commodities were assessed at increased rates ranging from 20% to 100%. For details see *H.M.C. Var. Coll.*, viii. 192: G. O'Brien, *Economic history of Ireland in the seventeenth century*, p. 62.

[8] See above, p. 37.

[9] Rushworth, *Trial*, p. 249.

of nearly £5,000.[1] For the financial year 25 March 1632–25 March 1633, the total yield from the customs was £22,563 out of which the farmers had to pay a total of £17,594, which included payments of £11,000 to the treasury and a pension of £4,500 to the Duchess of Buckingham.

During the next two years, the profits increased further. In 1635 Mountnorris stated that they rose from £4,951 in 1632–3 to £8,373 in 1633–4 and £20,019 in 1634–5.[2] If expenses remained constant at £17,000, these figures are confirmed by those given in 1641 which show gross totals of £22,553, £25,846 and £38,174 during the three years 1632–5. They are also confirmed by figures given by Sir Arthur Ingram.[3]

Clearly the revenue from customs duties was increasing beyond all expectation. The farm, however, remained fixed at the 1632 level. The question was bound to arise whether this state of affairs should be allowed to continue, in which the lion's share of the profits went to the customs farmers and not to the hard-pressed administration. Ingram and Mountnorris may have felt that after the lean years they were entitled to all they could get, but no lord deputy could ignore the fact that the total yield from the customs was already equal to a half of what the total revenue had been in 1628. There was thus a split among the farmers, and with so great a prize at stake it was not surprising that it should have been most bitter. During the course of the struggle, Mountnorris, who had been Wentworth's political associate since 1632, was in fact condemned to death. The custom farm, indeed, was not merely the most lucrative reward of political power; it was reaching the stage in which the customs farmers would have the disposal of an extremely large revenue and would possess the political power which went with it. In engaging in a struggle for control of the customs farm, Wentworth was fighting for political power itself.

Ultimately, however, victory lay with the lord deputy though he was forced to visit England first. Sir Adam Loftus replaced Mountnorris as vice-treasurer, paying £6,000 for the office.[4] Mountnorris also ceased to be a farmer and Ingram compounded out for £7,000.[5]

From 1636 therefore the position was as follows. The customs

---

[1] H.M.C. Var. Coll., viii. 194.
[2] Cal. Clarendon Papers, i. 362.
[3] H.M.C. Var. Coll., viii. 195.
[4] Liber. mun. pub. Hib., pt. 2, 45.
[5] Strafford's letters, ii. 21.

were still farmed at the rate of £15,500, but the profits were divided in the proportion of five-eighths to the king, a quarter to Wentworth, and an eighth to Sir George Radcliffe.[1] In 1636-7 the profits were worth £40,000 which was divided up as follows:

King's Rent		£15,500
Cost of managing the customs		£3,000
Profits £21,500.	King 5/8	£13,500
	Wentworth 1/4	£5,400
	Radcliffe 1/8	£2,600[2]

Thus the chief losers by the change of 1636 were Mountnorris and Ingram. Mountnorris five years later played a prominent part in the attack upon Wentworth at the trial in combination with his former enemy of 1632, Ranelagh.

Here mention may perhaps be made of a personal quarrel between Wentworth and Ingram which undoubtedly influenced the former's attitude when the customs business came to a head. Wentworth and Ingram were neighbours in Yorkshire and their relations seem to have been good in 1632. In 1634, however, Wentworth suspected Ingram of trying to break into the collection of recusancy fines in the North of England for which Wentworth, as lord president of the North, was the farmer.[3] The result was a violent quarrel between the two men and for the time being at any rate Wentworth held the whip hand as the Customs Farm episode proved. At Wentworth's trial, however, the positions were reversed and Ingram joined in the attack upon the man who had dismissed him from the Irish Customs Farm.

It was a year before there was any rise in the yield from the customs but when it did come the increase was very remarkable. The figures for the next three years were as follows:

1637-8	£57,387
1638-9	£55,582
1639-40	£51,874

There is little doubt that the greater efficiency of the new farmers was responsible in large measure for this increase. By August 1638 Wentworth had brought every outport under the control of the farm. Charles Monck, surveyor-general, was sent to

[1] Ibid., ii. 136-7. Wentworth to Laud, 27 Nov. 1637. Presumably Michaelmas 1636 to Michaelmas 1637.
[2] Ibid.
[3] The business is discussed fully by J. Cooper in *Econ. Hist. Rev.* (1958).

Ulster to examine the state of affairs there and his report made it clear that re-organisation there was very much overdue. He noted that in many of the ports, the essentials for efficiency were lacking—an office, a warehouse and a pair of scales. His remarks make it clear that smuggling was practised on the widest scale and that frequently customs were exacted at a rate much lower than that in the official book of rates. The improved administration which Wentworth brought to the customs made it possible as never before to close loopholes or outports farmed by an independent farmer who could offer favourable terms to merchants and thereby draw off trade from the stricter ports under royal control, as Goodwin did in Londonderry.[1] Wentworth was conscious of this danger[2] but by August 1637, once the customs of Strangford had been recovered by the Crown, only Carrickfergus remained independent, where the customs were farmed out to the corporation.[3] A year later Wentworth reported that Carrickfergus had been secured.[4] He estimated that the customs of Down and Antrim had not reached £2,000 per annum despite 'all our Endeavours of improvement',[5] but there was a factor which may be taken into consideration in explaining the rise 1636/7 to 1637/8. It was through these ports that much of the linen yarn from Ulster was exported to England though the figures do not show a remarkable rise until the next year.[6]

Another reason for the increased customs which at first appears important, appears less so on closer scrutiny. At a meeting of the Irish committee of the privy council in July 1636 it was agreed to buy in the rights of the Duchess of Buckingham, Endymion Porter, John West and the Earl of Carlisle.[7] The two former enjoyed pensions upon the Irish customs after collection. Even if their rights had been re-acquired by the king, the total customs receipts would not have risen. The direct benefit would have been felt only in the royal income in Ireland, to which the Duchess's customs pension in particular, £4,550 per annum,[8] would have meant a considerable increase. In fact, however, the negotiations fell through. A start was made, but in July 1638 the bargain with the Duchess was called off: later in the year, when the money was

[1] P.R.O.N.I., T.615.   [2] *Strafford's letters*, ii. 91.
[3] Ibid.   [4] Ibid., ii. 205.   [5] Ibid., ii. 223.
[6] See Fig. 4, p. 158.
[7] *Cal. S.P. Ire., 1633–47*, p. 136. Cf. also Grace 11.
[8] *Strafford's letters*, ii. 8.

needed to pay for an increase in the army, Wentworth referred to the incident ironically.[1] However, the total customs yield would not have been affected by these arrangements, since the Duchess was paid after collection had taken place.

It was otherwise with the rights of John West and the earl of Carlisle. West enjoyed a monopoly of licensing the export of what was technically a prohibited commodity—linen yarn, while Carlisle enjoyed a similar monopoly for licensing the sale of wine and *aqua vitae* and for collecting the imposition upon the import of wines into Ireland. This last would have brought a noticeable increase to the customs had it been acquired by the crown. Wentworth estimated the possible increase at £2,000.[2] He entered into negotiation with the countess of Carlisle[3] and in December 1637 he was authorised by the king to pay her £16,000 sterling in compensation for the surrender of her husband's rights.[4] A month earlier a payment of £2,000 was authorised for the surrender of John West's patent.

So far two examples have been given of the way in which Wentworth introduced a greater degree of centralisation into the running of the customs farm, namely the bringing of the Ulster outports into the general customs farm and the buying up of Carlisle's wine patent. In addition to this he took measures to prevent smuggling, the success of which it is difficult to measure. All of these factors played a part in bringing about the startling rise in customs receipts. The complaints of the merchants in 1640 after Wentworth's fall showed how this unaccustomed administrative pressure was felt as a legitimate grievance but from the financial point of view of the administration it was a success. The lord deputy, however, was fortunate in the time he chose. It is most unlikely that so great an increase in customs revenue should be at all possible without an improvement in trade. The figures for what was financially the most important branch of Irish trade, the export of wool to England, are not conclusive on this point but they do suggest something more than merely a more efficient system of licensing. If these were good years for the Lancashire linen manufacture the increased demand for supplies of linen yarn from Ulster would naturally be reflected in increased

---

[1] Ibid., ii. 234.   [2] Ibid., ii. 8.   [3] Ibid., ii. 71.
[4] *Cal. S.P. Ire., 1633–47*, p. 175, i.e. £2,000 at eight year's purchase. Knowler, ii. 76. See also 76 ff.; 175. The earl of Carlisle died in 1636.

customs duties and the same would hold for exports of raw wool to Devon. If this was the case, then some of the credit for the increased yield from the customs must go to forces which were beyond the lord deputy's control.

For all this administrative efficiency there was a political price to be paid as was to be seen in the Irish Remonstrance of 1640. The discontent among the merchants was one of the unifying factors among the opposition groups to Wentworth's administration, particularly as they realised that a high proportion of the revenues were going to him as private profit. Taken in conjunction with the tobacco monopoly the customs farm was one of the main reasons for Wentworth's unpopularity.

(v) SUMMARY

Some general remarks must now be made in summing up the economic aspect of Wentworth's administration. Had Wentworth an economic policy? The answer implied in the foregoing pages is that he had not, in the sense of a well-defined body of principles over and above the particular economic episodes which have been described. It has been said that the object of the economic policy of sixteenth and seventeenth century governments was

the creation of an industrial and commercial state in which by encouragement or restraint imposed by a central authority, private and sectional interests should be made to promote national strength and independence.[1]

There is a good deal to be said for this as a historical generalisation. Certainly the centralisation and regulation introduced in Ireland by the English administration in the early decades of the seventeenth century was not unique in Europe. On the other hand, this definition of mercantilism is open to criticism on several grounds. It exaggerates the freedom of action, for example, which was open to particular governments. The regulation of the Irish wool trade was not something consciously adopted by Wentworth as an economic policy, so much as part of an economic situation which he could not escape. The initiative did not lie even with the English privy council, which could hardly fail to take steps to safeguard the interests of England's most important industry.

[1] *Palgrave's Dictionary of political economy* under 'Mercantilism'.

To speak of Wentworth's economic policy in this connection is to overstress his significance. His interest in wool licences was a financial one.

The same may be said of the other examples of economic activity which have been discussed. The customs farm, the Court of Wards and the plantation of Connacht were institutions and ideas bequeathed by the previous generation and were primarily financial in character. If Wentworth had a general economic intention, it was to bring some degree of financial stability to the Irish administration, while ignoring the political cost. It was not surprising that in 1640 he should be blamed for the decay in trade, unjustified though the charge might be.

There were, it is true, 'projects' of an economic character during Wentworth's deputyship, but their significance has been exaggerated. Wentworth's letters concerning the encouragement of Irish trade with Spain, his intervention in the linen trade, his attempt to keep going a government-financed ironworks— all these were minor activities, which came to nothing. More typical of his administrative intervention was the setting up of a tobacco monopoly, as a financial not a commercial expedient, to control the sale of tobacco on much the same lines as the French *gabelle* on salt. Even here, however, Wentworth merely introduced into Ireland a monopoly which already existed in England.

Finance, therefore, was the mainspring of Wentworth's economic policy. With this went centralisation and greater efficiency. The bringing in of Ulster into the general customs farm for example was not an end in itself but a means of increasing the financial yield of the great customs farm. On the other hand, Wentworth resisted the tallow monopoly, suggested by Portland in 1634, on mercantilist grounds, as part of a scheme to make English soap, because of the effect which such a scheme would have had upon the financial prosperity of Ireland. In this case he stood out for the 'sectional' interests of Ireland against the plausible case of the commonwealth's good. In short, Wentworth's mercantilism did not run deep. He shared the contemporary climate of opinion and paid lip service to general principles, but his real ability was that of an administrator concerned with increasing the efficiency of the financial machinery already at his disposal. During his deputyship, revenues rose from E£40,000 to E£80,000, an improvement which was due largely to the customs farm, the

Court of Wards and the tobacco monopoly.[1] In 1633 the lord
deputy had been dependent upon a subsidy of £20,000 per annum
in order to make ends meet. Within five years, revenues were in
excess of expenditure and a large debt had been paid off. This was
a remarkable administrative achievement. Finance was not an
aim in itself, however. It was the means which made possible
freedom of action for the lord deputy. It was indeed largely
because of his financial measures that Wentworth was able to go
ahead with more far-reaching religious and political policies,
despite their unpopularity.

[1] Cal. S.P. Ire., 1625-32, pp. 418-19; ibid., 1647-60, pp. 234-5.

12

PERSONAL PROFIT

PUBLIC finance in the seventeenth century was not incompatible with private profit. It has long been known that Wentworth acquired lands in Ireland during his years of deputyship there, and that most of this property remained in the hands of his descendants after the Crown regranted the lands which were forfeited by Strafford's attainder in 1641 to his eldest son. Thus it came about that Charles Watson-Wentworth, Marquis of Rockingham, was one of the great absentee landlords of Ireland during the eighteenth century.[1] The exact extent and value of Wentworth's property, however, and the way in which it was acquired have never been fully investigated.[2]

Few Englishmen went to Ireland in the early seventeenth century save for the purpose of acquiring land. Most of the exceptions to this general rule came from the ranks of the English clergy, appointed to benefices in the Church of Ireland, but members of the expanding English administration in Ireland and old soldiers from Elizabeth's Irish armies usually found themselves a large estate, sometimes by direct Crown grant, rarely by purchase. In the race for the pickings which accompanied the confiscations in Ulster and elsewhere during these years, propriety and custom seldom held the lord deputy back, though subordinate officials, such as Richard Boyle and Adam Loftus, proved more successful in the race to establish themselves as great landowners.[3] Of Strafford's three predecessors, Chichester (1604–15), St. John 1616–22) and Falkland (1622–9), however, only Chichester seems to have acquired land during his deputyship. His holding as a

[1] Cf. 'A letter from the Marquis of Rockingham on the proposed absentee tax of 1773' in *Irish Historical Studies*, viii. No. 32 (Sept. 1953).

[2] A good deal of this information in this chapter is derived from the survey of Wentworth's estates made *c.* 1656 (now Vol. 41, Strafford MSS., Sheffield City Library). Cf. also J. Cooper 'The Fortune of Strafford' in *Econ. Hist. Rev.* (1958).

[3] See T. Ranger, 'Richard Boyle and the making of an Irish fortune, 1588–1614' in *I.H.S.*, x. no. 39 (Mar. 1957).

planter in Ulster was 1,300 acres in Co. Tyrone[1] but he also had
been granted the barony of Inishowen (Co. Donegal),[2] which was
a vast holding of *c.* 50,000 acres. St. John also was a planter, in
Co. Armagh, but he acquired his holding before his appointment
as lord deputy.[3] Falkland had the ill luck to be appointed at a time
when official opinion in England was opposed to any further
plantation and the outbreak of war in 1625 may also have reduced
his enthusiasm for an estate in Ireland. But there was no hard and
fast ordinance, such as was the case in the Spanish American
Empire, against a chief governor acquiring land in the territory
to which he was appointed. The extent of Strafford's acquisitions
in Ireland, however, aroused a good deal of criticism even during
his deputyship. Strafford admitted this in a letter to Laud in 1637
but he dismissed the charges as grossly exaggerated.[4] At this
date he admitted to having spent £12,000 to £13,000 on estates
which were bringing in less than £1,000 a year rents, and he
expected his great house to cost in the region of £6,000.[5] He also
stated that his debts had risen by £7,000 since he came to Ireland.
By 1640, however, there is no doubt that his scale of buying and
spending had reached more lavish proportions. In 1642 it was
held against him by a critic that he 'got more in three years than
all his predecessors did in twenty'.[6] Sir Thomas Roe's judgment
on Strafford was that he was 'a servant violently zealous in his
master's ends and not negligent of his own'. On the other hand
Wentworth professed to be violently shocked in 1633 upon his
arrival in Ireland. 'I find myself in the society of a strange people,
their own privates altogether their study without any regard at
all to the public.'

For all his protestations, however, Strafford by 1640 had
acquired estates in Ireland, amounting to nearly 34,000 acres
(excluding 23,500 described as waste).[7] Of these, 14,000 acres
(excluding 10,000 acres of waste) were by royal grant; the remainder cost him £35,000. In addition, he had built a large house
near Naas, which cost £22,000 and which in its frontage of

[1] Hill, *Plantation in Ulster*, p. 315.
[2] Cf. R. M. Young, *The Town Book of Belfast, 1613–1816*, p. 226; R. C.
Simington (ed.), *Civil Survey*, iii. 2–11.
[3] *Cal. S.P. Ire., 1615–25*, p. 221.
[4] *Strafford's letters*, ii. 105.   [5] Ibid., 105.
[6] B. M. Egerton MSS. 917. 'A discourse between two counsellors of State'.
[7] Cf. Strafford MSS., vol. 40.

360 ft. was larger than Hatfield (220 ft.) and Longleat (260 ft.)
This was no small reward for a deputyship of seven years.
Richard Boyle himself could hardly have bettered it in so short a
time.

So bald a statement of the extent of Strafford's Irish property,
however, conveys a misleading impression. Much the greatest
part of these estates lay in Co. Wicklow which, save for a narrow
coastal strip, is a hilly area, not unlike the Derbyshire moors so
near to Strafford's Yorkshire manor of Wentworth Woodhouse.
Of the five parcels of land acquired by Wentworth, four lay in Co.
Wicklow. They were the manors of Newcastle, Wicklow and
Fairwood and the half barony of Shillelagh.[1] Of these, the manors
of Newcastle and Wicklow contained some of the good land near
the coast, but all of them contained a high proportion of poor
grazing and of waste. The fifth estate was very different in
character. It consisted of various parcels grouped near the town
of Naas, Co. Kildare. This land, though not far in terms of
distance from the Wicklow hills, was comparatively rich. Here
Strafford was among wealthy old-established old English proprietors 'inside the Pale' which at this point faced due east towards
Wicklow. Much of his Wicklow estates on the other hand lay
within a Gaelic Irish area, occupied by the O'Byrnes, who had
extended their effective control in the fifteenth century only to
see it substantially diminished during the attempted plantations
of the early seventeenth century. It was at Naas, among the old
English, that Strafford chose to build his great house. Here his
land was to cost him £4 an acre compared to 16s. an acre in
Shillelagh (excluding waste) and 25s. an acre in Fairwood
(excluding waste).

The question now arises as to how the land was actually acquired.
Of his five parcels, Wentworth obtained three by purchase and
the remaining two by Crown grant. By English standards,
however, the only real purchases took place within the Pale.
Here, in Kildare, Wentworth's representatives bargained with the
actual proprietors of particular estates and for a total outlay of
£13,700 acquired the 'manor of Elsmore'. Sir George Radcliffe,
William Billingsley, Joshua Carpenter and Bartholomew Pesely
acted as the lord deputy's agents in the matter. The property

---

[1] Cf. L. Price, 'The Barony of Shillelagh' in *Journal of the Royal Society of
Antiquaries of Ireland*, lxxxvi. 77–83 (1956).

included houses and messuages in Naas itself, tithes of neighbouring rectories, as well as a total of 3,580 acres. The rent roll brought in £989 in 1638.[1] Wentworth did not acquire the property in one piece of bargaining, but as a result of individual negotiation with a dozen different proprietors, carrying such old English names as FitzGerald, Eustace, Herbert, Aylmer, Sherlock, Delahyde and Wogan.

It was different with the estates in Wicklow. Here, Wentworth's financial outlay was tantamount to speculation rather than purchase. Fairwood and Shillelagh were acquired by cash payment, and the manors of Newcastle and Wicklow were granted by royal patent, but in all four instances Wentworth was acquiring plantation land. What the planter normally gained in such cases was opportunity to collect and increase rents over a vast area as much as the property itself. Wentworth's interest in Wicklow would require explanation were it not for the fact that it was only in this county that opportunities for speculation existed on a grand scale, so near to Dublin. Elsewhere in Co. Dublin, Kildare and Meath for example, land was available only at a high price. Wentworth chose to speculate in Wicklow rather than further afield as George Radcliffe did in the plantation of Connacht. In doing so, however, he was merely following in the footsteps of such expert 'adventurers' as Sir William Parsons, Viscount Loftus and Viscount Ranelagh, all of whom had acquired land in Wicklow in 1628.[2]

The grant of land in Wicklow to Wentworth in 1638 was the last stage in the story which had been dragging on for the previous twenty years, and in view of the numerous references to 'Birnes' Country' in Wentworth's correspondence it is perhaps worthwhile making its main outlines clear. Central Wicklow had never been under English control; in fact during the fifteenth century, the Gaelic Irish families of O'Byrne and O'Toole had greatly extended the area over which they enjoyed effective lordship.[3] By the

[1] FitzWilliam deeds D.1474 (1). I owe this reference to the kindness of Mr. John Cooper.

[2] *Cal. Patent Rolls Chas I.* ed. Morrin pp. 356-7.

[3] Cf. L. Price, 'The Byrne's Country in County Wicklow' in *J.R.S.A.I.*, lxvi. 41-66 (1936); L. Price, 'The case of Phelim MacFeagh O'Byrne and the lands of Ranelagh', ibid., lxxiii. 50-9 (1943); Sean MacAirt (ed.) *Leabhar Branach: the Book of the O'Byrnes* (Dublin 1944), reviewed in *I.H.S.*, v. 249-53; B. G. MacCarthy, 'The riddle of Rose O'Toole' in S. Pender (ed.) *Feilscribhin Torna* (Cork, 1947), pp. 171-82.

mid-sixteenth century, two branches of the O'Byrne family had emerged. The senior branch occupied the better land, running up the coast from Arklow to Delgany, including the small town of Newcastle, but excluding Wicklow. This branch (the O'Byrnes of Crioch Branach) were more exposed to English pressure than the junior branch and accepted an English seneschal at Newcastle in 1566. During the troubled last two decades of the sixteenth century most of these O'Byrnes remained at peace and in fact took the English side against Hugh O'Neill. For this attitude, their hostility towards the junior branch of the family was mainly responsible. The other branch of the O'Byrnes, which was led into rebellion in 1580 and again during Hugh O'Neill's war by Feagh McHugh O'Byrne,[1] occupied the more mountainous region of east and south Wicklow, including the areas of Ranelagh and Cosha. Rebellion did not lead to confiscation, however, as the O'Byrnes made peace with Mountjoy in 1601, but neither did it lead to a secure title and during the first decades of the seventeenth century Wicklow lay exposed to the possibility of plantation, a threat which applied to 'Birnes' Country' proper, that is the area of Crioch Branach, quite as much to the junior branch, who remained in uneasy possession of Ranelagh and Cosha.

In 1617, after much negotiation, Phelim McFeagh O'Byrne, head of the junior branch, was confirmed in his title to Ranelagh and Cosha, but he was not left long undisturbed. In the same year, a grant of Cosha was made to Sir Richard Graham, an old officer of Mountjoy's army and a legal struggle developed between himself and Phelim O'Byrne. The verdict went against the O'Byrnes, as a result of which an attempt was made, with Falkland's approval, to plant Ranelagh in 1628. During the course of this second episode the O'Byrnes were imprisoned in Dublin Castle and, as a consequence of the scandal which followed, Falkland was recalled. A group of undertakers still remained in possession of 8,000 acres in Ranelagh, among them Parsons and Loftus. So far, only Cosha and Ranelagh had been affected; 'Birnes' Country' remained unplanted.

Much of this land was eventually to become Wentworth's property. Cosha was acquired by Wentworth by purchase from Graham's son, William in 1637. Other minor partners of Graham

---

[1] Cf. L. Price, 'Notes on Feagh McHugh O'Byrne' in *Kildare Arch. Soc. Jn.*, xi. 134–75.

N

in the bargain were Sir William Parsons, the earl of Meath, Richard Bellings and Edward Wingfield, all of whom had been involved in the case of the O'Byrnes in Falkland's time. The estate consisted of *c.* 5,500 profitable acres, plus *c.* 5,000 acres of waste. Rents brought in *c.* £700. The total expenditure on Wentworth's part was £8,900, of which £5,800 went to William Graham. Cosha was referred to in legal documents as the manor of Fairwood. In acquiring it Wentworth was taking over the rights of the original speculator Graham.

Wentworth's second acquisition by purchase was the half barony of Shillelagh which lay south of Cosha and where lay the hunting park to which Wentworth often referred proudly in his correspondence. The title to this area was granted to Sir Henry Harrington in 1581. In 1607 he leased it.[1] In 1637 the title was held by Calcott Chambers, who had leased it to Philip Percival, clerk of the Irish Court of Wards and Liveries. The rents from Shillelagh were estimated in the 1656 Survey at £1,100 a year, 'beside yearly in Pipestaves and Timber' £1,000 a year. Of the total acreage of nearly 24,000 acres, over 10,000 were arable and pasture and 5,600 woodland. The proportion of hunting park was comparatively small, under 3,000 acres.[2]

In purchasing Cosha and Shillelagh, Strafford had acquired 'planted' land at what were abnormally cheap rates by comparison with England or even Kildare. They were only possible in a country in which the English government was attempting a territorial revolution for its own political and strategic reasons. Strafford undertook several new plantations during his deputyship but the only one from which he derived any personal profit was the attempt made to plant the coastal strip of Wicklow running south of the Delgany river to north of the town of Arklow, known as Birnes' Country. The scheme originated with James Hay, earl of Carlisle, who bought the manor of Newcastle from Sir William Harrington, son of the former Crown seneschal of Newcastle, and in addition acquired a Crown patent to Birnes' Country.[3] At this date the manor was rented to John Wolverston at £350 a year.[4] However, during the Spanish war, in 1628, the

---

[1] *Cal. Patent Rolls, Jas I*, p. 253.

[2] The remains of Strafford's hunting lodge are still to be seen near Tinahely, where they are known locally as 'Black Tom's Cellars'. L. Price, *Place Names of Co. Wicklow*, ii. 91.

[3] *Cal. Patent Rolls, Chas I*, ed. Morrin, p. 399.   [4] 1656 Survey.

Carlisle grant was rescinded and the Crown's intention was now stated to be the confirmation of the freeholders' titles in Birnes' Country in return for an annual rent of £150 a year.[1] With the coming of peace in 1630 the goodwill of the inhabitants no longer seemed so vital and the earl of Carlisle attempted to press his original claim. For this purpose his acquaintance with Strafford proved useful and the new lord deputy promised to use his good offices in this matter on Carlisle's behalf.[2] In July 1635 Strafford informed Carlisle that he hoped to raise £15,000 from the tenants made up of £5,000 for the manor of Newcastle and £10,000 for the patent to Birnes' Country.[3] He seemed to envisage that Carlisle would surrender his titles to the Crown in return for this sum, while the tenants would in return obtain secure titles from the Crown. Part of the bargain took place as arranged. Carlisle surrendered to the Crown for £15,000[4] and the gentlemen of the territory paid the money in.[5] Carlisle's death in 1636 appeared to round off the transaction and one would expect to hear little more of it.

In fact, however, Strafford's part in the business was only just beginning. From 1636 onwards a proposed plantation of Birnes' Country was repeatedly mentioned in Strafford's correspondence as a potential source of revenue to the Crown.[6] In writing to Laud in 1637, Strafford said that 'the contract made for my Lord of Carlisle's interest in the Byrnes is believed here to be for me but in truth (I dare impart it to your Grace) his Majesty full well knows it is for himself'.[7] Strafford claimed to have rejected 'a Bargain of so Mighty a Profit' and to have put the interests of the Crown before his own. He did not, however, go unrewarded. He was granted the manor of Newcastle and the manor of Wicklow, newly created out of part of Birnes' Country. Together these amounted to 9,000 profitable acres (excluding 10,000 acres of waste) of what the 1656 Survey described as 'a rich and healthful soyle situate upon the sea coast and within 18 miles distant from Dublin'. In 1656 the rents of the Manors of Newcastle and Wicklow were estimated respectively at £500 and £1,078 a year. Clearly there had been a sharp rise in rents since 1628. The Crown

[1] *Cal. Patent Rolls, Chas I*, ed. Morrin, p. 400.
[2] *Strafford's letters*, i. 179.
[3] Strafford MSS., vol. 8, f. 247.
[4] 1656 Survey.
[5] Strafford MSS., vol. 10, ff. 2–3.
[6] *Strafford's letters*, ii. 8.
[7] Ibid., 175.

itself seems to have gained £2,000 a year in rents[1] from the remaining territory of Birnes' Country, which amounted to over 60,000 acres not all of which were profitable.[2]

The story of Birnes' Country is a complicated one and not all of its main features are clear. Strafford, for example, referred at his trial to the Crown paying £15,000 for land[3] which suggests the possibility that the gentlemen of Birnes' Country were refunded their money. Strafford's own motives were mixed and the proportion of public gain and private profit is a matter for conjecture. Those who were worst off were the tenants of Birnes' Country and it is understandable that the rebellion of 1641 should find a ready response here. Those who did benefit were Strafford, Lady Carlisle and perhaps, the Crown. The whole episode, however, does suggest that Strafford was playing a similar kind of game in Irish land to that of men whom he criticised so severely when he first landed in the country. He is often considered to have acted on a plane different from that of other lords deputy and from the normal type of new English land speculator in Ireland and though it is true that he did not dabble like Boyle, Loftus and many others in church lands and impropriations, the picture which emerges is not that of the complete idealist of some modern commentators.[4]

Finally, mention must be made of the great house at Jigginstown. The cost of this far exceeded Wentworth's expectations and according to the 1656 survey cost some £22,000. Its plan was simple, a long three-storey building with two square wings; twenty-four large windows (6 ft. wide by 25 ft. high) made up the first floor together with two entrances, each with a flight of twelve steps. The ground floor consisted of a row of windows designed to provide lighting for the large cellars. The brickwork some of which still survives was excellent and there were also some marble columns and pavements. By the 1650's, however, the house was in ruins and most of the lead and iron used in its construction had been removed for use as ammunition. A house

---

[1] Rushworth, *Trial.*

[2] The present baronies of Newcastle and Arklow total 119,000 acres, but Birnes' Country in the early seventeenth century did not include the so-called 'shires of Arklow', to the south. Birnes' Country proper probably extended to 80,000 acres or more.

[3] Rushworth, *Trial.*

[4] H. O'Grady, *Strafford and Ireland*; C. V. Wedgwood, *Strafford.*

built on such a scale may be taken as further evidence if such
were of Wentworth's confidence in the permanence of the existing order.

In the form of a table, Wentworth's expenditure during the
years 1637–40 may be set down as follows:

	Acreage	Waste	Cost	Rents	Date
Kildare					
Manor of Elsmore	c. 5,000	—	£13,700	c. £980	1638
Wicklow					
Manor of Fairwood (Cosha)	c. 5,500	c. 5,000	£8,900	£700	
Half-barony of Shillelagh	c. 16,000*	c. 8,000	£13,200	£2,100†	
Jigginstown House	—	—	£22,000		
Total by purchase	c. 26,500	c. 13,000	£57,800	£3,780	
By royal Grant					
Wicklow					
Manor of Newcastle	c. 2,800	1,700	[£15,000]	£500	
Manor of Wicklow	c. 6,200	8,500		£1,200	
	9,000	10,200		£1,700	
Total	35,500	23,200	£57,800	£5,480	

* Including woodland.
† Including income from pipestaves.

In view of this expenditure the question naturally arises as to
the sources of the income which financed it.

No actual accounts survive but there is sufficient evidence to
give some indication of Wentworth's income in Ireland. It
seems to have derived from three main sources, his salary as
lord deputy, his share of the profits from the customs farm and
thirdly, the profit from the tobacco monopoly. Of these the first
was least important. As lord deputy Wentworth was entitled to
an official income of £2,000 a year, plus travel expenses.[1] This
had been Falkland's peacetime salary, though in time of war, it
had risen to £5,000. Lord justices, who acted in the lord deputy's
absence, were paid at the rate of £100 a month each. Later, in
1640, when Wentworth returned to Ireland as lord lieutenant,
he was paid at the rate of £5,000 a year, But as he stayed only for
six weeks he was entitled only to £444, a sum which was still
owed to his son after 1650. It is difficult to surmise how much of

[1] At the end of the sixteenth century, the deputy's official salary was £1,000
a year. *Lib. mun. pub. Hib.*, ii. 5.

his salary was spent in ordinary living expenses, but probably most of it went towards maintaining the dignity of Wentworth's office, which he himself was not the one to underplay. In any case, what was left over, could have gone little way towards the expenditure of £35,200 which was incurred for the acquisition of his estates in Wicklow and Kildare. For this and for the building of the great house much larger sums were necessary. They were supplied from the profits of the customs farm, particularly after 1637, when much of Wentworth's heavy spending took place.

Before Strafford's appointment as lord deputy, the Irish Customs brought in approximately £12,000, of which the farm accounted for £6,000, while the remaining profits were shared equally between the Crown and the farmer, the Duchess of Buckingham. In 1632 after much negotiation, a new arrangement was agreed upon and Strafford, with the backing of Sir Arthur Ingram and Viscount Mountnorris, vice-treasurer of Ireland, offered a new rent of £15,500 plus a large fine which seems to have been £28,000.[1] The Duchess herself received as compensation a pension of £4,500, paid out of the profits of the farm.[2] The new farmers had gambled on increased receipts and on the fact that the Duchess's farm had only four years to run, leaving them with the reversion for eleven years. Their confidence was rewarded. Thanks to an increased scale of customs duties and a revival of trade, total receipts for the Irish customs rose to £22,500 in 1633 and £25,846 in 1634. The farmers made a corresponding profit which Mountnorris estimated at £4,950 and £8,370.[3] It was not until 1635, however, that there was a really remarkable increase in receipts when in the half-year 1635 the farmers made £9,700 profit and in the whole year over £20,000. This was the moment that Strafford chose to get rid of his fellow partners and re-allot their shares to the Crown. Under the new arrangements five-eighths of the profits were to go to the Crown, while Strafford and Sir George Radcliffe retained two-eighths and one-eighth respectively.[4]

[1] On at least two occasions Strafford referred to the farmers having to pay a fine of £28,000 (Knowler, ii. 137; Strafford MSS., vol. 7, f. 160), though elsewhere £8,000 is the sum mentioned. It may be that the Duchess's pension was paid by the farmers eventually even though it was paid first out of the farm.

[2] H.M.C. Var. Coll., viii. 195.   [3] Cal. Clarendon Papers, i. 362.
[4] Strafford's letters, ii. 136–7.

The receipts from the Customs continued to rise during the next four years to £38,174 in 1635–6, £38,889 in 1636–7, £57,387 in 1637–8, £55,582 in 1638–9 and £51,874 in 1639–40.[1] It must have been during these years that the lord deputy recouped with interest his share of the fine of £28,000.[2] During the early years of the farm Strafford's profits would not have covered his initial outlay of £7,000 until 1635.[3] From then on, however, it is safe to estimate his share of the profits at a quarter of the total receipts after the Crown rent of £15,500 and running expenses of £3,000 had been deducted. On this basis, which has Strafford's own state-ment for its justification, his personal profits may be set down as follows:

1635–6	£4,000
1636–7	£4,000
1637–8	£9,700
1638–9	£9,250
1639–40	£8,300
Total	£35,250

In 1637, however, the increase in customs receipts could hardly have been foreseen and Wentworth may well have felt the need for another source of income. Even before that date, he had looked round for other ways of making money. For example, in 1634, he had instructed his agent Joshua Carpenter to fit out a ship for trade with Spain and in the same year he lost money attempting to set up an iron-manufacture; he wrote that he expected to be £600 out of pocket 'and if I be once so fortunate as to recover myself, if any man take me a Merchant Adventurer againe, I am much mistaken.'[4] In 1636, his well-known, if ill-fated attempt to set up the manufacture of linen cloth was part of the same pattern. In this venture he lost £3,000, according to his own statement at the trial. It is noticeable that in all three instances, Wentworth combined an insistence upon public interest, with the opportunity of private profit.

Outside the customs farm, however, Wentworth's largest

---

[1] *Cal. S.P. Ire., 1633–47*, p. 273.
[2] Sir Arthur Ingram received £7,000 when he left the farm. *Strafford's letters*, ii. 21. As he had held, like Strafford, a quarter share, this would appear to be repayment of his share of the fine. Only £2,000 seems to have been paid off the fine as a first instalment. Cf. *Cal. S.P. Ire., 1647–60*, p. 239.
[3] *Strafford's letters*, ii. 137.
[4] Strafford MSS., vol. 3.

financial venture was the tobacco monopoly. Wentworth had
already suggested this in 1634;[1] he formally proposed it again in
1636;[2] finally, in November 1637, he informed Charles that, in
default of any other offer, he had agreed to offer, himself, £7,000
for the first five years and £12,000 for another six years in return
for a monopoly.[3] (A similar tobacco monopoly had just been set
up in England.) Wentworth made out that he entered into the
agreement unwillingly, but this disclaimer need not be taken too
seriously.

It is difficult to estimate how much actual profit Wentworth
made out of the tobacco monopoly. On paper, the idea behind
the scheme was that the monopolists should be allowed the sole
right of importing tobacco into Ireland. Merchants outside the
monopoly were required to pay an import to the patentees of
6d. a lb., plus 18d. customs duty.[4] Wentworth's own tobacco paid
proportionately much less. The monopolists thus made their
profits from the sale of tobacco and from collecting additional
duties imposed upon their commercial rivals. The capital for the
monopoly was provided for by a secret agreement between Wentworth and the King. Wentworth was to be allowed to borrow,
over a period of three years, the sum of £40,000 from the Exchequer. Adam Loftus, the vice-treasurer, denied any knowledge
of the arrangement, but he admitted that Radcliffe had borrowed
£24,000 in 1638 from the profits of the Customs Farm.[5] The
money was spent upon tobacco which was then stored in 'magazines' at Dublin, Youghal, Cork and Galway. In part the scheme
was a form of rudimentary excise, but it was also state commerce
on a grand scale in view of the fact that the Irish revenues as a
whole totalled only £84,000.[6]

Had Strafford not fallen from power before the monopoly had
come to full efficiency it is probable that the profits would have
been as great as those from the Customs Farm. They were indeed
stated by the opposition at the trial to have been in the region of
£100,000,[7] making an average over three years of over £30,000.
This is hard to accept even if due allowance is made for the fact
that the monopolists were making a profit of over 100 per cent

[1] *Strafford's letters*, i. 192.   [2] Ibid., ii. 8.   [3] Ibid., ii. 135.
[4] Rushworth, *Trial*, p. 403.   [5] Ibid., p. 115.
[6] *Cal. S.P. Ire., 1647–60*, p. 234.
[7] Rushworth, *Trial*, p. 402.

upon every pound of tobacco sold. Strafford himself stated that there had been a loss of £6,000 over the three years.[1] His figures of £86,000 expenditure and £80,000 income implied an average yearly of £28,000 expenditure and £26,000 income. That considerable sums were involved and that large stocks of tobacco were held is shown by the estimates made in 1656 of official debts owed to Strafford for the use of his tobacco as payment in kind for government troops during the years 1642–4.[2] These official debts, which make it clear that the tobacco monopoly was a personal venture of Strafford's were estimated at £18,000. To them can be added arrears owed to Strafford by his agents in the various ports, amounting to a total of £28,500. Thus the total debts owed to Strafford from this ill-fated monopoly can be reckoned at something in the region of £45,000. He himself had repaid the Crown loan of £24,000 in 1641,[3] but it is doubtful whether his heirs recouped the tobacco debts. All in all it is difficult to resist the conclusion that the tobacco monopoly was a disastrous failure which probably consumed much of the profits that Strafford had made in other ways. This was in the future, however; in 1639 Strafford's income from Irish sources was in the region of £13,000 per annum. This placed him among the richest men in England. As lord deputy he had succeeded in acquiring an Irish income for himself which was of the same order of magnitude as that which Bramhall had raised, after so much effort, for the episcopal revenues of the church. It was certainly an income much larger than that from his Yorkshire lands, which brought him in about £6,000 a year.

Strafford's preoccupation, if that is not too strong a term, with the making of money and the acquisition of property compels some reassessment of the extent to which his political idealism may be taken seriously. He pictured himself in his letters as a man above the normal play of selfish ambition and his whole conception of the policy of 'thorough' rested upon its claim to cut through a world of vested interest. But there was a more mundane side to it all, and in fact so far from being as exceptional as he liked to persuade others, and perhaps himself, Strafford was typical of the general run of seventeenth-century politicians. He was close in spirit to his adversary Richard Boyle, for all the

[1] Ibid., p. 410.   [2] 1656 Survey.
[3] Rushworth, *Trial*, p. 115.

gibes which he levelled at him. But though ultimately we may be prepared to place Strafford nearer to Boyle than to Colbert, it should in fairness be borne in mind that Colbert himself made a not inconsiderable fortune from his chosen trade of politics.

13

THE DOWNFALL OF WENTWORTH'S
ADMINISTRATION

(I) OPPOSITION IN ULSTER

IN May 1639 Laud made a speech in the Star Chamber where
Sir Piers Crosby was on trial for libelling the lord deputy.
'The State', he declared, 'doth not owe a little to my Lord Deputy
that the kingdom of Ireland is kept in that great peace and security;
for at this day (God be thanked) that Kingdom is at peace, notwithstanding the Multitude of Scots in that Kingdom and those
rebels that are within an hour and half's passage of Ireland. No
part of England is in more security than they are at this time and
under God and the King, I can attribute it to nothing but the
wisdom, courage, and care of my Lord Deputy and therefore
God forbid offenders against his reputation should go away without exemplary punishment.' [1] Appearances were deceptive,
however, and for all its seeming peace Ireland was in a state of
unstable equilibrium. Wentworth had succeeded in imposing his
will upon the four sections of society in Ireland–Gaelic Irish,
Ulster Scots, old English proprietors and new English planters—
but everywhere there was a discontent which only fear prevented
from emerging. What is surprising, indeed, is that the opposition
to the lord deputy was not more effective. But it was hard to
envisage a situation in which the piecemeal opposition of Boyle,
Mountnorris, Clanrickarde, Westmeath and the Ulster Scots
would be in a position to combine. Wentworth, himself, had no
vision of future catastrophe, as his extensive purchases of land
during these years showed, [2] and he had good reason for his confidence, if economic prosperity was any guide. In England, he
could count upon the support of Charles I and his two chief

---

[1] *Works*, vii. 649–50.
[2] In August 1639, he wrote to the dowager Countess of Clare explaining
that he was buying land for his son in Ireland. She was the grandmother.
Strafford's letters, ii. 380.

ministers, Laud and Cottington, which had not been the case during Portland's lifetime. By the end of 1640 however, the whole system of absolutism which had been attempted on the French model, had collapsed throughout the three kingdoms, though it was something of a tribute, that Strafford's Irish system should be the last to collapse and that Charles I should be haunted throughout the civil war period by the hope of aid from Ireland.

In 1639, every section of society in Ireland had deep-seated grievances against the administration, but by a strange paradox discontent was most acute in Ulster where the policy of plantation had been most successful. However for the unrest in the English plantation of Co. Londonderry, Wentworth bore only a minor share of the responsibility. The source of the trouble went back to 1635, when the decision of the Star Chamber had gone against the London companies for failing to comply with the conditions of their agreement with the Crown.[1] In 1637, they yielded up their rights and agreed to pay a fine of £12,000 in return for a pardon.[2] The fate of the forfeited lands remained undecided for four years and then in 1639 royal agents were appointed to collect the rents. It is conceivable that the actual tenants, as distinct from the London companies, might have had little reason to resent the change of landlord. In fact, however, the agents, Whitfield and Fotherley, added to existing discontent by demanding higher rents,[3] while at the same time they dispossessed important proprietors, such as Beresford, Freeman, Stone, and Moore, of their estates.[4] The increased rents went to defray the costs of Wentworth's army which was stationed in the north.[5]

Wentworth and Bramhall were strongly critical of the agents' 'rackinge of it for the odd thousand or fifteene hundred pounds' on the grounds that it caused 'a great clamour'.[6] They were also opposed to any measures which would strengthen the Scottish planters at the expense of the English. In this they could rely upon the support of Laud, who judged it 'no time to weed the English out of Londonderry to make room for more of that leaven',[7] i.e. the Scots. On this particular issue the combined influence of Laud and Wentworth did not prevail. But even if

[1] Moody, *The Londonderry plantation*, pp. 365–9.
[2] Ibid., p. 385.   [3] Ibid., p. 399.   [4] Ibid., pp. 402–3.
[5] Ibid., p. 404.   [6] Ibid., p. 401.
[7] *Works*, vii. 444.

Wentworth did not back government policy over Londonderry, as lord deputy, it was his task to carry it out and in the minds of those who suffered by it he inevitably bore the blame. Discontent among the English planters in Ulster was to play its part in bringing about the final collapse of Wentworth's administration when the time came for action in 1640.

In 1639, however, unrest among the Scottish planters was of greater urgency than that among the English. Bramhall's Laudian religious policy was responsible for much of this but the situation took a turn for the worse, from the point of view of the administration, when resistance occurred in Scotland to proposed religious innovations. In February 1638 the National League and Covenant was drawn up by the Scottish Presbyterians and it was too much to expect that the Ulster Scots would remain unaffected by this development. Even the English puritan Sir John Clotworthy went to 'salute the Kirk at Edinboro' in 1638.[1] Wentworth acted with characteristic promptness. He raised additional troops and stationed them at Carrickfergus to deal with any eventuality that might arise. The strength of this force in May 1639 was 2,000 foot and 1,000 horse; Wentworth estimated the number of Ulster Scots at 100,000.[2] At the request of Charles I some 500 troops were sent to garrison Carlisle and so to secure the western flank of the English border with Scotland. At the same time, May 1639, an attempt was made to ensure the loyalty of the Ulster Scots by compelling them to take an oath denouncing the National League and Covenant.[3]

Wentworth himself could not understand the Scots' violent antipathy to things which were in his view 'purely and simply indifferent.'[4] He regarded disobedience to so excellent and Christian a ruler as lamentable, the more so because it was preached in a Protestant church and he asked the earl of Argyll, 'could Bellarmine, Mariana with all the rest of that rebellious college do more'?[5]

He did not, at any rate in 1639, regard the Scottish troubles as more than a temporary difficulty facing the government and he therefore opposed such desperate remedies as the arming of

---

[1] According to Laud. *Works*, vii. 464.
[2] *H.M.C. Cowper MSS.*, ii. 230.
[3] For the text of the so-called 'Black Oath', see *Strafford's letters*, ii. 345. See also Strafford MSS., vol. 7, f. 178.
[4] *Strafford's letters*, ii. 210.   [5] Ibid.

20,000 Ulster Irish under the command of the earl of Antrim. As he wrote to secretary Windebank in March 1639, 'what sudden outrage may be apprehended from so great a Number of the native Irish, Children of habituated rebels, . . . armed with our own weapons'?[1] He was also afraid that if Antrim's venture failed, the earl of Argyll would land in Ulster and rouse the Northern Scots. Wentworth's doubts about the earl of Antrim were justified if the list of Antrim's supporters was any indication, since it included Sir Phelim O'Neill and others who were to rise in Ulster eighteen months later.[2] Wentworth's views were temporarily disregarded and Antrim received the backing of Charles for his scheme of providing a military diversion on the coast of Kintyre.[3] In June 1639, however, the lord deputy was still expressing his hostility to a scheme which carried such 'great and dangerous consequences.'[4] In that same month, Charles opened up negotiations with the Scots and by the treaty of Berwick it was agreed that their army should disband in return for Charles's assurance that the General assembly should decide upon matters of church organisation and discipline. For the moment the pressure upon Ulster was relieved and the need for Antrim's expedition was taken away.

In July Charles decided that the respite was only temporary and in preparation for stronger measures summoned Wentworth back from Ireland.[5] Wentworth had, indeed, already given as his opinion that if rightly handled the situation could easily be brought to a satisfactory conclusion.[6] This was a sad overestimate of the king's military resources. Wentworth's influence was to be thrown upon the side of an adventure which was to end in his execution in May 1641.

By October 1639, Wentworth was in England, and during the next winter a plan was drawn up to raise an army of 8,000 men in Ireland, which was to be transported to Scotland by the end of June 1640. England was to provide 500 horse and 2,000 foot.[7]

Wentworth's new army, unlike the smaller one already in existence, consisted largely of Catholics. It was officered, however, mainly by Protestants. Of the eight colonels in command, all except one were new English, while only a dozen of the junior

---

[1] *Strafford's letters*, ii. 304.   [2] Ibid., ii. 306.   [3] Ibid., ii. 323.
[4] Ibid., ii. 359.   [5] Ibid., ii. 373.   [6] Ibid., ii. 271.
[7] Ibid., ii. 400-1.

officers were old English.[1] They included Theobald Taaffe, the two Sir James Dillons, John Barry and Rory Maguire, all of whom were to play a part in the rising of 1641. This as yet was in the future, but it was ironical that Wentworth, having foreseen the dangers which might arise if the earl of Antrim were allowed to raise an army, in fact created himself a similar instrument. Had this army ever left Ireland the rebellion might not have taken place.

Early in 1640 Wentworth's over-confidence may well have been the decisive factor in leading Charles to overreach himself. He does not seem to have realised how much bitterness he had created in Ireland and how weak his position in fact was. His short return visit to Ireland in March 1640 led him to inform the king that he would not 'suffer this Nation to cool on my Hands whose Zeal is all on fire to serve your Majesty'. He also assured Charles that the Irish parliament newly summoned on 16 March had voted four subsidies 'with all possible cheerfulness'. The next six months, however, were to show that Wentworth had erred on the side of gross over-confidence. He left Ireland immediately after he had prorogued the Irish parliament on 31 March, without realising how soon the collapse of his administration would take place.

(ii) OPPOSITION IN PARLIAMENT

As his deputy in Ireland, Wentworth left his cousin Christopher Wandesford, who had joined with him in the attack on Buckingham in the early years of Charles I's reign and had then followed Wentworth to Ireland. He had been in Ireland since 1633, when he had been appointed Master of the Rolls. He was soon to find that the situation in Ireland was much less simple than Wentworth had believed. The first hint of trouble came in June when Parliament reassembled. The session lasted only just over a fortnight[2] but during that time Wandesford found himself forced to make concessions, which amounted to a direct reversal of important decisions taken by Wentworth. In the first place the house of commons ordered that writs should be issued to the sheriffs of the seven Anglo-Irish boroughs which Wentworth had succeeded

[1] For a list of the officers, see T.C.D. MS. F.3.15.
[2] 11–17 June 1640.

in excluding from the house in accordance with the plan he had
outlined to the king in 1635.[1] The boroughs concerned were
Newcastle, Naas, Ardee, Fore, Bannow, Taghmon and Clonmines and the only result of the decision could have been to increase the Anglo-Irish representation in the house of commons.
This could be interpreted as a move by Wandesford to gain control
of the house by an alliance with the Anglo-Irish, were it not for a
letter which he wrote at this time to Wentworth in England.[2]
It appears from this that Wandesford had lost control of the
house and that the concession to the Anglo-Irish was not part of
a deliberate policy but had been forced upon him. 'The Proceedings in the House of Commons,' he wrote, 'notwithstanding the
good order you left them in . . . grow worse and worse every
day: neither hath these layte debates concerning the declaration[3]
been prosecuted by the Irish onley but those of our own partye
(as we call them) have joined apparently with them insomuch as
Serjeant Sambadge (one of the five[4] appointed to draw the
Declaration) was left alone in his modest opinion for the King. . . .
Howsoever they grow so intemperate that they must and shall be
dissolved and that upon Monday next.' The Anglo-Irish could not
have forced this motion through the house against the wishes of
the deputy, without the support, tacit or otherwise, of a considerable section of the new English or 'Protestant' party (or
parties).[5] In the light of Wandesford's letter, therefore, it would
seem that a movement of opposition to the deputy had appeared
in the house, in which Anglo-Irish and some new English
combined.

This inference is confirmed by two other facts—the dropping
of the bill to confirm the plantation of Connacht and the change in
the method of levying subsidies. The basis of the legislative
programme which this parliament had met to consider was the
passing of an act for the securing of the plantation in 'the several
counties of Roscommon, Sligo, Mayo, etc.'[6] The bill was first

[1] See above pp. 66–7 .

[2] Wandesford to Wentworth. 12 June 1640. Bodleian Add. MSS. C, 286,
p. 25. T. D. Whitaker, *The Life and original correspondence of Sir George Radcliffe*,
pp. 249–51.

[3] 'A declaration concerning the levying of subsidies in a parliamentary
way.' *Commons jn. Ire.*, 10 June 1640, p. 145.

[4] The other four were John Bysse, recorder of Dublin, Geoffrey Browne,
Nicholas Plunkett and James Cusacke.

[5] See below, pp. 194 ff.   [6] *Commons jn. Ire.*, p. 124.

read on 1 June and after being discussed in committee, it was read a second time on 8 June. From then on, however, no more was heard of it; the most likely explanation seems to be that this disappearance represents further evidence of an alliance between the Anglo-Irish and other sections of the house. The sending of writs to the Anglo-Irish boroughs and the dropping out of sight of the plantation indicate concessions to Anglo-Irish opinion in the interests of a wider movement of opposition in which Catholic and Protestant joined. On 13 June another of Wentworth's decisions was rescinded, when the house declared that subsidies were to be levied 'in a moderate parliamentary way after an easy and equal rate of each man his estate': thus the method which Wentworth had adopted in 1635 of imposing a fixed sum upon each county in order to ensure a subsidy of £40,000 was dropped.[1] In its stead, everybody having lands or other profits of the yearly value of £30 was to be assessed in the subsidy book at £3 and was to pay 4s. in the £ or 12s. in all: a similar assessment was to be made for larger incomes.[2] On 15 June the house was given further time to consider its grievances before being adjourned two days later.

By the middle of 1640, therefore, discontent in Ireland had begun to express itself openly in parliament. The atmosphere of June was very different from that of March. But the situation in which the Irish administration found itself did not improve as time went on, and if anything, its freedom of action was increasingly curtailed by the need to placate the new English and Anglo-Irish opposition if the Ulster Scots were to be kept under control. The worsening position of the king in England, culminating in the defeat at Newburn on 28 August, made it more necessary than

[1] The application of the subsidy to the whole country was a novelty in seventeenth-century Ireland. The original parliamentary subsidy, which had been confined to areas under English control had become increasingly unimportant in the sixteenth century: in 1574–5 it brought in only £200. It was replaced by cess, a system of military taxation, which was 'a regular imposition of the administration . . . without intervention by Parliament' (D. B. Quinn, 'Irish parliamentary subsidy in fifteenth and sixteenth centuries' in *Proc. R.I.A.*, sect. C, xlii, no. 11, 219–46 (July 1935)). The first subsidy on the English model and levied on the whole country was granted by the Irish parliament in 1615. (*Cal. S.P. Ire., 1615–25*, p. 49). The work of assessing the whole country did not begin until August of that year (ibid., p. 85). Sir Thomas Ridgeway expected it to bring in £30,000 (ibid., op cit.).

[2] *Cal. S.P. Ire., 1633–47*, p. 251. 20 Oct. 1640. Cf. also *Commons jn. Ire.*, p. 170.

ever to contain the discontent of the Ulster Scots. The need for
a large standing army in Ulster placed Wandesford in the hands
of the Irish house of commons and made it extremely difficult
for him to withstand any movement for redress of grievances. The
situation in England which in November made Pym's parliamentary position almost impregnable—namely the need to find money
to pay the Scottish occupation forces in the northern counties—
was paralleled earlier in the year in Ireland by the need to finance
the standing army in Ulster. The fact that this Irish standing
army was regarded by Wentworth as a card in the king's hand
which might be played in England, made Wandesford's position
vis-à-vis opposition in the Irish house of commons all the more
difficult, and in the last analysis deprived him of any means of
taking measures against such opposition. In the interests of the
wider policy of Charles I, it was all important to keep royal power
in Ireland comparatively untouched, even at the cost of yielding
over such measures as the plantation of Connacht, a reversal of
policy which went to the heart of Wentworth's administration.
And therefore in spite of the certainty that it would be difficult
to control, the Irish parliament was summoned to meet on
1 October: it was the lesser evil, the alternative being the possible
intervention of the victorious Scottish armies in the interests
of their persecuted fellows in Ulster.

(III) THE PARTIES IN PARLIAMENT

Some attempt must now be made to indicate the balance of
forces in the 1640 house of commons. If a division is made upon
religious grounds, then, out of a house of 240, the Protestant
members numbered slightly less than three-quarters, while the
Catholics, including both Anglo-Irish and the few Gaelic Irish,
numbered seventy or slightly more than a quarter. Had protestantism been a sign of loyalty to Wentworth's administration, the lord
deputy's party would have enjoyed an unassailable majority and
the position in 1640 would have been much more favourable than
it had been in 1634. In his first parliament, Wentworth had been
able to call upon the support of the Protestant new English
members of the house when, during the crisis of the second session,
the Anglo-Irish party had seized control for a few days; Wentworth's administration however had caused a radical change of

attitude towards the administration, on the part of many of the Protestant 'planter' class.

What requires elucidation is how it came about that in a house numbering 240, the Anglo-Irish, whose strength was only seventy, were able to control the house in alliance with a planter opposition group or groups. For this to occur it was necessary for them to win over an approximately equal number of votes in addition to their own.[1] The composition of the committee, which was nominated to take the Remonstrance in December 1641 to England, may be regarded as throwing some light upon this question and can be taken as a rough guide to the relative strength of Anglo-Irish and new English, in the general anti-Wandesford opposition. Of the thirteen members, seven were Anglo-Irish and six were new English.[2]

The membership of the Anglo-Irish party in the house as a whole may be safely deduced from their religion.[3] Their leaders, apart from those who went to England with the Remonstrance, can be seen in the membership of the impeachment committee of June 1641. Of this committee, which numbered sixteen members, nine were Anglo-Irish:

Patrick Darcy (Bannow)
Garrett Cheevers (Co. Wexford)
Maurice FitzGerald (Co. Kildare)
Richard Blake (Co. Galway)
Richard Barnewall (Co. Meath)

Christopher Bellew (Co. Louth)
Sir John Dongan (Newcastle, Co. Dublin)
Brian O'Neale[4]
John Taylor (Swords)

The prominence of these men as leaders is confirmed by an examination of the membership of the various committees of the house during the year 1641.

---

[1] On the assumption that the house was fully attended. In mid-1641, however, for a most important division only 120 members were present. *Commons jn. Ire.*, p. 239; cf. App. for members of the 1640 parliament.

[2]

Anglo-Irish	*New English*
Sir Donough MacCarty (Co. Cork)	Sir Hardress Waller (Co. Limerick)
John Walsh (Waterford)	Sir William Cole (Co. Fermanagh)
Nicholas Plunkett (Co. Meath)	Sir James Montgomery (Co. Down)
Nicholas Barnewall (Co. Dublin)	Edward Rowley (Co. Londonderry)
Thomas Bourke (Co. Mayo)	Simon Digby (Philipstown)
Sir Roebuck Lynch (Galway)	Richard FitzGerald (Strabane)
Geoffrey Browne (Athenry)	

[3] Darcy was one of the three agents who had been sent over to England to oppose the Galway plantation in 1635. His presence on the committee suggests links with Clanrickarde. Cf. *D.N.B.*

[4] His seat is not given.

It is difficult to speak with the same certainty of the composition of the new English opposition groups. Neither religion nor name nor office (or lack of it) are a safe guide here. No division lists have survived and very few speeches. Some conclusions may be drawn, however, from the composition of the impeachment committee of June 1641. This was a smaller committee than the original one which had been selected in February 1641 and in the meantime the king and the lords justices had made their wishes clear that the impeachment should be dropped. The fact that some new English (as well as the Anglo-Irish mentioned above) persisted in the face of royal displeasure is a sign of their determination.

One of the most prominent members of this committee was Audley Mervin (Co. Tyrone) nephew of Lord Castlehaven and brother-in-law of Rory Maguire. There were at least two possible reasons for his opposition to Wentworth's administration. In the first place he was related to Piers Crosby[1] who had clashed with the lord deputy on more than one occasion and who had come before the Star Chamber[2] and secondly, Mervin himself may well have suffered under Wentworth for his failure to fulfil the articles of plantation on the Castlehaven lands in Co. Tyrone, in the precinct of Omagh, where, apparently, little serious attempt had been made to introduce English tenants.[3] Bramhall's religious policies must also be taken into consideration.

Another member of the committee was Oliver Jones (Athlone), who was almost certainly related to Roger Jones, Viscount Ranelagh, lord president of Connacht.[4] If this relationship could be definitely established, Oliver Jones would take his place as another member of the Ranelagh-Clotworthy group, which had a footing in both Irish and English parliaments during this crucial period. The impeachment of Wentworth in England and of his associates in Ireland was synchronised largely because such links as Oliver Jones existed.

Simon Digby was another member. In view of the fact that John Digby, earl of Bristol, was associated with the movement against Wentworth in 1640 and George Digby his son was one of the managers for the impeachment of Wentworth, Simon Digby offers interesting possibilities for investigation. He had gone over with

---

[1] Crosby married the dowager countess of Castlehaven.
[2] *Cal. S.P. Ire., 1633–47*, p. 214.   [3] Hill, *The Plantation in Ulster*, p. 535 n.
[4] The official seat of the lord president of Connacht was Athlone.

the agents for the Remonstrance but he returned to Ireland early in 1641.[1] In the absence of evidence, only guesses can be made, but it is possible that he played a part in co-ordinating the opposition on both sides of the Irish Sea.

Apart from these three members, there must have been a considerable number of members from Ulster to form a hard core of opposition, in view of the history of that province under Wentworth.[2] Another fact may also be taken into consideration, namely that office holders like Ranelagh and Parsons, though they were members of the administration, were willing to take advantage of the increasing embarrassment of the lord deputy and their example would be followed in the commons. Unquestioned support of the deputy during the first session, while Wentworth was present, easily turned to a lukewarm attitude in the second. In the complex situation of mid-1640, abstention from voting could embarrass Wandesford as much as direct opposition. Thus it can be seen how Wentworth's own party, consisting of office holders elected under his influence, might easily melt away during the second half of 1640 when it became more and more obvious that his star was on the wane.

Nevertheless there was a group of members upon whose loyalty Wentworth could rely. They included in the first place those who were closely associated with him in the administration—George Radcliffe (Co. Sligo), Philip Mainwaring (Carysfort) and John Borlase (Belturbet). All of these had been brought over from England by Wentworth.[3] With them may be linked the three Wandesfords who sat for Inistiogue, Clogher and Lifford, Thomas Radcliffe (Sligo) and Captain John Borlase (Enniskillen). Other members of the deputy's party were Robert, Lord Dillon of Kilkenny West (Trim) who was a defence witness at Wentworth's trial,[4] Lucas Dillon (Co. Roscommon), and Adam Loftus (Newborough), with their various associates. Two Yorkshiremen could also be relied upon by the deputy; Sir Thomas Wharton[5] (Callan)

---

[1] He was back in the Irish house of commons for the session beginning 11 May 1641. *Commons jn. Ire.*, p. 204.

[2] See above, p. 78, 116, 185.

[3] John Borlase had been specially summoned to be master of the ordnance, a post which Piers Crosby hoped for. Strafford MSS., vol. 8, 29 May 1634.

[4] Rushworth, *Trial*, p. 191.

[5] Brother of Philip, 4th Lord Wharton. Burtchaell, *Kilkenny Members of Parliament*, pp. 36–7.

who was a personal friend of Ormonde and Robert Maude
(Inistiogue), son-in-law of Christopher Wandesford. Thomas
Little, father and son (Cashel and Banagher), and Joshua Carpenter (Carlingford) had been closely connected with the deputy,
in particular over the tobacco monopoly. Maurice Williams
(Askeaton) was Wentworth's personal physician. William Sambach (Carrickfergus) proved his loyalty during the second session.[1]

With this personal following in the Irish house of commons and
with the general support of the office holders it was not surprising
that Wentworth was able to run the first session as he wished. As
time went on, however, the position of the administration clearly
deteriorated. The eclipse of the deputy is borne out by a simple
comparison of the composition of the committee of privileges[2]
which was formed during the first session, at a time when Wentworth's power was still unshaken, with any of the larger committees in the third session. In March 1640, out of a total membership of sixty-one in the committee of privileges, only nine were
Anglo-Irish, whereas at least twenty-four had definite official connections. Of these, twelve belonged to Wentworth's inner group.
A year later in February 1641 the committee formed to administer
the levying of the subsidies contained none of Wentworth's
group.[3] This committee numbered twenty-five of whom eleven
were Anglo-Irish. Another committee formed at the same time to
draw up charges against Carpenter numbered twenty-three,
twelve of whom were Anglo-Irish.[4]

So far we have distinguished three main groups in the Irish
house of commons; firstly the Anglo-Irish, secondly the convinced
new English opposition and thirdly the party of the lord deputy.
The history of the year 1640 showed the gradual defeat of the lord
deputy's party and the rise of the other two to control the house.
But as time went on the position became more complicated. The
execution of Wentworth in May 1641 removed the main danger,
so far as Ranelagh, Parsons and Clotworthy were concerned. They
presumably hoped that they would inherit the position and power,
if not the policy, of Wentworth, hence the influence of the lords
justices now began to make itself felt in the house. The field upon
which they chose to do battle was the impeachment proceedings.[5]
Impeachment was a new political expedient in Ireland and Parsons

[1] See above, p. 190.   [2] *Commons jn. Ire.*, p. 137.
[3] Ibid., p. 171.   [4] Ibid., p. 172.   [5] See below, p. 211.

clearly felt that if it were allowed to proceed unchecked an effective political weapon would be placed in the hands of the opposition. Two of his former colleagues in the Court of Wards, Bolton and Lowther, were being impeached along with Bramhall and Radcliffe and Parsons himself was a not unobvious choice for a future impeachment. In the middle of 1641, therefore, the Irish administration, under Parsons and Borlase, tried to regain control of the house of commons.

The trial of strength took place on 23 June 1641.[1] The speaker of the house reported that the lords justices did not wish the impeachment proceedings to be proceeded with. The house went into a grand committee to discuss the question and a dispute arose as to which member should take the chair. There were two rival candidates, one, Hugh Rochfort (Fethard, Co. Wexford), who belonged to the Anglo-Irish party,[2] the other Robert Brereton (Old Leighlin) who had official connections. The split between the 'administration' and 'opposition' was revealed also in the tellers: St. Leger, lord president of Munster, and Sir James Ware on the one hand, and Audley Mervin and Richard Barnewall on the other. The importance of the tellers also perhaps may be taken as evidence of the importance of the occasion. The result of the voting was in Rochfort's favour, on the first count by 67 to 56 and in the second by 64 to 56.[3] From this, three conclusions may be drawn. In the first place, only half the members still seemed to be attending the house, which was not surprising in view of the unprecedented length of this parliament. Secondly, the gap between the administration and the opposition was by no means large. Thirdly, the opposition for the moment still retained the initiative, but as times became more 'normal', the pendulum would tend to swing back in favour of the administration. In June 1641, however, it seems clear that there was still a political alliance between the Anglo-Irish and a group of new English. This is indicated by the membership of the impeachment committee and by the fact that Audley Mervin acted as teller along with the Anglo-Irish Richard Barnewall. How long that alliance was likely to last it was impossible to say.

[1] *Commons jn. Ire.*, p. 239.
[2] He was expelled from the House in June 1642, along with the other Confederates.
[3] *Commons jn. Ire.*, p. 239.

The third party in the commons was that of the administration, which, for the first time since June 1640, was beginning to assert itself with any degree of success. Parsons and Borlase were now endeavouring to restore the authority of the administration to the level which it had achieved in the first session under Wentworth. The rising of Phelim O'Neill came at just the right moment for it to be used by Parsons against his political opponents. He was presented with an opportunity to split the alliance of the old English and new English opposition parties.

14

THE IMPEACHMENT OF WENTWORTH

WE may now return to the chronological history of events during the second half of 1640 and the first half of 1641.

On 1 October 1640 the Irish parliament met for its third session.[1] Before the adjournment took place in June, a Committee of Grievances had been set up, consisting largely of those members who lived near Dublin. Out of a total of thirty-five, there were at least a dozen members, with strong official connections, including Borlase, Parsons, Sambach, Usher, Davis, Ware and one of the Wandesfords, whereas there were only three 'opposition' members from Ulster and only six Anglo-Irish.[2] The large official element in this committee made it an unlikely instrument for any opposition group and it is certain that any planning ahead by the opposition did not take place in this committee. Subsequent events in November, however, made it clear that there was co-ordination between Pym's party in England and some of the Irish opposition in Ireland.

The machinery by which this co-ordination was brought about can only be guessed at. It is clear, however, that Sir John Clotworthy played an active part in linking together opposition elements in Ireland with those in London. He himself was related by marriage to Pym and he was also a son-in-law of Viscount Ranelagh.[3] In his own person therefore, he provided a connection with the Boyle-Ranelagh-Coote group in Ireland and the Puritan party in England. He was also an Ulster planter in his own right, he was the agent in Ulster of the London Companies and he had a more personal grievance against Wentworth in that his wife had suffered imprisonment during the recent persecution of Presbyterians in Ulster. It was more than a coincidence that Clotworthy should be elected to the Long Parliament as member for Maldon, Essex, a borough which was under the control of the earl

[1] 1 Oct. 1640–5 Mar. 1640/1.   [2] *Commons jn. Ire.*, p. 149.
[3] For a sketch of his career, see M. F. Keeler, *The Long Parliament*, p. 136.

of Warwick, a close political associate of Pym. To make doubly
sure that Clotworthy would be present at Westminster for the
opening of Parliament, he was also found a seat at Bossiney in
Cornwall. (Not far away at Callington, another critic of Wentworth, Sir Arthur Ingram, found a seat.)[1]

The presence of Clotworthy in Pym's party was a sign that
Wentworth's Irish administration was to be used against him.
There was only one constitutional method of bringing down a
king's minister, namely, impeachment, which had been used
successfully against Cranfield in 1624, though it had failed
against Buckingham in 1626. Pym's difficulty was to find convinc-
ing charges, especially as Wentworth had exercised power in
England for only a year. The real charge, in fact, against him was
what he might do in England, not what he had done. It was
obvious, therefore, that Wentworth's record in Ireland would
have to form the main basis of the impeachment. In fact, out of
the twenty-eight articles of the impeachment, over half were concerned with Wentworth's behaviour as lord deputy.

It is clear, from the articles of the impeachment, that it was
primarily the grievances of the planters against Wentworth,
which were regarded as important. It was they, the conquerors,
who resented the lord deputy describing Ireland as a conquered
nation which the king could dispose of as he pleased (Article IV).
Other articles referred to the ill-treatment received by Richard
Boyle, by Mountnorris, by Viscount Loftus, and by the planters
of Munster and Ulster. Wentworth was also accused of favouring
the papists and threatening the Ulster Scots. The whole tenor of
these articles relating to Ireland was to stress the way in which the
lord deputy had attacked the interests of the new English and the
Ulster Scots. They showed clearly that the old English had no say
in deciding the policy of the opposition in England. There was
no old English equivalent of Clotworthy to put their point of
view and their grievances were in fact largely ignored in the
articles of the impeachment. Eventually they were to find that in
defeating Wentworth they were merely helping to restore to
power the planter groups in Ireland whom Wentworth had for a
time displaced. All this, however, was in the future. For the
moment they were content to go along with Pym in bringing

[1] For a sketch of his career, see M. F. Keeler, *The Long Parliament*,
p. 229.

about the downfall of the hated lord deputy, who only a few months before had seemed securely in power. From November 1640 the attack upon Wentworth's administration was launched on both sides of the Irish sea.

In Ireland, parliament was summoned early in October, a full month before the Long Parliament met in England. During this month Wentworth was still the king's chief minister and his fall from power was by no means predictable. It was not surprising, therefore, that Wandesford had not accepted his defeat in the June session as final. He was determined not to give way over the plantation of Connacht and the Commission for Defective Titles and made no attempt to issue writs for the seven old English boroughs excluded from parliament. The opposition were not content with this and on 6 October a letter was sent to the lord chancellor asking 'in the name of this House' why no election writs had been issued. It was a sign of the mixed character of the opposition group that this message was presented by a combination of old English and new English, the members for Co. Limerick, Sir Edward FitzHarris and Sir Hardress Waller. A fortnight later, the question was still undecided.[1] Meanwhile relations between the lord deputy and the house had deteriorated still further, over the subsidies question. On 17 October, the house went into committee to discuss the method by which the three remaining subsidies were to be collected, and three days later detailed instructions were entered into the orders of the house. These were clearly opposed to the method which Wentworth had introduced in 1635 and which had been objected to in the June session. Wandesford refused to give way on the point and the offending page in the Commons journal was removed.

In all this, Wandesford was playing into the hands of Pym. He made no attempt to conciliate the Anglo-Irish and thereby divide the opposition against himself. The result, by the middle of October, was a deadlock, the resolution of which may be sought in the turn which events had taken in England. The Long Parliament met on 3 November 1640. In the Irish house of commons, the opposition presented its Petition of Remonstrance four days later.[2] The terms of the Remonstrance were in remarkable contrast with the later articles of impeachment in that they gave expression to the grievances of the old English as well as those of the planters.

---

[1] *Commons jn. Ire.*, p. 157.   [2] Ibid., p. 162.

Its complaints against Wentworth were numbered under sixteen heads—the decay of trade which was attributed to increased impositions; the arbitrary deciding of civil causes before the lord deputy and the proceeding in civil causes at the council chamber; the denial of the Graces, in particular, the statute of limitations; the extra-judicial voiding of letters patent; the monopoly of tobacco and other monopolies; the cruel usage of the city and inhabitants of Londonderry; the late erection of the Court of High Commission; the exorbitant fees of the clergy; the increased debts of his majesty in Ireland; the need for the permission of the lord deputy in order to leave the country, the 'quo warranto' proceedings against many ancient boroughs to show cause why they should send burgesses to parliament; the lack of freedom in parliament owing to the 'powerfulness' of some ministers of state; the immoderate fees in the courts of justice; finally, the decay of the gentry and the merchants, while farmers of the customs and others were greatly enriched.

The Remonstrance had been drafted with an eye to English politics. It emphasised those features of Wentworth's administration, which would have been equally criticised in the English house of commons—monopolies, High Commission, arbitrary government, the fate of the Londonderry plantation, the increased impositions and the attack upon what were described as 'many antient boroughs'. On the other hand, Anglo-Irish grievances which might have proved to be an embarrassment to Pym's party in the English house of commons were not stressed. The plantation of Connacht and the treatment of the Galway jury were not explicitly mentioned nor were the religious grievances of the Catholics, though they were implied in the general complaint about the denial of the Graces. The only Grace to be specifically mentioned was that referring to the Statute of Limitations and the implication here was that Wentworth had denied to the Irish the benefit of an English statute which had been passed in James I's last parliament.

Thus the Remonstrance was not either exclusively old English or new English. Its very existence showed that in Ireland there was a political alliance between these two groups. On arrival in England, however, only the planters' grievances in the document eventually found their way into the articles of impeachment.

By the time all the Irish agents had arrived in London, it was mid-December.[1] The attack upon the lord deputy had been launched a month before. On 6 November, the third day of the parliament, it was decided that Irish affairs should be referred to a committee of the whole house.[2] Sir John Clotworthy and his fellow member for Maldon acted as tellers. Five days later the committee to draw up charges against Wentworth was selected and on the same day freedom of passage between Ireland and England which since 1635 had depended upon the permission of the lord deputy[3] was requested. This was granted by the English privy council on 12 November,[4] making it possible for the Irish agents to cross.

Of the thirteen agents who made up the committee which took the Irish remonstrance to England after Wentworth's fall only four came from Ulster, but their influence, allied to that of Clotworthy, was to prove more effective than that of the majority. Edward Rowley (Co. Londonderry) was brother-in-law of Sir John Clotworthy and was related by marriage to Sir Tristram Beresford, who had recently been deprived of his estates;[5] Rowley as patentee for the customs of Down and Antrim had personally suffered financially when they had become incorporated within the general customs farm. Sir William Cole (Co. Fermanagh) had been associated from the beginning with opposition to the deputy and had been imprisoned by his orders before Wentworth had ever arrived in Ireland.[6] Richard FitzGerald (Strabane) despite his Anglo-Irish name, was new English by sympathy and in 1642 was the accredited agent of the lords justices by whom he was sent with dispatches to England.[7] The fourth Ulster member on this committee was a Scot, Sir James Montgomery (Co. Down) who had played safe while Wentworth was at the height of his power and had in fact signed the petition asking the lord deputy to devise some method by which the Ulster Scots could prove their loyalty to the king. When it became clear that Wentworth's power had declined, he showed his true colours. The political situation was most delicate and it must have been by no means clear what was the best course of action for the old English to adopt. They

---

[1] Carte MS (Bodleian), vol. 67, f. 63. 19 Dec.   [2] *Commons jn.*, ii. 21.

[3] Steele, *Tudor & Stuart proclam.*, ii. 35. 17 Sept. 1635.

[4] *Commons jn.*, ii. 27.

[5] Moody, *The Londonderry plantation*, p. 403.

[6] *H.M.C. Var. Coll.*, viii. 37.

[7] *H.M.C. Ormond MSS.* (new series), ii. 231; *Cal. S.P. Ire., 1633–47*, p. 188.

could not turn their back on their new English allies without
destroying their parliamentary majority in Dublin; on the other
hand they could expect far less from Pym and Clotworthy than
could Cole, Rowley and the other new English agents. Their best
hope of having their own particular grievances remedied, in
particular the rescinding of the plantation of Connacht, might
well have appeared to be with the king and the privy council,
in which Cottington still remained influential. Until Strafford was
removed from the scene, the old English were in a cleft stick.
The king for his part naturally wished to keep Wentworth's 'new
army' in existence in Ireland, as a card which might strengthen
his hand and since it consisted mainly of Catholics, his best hope
of doing so seemed to lie in enlisting the support of the Catholic
Anglo-Irish.

The first change which came about as a result of the arrival of
the agents, was the dismissal of Robert, Lord Dillon of Kilkenny
West, who had been one of Wentworth's closest associates, especially since the great political changes of 1635 and who had been
chosen as one of the lords justices after Wandesford's death.
Dillon was replaced by John Borlase, who also had close links
with Wentworth, but who was much less of a danger politically to
the opposition than Dillon would have been. The appointment of
Borlase, however, showed that the privy council were not prepared
to capitulate completely, even though they did not stand by Lord
Dillon. Borlase was a compromise candidate. There is no evidence
as to whether the Irish agents pressed for any other candidate as
their own preference.

By March 1641, differences of opinion had become unmistakable among the agents. John Barry, who was in London seeking
permission along with other Irish colonels to take 1,000 men into
the Spanish service, wrote to Philip Percival, brother-in-law of
Richard FitzGerald, one of the agents, giving some account of the
proceedings of the committee.[1] From the evidence of this letter it
seems that two Catholic Anglo-Irish members of the committee,
Barnewall and Plunkett, had been engaged in private negotiation
with the king; thanks to the influence of Cottington and others
favourable to the Catholics, they had been successful in bringing
about a reversal of the plantation of Connacht. Barry made out,
on the other hand, that other members of the committee were in

---

[1] *H.M.C. Egmont MSS.*, I, i. 129. 18 Mar. 1640/1.

favour of continuing the policy of plantation. It seems clear that at this date there was a rift appearing among the agents between the Anglo-Irish and the new English over the land question.

The artificiality of the alliance was emphasised by the policy of Pym's party in the house of commons. On 11 February 1640/1, Sir John Clotworthy and Sir Walter Erle reported to the house on the existence of the papist army in Ireland, 8,000 strong, of which Wentworth was still technically in command.[1] A genuine fear of Popery and the political need to provide a highly emotional background for the approaching impeachment of Wentworth combined to produce a continuous demand throughout March and April for the disbanding of the Irish army.[2] It was most unlikely that the grievances of the Anglo-Irish would be sympathetically listened to in this atmosphere. Pym himself had to handle the topic of Irish land titles at Wentworth's trial in a most delicate manner. His charge against Wentworth did not descend to particularities but kept to the general line that all men should be preserved in their estates and that if Wentworth had had his way, English land titles would have been in as much danger as Irish.

Wentworth's trial began on 22 March 1641. Before it had come to an end, the king had taken decisions which implied a complete reversal of Wentworth's policy in Ireland. The remonstrance had been first read to the king in council on 3 January 1640/1.[3] Three months to the day later, on 3 April 1641, Charles signed a letter which showed how successful the negotiations of Barnewall and Plunkett had been. The letter[4] declared that the Graces were to be enjoyed by 'all and everyone of our subjects' of Ireland. It requested that bills should be transmitted to cover the five specific points mentioned in the letter; these included the granting of free trade in corn with the king's dominions and those countries in amity with him, the passing of a statute of limitations on the lines of the English statute of 1624 and lastly the securing of the estates of the inhabitants Connacht, Clare, Limerick and Tipperary, since the royal intention was 'to forgo and discharge our intended plantations therein notwithstanding any office there found'.

All this had not prevented the Anglo-Irish from playing some part in the trial of Wentworth, but their role was a very minor

---

[1] *Commons jn.*, ii. 82.   [2] Ibid., pp. 99, 117, 119.
[3] *Cal. S.P. dom., 1640–1*, p. 406.
[4] Printed in *Commons jn. Ire.*, pp. 211–12.

one, by comparison with that of Ranelagh, Clotworthy, Sir Robert King, Mountnorris, Wilmot and the earl of Cork, all those in fact who, at Wentworth's coming to Ireland, had lost so much power in various ways. Viscount Roche, Donogh MacCarthy and Roebuck Lynch were witnesses on the charge that Wentworth had refused licences for visits to England.[1] John Walsh, Patrick Gough and Nicholas Plunkett were witnesses against the tobacco monopoly.[2] Nicholas Barnewall was a witness on two counts— Wentworth's alleged intimidation of the Irish house of commons in 1634[3] and his design against Scotland.[4] Their combined efforts, however, did not add up to a great deal against the background of the whole trial. It was natural that this should be so. In the first place, Pym could not afford to make too much use of Papist witnesses. Secondly, the negotiations with the king were going too successfully for the Anglo-Irish to want to prejudice their chances by supporting measures which could only embarrass Charles.

The question must now be asked how it came about that the Irish committee remained in England after April. Two reasons may be suggested. Firstly, the king's letter of 3 April had made no mention of the Londonderry plantation. The question had come before the house of commons early in March,[5] but it was not until August that the report of the commons committee was made known.[6] Their decision was wholly favourable to the London companies and the new English members of the Irish committee might well feel that it would be only a short time before the privy council could be prevailed upon to reverse the adverse Star Chamber decision of 1635. In the event it was not until after the Ulster rising of October that Charles finally gave way.

The old English members of the Irish committee for their part could not very well return to Ireland until the formalities had been completed in connection with the legislation mentioned in the king's letter. In order to comply with Poynings' Law, the legislation drawn up by the Irish privy council, had to be forwarded to England for approval by the English privy council before it could be submitted to the Irish parliament itself. The king's letter of 3 April thus merely marked the initiation of a legal process, which

[1] Rushworth, *Trial*, pp. 460 ff.   [2] Ibid., pp. 401 ff.
[3] Ibid., p. 112.   [4] Ibid., p. 534.
[5] Moody, *The Londonderry plantation*, p. 411.   [6] Ibid., p. 413.

was liable to take months. In view of the previous history of the Graces, it was natural that the agents should prefer to remain in London until the approval of the English privy council had been given.

Simon Digby and Geoffrey Browne took the royal letter to Ireland almost immediately. By 12 May, the required bills had been drawn up and had been sent over to London.[1] After this, progress was very slow. In view of the revolutionary atmosphere which existed in London, during and after Wentworth's trial, Irish affairs did not have the same priority for the English government as events nearer home. On 10 June, the Irish parliament petitioned for the bills to be returned to Ireland but there was no immediate response to their request. Some action was taken on other matters a month later when the king in council gave his decision upon the terms of the Irish remonstrance and ordered them to be entered in the acts of the Council.[2] The Court of High Commission was to be abolished. Customs rates were to be reduced and the statutes concerning the export of wool were to be repealed. The lord deputy and the other high officers of state were to be prohibited from taking up the farm of the customs. A decision over the Londonderry plantation was postponed on the ground that the matter was now in the hands of the English parliament. Still, however, the bills for the statute of limitations and the reversal of the plantation of Connacht failed to appear.

News of the English privy council decisions reached the Irish house of commons on 21 July 1641. But until the two bills arrived, the opposition was opposed to an adjournment.[3] In fact it was not until the 27 August that Lord Dillon reported to secretary Vane that the Irish committee had at last landed in Ireland with the two bills. All seemed well. Dillon wrote that 'the happie conclusion of the troubles . . . of that side is *instar omnium* and by the influence thereof I dare boldly saye his Majesties affairs in Ireland wilbe sufficiently quieted and secured maugre any opposition to the contrary'.[4] Meanwhile with the assistance of the 'Protestants' the lords justices had managed to adjourn the Irish parliament on

[1] Lords justices to Secretary Vane, 8 May 1641 (P.R.O., S.P. 63/259/f. 62. *Cal. S.P. Ire., 1633–47*, p. 282).

[2] *Cal. S.P. Ire., 1633–47*, pp. 317–22.

[3] *Commons jn. Ire.*, p. 263.

[4] Dillon to Vane, 27 Aug. 1641 (P.R.O., S.P. 63/266/f. 207; *Cal. S.P. Ire., 1633–47*, p. 340).

P

August 7.[1] Until parliament met again in November, after the harvest had been gathered in, the bills would have to wait. But a delay of three months seemed harmless enough. For the first time for twelve months the sky seemed comparatively clear on both sides of the Irish sea.

[1] Lords justices to Vane, 26 Aug. 1641 (*Cal. S.P. Ire., 1633–47*, p. 339).

15

AFTERMATH IN IRELAND

THE departure of the Irish agents for London in November 1640 meant that the Irish sub-plot became caught up in the main drama in a more direct manner than hitherto. This had the effect of taking out of Ireland the discussion of those political issues which were of major importance. For the moment, all was centred on London. The trial of the former lord deputy of Ireland and the redress of Irish grievances—these things were to be decided not in Dublin but in London. Direct action in the Irish parliament itself, so far as these questions were concerned, had gone as far as it could. The most that could be done at the moment was to keep in close contact with London, in case more information from Ireland should be required by those who were preparing the impeachment against Wentworth. Hence, almost as soon as the Irish house of commons had reassembled in January 1640–1, specific measures were suggested by the opposition majority to ensure this. The speaker was empowered to grant warrants for posthorses in England, or to press any ship into service, should extraordinary speed be required.[1]

But though the main drama was being staged in London, political questions in Ireland had their own intrinsic interest and importance. The Irish parliament sat from January 26 to March 4, and from May 11 to August 7. As time went on, the return of the agents from England began to be awaited with increasing impatience, but this was not the only political issue. It could hardly be expected that events in London, where drastic constitutional change was so much in the air, should have no influence in Dublin, and that the Irish parliament should confine itself to the details of financial administration, until the agents returned with the royal decisions upon the November Remonstrance. The house did occupy a good deal of its time with such things as the investigation of the tobacco monopoly set up by Wentworth in 1637 and

[1] *Commons in. Ire.*, pp. 167–8.

with taking decisions upon particular petitions which were presented to it. But it also concerned itself with two matters, which
had far-reaching constitutional implications, similar to those
which in England were implied by the Triennial Act and the
abolition of the Prerogative courts.

On 16 February 1640/1, twenty-one questions, which had
already been discussed and amended in the Grand Committee of
the house,[1] were drawn up in final draft for presentation to the
lords.[2] Two days later a small group, led by Sir Richard Blake, one
of the most prominent Anglo-Irish members in the house,
delivered the document at the bar of the lords and asked the lords
to order the judges in writing to answer the questions put to
them. Though the constitutional niceties of the relationship
between lords and commons were observed, it was more than
probable that the Anglo-Irish lords of the Pale, Gormanston,
Fingall, Slane and Netterville were working together with the
gentry of the Pale and elsewhere, men like Richard Blake,
Nicholas Barnewall and Nicholas Plunkett. Even though there is
no direct evidence it is difficult to believe that there was no
informal contact between the Anglo-Irish members of the lords
and commons.

The twenty-one questions were the so-called *Queries*, beginning
with the question 'whether the subjects of this kingdom be a free
people and to be governed only by the common laws of England
and statutes of force in this kingdom',[3] and going on to put more
specific questions, which clearly aimed at making an arbitrary
administration, like Wentworth's, legally impossible for the
future. The Court of Castle Chamber, the granting of monopolies,
the power of proclamations to alter the law—these and other
specific matters formed the basis of the document, upon which the
verdict of the common law judges was request. The *Queries* were
an attempt to have what were claimed to be the fundamental laws
of the kingdom restated in an unmistakable manner.

The form of this document was unusual, in that it resorted to
questions instead of direct statement, unlike the Petition of Right in
England in 1628. There were two advantages in this way of proceeding. In the first place, the house could claim that it was not
instituting any change, but merely seeking information about the

---

[1] *Commons jn. Ire.*, p. 173.   [2] Ibid., p. 174.
[3] Ibid., pp. 174–5.

fundamental laws of Ireland. Secondly, since the house was not proceeding by way of statute, it avoided the necessity of conforming to the conditions of Poynings' Law. The danger of delay in the English and Irish privy councils was by-passed. In the form of the *Queries* and the character of the individual clauses may be seen the hand of the common lawyer. The legal element in the Irish opposition was as important as in its English counterpart.

No answer to the *Queries* had been made by the time parliament was adjourned early in March. But within a few days of being presented, the *Queries* had been followed up by further constitutional innovation. On 27 February 1640/1, a committee of the commons, led by Audley Mervin, informed the lords of its intention to impeach Richard Bolton, lord chancellor, John Bramhall, bishop of Derry, Gerard Lowther, lord chief justice of the court of common pleas, and Sir George Radcliffe, former secretary of the lord deputy. This may be regarded partly as an Irish parallel to the impeachment of Wentworth and an attack to reinforce Pym's own attack on the lord deputy by an indictment of Wentworth's associates; and partly as an attempt to bring pressure on the judges to answer the *Queries*.

Impeachment as such was a constitutional innovation in Ireland.[1] The only argument which could be brought in support was argument by analogy from England. In the existing situation, hard-pressed financially as they were, the lords justices were in no position to defeat the opposition. Despite the efforts of Ormonde in the lords, Bolton and Lowther were ordered, on 4 March, to be committed 'by most voices'.[2] Radcliffe was already in prison in England.[3] The new English Lord Lambart played a prominent part in pressing home the attack in the Irish house of lords.[4]

At this point, parliament was adjourned, in spite of protests, until May. Clearly the administration had decided upon delaying

---

[1] Even in England, the re-invention of impeachment as a political weapon after well over 150 years of disuse was tantamount to a constitutional revolution. Cf. M. V. Clarke, *Fourteenth-century studies*, pp. 266–9.

[2] *Lords jn. Ire.*, pp. 165 ff.

[3] *D.N.B.* Bramhall was also imprisoned, but was released thanks to the influence of Ussher. Cf. *D.N.B.* under 'Bramhall'.

[4] *Lords jn. Ire.*, p. 166. 27 Feb. 1640–1. Charles, Lord Lambart, later earl of Cavan, was son of Oliver Lambart who had fought with Mountjoy. He sat for Bossiney, Cornwall in 1626 and 1628–9, one of the two boroughs that Clotworthy had in 1641. He was son-in-law of the earl of Radnor. Close investigation might reveal links with the English opposition.

tactics, with regard to the impeachments and for that matter the *Queries*. Were the impeachments allowed to proceed unchecked, a new weapon would be placed in the hands of the Irish opposition, and the next to suffer might well be Parsons and Borlase themselves. When parliament met again, however, the *Queries* and the impeachment continued to be pressed home by the opposition. On 13 July the house of commons was still debating the *Queries* and on 26 July, as part of an attempt to take the issue further, the house voted on each of the Queries, 'nullo contradicente'.[1] More dangerous from the point of view of the administration was the fact that the opposition was still persisting with the impeachments. On 23 June, the lords justices had made it clear that they were against this development; but at a trial of strength, in a house of 120, they could not muster enough votes and were defeated by a small margin.[2] On 30 June, the lords justices informed secretary Vane that the commons were still determined to impeach the lord chancellor, Bolton, and the lord chief justice of common pleas, Lowther.[3] Three weeks later, according to Parsons, the house was still pressing hard for 'judicature'.[4] The commons impeachment committee was authorised by the house to seek permission to inspect all official records from 1633 to 1641.[5] The impeachment committee was equally balanced between Anglo-Irish and new English, thus showing that the alliance between the two groups persisted even in the face of the displeasure of the administration. The membership was as follows:[6]

Anglo-Irish	New English
Patrick Darcy	Audley Mervin
Garrett Cheevers	Simon Digby
Maurice FitzGerald	Archibald Hamilton
Richard Blake	Peregrine Bannister
Richard Barnewall	Oliver Jones
Christopher Bellew	William Cadogan
Brian O'Neale	Matthew Derenzi
John Dongan	
John Taylor	

Right up to the adjournment of the house on 7 August, the *Queries* and the impeachments remained live issues, causing tension between the administration and the opposition groups.

[1] *Commons jn. Ire.*, p. 269.   [2] Ibid., p. 239.
[3] *Cal. S.P. Ire., 1633–47*, p. 308   [4] Ibid., p. 323.
[5] *Commons jn. Ire.*, p. 249.   [6] Ibid., p. 249.

Two other matters may now be mentioned—firstly the financial weakness of the administration. In June 1641, crown debts in Ireland stood at £140,000, a figure higher than that at the beginning of Wentworth's deputyship, despite the fact that he had managed to pay off the main debt. Income from customs, the Court of Wards, plantations and granting licences for the sale of wine, etc., had fallen considerably.[1] The parliament had taken measures in February for the levying of the second and third subsidies as a result of a letter from the agents, advising the opposition to show goodwill. But in June the subsidies were reported to be late coming in and, presumably as a result of the changed method of collection, to be small in amount.[2] While it lacked money, the administration could do little but employ delaying tactics and this in fact was what Vane himself advised in August 1641, so far as the *Queries* were concerned.[3]

In the second place, the fate of Wentworth's army remained to be solved satisfactorily. The clamour in the English parliament was met in May 1641, when the army was formally disbanded.[4] In fact, however, the 8,000 men did not disperse, since it was probable that they would be taken into the service of the king of Spain. One contingent of 1,000 men, under the command of Colonel Christopher Bellings, actually did leave before the month was out,[5] but no others had left by the end of June, although the colonels concerned had actually been granted their warrants. In the event, however, the foreign policy of England took an anti-Hapsburg turn, with the result that the remaining troops were forbidden to go abroad. On 30 July 1641, the reasons given for the withdrawal of the warrants to the colonels were set down in the Commons journal.[6] The commanders concerned still had hope in view of the non-committal answer given by the king on 8 August.[7] 7,000 trained men were therefore still waiting to leave Ireland for service abroad during the weeks following the adjournment of the Irish parliament.

To conclude, none of the issues which had occupied the attention of the Irish parliament during the first eight months had

[1] *Cal. S.P. Ire., 1633–47*, p. 299.
[2] Ibid., p. 299.   [3] Ibid., p. 340.
[4] Ibid., p. 290.
[5] Gilbert, *Ire. confed.*, i. 217–19.
[6] *Commons jn. Ire.*, pp. 276–7.
[7] Gilbert, *Ire. confed.*, i. 224–5.

reached a definite decision. The bills for Connacht and the Statute of limitations, which would have helped to ease the tension, had not yet arrived. They did arrive, it is true, before the end of August, but they had still to pass through the Irish parliament, and the lords justices were advising the king to be in no hurry to give his final approval.[1] The *Queries* still hung fire, and so did the impeachments. Finally, the army of 7,000 men, raised by Wentworth early in 1640, waited impatiently for permission to go abroad.

It was against this background of distrust and antagonism between the administration and the opposition that the rising in Ulster took place at the end of October.[2] The reasons for this lie outside the scope of the present work, and its whole history is far too entangled for short and summary treatment. One point may be made, however, that the Anglo-Irish showed no enthusiasm for the rebellion. At an emergency meeting of the Irish parliament[3] held on 16 November 1641, Thomas Bourke, Richard Bellings, Patrick Darcy, Nicholas Plunkett, James Cusack, Hugh Rochfort, Tibbot Taafe and John Bellew—all prominent Anglo-Irish members of the commons—were all present. Thomas Bourke declared that the house would not lose a day in taking a decision to vindicate the king's honour against the rebellious factions of the north. Patrick Darcy referred to the rebels as 'the enemy'. They all opposed the prorogation of parliament till January, since this would leave the initiative at a crucial period in the hands of the administration.

Parliament was prorogued, however, and by the time it met again on 11 January, the lords of the Pale were in arms. On 8 December 1641 Lords Fingall, Netterville, Gormanston, Slane and Richard Barnewall, James Bathe and Nicholas Darcy issued the 'Humble Apology' of the English Pale for taking arms.[4] The earl of Westmeath refused to join them. Nicholas Barnewall fled to England. Lord Howth and Lord Dunsany threw in their lot with the administration. The choice in fact was a difficult one to make, but it had to be made. The Catholic Anglo-Irish had to

---

[1] *Cal. S.P. Ire.*, *1633–47*, pp. 328–9.

[2] In August 1638 Wentworth had heard rumours that there would be a rising at the slightest sign of unrest. Wentworth to Argyll, 28 Aug. 1638. Strafford MSS., vol. 10, f. 168–70.

[3] The house of commons numbered seventy. *Commons jn. Ire.*, p. 291.

[4] Gilbert, *Ire. confed.*, i. 237–41.

choose between Protestant English planters and Catholic Ulster Irish. In the end, most of them joined the Ulster Irish in an alliance which always remained uneasy.[1]

[1] The Adventurers Act of Feb. 1641/2 passed by the English parliament helped to preserve the alliance since it made no distinction between Gaelic Irish and old English but lumped all together as Irish rebels, whose land was to be confiscated.

16

CONCLUSION

THE historical importance of Strafford's deputyship has generally been recognised, but its novelty has been either exaggerated or misunderstood. More often than not emphasis has been placed upon his land policy or his economic policy. On the one hand, he has been seen as a lord deputy who acted in the interests of the smaller proprietors against the greater, and on the other as a statesman who, though he crushed the Irish woollen trade yet was sufficiently farsighted to establish linen as a substitute. Alternatively, he has been seen as leading a crusade against the vested interests of a corrupt society in the name of a higher, traditional social code. There is little justification for these points of view. The supposed violent contrast between the land policies of Strafford and those of his predecessors did not exist. It is significant that though Richard Boyle was in political disgrace, Strafford made no attempt to dislodge planters like Parsons, Coote and Jones from their niche in the administration. Parsons remained as master of the Court of Wards and the activity of the court went on unchecked. The policy of plantation which had been temporarily halted under Falkland was continued under Strafford and the general effect of his land policy was to increase the sense of insecurity among a class which had so far been unaffected, namely the old English gentry. By 1640, Strafford himself had become a planter with great estates in Ireland and formed a part of the same group which he had so bitterly criticised on his arrival in 1633.

Nor can it be maintained that Strafford's economic policy marked a departure from that of his predecessors. His attitude towards the Irish woollen industry was essentially the same as that which had been followed for over half a century. His linen scheme was a private monopoly typical of the period and for the short time that it was in operation seems to have had a disastrous effect upon the export of linen yarn from the ports of the north-east coast. Its importance has been exaggerated out of all proportion by historians looking for profound policies where none existed. Strafford's economic schemes, the customs farm, the tobacco farm and the linen monopoly, contained little that was new. They were typical examples of the way in which during this period public enterprises were combined with private profit. Strafford may have been critical of the standards of his day in this matter but his own practice was not so very different from that of Richard Boyle. In no instance can it be said that thoughts of private profit were far from Strafford's mind. If he is not to be condemned for this, then his own criticisms of his fellow courtiers cannot be taken as seriously as he himself intended.

The real novelty of Strafford's deputyship lay elsewhere. It was, in the first place, an attempt by a prominent member of the English privy council at direct colonial administration of the whole island. Unlike his immediate predecessors, Strafford was an important English politician in his own right and he enjoyed the confidence of the king and of Laud throughout his whole period of office. This was in itself a novel departure, which brought in its train a great change in Anglo-Irish political practice. It made extremely difficult what had become the usual tactic of opposition, namely to go behind the lord deputy's back to Whitehall. This had often succeeded under Falkland but failed in every case under Strafford. The letters which passed between the lord deputy and the king were not only extremely numerous, they also reveal that for the most part Strafford could rely upon the support of Charles I, even when Portland was his bitter critic. Neither Boyle, nor Mountnorris, nor any of the Catholic old English gentry made any real headway in England during these years. The solitary exception was Clanrickarde, the plantation of whose lands was reversed during the Scottish crisis of 1638–9.

The second novel feature of Strafford's deputyship lay in the field of financial administration. For the first time since the later middle ages, the English government was not called upon to make a substantial contribution to the Irish exchequer or to give way on important issues in return for a subsidy from the Irish parliament. Strafford was successful far beyond the dreams of Chichester or Falkland in solving the financial problem and it was this success which made possible the freedom of action enjoyed

by the administration during these years. Financial success however, was only gained at a price. Fiscal pressure upon the gentry
and merchants combined with an unsettling land policy to create
a potentially dangerous situation among the old English, while
at the same time the absence of any reason for constraint made
Strafford contemptuous of opposition in other quarters. The
seeds of eventual disaster lay within Strafford's financial achievement. Had he not been so successful he might well have been
forced to recognise the existence of political realities which were
in the long run to prove too strong for him.

Finally there was Strafford's religious policy. For the first time
since the Reformation the persecution of Protestants took place
in Ireland at the hands of the Court of High Commission.
Strafford's links with Laud, which were a political asset in the
internal politics of the English Privy Council, proved to be a
liability in Ireland, since they committed him to a policy which
ran counter to the accepted Protestant norm in Ireland. Over
doctrine, discipline and the resumption of church lands and
impropriate livings, Strafford aroused the sternest opposition,
particularly among the Scottish Puritans of Ulster. Strafford's
religious policy was carried out without a real possibility of it
striking permanent roots and though, given the existence of
Charles I and of Laud, it was bound to be attempted, it is difficult
to resist the conclusion that it was almost completely miscon-
ceived. The Catholics benefited from continued toleration but
not so much on principle as because the lord deputy felt his
hands were sufficiently full without this additional problem.

With policies destined to arouse grave discontent, it was calami-
tous that a man of exceptional administrative ability should have
been chosen to carry them out. Strafford's very talents proved to
be the source of disaster in themselves and he succeeded in a way
that was beyond his immediate predecessors in increasing the ten-
sions of a political society already strained beyond the normal
even for the early seventeenth century. Yet it would be unjust
to lay wholly at Strafford's door the blame for the decade of
disaster which followed his fall from power. It may even be maintained that his deputyship postponed what was almost inevitable,
since the indiscriminate pressure which he exercised on so many
groups had the effect of uniting against him, however temporarily,
the diverse elements of Irish political life. The rising of the dis-

possessed Irish in Ulster had nothing to do with Strafford and was bound to have taken place sooner or later. What is surprising is that it did not occur in 1625 during the Anglo-Spanish war, when opportunity to reverse the plantation presented itself. Had it occurred in 1625 it is probable that the Catholic old English would have refused to join the Ulster Irish against the administration. Fifteen years later, however, the old English had experienced the results of complete exclusion from power, and Strafford's land policy had given them misgivings for the future. In 1641, they rose in protest against the lord justice, Sir William Parsons, who stood for Strafford's land policy at its most sinister.

By the middle of 1641 it was clear that Strafford's deputyship had been a failure. His policies, religious and otherwise, had been reversed in every important feature. Connacht was never to be planted with English settlers as he had envisaged; instead, by a strange irony it became the refuge of those old English proprietors who were driven out of Leinster and Munster by Cromwell. In religious matters, Strafford's policy had an adverse effect upon the interests of the church which he had favoured and his vision of absolute monarchy, operating as the only completely free agent in a world of vested interests, did not survive his death. Eventually, the English government was forced to compromise with Mammon and to govern throughout the eighteenth century by means of the same kind of established interest which Strafford had attacked.

The reasons for so overwhelming a failure are obvious enough. Strafford was attempting to impose unity where none existed. If there was a solution to the problems of the English government in Ireland, it did not lie in the direction of 'Thorough'. It was almost in the nature of colonial government that so drastic a policy should fail, since it took little or no account of the realities of the situation. An English lord deputy was essentially a new-comer who could hardly hope to govern without the assistance or consent of existing groups. Every previous lord deputy had been forced to recognise that his powers were limited and that if he wished to carry out a policy, it must be in alliance with one or more of the established interests. In choosing to aim at setting the authority of the Crown above the play of politics, Strafford was acting under the influence of Charles I. In a sense, he was another Buckingham, going even further than his predecessor in ignoring the need for concession and compromise. The influence of the king upon him, however, can be, and has been, exaggerated. Strafford ran on ahead of his master, who was exposed to other, less determined influences, such as the Queen, Cottington and Holland. Wentworth's request for an earldom in 1635 was refused by Charles I, and over such issues as the customs farm and the Galway plantation, his policy was subject to criticisms which the King did not brush aside, and which Wentworth was required to answer.

Strafford's Irish policy was successful for a time but its eventual failure could be anticipated. The decisive factor was that of religion. Political absolutism was one thing, religious absolutism was another. Had Laudianism not been in power in England, Strafford might well have been able to rely upon the support of the Ulster Scots and the new English puritans. As it was, however, his Laudian church policy cut him off from the very alliance with the Protestants, which his policy of plantation in Connacht and elsewhere made essential. Some freedom of policy was possible; the absolute freedom which Charles I and Strafford aimed at was not. The surprising thing perhaps is that Strafford achieved so much of what he set out to do; had administrative ability been sufficient, his deputyship would have been a landmark. He was the first lord deputy to succeed at any rate for a time in carrying out a policy which had been conceived in England without regard for existing interests in Ireland. To regain the financial and political initiative in Ireland for the English privy council was a considerable achievement which only a man of Wentworth's abilities could have brought to completion. But it was all achieved at too high a price. Even where religion was concerned the same judgment must apply. It is true that Bramhall returned to Ireland as archbishop of Armagh in 1660, but the majority of Protestants preferred dissent to uniformity. Laudianism died in Ireland in 1640 and the Church of Ireland, which was restored under Charles II, became part of the defensive structure of a ruling class. The oath of supremacy and the sacrament were made into political tests to keep out the majority, not to force them in.

The unity which Wentworth had attempted to impose upon Ireland proved to be extremely short-lived and less than six months after his death had completely dissolved. It proved impossible to unite a country so deeply divided by religious and local loyalties. By 1642 there were to be two centres of administration and at least four armies all fighting for different aims in the name of the king. Wentworth's deputyship, spectacular as it was, had passed almost without leaving a trace. Yet the contending parties after 1642—Ulster Irish, Anglo-Irish, New English and Ulster Scot—were all striving to obtain for themselves the sovereignty which he had exercised. Those who eventually inherited it, after two decades of bitter struggle, were the descendants of those new English whom Wentworth had temporarily driven from power during the thirties. It was Roger Boyle, Viscount Broghill and Sir Charles Coote, sons of the Boyle and Coote of Wentworth's deputyship, who were in a position to dictate terms to Charles II at the Restoration. Broghill, not Ormonde dictated the Act of Settlement confirming, in the main, the Cromwellian settlement. In doing so he acted as the representative of the new English of Wentworth's time, who against Charles and Cromwell alike succeeded in maintaining their position in Ireland.

By comparison, the old English who had been so powerful in 1633 on Wentworth's arrival suffered a catastrophic political decline, which except for an Indian summer under James II was destined to be permanent. Wexford, Drogheda and the other main ports lost their Catholic populations under Cromwell and never again regained their old English character. The old English gentry suffered the same fate as the Ulster Irish and with a few exceptions found themselves swept from the land which they had held in Leinster and Munster. From their ranks were to be drawn many of the 'Wild Geese' which served with distinction in the armies of France and Spain. The Ulster Irish who headed the revolt in 1641 also failed to recover their old position and they found the task of overthrowing the plantations too much for their military resources despite the ability of Owen Roe O'Neill.

It would be too much to expect that a great part of Wentworth's policies should survive when all else changed. No lord deputy exercised again the power which he had, not even the deputies of the Lord Protector. After the Restoration, the real core of political power rested with a comparatively small group of landowners and it was with these that every chief governor had to come to terms. Wentworth's period of office proved to be a passing interlude between the two great revolutions of seventeenth-century Ireland—the Ulster Plantation and the Cromwellian Settlement. On the other hand, it may be suggested without undue paradox that he was the first and last lord deputy of Ireland.

APPENDIX I

MEMBERSHIP OF THE 1634 PARLIAMENT

IN 1585 the membership of the Irish house of commons stood at
126.[1] In 1613 it had increased to 232. The main reason for this
increase lay in the creation of 40 new boroughs to represent the
new planter interest; of these 18 were in Ulster and the remainder were
scattered over the planted areas of the rest of Ireland. Of the 232
members in 1613, 100 were Catholic and 132 were Protestant, a marked
change since 1585 when the Catholics had been in a complete majority.
By 1634 further changes had taken place, though by no means as
revolutionary as those which had occurred in 1613. It is proposed in
this appendix to examine county by county the membership of the
1634 parliament as a method of throwing light upon the balance of
political forces in Ireland during Wentworth's deputyship.

Numerically, the strength of the Commons rose from 232 to 256.
The preponderance of Leinster, a legacy from the days when the Pale
had provided most of the members, continued. In 1613, the number of
members from the Leinster counties and boroughs had been 88, compared with 54 from Munster, 26 from Connacht and 64 from Ulster.
In 1634, 106 members were returned from Leinster, 56 from Munster,
28 from Connacht and 66 from Ulster. If we examine each province
in turn it cannot be said that there had been any dramatic changes since
1613, so far as the representation in the house of commons is concerned.
In 1613, of the 88 members returned from Leinster, 55 were Catholic
and 33 Protestant; Protestant members were returned for the city of
Dublin and Trinity College, for Trim and Carlingford, for the 'planted'
King's County and Queen's County and for those Leinster boroughs
which had been newly incorporated in 1613, namely Carlow, Newcastle, Kilbeggan, Enniscorthy, Fethard and Wicklow. Athlone incorporated in 1608 also returned two Protestant members. The
remaining old boroughs and the unplanted counties returned Catholics.[2]

In 1634 the balance remained roughly the same. Of the 18 new
members, authorised or not, nine were Catholic and nine Protestant.
The question whether the 'Catholic' boroughs of Fore, Taghmon,

[1] T. W. Moody, 'The Irish Parliament under Elizabeth and James I' in
R.I.A. Proc., xlv, sec. C, no. 6 (1939).
[2] Athy returned one Protestant and one Catholic.

Bannow and Clonmines had the right to send members to parliament was disputed, but their members seem to have been allowed to remain until near the end of the parliament, before the decision went finally against them. If these new members are left out of account for the moment, there was no alteration in the relative position of Catholics and Protestants. Certain gains and losses cancelled each other out. The Catholics made gains at Newcastle (2 seats), Wicklow (1 seat) and Trim[1] (1 seat); the Protestants made gains at Kildare (2 seats), Athy (1 seat) and Callan (1 seat). If the new members are included, of the grand total of 106 for Leinster, 63 members probably were Catholic and 38 Protestant, while the religion of five remains uncertain for lack of direct evidence.

Munster in 1613 had returned 34 Catholics and 20 Protestants. In 1634, 30 Catholics were returned and at least 25 Protestants (the religion of two members remains doubtful).[2] The boroughs which had been incorporated in 1613 returned Protestant members in 1634 as they had done in 1613; Co. Limerick, however, where there had been a disputed election in 1613, and where two Protestants surprisingly had been returned, in 1634 sent two Catholic members to parliament. In Co. Cork, however, the lord president of Munster was elected as senior county member; and in Cashel, Thomas Little, Wentworth's secretary, was elected. In Dungarvan also at least one Protestant was elected. Co. Kerry returned two Protestant members in 1634 though the election of Sir Thomas Harris was later successfully challenged.

In 1613, 12 Catholics and 14 Protestants had been returned for Connacht; in 1634, 12 Catholics were returned and 16 Protestants. The new borough of Jamestown accounts for the increase of Protestant representation. The Catholics gained a seat for Co. Roscommon and at Tuam, but since they lost the two seats for Co. Leitrim the balance remained the same. There is some uncertainty about who actually sat for certain counties and boroughs, owing to discrepancies between the printed lists, but this does not affect the general picture of the religious position.

Ulster, as could be anticipated, remained an overwhelmingly Protestant bloc; however, whereas in 1613 one Catholic had been elected for Co. Monaghan, in 1634 two were, both being MacMahons and regarded as loyal Irish by the administration.

Taken by and large, therefore, the relative position of Catholic and Protestant remained in 1634 what it had been in 1613. Whereas in 1613 of a total membership of 232, 100 were Catholic and 132 were Protestant, in 1634 of the membership of 256, 107 were Catholic and 143

[1] Lord Dillon of Kilkenny West, the second member, was a Protestant.
[2] Though it seems probable that Boethius Clancy, who sat for Clare in 1613 and 1634, was Catholic. Cf. B. Jennings (ed.), *Wadding Papers*, p. 237.

Protestant, while the religion of six remains uncertain. Thus if the Protestant members remained united and attended the house regularly, they possessed a safe working majority.

LEINSTER

It is difficult to divide the counties of Leinster into simple categories to make for easier description. Certain counties of the 'Pale' such as Louth, Kilkenny and Meath were largely untouched by new English influence; others like Kildare, Dublin and Wexford returned both new English and old English members. Yet other counties like Carlow and Wicklow which lay on the borders of the Pale provided a mixture of Irish as well as old and new English, while planted counties like King's and Queen's counties returned new English representatives. Longford, though 'planted', returned Irish and new English but no old English. Few generalisations can be made therefore about Leinster and some attempt must be made to treat each county as a separate entity.

Louth

Louth County	*Sir Christopher Bellew; Christopher Dowdall*[1]
Drogheda	*Thomas Peppard; Richard Brice*
Ardee	*Thomas Kippoke; John Dowdall*
Dundalk	*Peter Clinton; Oliver Cashell*
Carlingford	John Travers; Joshua Carpenter

The representation of Louth was almost entirely in the hands of the Anglo-Irish, the only exception being the borough of Carlingford. Both of the members for the county of Louth were important land-owners[2] and both could trace a long family connection with Ireland. A Philip Bellew was canon of St. Mary of Duleek in 1288,[3] while a John Dowdall is mentioned in the Patent Rolls in 1388.[4] The two members for Drogheda were both described as merchants. One of them, however, possessed a name which went back to the early days of the Norman invasion, and while there is no reason to assume that this merchant family in Drogheda was anything more than distantly related to Peter Peppard who was chief governor of Ireland in 1192, still no Peppard would regard himself as a newcomer to Ireland. The name appears in 1539, if not before, in connection with Drogheda.[5] Peppard's fellow member, Richard Brice, seems to have belonged to a newly-established family in Drogheda which even in 1641 held no land in

---

[1] Catholic names are printed in italic throughout.
[2] Book of Survey and Distribution: co. Louth (R.I.A. copy).
[3] *Cal. doc. Ire., 1285-92*, p. 183, no. 416.
[4] *Cal. rot. pat. Hib.*, p. 138, no. 25.   [5] *Cal. S.P. Ire., 1509-73*, p. 49.

Louth. In the obvious collections of documents the name does not occur before 1608; Richard Brice himself is mentioned as a witness at an inquisition held at Santry, Co. Dublin, in June 1615.[1]

Of the two members for Dundalk, one, Peter Clinton, belonged to one of the oldest-established families in the county.[2] The Dowdstown branch of the family to which he belonged seem to have first become prominent in Elizabeth's reign, though the name itself goes back to 1200. In a deposition of 1642 he was referred to as a lawyer[3] and in the same year he was to be indicted, along with other Anglo-Irish members of the house of commons, for high treason.[4] His fellow member, Oliver Cashell, belonged to a family which first appeared in connection with Dundalk in 1434;[5] by the mid-seventeenth century, however, the Cashells were prominent landowners in Louth.[6] A Cashell sat for the borough in 1613 and Oliver Cashell was to reappear in 1640; he and John Bellew were to take the Remonstrance to England in November 1640.[7]

The members for Ardee could also trace a long connection with the county. One was a Dowdall, member of a family which had provided a member in every parliament since 1559. Thomas Kippoke belonged to an important local family, which is mentioned as early as 1283 with this part of Ireland.[8] Thomas Kappocker or a namesake joined the Confederates in 1642.[9]

The great exception to all this was the borough of Carlingford, which being a military garrison, returned members favourable to the administration. Joshua Carpenter was associated with Wentworth in the tobacco monopoly for which he was to be expelled from the house in February 1641.[10] It seems likely, therefore, that in 1634 he—and his fellow member—owed their election to the influence of the lord deputy and would form a section of the small party with which he hoped to hold the balance of power in the house.

---

[1] *Inq. cancell. Hib. repert.*, Jas. I, Dublin, no. 28. The name also occurs in 1637 in connection with some dealings with Robert Barnewall, ibid., Chas I, Dublin, no. 55.

[2] J. B. Leslie, 'The Clinton family in co. Louth' in *Louth Arch. Soc. Jn.*, ii. 398–412 (Nov. 1911).

[3] Ibid., loc. cit., 404.

[4] Ibid., loc. cit.

[5] *Cal. rot. pat. Hib.*, p. 257 no. 52.

[6] Book of Survey and Distribution: Co. Louth (R.I.A. copy).

[7] Rushworth, *Trial*, p. 15.

[8] *Cal. doc. Ire.*, *1285–92*, p. 46. A receipt roll of Michaelmas 1285 records a payment of half a mark by Geoffrey de Keppok.

[9] T. Gogarty (ed.), 'County Louth Depositions, 1641' in *Louth Arch. Soc. Jn.*, iii. 169 (Dec. 1913).

[10] *Commons jn Ire.*, p. 183. 24 Feb. 1640/1.

Meath.

Meath County	*Nicholas Plunkett; Patrick Hussey*
Trim	*Robert, Lord Dillon; Valerian Weasley*
Athboy	*Richard Browne; Peter Tyrrell*
Navan	*Laurence Dowdall; Patrick Darcy*
Kells	*Walter Evers; Adam Cusack*

Meath was a county similar to Louth, a 'Pale' county in which the old English ascendancy was undisturbed and English traditions of administration had a long history. The only exception was Robert, Lord Dillon of Kilkenny West, who had thrown in his lot with the new order of things. His connection with Trim was a local one; he is described as being of Moymet, which lies two miles north of the town, in the vicinity of which Lord Ranelagh and Sir Arthur Loftus held land.[1] Trim had returned two new English members in 1613 but in 1634 one was Anglo-Irish, Valerian Weasley, who held land in Kildare as well as in Meath near Trim.[2]

The county members for Meath belonged to the old English families of Plunkett and Hussey, both of which had long connections with the county and the members for the remaining three boroughs belonged to similar families. Richard Browne sat for Athboy, a borough for which a Browne had been elected in two previous parliaments; he held land in the neighbourhood of Athboy,[3] but his fellow member derived from Westmeath. A Tyrrell, however, had sat for Athboy in 1585 and the nearness of the borough to the borders of Westmeath makes Tyrrell's election explicable.

The members for Kells belonged to Catholic families which held land in Meath. Laurence Dowdall sat for Navan, in the barony of which he was a prominent landholder. His fellow member, Patrick Darcy, had links with the town. He was later to play a part in the opposition to Wentworth over the Galway plantation.[4]

In Meath, as in Louth, county and borough members formed a homogeneous grouping, linked by family and religious ties and with strong and ancient local attachments to the area which they represented in parliament.

[1] *Civil Survey*, v. (Co. Meath), p. 168.
[2] Ibid., viii. (Co. Kildare), p. 133; ibid., v. (Co. Meath), p. 174.
[3] Ibid., v. (Co. Meath), p. 214.
[4] See above, p. 92. Patrick Darcy (1598–1668) born co. Galway: opposition leader in 1640 parliament. In 1646 took part in negotiations towards First Ormonde Peace. *D.N.B.*

Kilkenny[1]

Kilkenny County	Edward Butler; Robert Grace
Kilkenny	Robert Shee; David Rooth
Callan	Lord Henry Maltravers; Edward Comerford
Inistiogue	Griffin Murphy; James Dulan
Gowran	John Huckett; James Keely
Thomastown	Patrick Sherlock; James Walsh

Kilkenny was the third and last county of Leinster which it can be said was largely untouched by new English influence. The members for the county and boroughs for the parliament of 1634 were still as homogeneous in character as they had been in 1613 and before and as they were to be, for the last time, in 1640. They were Catholic landlords or merchants with a long tradition of loyalty to English methods of government and it was no accident that the confederates established their parliament and centre of administration here after '1641'.

The Butlers dominated Kilkenny and of the county members one was a Butler, though curiously enough this was the first time this had occurred since 1559. Sir Edward Butler's daughter married a Kavanagh from Co. Carlow so that here again hard and fast distinctions cannot be drawn between Anglo-Irish and Gaelic Irish. The remaining members were indeed a mixture of both.

The great Anglo-Irish families of Grace, Rothe, Archer and Shee dominated the parliamentary representation of the town and had a quasi-monopoly: in 1559 Shee and Archer were elected; in 1585 Rothe and Shee; in 1613 Archer and Langton; in 1634 Shee and Rothe; in 1639 Archer and Rothe. The Comerfords, a family like the Shees with a strong legal tradition, dominated Callan in the same way and a Comerford sat for this borough in 1585, 1634 and 1639; they were the types of a class which the coming of the new English had excluded from the administration and from high legal office. The remaining members for the boroughs of Kilkenny also had local connections. The only stranger was in fact Lord Henry Maltravers[2] whose seat in Callan presumably reflects the influence of the lord deputy, exercised through the medium of the earl of Ormonde.

To sum up, these three counties of Louth, Meath and Kilkenny

---

[1] Cf. G. D. Burtchaell, *Members of parliament for the county and city of Kilkenny*, and W. Healy, *History and antiquities of Kilkenny*.

[2] Maltravers wrote to Ormonde, 23 Aug. 1634, 'I beseech you my lord that some other may be chosen burgess in that place which you did mee the favour to have me chosen in'. N.L.I., Ormonde MSS. 2304, f. 235. Maltravers had been visiting Ireland on behalf of his father Arundel, member of the Irish committee of the privy council, who had been putting forward far-fetched claims to Leinster.

may be classified as Anglo-Irish, but there were four other Leinster counties in which Anglo-Irish control, to a greater or lesser extent had been affected by the introduction of new English elements, and it is to these four that attention must now be turned—Dublin, Kildare, Westmeath and Wexford.

Dublin

Dublin County	*Sir Nicholas Barnewall; Sir Thomas Luttrell*
Dublin	Nathaniel Catelin; Alderman Richard Barry
Trinity College	Sir James Ware; James Donnellan
Swords	*Lucas Nettervill; Richard Barnewall*
Newcastle	*Sir John Dongan; Patrick Sherlock*

In the representation for this county, there is a clear and obvious division between the city of Dublin and the rest of the county. The two members for the city were Wentworth's official candidates,[1] one of them, Catelin, becoming speaker of the house. The members for Trinity College, James Ware and James Donnellan, were also nominees of the lord deputy[2] and both of them were office-holders. After the Restoration, Donnellan was to become chief justice of the court of common pleas.[3]

The members for the county were the two most distinguished members of the distinguished Anglo-Irish families of Barnewall and Luttrell, and with them also can be linked the members for Swords. The borough of Newcastle was linked with Kildare rather than Dublin. It had been incorporated in 1613 and had returned two new English members, but in 1634 its members were two Catholic landowners from Kildare, who had some land in Co. Dublin and therefore fulfilled the qualification of residence upon which the old English party in the commons had insisted in 1613.

Kildare[4]

Kildare County	*Sir Nicholas White; Maurice FitzGerald*
Kildare	Christopher Wandesford; Philip Pillsworth
Naas	*Christopher Sherlock; William Archbold*
Athy	Maurice Eustace; Edward Blount

Kildare was a county which had long lain under the control of the old English. They still maintained control, a fact which is reflected in the members for the county, though two of the three boroughs returned new English. Maurice FitzGerald belonged to the old Geraldine house

---

[1] Wentworth to Coke, 24 June 1634, *Strafford's letters*, i. 270.
[2] J. W. Stubbs, *The History of the university of Dublin*, p. 68.
[3] Ball, *Judges in Ireland*, i. 337.
[4] Cf. T. U. Sadleir, *Kildare members of parliament 1559–1800*.

which had long been established in Kildare. The links of his fellow member with the county were however of more recent origin. Sir Nicholas White's connection with Leixlip did not go back further than the reign of Elizabeth[1] when in 1568 his grandfather had been granted the lands of the dissolved abbey of St. Katherine, near Leixlip. The Whites are indeed an example of a family which had acquired the position of landed proprietors as a result of their connection with the crown, Sir Nicholas White senior having been Master of the Rolls.

Most of the Eustace family were Catholic but Sir Maurice Eustace, most of whose lands were near Naas, was the exception in belonging to the new religion.[2] Athy lay on the borders of the county and its nearness to the planted Queen's County may account for its returning two new English members. Kildare as the seat of the bishopric may be regarded as the centre of new English influence. Philip Pillsworth's links with the borough were ecclesiastical in character; it is true that the Pillsworth family held some land in the county but hardly enough to make it of sufficient standing to be of parliamentary status, without some additional factor entering in. Pillsworth was in fact the eldest son of William Pillsworth, Bishop of Kildare (1604-36).[3] Christopher Wandesford probably owed his election to the influence of the lord deputy alone.

Kildare in short was a county in which the majority of the proprietors were old English and Catholic, while Athy and the town of Kildare were outposts of new English influence.

Westmeath

Westmeath county	*Sir James Dillon; James Dillon*
Mullingar	*James Christabel; Edward Pettit*
Athlone	James Coman; Edward, Lord Brabazon
Kilbeggan	Robert Birley; Edward Keating
Fore	*Sir Lucas FitzGerald; Thomas Nugent*

Two members of the old English family of Dillon were returned as members for county Westmeath.[4] Like the Butlers and the FitzGeralds a section of the family embraced the new religion and it is often difficult to decide which religion, Catholic or Protestant, any particular

---

[1] G. D. Burtchaell, *Members for Kilkenny*, pp. 6-7.

[2] The most likely explanation of this seems to be that one branch of the Eustace family embraced the new religion rather than that Maurice Eustace was a member of a family which had newly arrived in Ireland. Maurice Eustace of Castle Martin was a papist (Civil Survey, viii. p. 53); only the Harristown branch were Protestant. John Eustace of Harristown was Constable of Naas in James I's reign: this Maurice Eustace was his eldest son.

[3] Sadleir, *Kildare members*, p. 102.

[4] P.P. list gives Sir Luke FitzGerald as the only member for the county.

Dillon belonged to, especially as the Christian names 'James' and 'Lucas' are so common. It seems likely that the first member for the county was Sir James Dillon the elder, who had been associated with the Catholic protest against the 'Mandates' in 1605.[1] He was also to be prominent during the wars on the side of the confederates.[2] (It is difficult to believe that he was the Sir James Dillon who was in correspondence with Falkland in 1632 over the suggested plantation of Connacht.[3] A more likely person was Sir James Dillon 3rd earl of Roscommon, who was a Protestant and whose son, born in 1633 was given the name 'Wentworth'.)[4]

The James Dillon who was second member for the county may well have been Sir James Dillon the younger who is often confused with his namesake.

Of the remaining members three seem to have been Catholic. The borough of Fore appears for the first time in 1634 and may be regarded as an attempt on the part of the Catholics to increase their representation in the county, in much the same way as was being done in Wexford. The Nugent family who were prominent proprietors in Westmeath and who had been granted Fore priory in 1588 were probably behind the move. One of the members for the borough belonged to the Nugent family; (the other was Sir Lucas FitzGerald who had a good deal of landed property in the county[5] and who became a confederate after 1641.[6] One of the members for Mullingar belonged to a Catholic family which held land there in 1640[7] but lost it at the Restoration; in 1627 they were sufficiently prominent for Adam Pettit to be appointed one of the tax commissioners for the county.[8] James Christabel, the second member for Mullingar, may also have been a Catholic.

The other two boroughs, Athlone and Kilbeggan, were of a different character. Athlone, commanding the crossing of the Shannon and a place of great strategic importance, was a garrison town; it was therefore not surprising that one of its members, Edward, Lord Brabazon[9] should have had links with the administration. Fifteen miles away on the river Brosna the borough of Kilbeggan was under the control of the son of Lord Lambart, one of Elizabeth's soldiers, who had been granted the abbey lands of Kilbeggan.[10] Lambart's son had been raised to the peerage as earl of Cavan and he had therefore no need to sit

[1] Bagwell, *Stuarts*, i. 26.
[2] Gilbert, *Ire. confed.*, vi. 80. Cf. also *D.N.B.*   [3] See above, p. 88.
[4] Cf. *D.N.B.*, under 'Wentworth Dillon'.
[5] Westmeath, *Book of survey and distribution* (1852), pp. 5, 6, 27, 31, 65, 121,
[6] Gilbert, *Ire. confed.*, iii. 40. He was a member of Sir James Dillon's regiment, ibid., vi. 80.
[7] Westmeath, *Bk. of survey and dist.*, p. 28.
[8] *Cal. S.P. Ire.*, *1625–32*, p. 251.   [9] Cf. Burke, *Peerage*, under 'Meath'.
[10] His house was there. *Cal. S.P. Ire. 1625–32*, p. 34.

himself, but the two members for Kilbeggan inevitably were new English and one at least, Edward Keating, was an office holder; he was Comptroller of the Pipe.[1] Kilbeggan was a borough typical of those which had been created in 1613 and which were in reality garrisons protecting small plantations and without any roots in an environment which was largely hostile to them.

Westmeath, like Kildare, was an Anglo-Irish county in which the boroughs of Athlone and Kilbeggan marked the beginnings of new English infiltration.

The next group of counties to be discussed are those which had been planted; King's County and Queen's County in the sixteenth century and Longford and Wexford in the early seventeenth.

King's County

King's County	Sir William Colley; *Terence Coghlan*
Philipstown	Robert Leicester; Thomas Moore
Banagher	Sir Edward Bagshawe; Richard Pigott

This area, though nominally planted in the middle of the sixteenth century, remained in an unsettled condition until Mountjoy's campaign of 1601. The O'Mores, the O'Connors, the O'Dempseys[2] and other Irish families still remained in the area and must have formed the majority of the population, but their existence is not reflected in the returns to parliament. Terence Coghlan, however, was a Catholic who fought with the confederates in 1642[3] and his local ties were sufficiently strong for him to be re-elected to the parliament of 1640. The other members for the county, however, belonged to families which were granted land at the time of the original plantation in Mary's reign or had acquired land since by purchase or other means. Sir William Colley's estates were near Edenderry: he was a grandson of Archbishop Adam Loftus but the family originally seems to have been Anglo-Irish in character; Robert Cowley or Colley was Master of the Rolls in 1538.[4] Robert Leicester sprang from a planter family which had prospered and acquired more land;[5] Thomas Moore also was related to the Moores

---

[1] *Liber. mun. pub. Hib.*, pt. 2, p. 65.

[2] The territory of the O'Dempseys, Clanmalier, in the south east of Queen's County remained unplanted. Butler, *Confiscation*, p. 15.

[3] *Cal. S.P. Ire., 1633–47*, p. 403; Gilbert, *Ire. confed.*, iii. 215.

[4] The name Henry Coly occurs in the patent rolls in 1310 (*Cal. rot. pat. Hib.*, p. 16, no. 63.): in an account for the year 1542, several Cowleys are mentioned (*Cal. S.P. Ire., 1509–73*, p. 62). Henry Colley acquired his land in King's County in 1562 (R. Dunlop, 'The plantation of Leix and Offaly', *E.H.R.*, 1891, p. 35). He was seneschal of the county and constable of the fort of Philipstown until 1576. *Lib. mun. pub. Hib.* pt. 2. p. 128. His fellow member Richard Pigott had links with the neighbouring Queen's County.

[5] R. Dunlop, 'The plantation of Leix and Offaly' in *E.H.R.*, 1891, p. 95.

who were planters in Elizabeth's reign.[1] Sir Edward Bagshawe appears to have held no land in the county and we may infer from this that he owed his election to official influence; he was receiver of customs for the port of Dublin from 1624 onwards[2] and held land in Co. Dublin.[3]

Queen's County

Queen's County	Sir Piers Crosby; John Pigott
Maryborough	Sir Walter Crosby; Sir William Gilbert
Ballinakill	Richard Blacknall; John Ingersoll

All the members for Queen's County and its boroughs were new English in character. The Crosbys may have been of Irish descent but their link with the county was new English; Sir Piers Crosby was the son of Patrick Crosby who had been granted land in the county because of his scheme for transplanting native Irish families to county Kerry.[4] John Pigott of Dysart, his fellow county member, belonged to the family which had taken over Dysart O'Lalor, formerly the main stronghold of the O'Lalor family; he was to be killed defending it in 1646.[5] Sir Walter Crosby was the eldest son of John Crosbie, Bishop of Ardfert. Sir William Gilbert of Kilminshy had been appointed Constable of the fort of Maryborough in 1622;[6] there is thus no difficulty in explaining why he should sit as a member for the borough in 1634. The Gilberts and the Pigotts were still prominent in the area in the mid-eighteenth century.

The remaining members for Queen's County are more difficult to 'place'. The appearance of Blacknall and Ingersoll may be due to the ironworks at Mountrath.

The representation of Queen's County in 1634 left no doubt that the area was 'planted' with new English, though by comparison with the native Irish inhabitants they must have been comparatively few in number.

Longford

| Longford County | Roger Farrell; Faigney Farrell |
| Johnstown | John Ware; Edward Blaghan |

Longford was an area in which a significant change had taken place since the Parliament in 1613, a change reflected in the appearance of the borough of Johnstown.

The 'county' was a recent administrative creation and was in fact

---

[1] Ibid., op. cit.　　　　　　[2] *Liber mun. pub. Hib.* pt. 2, p. 147.
[3] *Civil Survey*, vii. (Co. Dublin), p. 163.
[4] Cf. *Kerry Archaeological Magazine*, iv. 1–15; 94–105.
[5] J. O'Hanlon and E. O'Leary, *History of Queen's County*, i. 270–1; ii. 524.
[6] *Liber mun. pub. Hib.*, pt. 2, p. 127.

the territory of the O'Farrells, who had come to terms with Elizabeth in 1570 and by 'surrender and regrant' had acquired a title to their land which was valid in English law.[1] If parliamentary representation can be taken as a guide, the O'Farrells seem to have accepted the new situation and were represented in the various parliaments from 1585 to 1640, though the uncertain nature of their loyalty to the English crown was revealed in 1599.[2]

In May 1618 the project for the plantation of Longford was sent to the English Privy Council—and during the following years it took place. Only a proportion of the land was confiscated, however, and there were 142 'mere Irish' and Anglo-Irish names among those who were allotted land. The plantation was hardly a success in a numerical sense and probably all that happened was a minor curtailment of the pastoral farming which was the main feature of the native Irish economy. The uneasy existence of a few nucleated settlements of the English type in a largely pastoral area was reflected satisfactorily enough in the returns of the parliament of 1634. The county members were Gaelic Irish: the burgesses of the newly created borough of Johnstown were new English,[3] neither had anything in common and the precarious nature of the plantation was to be revealed in 1641 when the O'Farrells re-established their control over the whole territory.

Wexford

Wexford County	*Marcus Cheevers; William Esmond*
Wexford	*Patrick Turner; Richard Cheevers*
Ross	*Nicholas Dormer; Peter Rooth*
Enniscorthy	Sir Arthur Loftus; Thomas Newcomen
Fethard	Nicholas Loftus; Richard Parsons
Bannow	*Pierce Nevill; Walter Furlong*
Clonmynes	*James Brian; John Cullen*
Taghmon	*Thomas Rothe; David Hore*
Newborough	Sir Adam Loftus; Roger Lort

Wexford, like Longford, was a planted county—but with a difference. The northern baronies of Wexford were still, in the early seventeenth century Irish in character, while the southern baronies were old English. A list of Wexford names drawn up in 1608[4] brings out clearly this distinction between the two areas; but by 1634 northern Wexford had been planted, thus leaving Wexford divided between new English and old English. The old English boroughs of Wexford and Ross

---

[1] *Cal. Carew MSS.*, *1515–74*, pp. 406–8.
[2] *A description of Ireland*, ed. E. Hogan (1873), p. 115.
[3] I have assumed that John Ware was related to Sir James Ware.
[4] *Cal. Carew MSS.*, *1603–24*, pp. 31–5.

returned Catholic members to the parliaments of 1560, 1585 and 1613 and the tradition was continued in 1634. The situation, however, had been complicated by the creation of two boroughs in 1613—Enniscorthy, which lay within the area marked out for plantation, and Fethard, a port on the south coast of Wexford which, though lying outside the plantation area, seems to have fallen under new English control. These two boroughs were joined in 1634 by Newborough (Gorey) which lay well within the planted area. It was presumably as a conscious reaction against this increase of new English influence, that the old English elected two members each for the boroughs of Bannow and Clonmines, both of which lie near Fethard, and for Taghmon, which is in the vicinity of Wexford town. These elections can hardly have been accidental, though there is no evidence of any deliberate plan. One strong argument for it, however, is the fact that the political tradition in Co. Wexford was concentrated in the hands of a comparatively small number of families.

Most of the families which provided members in 1634 had provided them in one or more parliaments before that date. David Hore sat for Taghmon in 1634; a Hore had sat for Co. Wexford in 1559. Pierce Nevill and Walter Furlong sat for Bannow in 1634; Nevill was presumably related to the Nevill family of Ross Garland and it is significant that the name Nevill was still to be found in 1659 in the barony of Bargy, where Bannow is situated. The Furlongs were another old Wexford family and a Furlong had represented Co. Wexford in 1613 and Wexford town in 1585, 1613 and 1639–42. After the death of Richard Cheevers during the 1634 parliament he was replaced by John Furlong. The Furlongs also had some local connection with Bannow, as a John Furlong was portreeve there in 1608. A similar kind of continuity is provided by the names Dormer and Turner. A Dormer sat for Ross in 1559 and for the same borough in 1634 and 1639. A Turner had been Mayor of Wexford in the middle of the sixteenth century and sat for Wexford town in 1613 and 1634. The name Cheevers in 1634 is borne by two members; Marcus Cheevers sat for the county and Richard Cheevers for the town. This name does not occur explicitly in the lists for recent parliaments but the Cheevers were clearly a local family of importance. A Cheevers had been Mayor of Wexford in the early fifteenth century; Richard Cheevers had been mayor in 1628 and Nicholas Cheevers was to be mayor in 1641. This family also played a considerable role on the confederate side in the years following 1641; Marcus Cheevers was appointed chief justice by the confederates, while in 1647 two members of the family acted as collectors of money for the confederate armies, in Co. Wexford and Wexford town respectively.

Thus, politically speaking, the branches of half a dozen old English families controlled Co. Wexford and its two ancient boroughs. In 1613 their local position was challenged seriously for the first time. Stated in general terms, a class of merchants and gentry were confronted by a newly arrived class of administrators and soldiers. The plantation of northern Wexford may not have been felt as a serious threat to their own position by the old English, but after the 1613 parliament the far-reaching consequences of the creation of new boroughs like Enniscorthy and Fethard could hardly be ignored.

Who were the representatives of the new arrivals in the 1634 parliament? The Loftus[1] family who were among the patentees for the plantation of Wexford seemed to have the decisive say. Sir Adam Loftus, who sat for Newborough, was the eldest son of Sir Dudley Loftus, son of Adam Loftus, late archbishop of Dublin (1567–1605). His brother Nicholas sat for Fethard in 1613 and 1634. Sir Arthur Loftus, member for Enniscorthy, was grandson of Sir Dudley Loftus. Two other members probably sat for Wexford boroughs because of their connection with the Loftus family; Thomas Newcomen, brother of Sir Beverley Newcomen and himself a member of a successful administrative family, was associated as joint clerk of the pipe with Nicholas Loftus.[2] Richard Parsons, son of Sir William, comes into the picture because he and his father were associated with Sir Adam Loftus at this date as joint surveyors of the royal estates.[3] The new English representation in Co. Wexford, like the old English, was linked by family and other connections.

It remains to discuss the unplanted counties of Carlow and Wicklow.

Carlow.

Carlow County	James Butler; (Morgan Kavanagh) Sir Thomas Butler
Carlow	Sir Barnaby O'Brien; James Rowson
Old Leighlin	Sir Thomas Meredith; James Cusack[4]

County Carlow was in theory an unplanted county but lying as it did on the border of the Pale and occupying an important strategic position, it would hardly have remained untouched by the revival of English power under the Tudors. The representation for the county and boroughs of Carlow does throw some light upon the situation as it was in 1634. Carlow was 'the country' of the Kavanaghs and Morgan Kavanagh, who had been elected in 1613 and who was the son of Donnell Spaniagh Kavanagh, was returned as a county member, though his election was subsequently declared invalid.[5] The politics which lie behind this disputed election remain hidden.

[1] Cf. Burke, *Peerage*, under 'Ely'.
[2] *Liber mun. pub. Hib.*, pt. 2, p. 64.   [3] Ibid., p. 56.
[4] P.P. List gives Richard FitzGerald as second member for this borough.
[5] Cf. Rev. J. Hughes, 'The fall of the clan Kavanagh' in *J.R.S.A.I.*, 4th ser., ii. 282–305.

Morgan Kavanagh was replaced by Sir Thomas Butler and the two county members therefore belonged to that branch of the Ormonde family[1] which had been established at Tullow since the early days of the Norman invasion and had maintained its grip ever since, providing a link between the Pale and the Butler territory in Kilkenny and Tipperary. If the representation for the county proved that local power in Carlow was still in the hands of Kavanagh and Butler, numerically it was outweighed by the new English boroughs of Carlow and Old Leighlin.

The connection of Sir Barnaby O'Brien with Carlow lay in the fact that his father had been made Constable of the fort in 1604.[2] He was elected for Ennis also and when he gave up his Carlow seat, he was succeeded by the new English Edward Harman, grandson of the Nicholas Harman who had been named one of the first twelve burgesses of the borough.[3]

Old Leighlin had not been made a borough in 1613; and one of its members, Sir Thomas Meredith, presumably owed his connection to his being the second son of a former bishop of Leighlin, Richard Meredith (1589–97). James Cusack, his fellow member, was old English, but as he was a King's Counsellor at Law from May 1633 and shortly to be clerk to the Commission of Defective Titles, he probably owed his election to the influence of the lord deputy.

The Bagnalls, who had provided one of the county members in 1613, and the Hartpoles, who were to provide one of the representatives for the borough of Carlow in 1640, were conspicuous by their absence. Perhaps the Butlers were regarded by them as providing the strongest representation for the old English cause in parliament.

Wicklow

Wicklow County	Sir Robert Talbot; *Brian Byrne*
Wicklow	William Usher; *James Byrne*
Carysfort	John Hoye; Gerard Slingsby

Before 1613, only the port of Wicklow, in which Ormonde's influence was strong, had sent burgesses to parliament. In 1613, the county was represented for the first time by two members of the O'Byrne family.[4] The division of the representation in the 1634 parliament

[1] Sir Thomas Butler was an illegitimate son of Sir Edmund Butler of Cloughgrenan, Co. Carlow and of Roscrea, Co. Tipperary. Edmund was the second son of James, 9th Earl of Ormonde. G.E.C., *Complete Baronetage*, ii. 1625–49, p. 258. Cf. also E. St. John Brooks, *Knights fees, Counties Wexford, Carlow, Kilkenny*, p. 79.
[2] *Liber mun. pub. Hib.*, pt. 2, p. 118.
[3] R. Malcolmson (ed.), *Carlow parliamentary roll*, p. 60.
[4] For a fuller discussion, see above, chapter 12.

was an indication of the plantation of certain parts of the county, notably Ranelagh in 1628. The borough of Carysfort, named after Falkland, was created in 1628, with a corporation consisting of a dozen planters,[1] among whom Parsons, Loftus and Roger Jones were prominent. Gerard Slingsby was a member of the administration; John Hoye (Hoyde) was possibly a relative of Thomas Hoyde mentioned among the original burgesses in 1628.[2] What was surprising about the situation in 1634 was that the O'Byrnes were still sufficiently strong to muster two members out of six in the face of competition from the administration. They were more successful in 1634 than they were to be in 1640 but by then the plantation of Wicklow had taken a further turn. Needless to say, in Wicklow as in so many other counties, representation in Parliament provided little or no evidence as to the real wishes of the majority of the proprietors. It was almost entirely an administrative arrangement the artificiality of which was to be revealed in 1641 when the O'Byrnes joined in the revolt.

MUNSTER

Like Leinster, Munster in the early seventeenth century was a confused mixture of different strains, Irish, Anglo-Irish and new English. Politically speaking, however, and with the 1634 parliament taken as an index of political power, the Irish had ceased almost completely to count; numerically, they may have been predominant but power administrative and otherwise, lay almost entirely in other hands. There was a remnant which had been found on the winning side in 1601, the MacCarthy Reagh family of Co. Cork and the O'Briens of Clare, and these preserved their lands and form of society intact for another half century; in general, however, Irish power was shattered, though the plantation of Munster is a misnomer and only a proportion of the province had in fact been planted. The struggle for power lay between the old and new English; but there were no untouched centres of old English power in Munster. The failure of the Fitzmaurice rebellion had removed what had been the equivalents of Meath or Louth in southern Ireland. Kildare and Wexford offered the truest northern parallels for the situation in the south; in the one, the Anglo-Irish and the new English confronted each other without an intermediary; in the other, the same situation existed with the additional factor of a disturbed Irish population. Limerick and Tipperary were counties in which political power—and land, the source of political power, lay still in the hands of the Anglo-Irish. In Cork and Kerry, the new English were largely in control. In Waterford the struggle between Anglo-Irish and new English was still undecided. Clare was

---

[1] *Cal. Pat. Rolls, Chas I.*, pp. 417–22.   [2] Ibid., p. 418.

the exception; there the lion lay down with the lamb and the O'Briens
and the new English shared the parliamentary representation.

Cork

Cork County	Sir William St. Leger; *Sir Donough MacCarthy*
Cork	*Sir William Sarsfield; Sir Dominick Coppinger*
Youghal	*Edward Gough; Theobald Ronane.*
Kinsale	*William Galway; Jacob Roche*
Mallow	William Kingsmill; Thomas Betsworth
Baltimore	Lott Peere; Edward Skipwith
Bandon	Sir George Wentworth; William Wiseman
Clonakilty	Sir Robert Travers; Sir Philip Mainwaring

The appearance of Sir Donough MacCarthy[1] along with Sir William
St. Leger,[2] Lord President of Munster, is a sign of the persistence of
some Irish power in Munster. But the MacCarthy was a solitary figure
in 1634; in the parliament of 1613, a Barrett had also been county
member and in 1639 a Barrett was to sit again for Cork City. A
MacCarthy had sat in 1613 and was to sit in 1639 again, but all the
rest of the representatives for the county and boroughs of Cork were
either Anglo-Irish merchants or members of the new English administrative or planter class.

If the county representation was divided between the old and the
new, so also were the boroughs. The old ports of Cork, Kinsale and
Youghal had sent members to parliament in 1559, 1585 and 1613 and,
as in Wexford, the same family names tended to recur. The Coppingers
provided a member for Cork city in 1585 and 1634 and for Youghal in
1585 and 1615. A Sarsfield who sat for Cork city in 1634 had sat also
in 1585: William Sarsfield was town clerk from 1628 onward.[3] The
Meades who sat for Cork city in 1559 and 1585 may have seen their
political influence decline after the incidents attending the proclamation of James I, though Sir John Meade was mayor of Cork in 1628.
In Kinsale the Roches were by far the most important local family, if
the parliamentary lists are a safe guide: they provided two members in
the three Irish parliaments of the early seventeenth century. The family
was an old one in the town,[4] John Roche having been provost at the
end of the fifteenth century, and Andrew Roche at the beginning of
the sixteenth, while a Roche was still provost for the years 1625 and
1635. Galway also was an old Kinsale name.[5] No doubt too much

---

[1] G.E.C., *Peerage*, ed. Gibbs, under 'Clancarty'.   [2] Cf. *D.N.B.*
[3] R. Caulfield (ed.), *Council book of the corporation of Cork*, p. 141.
[4] F. O'Sullivan, *History of Kinsale*, p. 219.
[5] Ibid., op. cit. In 1525 George Galway was provost: in 1566 William
Galway was sovereign.

R

significance should not be attached to the mere recurrence of these names without other evidence and too much stress should not be placed upon the differences between the Anglo-Irish towns and the native Irish hinterland. But the two ports of Cork and Kinsale did represent a long-lived Anglo-Irish element in the county, which was still strong in 1634. Youghal, on the other hand, might well have been captured by the newcomers. The strong plantations and the ironworks and timber trade of the Blackwater valley made it inevitable that Youghal would become new English eventually; but the influence of Richard Boyle, exercised from his residence in the Bishop's palace, was not strong enough to bring about the election of suitable new English members. Gough and Ronane in 1634 replaced the old names of 1613, Coppinger and Forrest,[1] but they themselves were almost certainly Catholic, the number of voters in the borough was only 142.

The four remaining boroughs, Bandon, Baltimore, Clonakilty and Mallow, lay within those areas of Co. Cork which had been planted and it was understandable that they would return new English members.

Of the eight members who sat for these four boroughs, only two, however, had no connection with Munster; they were Sir George Wentworth and Sir Philip Mainwaring, who were recommended to the earl of Cork by the lord deputy. Of the remainder, three at least were office-holders who had some connection with Munster; William Wiseman was clerk of the peace in Co. Cork and Co. Waterford until his death c. 1636;[2] Sir Robert Travers was a judge in the Munster court of Admiralty in 1626;[3] Lott Peere held some kind of official post, probably that of secretary to the Lord President of Munster.[4] Thomas Betsworth and William Kingsmill also may have had some local connection as their names are found in connection with Munster after 1641.[5] The eighth member, Edward Skipwith, was possibly a relative of Henry Skipwith who in James I's reign had been Constable of Castlepark, Kinsale.[6] Thus the majority of even the new English seem to have had some local connection.

Of the 16 members for Cork, a clear majority lay with the new

---

[1] The Ronayne family were old established in both Cork and Youghal. For Gough, see Davis, *The Patriot Parliament*, p. 160.

[2] *Liber mun. pub. Hib.*, pt. 2, p. 171.

[3] *Cal. S.P. Ire., 1625-32*, p. 171.

[4] R. Caulfield (ed.), *Council book of the corporation of Cork*, p. 139.

[5] *Cal. S.P. Ire., 1633-47*, p. 409. A William Kingsmill was lieut.-colonel of foot in the parliament forces in Munster, 1646, ibid., p. 447, but in 1641 a new writ was ordered for Mallow because William Kingsmill was thought to be dying.

[6] *Liber mun. pub. Hib.*, pt. 2, p. 125.

English, even though the new boroughs were small, isolated centres in hostile surroundings, as 1641 was to show.

Limerick

Limerick County	*Sir Edward FitzHarris; Richard Stevenson*
Limerick	*Sir Geoffrey Galway; Alderman Dominick White*
Kilmallock	*John Fox; Simon Haley*
Askeaton	Sir Hardress Waller; Maurice Williams

This county had been planted but not to the same extent as Cork or Waterford, and the representation therefore was largely in the hands of the old English. The two county members, Sir Edward FitzHarris and Richard Stevenson, were both prominent Anglo-Irish landowners,[1] and the former[2] had played a part in the agitation of 1628: he had been one of the representatives sent over to England in that year. He was later to suffer for his enthusiasm by incurring the displeasure of the lord deputy. The members for the city of Limerick were also Anglo-Irish: they were prominent burgesses with important holdings within the city[2] and one of them, Sir Dominick White, was to play an active, though administrative, part, with the Confederates after 1641.[3] Both Simon Haley[4] and John Fox[5] were landed proprietors in the neighbourhood of Kilmallock: neither of them seem to have played a part in the Confederate cause.

The plantation of Munster had been largely confined, so far as Limerick was concerned, to the barony of Connell, an area which had been a centre of Geraldine power and had escheated to the crown after the Desmond rebellion. Askeaton lay in this barony and it was natural therefore that two new English members should be returned. It is possible that both of them owed their election to the influence of the lord deputy. Maurice Williams was Wentworth's physician,[6] while Sir Hardress Waller, though he had married the daughter of Sir John Dowdall of Kilfinney, Co. Limerick, had no land within this particular barony. It was perhaps this connection with Anglo-Irish land which made him support the agitation against the plantation of Connacht in 1641. His own connection with Ireland was recent, as he did not settle in the country until 1630.[7]

---

[1] *Civil Survey*, iv. (Co. Limerick), 243: for Stevenson, cf. ibid., 335. A Sir Edward FitzHarris was one of the parliamentary delegation which went to England in 1613. *Desiderata curiosa Hibernica*, i. 206–7.

[2] *Civil Survey*, iv., pp. 455–6.

[3] Gilbert, *Ire. confed.*, vii. 250.

[4] *Civil Survey*, iv. (Co. Limerick), 151.   [5] Ibid., 240.

[6] *Cal. S.P. Ire.*, *1633–47*, p. 193; A. B. Grosart (ed.), *Lismore papers*, series 1, iv. 30.

[7] *D.N.B.*; Burke, *Landed Gentry of Ireland*, p. 735.

County Tipperary and Cross of Tipperary

Tipperary county	*Thomas Butler; Theobald Purcell*
Clonmel	*Henry White; Geoffrey Barron*
Cross of Tipperary	*Sir Thomas Gough; Geoffrey Mockler*
Cashel	Thomas Little; *John Haley*
Fethard	*Thomas Everard; Thomas Haynes*

Here again the returns to the house of commons might give a mis-leading picture of the actual situation in Tipperary. Tipperary was in fact divided between Anglo-Irish and native Irish as clearly as Wexford had been. North Tipperary was largely in the hands of the O'Kennedys and other Irish septs, but, unlike Wexford, it remained unplanted, though a beginning had been made with the territory of Ely O'Carroll. The projected plantation of 'Ormonde' was an attempt to bring this area of North Tipperary under English control and it was supported by the earl of Ormonde because he, more than any other landlord, stood to benefit if his claims to overlordship over this territory—claims which the Gaelic resurgence of the fifteenth century had made extremely theoretical—could be translated into fact as an indirect result of plantation.

On the other hand, the members for Co. Tipperary and the Cross of Tipperary came from a restricted area in the south of the modern county, in fact from the area in which Ormonde enjoyed direct in-fluence. Cross of Tipperary was the area round Cashel which had been excluded from the palatinate of Ormonde and had formed a separate 'county', but Wentworth seems to have taken advantage of its weak position in his campaign to reduce the number of Catholic members and Cross of Tipperary went unrepresented in the parliament of 1639. The three boroughs of Cashel, Fethard and Clonmel all lay in the baronies in which the earl of Ormonde was the largest landlord. In fact, the parliamentary county of Tipperary was 'Ormonde's Tipperary': the Gaelic Irish who inhabited the hilly northern part of the county found no representation.

With one exception, the members were drawn from this restricted area. John Haley of Cashel is described as a 'Civilian' in the Civil Survey[1]—he does not seem to have held much land in the barony of Middle-third. On the other hand, however, Thomas Butler, Geoffrey Mockler and Thomas Everard were, excluding Ormonde himself, the most prominent proprietors in that barony. I have not been able to trace Thomas Butler's relationship to the earl of Ormonde, but his lands lay near Fethard.[2] The lands of Theobald Purcell[3] lay in the barony of

[1] *Civil Survey*, i. (Co. Tipperary), 251. A John Haley was a member of the Confederation of Kilkenny. Gilbert, *Ire. confed.*, iii. 215.
[2] *Civil Survey*, i. (Co. Tipperary), 150.   [3] Ibid., 80.

Eliogarty, where he, together with Ormonde himself, was by far the largest proprietor. The two county members were therefore large landed proprietors. Henry White belonged to the Whites of Clonmel who had provided members for the parliaments of 1559, 1585 and 1613.[1] Geoffrey Barron, on the other hand, though he is described as being of Clonmel, did not hold land in the barony of Middlethird; he held over 1,000 acres in the barony of Glenahery which is on the other side of the Suir from Clonmel, but most of it consisted of mountain (800 acres) and 300 of 'woody glen'.[2] Sir Thomas Gough, also described as 'of Clonmel', owed his links with the town, it would appear, to his family having acquired the lands of the abbey in Innislonaught which lay near Clonmel.[3] Geoffrey Mockler's land lay further north;[4] both he and Gough were among the most prominent proprietors for the county. Thomas Everard of Fethard also falls into this category.[5] Thomas Haynes, on the other hand, appears to have had little land in Tipperary, by comparison with his fellow members. He shared a holding of 700 acres with Geoffrey Mockler by virtue of a mortgage, but that seems to be his only landed connection.[6] He is, however, described as being 'of Fethard' and he may therefore owe his election to other factors.

The only 'non-local' element was Thomas Little, member for Cashel, who probably owed his election to the lord deputy's influence with Ormonde. Little was described by Boyle as 'my Lord Deputie's secretary'[7] and though he may have obtained a more lucrative post later as Escheator for Munster, at this date, as Wentworth's secretary, he was in an excellent position to bring influence to bear on his own behalf.

To sum up, therefore, nearly all the members for the County and boroughs of Tipperary derived from a comparatively restricted 'Anglo-Irish' section of the county. The native Irish lords went unrepresented, and the evidence would seem to point to the conclusion that the influence of the earl of Ormonde was bound to be an important factor, though nothing can be said with certainty on this point.[8]

[1] *Civil Survey*, i. (Co. Tipperary), 379; *Waterford Arch. Soc. Jn.*, iii. 55, 119.

[2] He was a nephew of Luke Wadding. *Wadding Papers*, ed. Jennings, p. 238. He was executed in 1651 after fighting in the Confederate wars. *D.N.B.* See also *Civil Survey*, vi. (Co. Waterford, etc.), 94.

[3] *Civil Survey*, i. (Co. Tipperary), 307; White, *Extents of Irish monastic possessions*, p. 337–9.

[4] Ibid., i. (Co. Tipperary), 251.   [5] Ibid., 250.

[6] Ibid., 210.

[7] A. B. Grosart (ed.), *Lismore papers*, series 1, iv, p. 30. Wentworth in a letter to Portland refers to 'my secretary Little'. 19 July 1634. *Strafford's letters*, i. 274.

[8] Cf. a letter of John Barry to Philip Percivall in Mar. 1640/1, when it was

County Waterford

Waterford County	*Jacob Walsh; John Power*
Waterford	*William Dobbins; Richard Strange*
Dungarvan	Sir Pierce Smith; *John Hore FitzMahowghe*
Tallagh	Sir William Fenton; Thomas Elwall
Lismore	James Barry; Stephen Crowe

Waterford was another county, which, as a result of the Desmond rebellion, had been partly planted. In this case the lands which had been declared forfeit lay mainly in the barony of Coshmore and Coshbride, where by far the largest proprietor was Richard Boyle, earl of Cork. The river Blackwater formed the boundary separating the eastern planted section of the county from the centre and west. These facts are clearly illustrated in the returns for the parliament of 1634.

Like Kilkenny and the counties of the Pale, Waterford was an Anglo-Irish county in which the vast majority of the proprietors were of Anglo-Irish descent, whatever may be said of the tenants. James Walsh and John Power were both substantial landowners. James Walsh is described as being of Ballygunner which lies on the extreme eastern side of the county, but his main holding of 2,000 acres lay in the Decies.[1] John Power, on the other hand, was the largest proprietor in the barony of Middlethird, with land of over 4,500 acres. Both the Power and Walsh families had a strong tradition of parliamentary membership; together with the Aylwards they were the Waterford equivalent of the great families of Kilkenny and Wexford.

At least one of the two members for Waterford town was a burgess with a holding in the town.[2] Richard Strange appears as holding 1,000 acres in the barony of Upperthird.[3] The James Walsh and John Power, who had holdings within the town, may also be the county members but there is no definite evidence to link them; and since the names are very common it would be unwise to draw definite conclusions in the absence of further evidence.

The representation for Dungarvan appears to have been divided between Catholic and Protestant: John Hore of Dungarvan was a prominent merchant of the town, whom the Civil Survey describes as an 'Irish Papist'.[4] Piers Smith, his fellow member, on the other hand appears to have no local connections with the town of Dungarvan. His lands lay near Youghal at Ballynatra, where he was a tenant of the

rumoured that parliament would be dissolved and a new one summoned: he intended to write to Ormonde 'to get me a place', *H.M.C. Egmont MSS.*, I, pt. i, 129, 8 Mar. 1640/1. Percivall advised him to try Lord Dungarvan for a letter instead, ibid., p. 130, 15 Mar. 1640/1.

[1] *Civil Survey*, vi. (Co. Waterford), 75.
[2] Ibid., vi. (Co. Waterford), 193.   [3] Ibid., 106.   [4] Ibid., 37.

earl of Cork.[1] Richard Boyle's property in and near Dungarvan was considerable and the probability is that he possessed some influence upon the election of one member for the town.

The other two boroughs of Tallow and Lismore lay more definitely within the planted area. The barony of the Decies was on the whole untouched; Coshmore and Coshbride on the other hand was a planted barony, and Tallow and Lismore which lay within it, were dominated by the earl of Cork, and his influence upon the election of members can be taken for granted. Sir William Fenton, member for Tallagh, was a brother-in-law of Boyle by his first wife.[2] Thomas Elwall, his fellow member, is described as a burgess of Tallagh[3] and probably therefore a nominee of Cork. There is no definite evidence as to the identity of James Barry and Stephen Crowe. They do not seem to have had any local connection with Lismore; though James Barry could be identified as the James Barry who was baron of the Exchequer in 1634 and returned after the restoration as chief justice of King's Bench with the title Baron Santry;[4] there is no trace of his name in the Civil Survey for the county.

In short the representation for the county and boroughs of Waterford is balanced between the old English and the new English. There seems to be no one dominating Anglo-Irish influence, though there is no reason why Ormonde's enigmatic influence should not have crossed the Suir;[5] on the new English side, however, the earl of Cork would appear to have exercised an influence commensurate with his position as a great proprietor.

County Kerry

Kerry County	Sir Valentine Brown; *John Fitzgerald*
Dingle	Dominick Rice; James Rice
Tralee	Sir Beverley Newcomen; Robert Blennerhasset[6]
Ardfert	David Crosby; Pierce Fitzjames Pierce

The possessions of the earl of Desmond had been declared forfeit in Kerry, with the result that parts of the county were planted. Naturally therefore planter's names are prominent among the members for Kerry. Sir Valentine Brown of Mohaliffe, not far from Tralee, was a member of a new 'planter' family. His fellow county member, however, was the

---

[1] Ibid., vi. (Co. Waterford), 20.
[2] Cf. *D.N.B.*, under 'Sir Geoffrey Fenton', (his father).
[3] P.P. List, p. 635.   [4] Cf. Ball, *Judges in Ireland*, i. 335-6.
[5] On 14 Nov. 1641 the Mayor of Waterford commended the town to the protection of Ormonde and the Lords Justices. Carte MSS. (Bodleian), ix, f. 425.
[6] Sir George Radcliffe was elected but apparently preferred to sit for Armagh.

Anglo-Irish John Fitzgerald, who replaced Sir Thomas Harris, when the original election was declared void.

The earls of Desmond had held central Kerry and it is precisely this forfeited area which is represented in the 1634 parliament. The boroughs of Dingle, Tralee and Ardfert all lay on the coast within a comparatively small area. The rest of Kerry being still unplanted lay, along with west Cork, still largely under the control of the native Irish, who went unrepresented in parliament. The Rice family had strong local connections with Dingle and were sufficiently new English in outlook for Stephen and John Rice to be regarded in 1613 as 'both burgesses and both Protestants'.[1] Robert Blennerhasset came from a new English planter family.[2] The connection of Sir Beverley Newcomen,[3] Admiral of Ireland, with Tralee was possibly through Sir Valentine Browne, Deputy-Vice Admiral of Ireland. The clearest position is that of David Crosby whose connection with Ardfert was due to his being second son of John Crosby, bishop of Ardfert.[4]

Thus it would appear true of Kerry, as elsewhere, that the new English interest was represented almost without dilution wherever the Anglo-Irish had been driven out; the native Irish went completely without representation.

County Clare

Clare county	Sir Daniel O'Brien; Boethius Clancy
Ennis	Sir Richard Southwell; Sir Barnaby O'Brien

If the number of members returned is a criterion, then Clare is unimportant when compared with the other counties in Munster. Cork returned 16, and even Kerry and Limerick returned eight, whereas Clare returned only four. As might have been expected in the Thomond country where O'Brien influence was so strong; one of the two county members was an O'Brien: Sir Daniel O'Brien who replaced Sir Barnabas O'Brien for the November session. Sir Daniel was later to be a confederate and member of the Supreme Council,[5] but the other

---

[1] Cal. S.P. Ire., 1611–14, p. 165.

[2] He sat for Tralee in 1613 also. John Blennerhasset was appointed baron of the exchequer in 1609. Liber mun. pub. Hib., pt. 2, p. 51.

[3] P.P. List gives Sir Robert Newcomen but the argument would still hold.

[4] He married the daughter of John Steere, his father's successor as bishop. Sir Walter Crosbie of Maryborough was his brother, cf. Burke, Landed Gentry of Ireland (1912). David Crosby clashed with Wentworth over the possession of church lands, cf. Kerry Arch. Mag., iv, no. 17, p. 2.

[5] J. Frost, History of county Clare, p. 378; Gilbert, Ire. confed., vi. 211. Barnabas O'Brien was absent in England: had he continued as a member, all four representatives for Clare would have been new English in sympathy.

three members would appear to be definitely new English in sympathy. Clancy had sat for Clare before in parliament and Boethius Clancy, though probably a Catholic, appears to have thrown in his lot completely with the newcomers. His reward seems to have been a prominent place in the administration of the newly formed county of Clare.[1] Sir Richard Southwell was one of the council of the President of Munster and was appointed deputy governor of Clare in 1640.[2] Apart from Sir Daniel O'Brien, the members for Clare were of a new English character and such as might be expected in the territory of Inchiquin.

CONNACHT

Galway county	*Sir Henry Lynch; Sir Robert O'Shaghness*[3]
Galway	*Sir Valentine Blake;*[4] *Alderman Nicholas Lynch*
Athenry	*Richard Martin; Dominick Browne*[5]
Tuam	Sir Thomas Rotherham;[6] (*Sir Valentine Blake*)
Leitrim county	Henry Crofton; Charles Reynolds
Carrick-on-Shannon	John Jackson; Thomas Cave
Jamestown	Sir Charles Coote; Sir William Anderson
Mayo county	*David Bourke;*[7] *Sir Thomas Bourke*
Castlebar	Sir Henry Bingham; Thomas Edmonds
Roscommon county[8]	Arthur Jones; Sir Lucas Dillon
Roscommon[9]	George Carr; Edward Deane
Boyle	Sir Robert King; Richard Scott[10]
Sligo county	*Tadhg O'Connor; Farrell O'Gara*[11]
Sligo[12]	Sir Roger Jones; Thomas Mansell

Connacht does not demand the same amount of discussion as the other three provinces; politically speaking it was much the least important, though in the years following the 1634 parliament it was to give rise to large questions of policy.

[1] Frost, op. cit., p. 323.
[2] Cf. Burke, *Peerage*, under 'Southwell'.
[3] P.P. List, p. 616, gives Sir Valentine Blake.
[4] Ibid., p. 616, gives Sir Thomas Blake, Bart; Valentine Blake was sick in second session: new writ issued, p. 34.
[5] Ibid., p. 617, gives David Burke.
[6] Ibid., p. 622, gives Sir Charles Coote only.
[7] Ibid., p. 627, gives Sir Roger O'Shagness.
[8] Ibid., p. 631, does not give Arthur Jones; only Sir Lucas Dillon.
[9] Ibid., p. 631, does not give George Carr; only Edward Deane.
[10] Ibid., p. 631, gives Robt. Meredith Esq.
[11] Ibid., p. 632, gives Sir George Radcliffe, who sat in 1639.
[12] Ibid., p. 632, gives Arthur Jones and Edward Southworth (of Athlone).

Only two of the five counties of Connacht had fallen, to any extent, under the influence of the new English—Leitrim which was planted and Roscommon which was not, but which lay more open to control than the remoter west. The Dillons of Roscommon had shown themselves to be supporters of the administration and it was no accident that Roscommon should have been chosen as the first county of Connacht (excluding Leitrim) in which a royal title to land should have been sought.

All the members for Leitrim were new English. Crofton and Coote were names which had occurred in previous plantations and were to recur in connection with later ones.[1] Thomas Cave had official connections. He had been master gunner of Ireland from 1615:[2] he was also comptroller of the customs for Dublin and Wexford.[3] At this date Carrick and Jamestown[4] can hardly have been more than extremely precarious outposts, and yet they returned the same number of members as Galway or Limerick. In Co. Roscommon also, with the exception of Lucas Dillon, all the members were new English. Arthur Jones, the other county member, owed his election not so much to any large estates as to the influence of his father, Lord Ranelagh, and lord president of Connaught from 1630 onwards.[5] The Books of Survey and Distribution provide no evidence for George Carr,[6] Edward Deane nor Richard Scott having any land in Connacht. They also may have owed their election to the influence of the lord president. Sir Robert King, however, was a proprietor in Roscommon, at least after the plantation,[7] and his election for Boyle points to a connection with Edward King, bishop of Elphin (1611–39), whose second son was named Robert. A Robert King was appointed muster-master general and clerk of the cheque in Ireland in 1618.[8]

In Mayo and Sligo there was a sharp division between the county members who sprang from the native Irish families, and the borough members who were new English. This probably gives an accurate picture of the position, Castlebar and Sligo town being merely isolated points from which the new English administration operated, or attempted to operate. Sir Roger Jones was governor of Sligo.[9] The

---

[1] Henry Crofton was member of the commission for settling the plantation of Longford (*Cal. S.P. Ire.*, *1615–25*, p. 280. Charles Coote was vice-president of Connaught from 1620: for his career; see *D.N.B.*

[2] *Liber mun. pub. Hib.*, pt. 2. p. 107.

[3] Ibid., ii. 153, 154.   [4] *Cal. S.P. Ire.*, *1615–25*, pp. 430, 448.

[5] *Liber mun. pub. Hib.*, pt. 2, p, 189.

[6] He was appointed Clerk of the council in Munster in 1636. Ibid., 187.

[7] *Book of Survey and Distribution*, ed. R. C. Simington (1949), pp. 130, 140–1.

[8] *Cal. S.P. Ire.*, *1615–25*, p. 193.

[9] W. G. Wood-Martin, *History of Sligo 1603–88*, p. 38.

connection of the Bingham family with Mayo dates from the closing decades of the sixteenth century, and the election of a Bingham for Castlebar requires no explanation. The Bourkes of Mayo, the O'Connors and O'Garas of Sligo provided the county members respectively; there was little surprising about this.

In Galway, on the other hand, the new English had made no penetration whatever. The county itself lay outside the sphere of the lord president of Connacht, and the only alien element in the parliamentary representation for the county, Sir Thomas Rotherham, member for Tuam, owed his position as Deputy-Governor of the town and county of Galway to his appointment by Clanrickarde.[1] Under the leadership of Clanrickarde, the powerful Anglo-Irish landed families of Lynch, Blake, Browne and Martin remained undisturbed in their parliamentary control. The Lynches sat for Galway town in the three parliaments of 1613, 1634 and 1640.

Taken on a general view, the parliamentary representation for Connacht gives a hint of what events lay in the future. Roscommon, though unplanted, was open to new English influence in a way in which Mayo and Sligo were not; but only Galway retained sufficient independence for it to be likely to resist the policy of plantation should it seriously be attempted.

ULSTER

Parliamentary representation in Ulster was dominated by two facts —the creation of 18 boroughs by James I[2] and the plantation which had been carried on with varying degrees of success since 1610.

In 1634, owing to the wide plantation which had taken place under James I, the position of Ulster was very different from that of the other three provinces. In Munster, despite plantation, the Anglo-Irish retained some measure of local power; in Ulster, the Irish retained practically none, though they were not displaced from the land in many areas. Almost without exception it was the planters, Scottish and English, who were represented in 1634. In east Ulster, where Scottish settlers were predominant, the parliamentary returns give some indication of the fact; on the other hand the return of English members was not necessarily a sign of sizable English plantations and perhaps the predominance of official candidates without local connections was evidence for the slight hold which the English possessed. It may be said with some certainty in fact that the Scots were under-represented

---

[1] *Liber mun. pub. Hib.*, pt. 2, p. 190.

[2] 40 new boroughs were created by James I between December 1612 and May 1613, of which 18 were in Ulster. T. W. Moody, 'The Irish parliament under Elizabeth and James I' in *R.I.A. Proc.*, xlv, sec. c, no. 6 (Dec. 1939), p. 54.

while the English administration were over-represented. The Irish were hardly represented at all; only two Gaelic Irish from Ulster were members of this parliament. So far as the parliament returns were concerned, Ulster might well have been populated by English and Scots, with the latter in a small minority, though the reality was otherwise; of the 66 members for Ulster, less than a sixth were Scottish. The events of 1641 were to bring out clearly the true situation: the struggle lay between Scots and Irish, the English being almost negligible.

Antrim

Antrim county	Arthur Chichester; John Clotworthy
Carrickfergus	Sir Thomas Hibbots; Henry Upton
Belfast	Charles Price; Thomas Bramston

The Antrim which was represented in the parliament of 1634 was a comparatively restricted portion of the whole county, namely that part which lay between Lough Neagh and Belfast Lough which was in the process of being colonised by English settlers. Most of the county was unplanted and still remained in the hands of the MacDonnells whose position in Ulster was analogous to that of the MacCarthys in Munster; they had backed the winning horse at the right moment. Unlike the MacCarthys, however, the MacDonnells had not a single representative in the house of commons. The 'county' represented in 1634 was Chichester's county, just as the two boroughs of Belfast and Carrickfergus were Chichester's boroughs; the rest of the county had no voice.

The planted area of county Antrim had been known as north (or lower) Clandeboye, before the division of Ulster into counties took place under Sir John Davies; and the two county members were in fact the two largest landowners of lower Clandeboye. Arthur Chichester's connection looked back to the lord deputy under whom the original plantation had taken place, and he was linked with Clotworthy[1] by their common Devon origins. Two of the members for the boroughs also had obvious local connections with the area. Henry Upton[2] was the agent of Chichester in 1632 at a meeting of the Belfast Corporation, and the Town Book of Belfast leaves no doubt that the influence of Chichester upon the affairs of the town was constant and not to be lightly disregarded. Henry Upton probably owed his election therefore to the influence of Chichester, and the likelihood is that his fellow member for Belfast, Sir Thomas Hibbots, though he is described as being 'of Kildare', owed his seat to the same source, or to the influence of the lord deputy. Thomas Bramston was sovereign of Belfast Corporation, and it was this which led to his election being declared invalid.[3]

[1] For Clotworthy, see *D.N.B.* and Burke, *Peerage*, under 'Massereene'.
[2] R. M. Young (ed.), *Town book of Belfast*, p. 2.
[3] He was replaced by John Ingersoll.

The evidence suggests that his election represents a possible reaction against Chichester's control. Captain Charles Price would appear to have owed his election to the influence of the lord deputy; he was Wentworth's confidential emissary, to whom Wentworth was still writing in frank terms in February 1635/6,[1] and he does not seem to have had any local links with the borough.

Down

Down county	Hugh Montgomery; James Hamilton
Downpatrick	Edward Kinaston; William Billingsley
Newry	Sir Robert Loftus; Sir Arthur Terringham
Bangor	Sir Arthur Bassett; Matthew Brabazon
Killelagh	Walter White; Paul Reynolds
Newtownards	Sir Edward Trevor; Sir Thomas Meredith

Like Antrim, Down did not fall under the 'plantation of Ulster'. Attempts had been made in the middle of Elizabeth's reign to rescue what had been the medieval earldom of Ulster from the control of the native Irish and immigrant Scots, but they had failed. The political future was to lie with the Scots, and the representation in 1634 gives some idea how far the process had gone by that date. The Hamiltons and the Montgomerys owed their foothold in Down to a bargain made with Con O'Neill, who was glad to evade the possibility of losing all his land on a charge 'of levying war against the Queen'. O'Neill was unable to maintain himself in the position which he had been granted and the remainder of his estates were gradually lost to his Scottish neighbours. The history of this episode has been told elsewhere,[2] and for our purposes it is sufficient to draw attention to the fact that Hugh Montgomery and James Hamilton owed their position as county members to their successful bargain earlier in the century.

As Co. Down was not included in Pynnar's survey of Ulster, it is difficult to ascertain how far this Scots infiltration had gone by 1634. The parliament of 1640 gives a clearer picture, when three Montgomerys and two Hamiltons were members for the county (1), Newtownards (2) and Bangor (2).

Of the other members for Co. Down it is difficult to speak with certainty. The Trevors had a strong local connection; Edward Trevor had an Antrim seat in the parliaments of 1613, 1634 and 1640, and in

---

[1] Strafford MSS., vol. 8, ff. 356–8. Cf. also *Strafford's letters*, i. 503. For a fuller account of Price's career, see M. F. Keeler, *The Long Parliament*, pp. 313–14.

[2] Cf. G. Hill (ed.), *The Montgomery Manuscripts*, pp. 21 ff.; cf. also D. A. Chart, 'The break-up of the estate of Con O'Neill' in *R.I.A. Proc.*, xlviii, sect. c, (Sept. 1942), 119–51.

1640 Marcus Trevor, his son, sat for Downpatrick.[1] The members for Newry probably owed their election to official influence. Sir Robert Loftus was son of the lord chancellor, and Sir Arthur Terringham had been governor in Dundalk, Carlingford and Newry since 1626.[2] William Billingsley sat for Downpatrick in 1634 and 1640, as an official without any local connection. A Brabazon sat for Bangor in 1613 and 1634, and a similar conclusion may be drawn from this. One of the members for Killelagh, Walter White, had been appointed deputy vice-treasurer by Mountnorris in 1625;[3] he was also an official of the court of wards and hence connected with William Parsons.[4]

What does not emerge from the parliamentary membership for the county is the strong hold which the Gaelic Irish still maintained in South Down. Using the Census of 1659 as a basis,[5] it has been shown that, inland, the population of the Mourne country was overwhelmingly Irish, though on the coast the relative strength of English, Scots and Irish varied according to their locality; it was significant that all the boroughs which returned members to parliament were on the coast. If a general conclusion does emerge from Co. Down, it would seem to be that actual occupation of the land was shared between Scots and and Irish, while such English as were elected, owed their election to their official influence or position in the administration.

Monaghan

| Monaghan county | *Art Oge MacMahon; Coll McBrian MacMahon* |
| Monaghan | Richard Blayney; Arthur Blayney |

MacMahon's country was unplanted and was alone among the counties of Ulster in returning members of the Gaelic Irish ruling class to parliament. The election of two MacMahons as members for the county is an indication that the land lay largely under the control of the powerful sept of MacMahon, and points to the development which might have taken place in Ulster generally had not the plantation intervened. In the crisis of 1625, Art Oge MacMahon was regarded as a person 'fitted to be employed against Tyrone and other Irish rebels';[6] later in 1641, however, the MacMahons were to join the forces of the Confederation.[7] The members for the borough of Monaghan had local

---

[1] Cf. G.E.C., *Peerage*, ed. Gibbs, under 'Dungannon' The town of Rostrevor derives its name from this family.

[2] *Liber mun. pub. Hib.*, pt. 2, p. 126.

[3] Ibid., p. 45.

[4] Ibid., p. 57.

[5] Cf. Estyn Evans, *Mourne Country*, p. 110; D. B. Quinn, *Belfast Natur. Hist. Soc. Proc.*, 1933–4, pp. 56–78.

[6] *Cal. S.P. Ire.*, *1625–32*, p. 73.

[7] Ibid., *1633–47*, p. 374.

connections, both being related to Lord Blayney who had been granted land in Co. Monaghan during the reign of James I.[1]

Fermanagh[2]

Fermanagh county	Sir William Cole; Sir John Hume
Enniskillen	Sir John Borlase; Paul Davis

This county consisted of eight baronies, one of which was allotted to Connor Roe Maguire, one of the ancient lords of the county who had been 'loyal'. Two baronies were allotted to English undertakers and two to Scottish. The remaining three were allotted to natives and servitors; the other two classes for which allowance was made in the plantation of Ulster.

The members for the county illustrate this division between English and Scottish settlers. The English interest was represented by Sir William Cole[3] who came originally from a Devon family and, as captain of the castle of Enniskillen and sheriff several times for the county, as well as being a large and successful undertaker, was well placed for election as county member. The same may be said of Sir John Hume who was of Scottish birth and who by purchasing land in addition to his own plantation had become the largest proprietor in the county with 4,500 acres.[4] It is perhaps not reading too much into the evidence to see Cole as the leader of the English element in the county and Hume of the Scottish. As in England, the county seats were divided between the two most powerful interests. On the other hand, the Gaelic Irish were ignored, and it was not until 1640 that a Maguire was returned as a member for the county.

The two members for the borough of Enniskillen were 'official' candidates, who do not seem to have any local connection with the county. Sir John Borlase had just arrived in Ireland where he had been appointed master of the ordnance in 1634.[5] Paul Davis was clerk of the Council along with William Usher;[6] he held land in the barony of Raphoe,[7] Co. Donegal, for which county he was to be elected in 1640. It would appear that the two borough candidates probably owed their election to the direct 'influence' of the lord deputy; otherwise it is difficult to explain why they should have been chosen for Enniskillen.

[1] G.E.C. *Peerage*, ed. Gibbs, under 'Blayney'.
[2] Cf. the earl of Belmore, *Parliamentary memoirs of Fermanagh and Tyrone*.
[3] Belmore, pp. 13–16.
[4] Ibid., pp. 19–23.
[5] *Liber mun. pub. Hib.*, pt. 2, p. 102; Strafford MSS., no. 8, 29 May 1634.
[6] Ibid., pt. 2, p. 83.
[7] *Civil Survey*, iii. (Cos. Donegal, Londonderry and Tyrone), 35.

Tyrone[1]

Tyrone county	Sir James Erskine; Sir Henry Tichborne
Clogher	Sir Henry Spottiswood; Edward Ascough
Dungannon	Sir Faithful Fortescue; John Perkins
Strabane	Richard FitzGerald; Charles Moncke
Augher	Robert Meredith; Richard Erskine

In Tyrone, as in Fermanagh, the division of the plantation between English and Scottish undertakers is reflected in the parliamentary representation. Sir James Erskine, however, was not an original undertaker and, though a Scotsman, he had purchased estates in a precinct which had been reserved for English undertakers, from Sir Thomas Ridgeway in 1622.[2] These estates included Augher, for which borough Erskine's son was elected in 1634. Sir Henry Tichborne, the other county member, seems to have acquired his land before 1629 from Captain Edney who was an original patentee within the precinct of Clogher, an area which had been allotted to English undertakers.[3] Thus, though neither Erskine nor Tichborne were original undertakers, the likelihood is that they did represent Scottish and English interests within the county.

The division of members for Clogher borough does not seem to represent an agreement between English and Scottish settlers. Sir Henry Spottiswood was the son of the Scottish bishop of Clogher, James Spottiswood (1621–44), but Edward Ascough had no obvious local connection with Tyrone and may have been an office holder. The fate of church lands in Co. Tyrone was a major issue in local politics, dividing Spottiswood from the Erskines and showing how racial unity did not rule out division on other issues.[4] The Grace concerning the restoration of Church lands would clearly have been an issue on which the Scots members for Co. Tyrone would be likely to take different sides in parliament; the struggle was one in which a prominent landlord had lost his life and was not restricted to friendly debate.

One member for Dungannon owed his election to family influence. Faithful Fortescue was son-in-law to Viscount Moore of Drogheda, but the influence of the Moores had not prevented him from being defeated at Dundalk.[5] His seat at Dungannon, which was probably in the nature of a second string such as Barnaby O'Brien and others possessed, he owed to family links with a Tyrone undertaker, Sir Francis

---

[1] Cf. Belmore, *Parliamentary memoirs*.
[2] G. Hill, *The plantation in Ulster*, p. 539, note ; Belmore, pp. 161–4.
[3] Ibid., p. 542, note ; Belmore, pp. 164–7.
[4] *Cal. S.P. Ire., 1625–32*, p. 180.
[5] E. Hawkins (ed.), 'Brereton's Travels in Ireland etc.', Chetham Soc., vol. I, p. 133.

Roe.[1] The precinct of Dungannon had been allotted in the plantation of Ulster to servitors and natives; in 1616 Roe enfeoffed his land in the precinct to, among others, Sir Garrett Moore, viscount Drogheda, as a trustee to administer the property for his lifetime. This presumably is the key to Fortescue's election in Dungannon. It is also worth noting that the Moores and Hugh O'Neill had been friendly. John Perkins,[2] his fellow member, had succeeded Sir Moses Hill in 1629 as provost marshal of Ulster; the military establishment at Dungannon is probably sufficient explanation for his election there.

The three remaining members for the boroughs of Co. Tyrone were office holders: Charles Moncke was surveyor-general of the customs;[3] Richard FitzGerald, deputy clerk of the crown in the court of King's Bench,[4] and Robert Meredith, chancellor of the exchequer,[5] as well as being son-in-law to Sir William Usher, Clerk of the Council. As in Co. Down, therefore, the evidence points to the Scots being established on the land, while the English owed their election to 'influence', official or otherwise.

Donegal

Donegal county	Sir William Stewart; Sir John Vaughan
Donegal	William Crofton; Gilbert Domvill
Lifford	Jerome Alexander; Roger Mainwaring
Ballyshannon	Thomas Leake; Michael Stanhope
Killybegs	Thomas Talles; James Galbreth

Here again the division of the plantation between English and Scottish undertakers is illustrated in the parliamentary representation of the county. Both Sir William Stewart,[6] a Scot, and Sir John Vaughan,[7] who was English, had large holdings in the county as a result of the plantation, and had sat in 1613 as county members. Of the remaining members, only one, James Galbreth, seems to have been a planter in Donegal; he was member for Killybegs, though his lands seem to have been further north in the barony of Raphoe.[8]

The 'official' nature of the other members for the boroughs of Donegal may indicate that plantation here was less successful than in those parts of Ulster, which were more accessible to England and Scotland. Apart from Lifford, the boroughs lay within a comparatively

[1] Belmore, p. 141; pp. 170–2.
[2] *Liber mun. pub. Hib.*, pt. 2, p. 194; Belmore, pp, 172–6.
[3] Ibid., pt. 2, p. 137.   [4] *Cal. S.P. Ire., 1633–47*, p. 188.
[5] *Liber mun. pub. Hib.*, pt. 2, p. 49; T. U. Sadleir, *Kildare members of parliament*, pp. 43–4.
[6] *Civil Survey*, iii. 30; G. Hill, *The plantation in Ulster*, p. 524; he also held lands in Tyrone, *Cal. S.P. Ire., 1615–25*, p. 221.
[7] *Cal. S.P. Ire., 1615–25*, p. 225.   [8] *Civil Survey*, iii. 31.

restricted area of south-west Donegal; the west and north-west were remoter still, and English administration can hardly have been effective here.

William Crofton, member for Donegal town, did have links with Ulster as he was auditor for the provinces of Connacht and Ulster;[1] he had sat for the same borough in 1613, though his landed connection appears to be with Sligo. He was linked with the Croftons of Roscommon, who had been associated with the plantation of Longford, and were also to profit from the plantation of Connacht. Gilbert Domvill, like Crofton, was a member of the administration: he was clerk of the decrees and recognisances,[2] and had sought election for Kildare in 1613.[3] The members for Lifford were of the same official character as Donegal and, for that matter, as the borough of Strabane which lay on the opposite side of the river.

Jerome Alexander was a lawyer of sorts,[4] and later he had enough influence with Adam Loftus to be nominated as a justice of assize, though the appointment was declared void by the lord deputy.[5] His fellow member, Roger Mainwaring, owed his election to the influence of the administration.[6]

The remaining members are less easy to place. Thomas Talles was to sit again for Killybegs in 1640, which suggests some local connection. Michael Stanhope may be related to Sir John Stanhope who was an undertaker in the neighbouring county of Tyrone. All in all, however, 'official' candidates would appear to have predominated in Co. Donegal.

Armagh

Armagh county	Sir William Parsons; Arthur Moore
Armagh	Sir George Radcliffe; William Hilton
Charlemont	Chichester Fortescue; John Bysse

Armagh was a planted county, in which both English and Scottish undertakers were allotted lands. There are radical differences, however, between the two lists of members, which makes it difficult to say who sat for the county and the various boroughs. William Hilton is common to both lists; at this date he was attorney-general for Connacht,[7] and

---

[1] *Cal. S.P. Ire., 1625–32*, p. 630.   [2] *Liber mun. pub. Hib.*, pt. 2, p. 28.

[3] T. U. Sadleir, *Kildare members of parliament*, p. 100.

[4] Ball, *Judges in Ireland*, i. 266 ff.

[5] *Strafford's letters*, ii. 68.

[6] I have assumed he was a relative of Sir Philip Mainwaring, whose brother was sheriff of Limerick in 1605, Burke, *Extinct Baronetage*, p. 336. Philip himself died unmarried, so that Roger could have been only a nephew or cousin.

[7] *Liber mun. pub. Hib.*, pt. 2, p. 191.

he was described as being 'of the abbey of Navan, Co. Meath'. He owed his election for Armagh to neither of these circumstances but to the fact that he married Anne, sister of James Ussher, archbishop of Armagh.[1] Hilton's name is, however, the only one which appears in the same position in both lists, apart from Chichester Fortescue, member for Charlemont, the seat which Faithful Fortescue had in 1613.

Arthur Moore appears as member both for the county and for the borough of Charlemont. Charlemont seems more likely as it was a borough with which the Moore family had been connected in 1613; Gerald Moore, son of Sir Edward Moore of Mellifont, had been granted land as a servitor in Armagh.[2] Faithful Fortescue's marriage into the Moore family provided a further link, as Dungannon, for which he sat, lay only five miles north-east of Charlemont.

George Radcliffe may have sat for the county or borough of Armagh; whichever it was, he can only have owed his election to the influence of the lord deputy. When he did acquire land in Ireland it was to be in Sligo, for which he sat in 1640.[3] John Dillon is given as member for the borough of Armagh by one list; this is borne out by his having lands in the county. John Bysse's connection with Charlemont can have been due only to official influence: he was recorder of Dublin.[4]

Sir William Parsons had lands elsewhere in Ulster, in Cavan, Fermanagh and Tyrone; he would appear to have had no direct links with Co. Armagh, though as one who had taken a prominent part in the plantation from the beginning, he would have had no difficulty in finding a seat in Ulster.

One thing is certain—that the Scottish undertakers, who had been granted as much land as the English, were not represented in Co. Armagh as they were in other counties of Ulster, though in 1640 a Hamilton was to sit for the borough of Armagh.

Cavan

Cavan county	Lucas Dillon; Sir Stephen Butler
Cavan	Allan Cook; Brockhall Taylor
Belturbet	Sir Arthur Blundell; Sir William Ryves

As in the other planted counties, land within different precincts was allotted to both Scottish and English undertakers. In Cavan, however, as in Armagh, the Scots went unrepresented. Of the English planters, Sir Stephen Butler of Belturbet was one of the most prominent.[5] The

[1] Ball, *Judges in Ireland*, i. 338.
[2] Though within the precinct of Orier, in the south-east of the county: Charlemont lay north-west.
[3] See above, 'The plantation of Connacht'.
[4] Ball, *Judges in Ireland*, i. 344.
[5] G. Hill ,*The plantation in Ulster*, p. 465.

election of the Anglo-Irish Sir Lucas Dillon suggests that in Cavan the control of the new English was not to be taken for granted. In 1613 there had been a disputed election, and in 1640 an O'Reilly was elected as county member, which would suggest that in 1634 a compromise may have been arrived at. In 1610 Sir John Davies had noted that 'the inhabitants of this county bordering upon Meath had many acquaintances and alliances with the gentlemen of the English Pale.' [1] Without further evidence, however, it is impossible to do more than draw attention to what the appearance of Lucas Dillon might indicate. His land lay at Trinity Island, not far from the town of Cavan, so that his local connection was quite strong.

The two members for Cavan borough also had local connections. Brockhall Taylor held land in the barony of Loughtee.[2] Allan Cook on the other hand would seem, like William Hilton, David Crosby and Sir Henry Spottiswood, to have owed his election to his ecclesiastical links. He was lay chancellor of the diocese of Kilmore and son-in-law of James Higate who had been archdeacon in the neighbouring see of Clogher and had then become bishop of the remote see of Kilfenora. Cook's position was sufficiently strong for him to resist the attempts made by Bedell to control his use of writs of ex-communication to dispossess the native Irish.[3]

The two members for Belturbet seem to have had no such local connections. Sir Arthur Blundell's estates lay in King's county.[4] Sir William Ryves was attorney-general and held no land in Cavan; presumably he at least owed his election to official influence.[5]

Londonderry

Londonderry county	George Cary; Tristram Beresford
Londonderry	Robert Ferries; Robert Goodwin
Coleraine	George Blount; Edward Rowley
Limavady	Arthur Newcomen; George Downing

In some ways the most interesting group of members was that returned by Londonderry. George Cary, member for Co. Londonderry, was originally of a Devon family and was recorder of Derry, probably without a break, from 1615 to 1639.[6] He was the son-in-law of his fellow county member, Tristram Beresford,[7] who played a prominent

---

[1] Hill, *Plantation*, p. 226.   [2] Ibid., pp. 460–1.
[3] *Two biographies of William Bedell*, ed. E. S. Shuckburgh (1902), pp. 36–7; cf. also, *Cal. S.P. Ire., 1633–47*, pp. 218–19.
[4] He is described as of Blundellstown (alias Lomclone), King's County in P.P. List, p. 608.
[5] Ball, *Judges in Ireland*, i. 336–7.
[6] T. W. Moody, *The Londonderry plantation*, App. F, p. 448.
[7] Ibid., p. 131.

part as the agent of the London Company against the enquiries which were made from time to time into the success of the Londonderry plantation.[1] Robert Goodwyn, member for Derry town, was a freeman of the Drapers' Company and collector of the customs for the company in that town;[2] in 1625 he had been a fellow agent of Beresford.[3] Edward Rowley, member for Coleraine, was probably a relative of the Rowleys who were included in the 1622 muster list for the town of Coleraine.[4] George Downing, member for Limavady, was described in 1618 as a chief tenant of the Fishmongers' Company;[5] he was joint sheriff of Derry in 1626. Here then was a distinct and united grouping in the 1634 house of commons; to them must be added the name of Sir John Clotworthy, member for Co. Antrim and son of a former sheriff of the county. He was one of the farmers for the Irish Society and later was to play a large part in the attack upon Strafford.[6]

[1] *Cal. S.P. Ire., 1615–25*, p. 470.
[2] *Londonderry and the London companies 1609–29*, p. 101.
[3] Ibid., p. 31.   [4] Ibid., p. 53.
[5] *Cal. S.P. Ire., 1615–25*, p. 222.   [6] *D.N.B.*

APPENDIX II

LIST OF MEMBERS OF THE PARLIAMENT
OF 1640

LEINSTER

CARLOW CO.	*Thomas Butler;* Oliver Eustace
Carlow	*Robert Hartpole;* Thomas Harman
Old Leighlin	Roger Brereton; *Thomas Davills*
DUBLIN CO.	*Nicholas Barnewall; Peter Barnewall*
Dublin	John Bysse; Richard Barry
T.C.D.	James Ware; William Gilbert
Swords	*John Taylor; George Blakeney*
Newcastle	*Sir John Dongan; Sir Henry Talbot*
KILDARE CO.	Maurice Eustace; *Maurice FitzGerald*
Kildare	Christopher Wandesford; George Wentworth
Naas	*Christopher Sherlock; Nicholas Sutton*
Athy	Sir Robert Meredith; Stephen Stephens
KILKENNY CO.	*Walter Walsh; Peter Butler*
Kilkenny	*Henry Archer; Peter Rooth*
Callan	Sir Thomas Wharton; *Edward Comerford*
Inistiogue	Robert Maude; John Wandesford
Gowran	Patrick Weames; *Peter Butler*
Thomastown	Michael Wandesford; Scafoule Gibson
KINGS CO.	William Parsons; *John Coghlan*
Philipstown	Simon Digby; John Moore
Banagher	James Lovell; Thomas Little
LONGFORD CO.	*James Dillon; Faugney Macross Ferrall*
St. Johnstown	Dudley Loftus; John Ware
LOUTH CO.	*Christopher Bellew; John Bellew*
Carlingford	Joshua Carpenter; Bernard Sanders
Drogheda	*Thomas Peppard; John Stanley*
Ardee	Henry Moore
Dundalk	*Oliver Cashell;* Nicholas Smith
MEATH CO.	*Nicholas Plunkett; Richard Barnewall*
Trim	Robert, Lord Dillon of Kilkenny West; *Patrick Barnewall*
Athboy	Richard Brown; *Walter Dowdall*
Navan	*Thomas Nangle;* Patrick Manning
Kells	*Robert Cusacke; Oliver Plunkett*

QUEENS CO.	Charles Coote; John Pigott
Maryborough	William Gilbert; *Nicholas White*
Ballinakill	William Wandesford; William Alford
WESTMEATH CO.	*James Dillon; Lucas FitzGerald*
Mullingar	Alexander Hope; *Edward Pettit*
Athlone	William Sommers; Oliver Jones
Kilbeggan	Robert Forth; John Warren
Fore	*John Nugent*
WEXFORD CO.	Arthur Loftus; Nicholas Loftus
Wexford	*John Furlong; Patrick French*
Ross	*Nicholas Dormer; Christopher Brook*
Newborough	Adam Loftus; William Plunkett
Fethard	*Hugh Rochfort; Nicholas Stafford*
Enniscorthy	William Swanton; Ralph Waddington
Taghmon	*Richard Barnewall*
Bannow	*Christopher Holywood; Gerald Cheevers*
WICKLOW CO.	William Parsons; William Ussher
Wicklow	Richard Parsons; John Hoy
Carysfort	(Philip Mainwaring) Walter Loftus; Francis Cosbie

MUNSTER

CLARE CO.	*Dermot O'Brien; Donagh O'Brien*
Ennis	Ralph Leventhorpe; Simon Thorowgood
CORK CO.	William St. Leger; *Donough MacCarthy*
Cork	*Andrew Barrett; Dominick Roche*
Youghal	*Edward Gough; Theobald Ronane*
Kinsale	*Patrick Roche; Philip Roche*
Mallow	William Kingsmill; Thomas Pigott
Baltimore	Bryan Jones; Henry Kneyveton
Bandon	Francis Slingsby; Anthony Dopping
Clonakilty	Robert Travers; Peregrine Banister
KERRY CO.	Valentine Browne; Edward Denny
Dingle	Christopher Roper; George Blundell
Tralee	Thomas Maule; Henry Osborne
Ardfert	David Crosby; Anthony Stoughton
LIMERICK CO.	*Edward FitzHarris;* Hardress Waller
Limerick	*Dominick White; Peter Creagh*
Kilmallock	William St. Leger; *John Power*
Askeaton	Maurice Williams; George Crofton
TIPPERARY CO.	*James Butler; Thomas Butler*
Clonmel	William Smith; Richard Geathing
Cashel	Thomas Little sen.; Patrick Boyton
Fethard	Thomas Hennessey; Patrick Vyne

WATERFORD CO.	Sir Richard Osborne; *John Power*
Waterford	*Richard Butler; John Walsh*
Dungarvan	Sir Richard Osborne; John Hore
Tallagh	John Ogle; John Barry FitzWilliam
Lismore	John Brown; Stephen Crowe

CONNACHT

GALWAY CO.	*Ulick Bourke; Richard Blake*
Galway	*Robert Lynch; Valentine Blake*
Athenry	*Geoffrey Browne; John Blake*
Tuam	Thomas Rotheram; Henry Bringhurst
LEITRIM CO.	Charles Coote, jun.; Humphrey Reynolds
Jamestown	John Gifford; Francis Hamilton
Carrick	George St. George; John Jackson
MAYO CO.	*Theobald Bourke; Thomas Bourke*
Castlebar	Henry Bingham; George Carr
ROSCOMMON CO.	Lucas Dillon; Henry Dillon
Roscommon	Robert Bysse; Walter Loftus
Boyle	Robert King; Richard Wingfield
SLIGO CO.	George Radcliffe; *Theobald Taaffe*
Sligo	Thomas Radcliffe; *Kean O'Hara*

ULSTER

ANTRIM CO.	Capt. Arthur Chichester; Roger Langford
Carrickfergus	William Sambach; John Davys
Belfast	William Wray; George Rawden
ARMAGH CO.	Faithful Fortescue; William Bromloe
Armagh	William Dixon; Archibald Hamilton
Charlemont	John Martin; Henry Browne
CAVAN CO.	*Philip FitzHugh Reilly;* Robert Baily
Belturbet	John Borlase; *Richard Ash*
Cavan	Alan Cook; Edward Lake
DONEGAL CO.	Ralph Gore; Paul Davis
Donegal	Andrew Wilson; William Dixon
Lifford	William Wandesford; Robert Netleton
Ballyshannon	Robert Meredith; *James Cusack*
Killybegs	Edward Torleton; Thomas Tallys
FERMANAGH CO.	*Rory Maguire;* William Cole
Enniskillen	John Borlase; Arthur Champion
MONAGHAN CO.	Richard Blaney; Nicholas Simpson
Monaghan	Arthur Culume; William Cadowgan
TYRONE CO.	Tobias Caulfield; Audley Mervin
Clogher	George Wandesford; Henry Manning
Dungannon	John Chichester; Thomas Madden

Strabane	Richard FitzGerald; James Galbreth
Agher	Robert Birron; William Peaslie
LONDONDERRY CO.	Henry Conway; Edward Rowley
Derry	Robert Stewart; Francis Butler
Coleraine	Charles Moncke; Edmond Cossens
Limavady	Audley Phillips; John Usher
DOWN CO.	Edward Trevor; James Montgomery
Newry	William Reading; Tobias Poynes
Downpatrick	William Billingsley; Marcus Trevor
Newtownards	George Montgomery; Hugh Montgomery
Bangor	John Hamilton; James Hamilton
Killelagh	Paul Reynolds; George Netleton

APPENDIX III

COMMISSION FOR DEFECTIVE TITLES 1636

4 May, 1636

Compositions made upon his ma^ts^ Commission of Grace for remedy of Defective Titles: the first summes being the old Rents formerly paid; the Second Summes, are the increase of Rents now added; and the Third summes are the Totalls of both, being the entire Rents now reserved and payable to his ma^ty^ by the persons heretofore mentioned (videlicet).

	Old Rents			*Increases*			*Totalls*		
	£	*s.*	*d.*	£	*s.*	*d.*	£	*s.*	*d.*
Edward Dowdall	9	16	6	10	3	6	20	0	0
Christopher Plunkett	6	5	0	3	15	0	10	0	0
Teig McCarty	0	18	9	4	1	3	5	0	0
William Dillon	14	10	0	15	10	0	30	0	0
Sir Robert Pygott	8	4	7½	7	17	1½	16	1	9
Alexander Cosby	21	17	5¼	21	9	11¼	43	7	4½
James Hovenden	5	0	1½	5	0	1½	10	0	3
Sr William Cooley bt	36	10	6¾	12	13	10¾	49	4	5½
Anthony Skelton	1	13	4½	3	6	9	5	0	1½
Thomas Beard	1	2	6	2	5	0	3	7	6
William Hethrington	1	3	3	2	6	6	3	9	9
Sir John Bowen kt	8	9	1½	8	9	1½	16	18	3
Thomas Hovington	11	9	6	9	2	7½	20	12	1½
George Graham	3	11	5¼	3	11	5¼	7	2	10½
Thomas Graham	7	13	2¼	7	13	2¼	15	6	4½
Sir Barnaby Brien kt	2	3	9	2	3	9	4	7	6
Thomas Keatting	0	12	6¾	1	5	1¾	1	17	8½
John Apprie	1	8	1½	2	16	3	4	4	4½
Sir Thomas Loftus kt	0	5	9¼	1	4	2¾	1	10	0
The Lord of Dunboyne	10	3	9¾	10	3	9¾	20	7	7½
Donogh McShane Creagh	0	7	6	1	2	6	1	10	0
William Savadge	1	2	6	3	7	6	4	10	0
James Fynne	0	9	6¾	0	19	1½	1	8	8¼
Summe	154	19	11½	140	7	9¼	295	7	8¾

	Old Rents			Increases			Totalls		
	£	s.	d.	£	s.	d.	£	s.	d.
Sᶦʳ William Gilbert bᵗ	0	19	10½	1	19	9	2	19	7½
Nicholas Sanchy	2	8	9	2	8	9	4	17	6
Robert Leyester	3	9	4½	3	9	4½	6	18	9
Sʳ Jasper Harbrt kᵗ	4	4	2¼	8	8	4¾	12	12	7
Thomas Davills	1	8	1½	2	16	3	4	4	4½
William Soare	0	15	11¼	0	15	11¼	1	11	10½
Alexander Barrington	4	0	0¾	4	0	0¾	8	0	1½
Edward Brereton	3	17	0¾	3	17	0¾	7	14	1½
Edward McColly Phillipps	1	8	1½	2	16	3	4	4	4½
Walter Baskerville	1	16	9	1	16	9	3	13	6
Cooley Phillipps	8	4	5	1	10	0	9	14	5
Maurice Tirrell	2	10	7½	2	10	7½	5	1	3
Thomas FitzGerald of Clonbolge	6	16	3¼	6	3	8¼	13	0	0
Michaell Doyne	0	5	0	1	5	0	1	10	0
James Garrett	0	16	10½	0	16	10½	1	13	9
James Earle of Ormond	7	13	9	7	13	9	15	7	6
Sʳ Hardres Waller kᵗ	27	7	7	8	17	6	36	5	1
Anthony Dowdall	4	11	0	1	2	6	5	13	6
Thomas FitzGerald of Imo	1	11	9	1	11	9	3	3	6
Sʳ John Gifford kᵗ	1	17	6	1	17	6	3	15	0
Charles o Connor	5	7	4½	5	7	4½	10	14	9
Geoffrey Fay	2	9	8½	0	10	3½	3	0	0
James Farroll	21	18	7½	4	4	9½	26	3	5
Peter Rooth & Henry Shea	0	15	0	2	5	0	3	0	0
Nicholas Dowdall	1	1	7½	0	7	2½	1	8	10
Sʳ George Harbert bᵗ	7	10	0	10	10	0	18	0	0
Sʳ George Radcliff bᵗ	5	5	6	3	7	10	8	13	4
John Dillon	3	16	3	0	12	6	4	8	9
Robert Hartpoole Esqʳ	26	3	7½	26	3	7½	52	7	3
William Parsons Esqʳ	37	16	10½	6	16	5½	44	13	4
The Lady Ann Parsons	13	0	5	2	14	2	15	14	7
Summe	211	9	0½	128	17	0	340	6	2

	Old Rents £	s.	d.	Increases £	s.	d.	Totalls £	s.	d.
Robert Park	24	17	5½	4	19	2	29	16	7½
Wm Hethrington of Balliroan	8	10	4½	8	10	4½	17	0	9
Richard Farroll	23	2	6	9	17	0	32	19	6
Richard FitzGerald	8	10	0	2	0	0	10	10	0
Hugh o Dallaghan	1	3	10½	0	4	5½	1	8	8
Cohegery Coghlan	1	11	2½	0	6	2	1	17	4½
James Dillon	4	16	4	0	16	11	5	13	3
Robert Dillon	7	16	5	1	9	8½	9	6	1
William Peisely	24	3	4	4	0	8	28	4	0
Samuell Price	4	8	5	0	12	6	5	0	11
Faghney McRoss Farroll	32	19	6½	6	0	1½	38	19	8
James McGarrett Farroll	2	6	2	0	8	11	2	15	1
The Lord Bishop of Ardagh	13	2	10½	2	1	8	15	4	6¼
Sr Richard Brown Kt	1	18	7	0	5	8½	2	4	3½
Terence Coghlan	5	18	10	3	15	9½	9	14	7½
John Byss Esqr	1	13	9	1	13	9	3	7	6
Roger Farroll	20	0	0	5	17	0	25	17	0
Hubert Dillon	4	5	4	0	15	11	5	3	3
Patrick Foxe	7	6	9½	2	15	3½	10	2	1
Matthew Derenzi Esqr	17	19	9¾	3	3	7	21	3	4¾
Peter Hussey Esqr	7	6	3	1	9	9	8	16	0
Edmond McHubert Farroll	1	8	5½	0	5	3½	1	13	9
Nathaniell Hollington	5	1	11	0	16	8	5	18	7
Sr Charles Coote Baronett	25	1	9	7	5	10	32	7	7
Sr John Straton bt	27	2	4¼	4	3	4	31	5	8¼
The Earl of Londonderry	14	4	1½	27	3	7	41	7	8½
Sir Piers Crosby bt	15	10	7¼	15	10	7¼	31	1	2½
Summe	312	7	0	116	9	9	428	6	9

	Old Rents			Increases			Totalls		
	£	s.	d.	£	s.	d.	£	s.	d.
Edward Bermingham	1	7	2¼	1	7	2¼	2	14	4½
Tho. FitzGerrald of the Vallie	20	10	0	20	10	0	41	0	0
Thomas Clarke	6	5	10½	1	0	10	7	6	8½
Hubert Dillon	3	1	3	0	16	6½	3	17	9½
Olyver Flood	1	10	9	3	1	6	4	12	3
Lisagh mcGillernon	7	9	2	1	9	10	8	19	0
John Farroll of Tyrlickin	3	10	0	0	14	2½	4	4	2½
James mcWilliam Carroll	2	10	0	0	9	5	2	19	5
Kedagh Farroll	0	14	3½	0	2	8	0	16	11½
Carbry Farroll	2	4	4½	0	8	7½	2	13	0
Magha McShane Farroll	1	12	7½	0	3	5½	1	16	1
Edmond Farroll	0	5	6	0	4	6	0	10	0
Connell Farroll	1	12	4	0	4	9½	1	17	1½
Edmond mcCormock Faroll	3	7	9	0	11	7	3	19	4
Teig mcCormack Farroll	1	7	6	0	4	11	1	12	5
Kadagh McGerald Farroll	2	11	3½	0	8	8	2	19	11½
Summa	59	19	10½	31	18	8½	91	18	7½

New Rents. Those subsequent Rents are reserved upon the new Composition made for His Ma^{ty} where no Rent att all was formerly reserved, viz.

	New Rents		
	£	s.	d.
Thomas Luttrell Gent.	5	0	0
Thomas Lyneham	0	6	0
James Knolles	12	0	0
John Archdeacon	7	10	0
Robert Wise	10	0	0
John Kennedy	7	12	0
Robert Allen	0	15	0
Phillipp Hoare	3	0	0
The Lo. Chichester	0	10	0
Thomas Nugent	2	12	6
John Verdon	1	0	3
Richard Barry	7	13	0
Luke Plunkett	3	0	0
John Fagan	0	6	6
Arminett Plunkett	0	2	3
Walter Plunkett	3	0	0
The Lo. of Hoth	0	3	0
Charles McCarty	6	0	0
John Ankehill	13	6	8
John Newgent	4	2	6
The Lo. Viscount Netterville	17	5	0
Thomas Nugent for James & Edmond Nugent	1	15	7½
John Newman	0	5	3
Richard Myles	2	3	6
Tho. Garrett Marshall	1	0	0
S^{ir} Richard Blake b^t	0	7	6
S^{ir} Robert Dixon b^t	4	11	0
S^{ir} Thomas Savadge b^t	10	13	9
S^{ir} Robert Meredith b^t	1	0	0
S^{ir} Robert Forth b^t	4	1	4½
Henry Warron	2	0	0
Peter Rooth	1	0	0
The Cittie of Dublin	1	10	0
James Bathe	2	18	1½
Summ of New Rents is	138	10	9½

Somme of the old Rents is £738 13s. 11½d.
Somme of Rents increased is £417 13s. 3½d.
Somme of New Rents is £138 10s. 9½d.

BIBLIOGRAPHICAL NOTE

(i) POLITICAL

THE bulk of the material available for writing an historical account of Wentworth's administration in Ireland is official correspondence, either written by the lord deputy or intended to be read by him. Subconsciously therefore the historian may come to look at all problems through Wentworth's eyes and it is for this reason that the main problem confronting him is to try to lay hold of non-official evidence whether Gaelic Irish, old English or new English.

The official view-point is most fully documented in Wentworth's own letters. By comparison with them, the collection of State papers, Ireland, in the English Public Record Office (S.P. 46) is meagre, the most important items being letters written in 1640, after Wentworth's fall from power, between officials in Ireland and the English secretary of state. Some of them are printed in M. A. Hickson, *Ireland in the seventeenth century* (1884), ii. 332–40.

Letters between Wentworth and the two English secretaries of state John Coke (1625–40) and Francis Windebank (1632–41), form a large proportion of the Strafford MSS., as also does Wentworth's correspondence with the various members of the Irish committee of the Privy Council, Richard Weston, earl of Portland, Thomas Howard, earl of Arundel, Francis Cottington, chancellor of the exchequer, and William Laud, archbishop of Canterbury. With Cottington and with Laud, Wentworth corresponded on a more informal plane than with the rest, and these letters provide some evidence for Wentworth's unofficial views. The largest and most important collection of the Strafford MSS. is now housed in Sheffield City Library, having been moved there from Wentworth Woodhouse in 1949. In their present uncalendared state, they consist of eleven letter books, containing copies of Wentworth's official correspondence. There are also eight books, arranged by date, containing original letters to Wentworth from 1627 to 1639. (The key to the code used by Laud and Wentworth is to be found on the flyleaf, vol. 7 of the letter books.)[1] A number of the other volumes in the Strafford Papers contain items of Irish interest, in particular volumes 23–4, and 34. A good proportion of the letters are to be found printed in W. Knowler (ed.), *The Letters and Dispatches of the Earl of*

---

[1] Cf. also W. Scott and J. Bliss (ed.), *The works of William Laud* (vi, pt. 1, 247).

Strafforde (1739). Other letters of Wentworth are to be found in *The Works of William Laud*, ed. W. Scott and J. Bliss, (1847–60), vi–vii, and in *Camden Miscellany*, viii. (1883) and ix. (1895) which contains a few letters edited by S. R. Gardiner and C. H. Firth respectively. The 'Berwick Letters', of which transcripts are to be found in the Public Record Office of Northern Ireland, contain ten letters of Wentworth to Bramhall (1634–9).[1] Many of the letters of secretary Coke are to be found in *H.M.C. Cowper MSS.*, vol. i.

For evidence as to a point of view independent of the lord deputy, it is perhaps inevitable that the new English opposition should provide more than old English or Gaelic Irish. The most important of these new English sources is the account of the impeachment of Wentworth in *The Tryall of Thomas earl of Strafford*, ed. J. Rushworth (1680). The attitude of the earl of Cork is indicated in his diary printed by A. B. Grosart in *Lismore Papers*, 1st series I–V, and his letters, a selection of which were printed by Grosart in ibid., 2nd series. The correspondence of Richard Boyle is now at Chatsworth; little of importance remains in the Lismore collection itself, now housed in the National Library of Ireland. In the Public Record Office of Ireland there is a letter book of Henry Cary, Viscount Falkland (P.R.O.I., MS. 2445), which is useful for the first year of Wentworth's administration.

The letters of Sir Arthur Ingram, who was involved in the Irish customs farm as well as other business, are now in Leeds City Library (Temple Newsam MSS.), partly calendared in *H.M.C. Var. Coll.*, viii. 1–191.

The papers of the Loftus family form part of the Drogheda collection in the National Library of Ireland, but they contain no important material for these years. Evidence for the dispute between Wentworth and Viscount Loftus over the marriage settlement of Loftus' eldest son, as a result of which Loftus was imprisoned, is to be found in *H.M.C. Report*, ix. 293 ff. The papers of Sir William Parsons at Birr (Parsonstown) were reported upon in *H.M.C. Report*, ii. 217 ff.: they contain little of interest before the outbreak of the 1641 rebellion; there is, however, a letter from Phelim Molloy dated 17 March 1641/2 appealing to Parsons to join the Catholics against 'the Puritants', a somewhat forlorn hope. The Massereene papers, now in P.R.O.N.I., which might have been expected to throw light upon Sir John Clotworthy's activities during the period of Wentworth's trial and before, are of no value for this period.

The relevant volumes of the Ormonde MSS. in the National Library

---

[1] Printed in E. Berwick (ed.), *The Rawdon papers* (1819). Cf. also *Huntington Library Bulletin* (April 1934) for a report upon the Hastings MSS. which contain much Irish material including letters from Laud to Bramhall.

of Ireland (N.L.I. MSS. 2304–7) contain some letters between Patrick Darcy and Ormonde at the time of the plantation of Connacht. There are also some of Wandesforde's letters to Ormonde in the same collection. The Carte MSS. in the Bodleian contain material relating to the plantations of Connacht and Ormonde, but little else of importance for this period.

One of the most valuable of the new English sources is the correspondence of Philip Percival,[1] calendared *H.M.C. Egmont Papers*, i. pt. i. Percival was clerk of the Court of Wards; his home was in Munster and he also played his part in the plantation of Connacht. One of his correspondents was John Barry, who was in London during the first half of 1641. Thanks to this, the *Egmont Papers* provide a few valuable letters during the crucial period of Strafford's trial, at a time when the Irish agents were in England, seeking redress of their grievances.

The old English evidence for Wentworth's deputyship is very scanty. There is nothing relevant in the papers of the families of Cusack, Dillon and Fingall, which have been deposited in the National Library of Ireland. There are, however, the letters of Clanricarde to Sir Henry Lynch (c. 1624–32), which throw light upon his attitude to the projected plantation of Connacht (N.L.I., MS. 3111). *The memoirs and letters of Ulick, Marquis of Clanrickarde* (1757) contain only material from October 1641 onwards. A pamphlet entitled 'A Discourse between two Counsellors of State, the one of England and the other of Ireland', printed December 1642,[2] gives a critical account of Wentworth's actions from the old English point of view. In the first volume of *History of the Irish confederation*, ed. J. T. Gilbert (1882–91) the attitude adopted by Sir Richard Bellings provides an example of a more favourable estimate to Wentworth on the part of at least one member of the old English gentry. The 'Apology of the Anglo-Irish' for rising in arms in 1641 is printed in *History of the Irish Confederation*, ed. J. T. Gilbert, i. 246–52.

During this period, it is easy to lose sight of Gaelic Irish opinion. The plantations of the early seventeenth century in large measure removed the ruling class of Gaelic Irish society in Ulster, Longford and elsewhere; and in the absence of their natural spokesmen, the Gaelic Irish case tended to go by default. They were barely represented in the parliaments of 1613, 1634 and 1640. Not until after 1641 was the strength of the Gaelic Irish to be fully demonstrated in the army of Owen Roe O'Neill; and therefore during the period of Wentworth's deputyship, the most the historian can do is to remind himself constantly of hidden Ireland[3] which lies beyond his largely English sources.

[1] B.M., Add. MSS., 46920–47213.   [2] B.M., Egerton MS. 917.
[3] Reference may be made to the 'Memorial of the Longford Irish' printed in M. Hickson, *Ireland in the seventeenth century*, ii. 293, and the 'Remonstrance of Phelim O'Byrne', ibid., 306.

T

(II) RELIGIOUS

The greatest gap in this field is a study of the Counter-Reformation in Ireland. To some extent, however, it has been filled by publications on particular topics. In 1954 Fr. Brendan Jennings published a comprehensive selection of the papers of Luke Wadding, the Irish Franciscan who enjoyed a great deal of influence in Rome under Urban VIII and Innocent XI (*Wadding Papers*, Irish Manuscripts Commission). The commemoration volume of essays, *Father Luke Wadding* (Dublin 1957), also throws a good deal of light upon Irish links with Spain and Rome. There is a good deal of useful material in P. F. Moran, *Spicilegium Ossoriense* (1874–84). The best survey of English state policy during this period is that given by R. Dudley Edwards in *Studies in honour of Michael ó Clerigh*, ed. Fr. Sylvester O'Brien, O.F.M. (1944). A recent article by P. J. Corish, 'Two contemporary historians of the Confederation; John Lynch and Richard O'Ferrall' (*I.H.S.*, viii, no. 31, March 1953), brings out clearly the clash between Anglo-Irish and Gaelic Irish ecclesiastics on the plane of historical writing. An additional group of articles by the same author in *Irish Theological Quarterly* (1951–4) illustrates the same point. Reference may also be made to several journals of local ecclesiastical history, of which *Seanchas Ardmacha* (Armagh) and *Reportorium Novum* (Dublin) are the most important. The *Proceedings of the Catholic Historical Committee* contain a good deal of information about material of Irish interest on the continent. Most valuable of all these periodicals is *Archivium Hibernicum*, in which many early seventeenth-century ecclesiastical documents have been printed. For a Franciscan history, see O'Brien, op. cit. The Capuchins are the subject of a forthcoming monograph by F. Martin, O.S.A., There is no satisfactory treatment of the Jesuits or the secular clergy during this period.

The standard works upon the Church of Ireland are: R. Mant, *History of the Church of Ireland* (1840) and the articles by G. V. Jourdan in W. A. Phillips (ed.), *History of the Church of Ireland* (1933). The Ussher Centenary number of *Hermathena* (1956) provides a valuable supplement to these. Ussher's letters were printed by C. Elrington in his edition of the *Works* (1864). Laud's letters (W. Scott and J. Bliss (eds.), *Works*) contain much material from the English point of view. Bramhall's letters to Laud are to be found in *H.M.C. Hastings MSS.*, iv, and there is also a selection of his papers in E. P. Shirley, *Papers relating to the Church of Ireland* (1874). The *Civil Survey*, ed. R. C. Simington, gives details of glebe land and tithes. The contemporary lives of Bedell, ed. E. S. Shuckburgh (1902), also contain information as to the way in which a diocese was run. A full bibliography is provided in W. A. Phillips, above.

J. S. Reid's *History of the Presbyterian Church of Ireland* though published as long ago as 1834 has stood the test of time remarkably well and there is still no fuller modern treatment of this subject.

(III) ECONOMIC

The economic history of Ireland in the seventeenth century, by and large, remains to be written and perhaps it can never be written in the same detail as that of a country like England, since so many Irish records of this period, public and private, have perished. Even such economic history as has been produced with the evidence available frequently lies open to the criticism that contemporary difficulties and problems in the relationship between England and Ireland loom far too large in the historian's interpretation of past events. This criticism may be made even of the standard work by G. O'Brien, *Economic history of Ireland in the seventeenth century* (1919).

The most important event—or succession of events—in Irish economic history during this period was the movement of colonisation by Scottish and English settlers. The political and legal background of this movement has been discussed in such books as G. Hill, *The plantation in Ulster*, and W. F. T. Butler, *Confiscation in Irish history* (1917). The wider economic background which made the plantations so much more of a reality in the early seventeenth century than they had been in the sixteenth, has been neglected. The reasons which compelled large numbers of Scots to cross into Ulster; the regions of England which provided the settlers for the Irish plantations; the links between the Irish plantations and the colonising emigration to the new world; the effect of unemployment or land hunger in England—the answers to these and other questions remain unknown. With the exception of T. W. Moody, *The Londonderry plantation*, there is no satisfactory treatment of the economic side of the plantations and their effect upon the economic life of the country.

The pattern of Irish economic life during this period outside the broadest generalities still remains to be discovered. The relative importance of pasture and arable, the flax-growing and wool-growing areas and the economic state of particular sections of the population, are the type of questions which may well be asked. Some of the evidence which will provide an answer is to be found in the *Civil Survey*, ed. R. C. Simington (1931–53). Unfortunately only the material for nine counties survives, Dublin, Donegal, Kildare, Limerick, Londonderry, Meath, Tipperary, Waterford and Wexford, but a good deal may be made of this, as a recent article by Dr. J. G. Simms suggests (*I.H.S.*, ix, no. 35, March 1955). *The Lismore Papers* (ed. A. B. Grosart), 10 vols., and the Egmont Papers (B.M., Add. MSS. 46920–47016) give information about the economic activities of two important Munster landowners. The successive surveys made of the Ulster plantation (cf. G. Hill, *The plantation in Ulster*) yield material for the north of Ireland. Only Connacht remains almost a complete *tabula rasa*, though even here the *Compossicion Booke of Conought*, ed. A. M. Freeman (1936), provides a useful starting point for speculation together with W. O'Sullivan ed., *The Strafford Inquisition of Co. Mayo* (1958).

For particular areas, the most important modern accounts so far deal with Ulster. They are T. W. Moody, op. cit., E. R. R. Green, *The Lagan Valley* (1949) and W. H. Hutchinson, *Tyrone Precinct* (1952). In *Mourne Country* (1951), E. Estyn Evans has provided a sketch of the historical geography of South Down. W. O'Sullivan, *Economic History of Cork City* (1937), and M. D. O'Sullivan, *Old Galway* (1942), are also of value. Many of the older local histories such as Hore's *Wexford* provide valuable economic details (cf. M. Wall (ed.), A handlist of Irish county and town histories, Irish Catholic Historical committee).

The financial history of Ireland during this period has not been written, although an attempt is made in this work to provide studies of what were two of the most important sources of the Irish revenue—the customs farm and the court of wards and liveries. The papers of Sir Arthur Ingram,[1] who was a prime mover in the first Irish customs farm, contain a good deal of information on this topic. Another source is a survey made in 1637 by the surveyor-general Charles Monck at the orders of the lord deputy (B.M., Harleian MS. 2138, no. 47; transcript no. 615 in P.R.O.N.I.). Some appreciation of the issues involved may be gathered from A. P. Newton's article, 'The establishment of the Great Farm of the English customs' (Trans. R. Hist. Soc., 4th ser., i. 129–56 (1918)). Various records of the court of wards are to be found in Trinity College, Dublin, and Public Record Office of Ireland. For a discussion, reference may be made to my article, 'The court of wards and liveries in Ireland, 1622–41' in *R.I.A. Proc.*, lvii, sect. C, no. 2. Both the customs farm and the court of wards illustrate the interconnection between political and financial history (and in the case of the latter, religious history).

The construction of a picture of Irish trade during this period suffers from the same shortage of evidence. There are no Irish port books, with the exception of a few copies for the years 1613–15, in the papers of Sir Arthur Ingram. These few, however, throw some light upon trade between Ulster and Scotland. For facts about trade between Ireland and England, the historian must rely largely upon the English port books for the western ports of England. The port books record

---

[1] Temple Newsam MSS., Leeds City Library.

the Irish commodities which entered England legally and are therefore open to the criticism that they do not take smuggled commodities into account. In the case of Bristol, moreover, the commodities exported to Ireland are not specified: the entry in the port book is normally 'so many "wares" valued at so much'. Nevertheless, details about the Irish cattle trade, wool trade and linen yarn trade may be obtained from the English port books as from no other source. The papers of Sir Matthew Derenzy, a customs official during this period, throw light upon the wine and tobacco trade (P.R.O., SP/46). A survey of the Irish wine trade with Spain and France in the year 1615 (*I.H.S.*, ix, no. 36, September 1955) gives a picture which was probably similar to that twenty years later (P.R.O., E122/196/14). The diary and letters of the earl of Cork (published in the *Lismore Papers*) provide evidence for trade in pig iron, wrought iron and pipe-staves between Munster and the continent and England. Information about Dutch interests in Irish trade may be obtained from the great collection of notarial records in the municipal archives of Amsterdam, though the number of documents which specifically refer to Ireland is small. The archives of Middelburg, the merchants of which are known to have traded with Ireland, were destroyed during the course of the second World War.

Of secondary sources, A. Longfield, *Anglo-Irish trade in the sixteenth century* (1929) and E. A. Lewis, *Welsh Port Books 1505–1603* (1927) though they refer to an earlier period provide material relevant for the early seventeenth century. Studies of ports and particular regions of England, which traded with Ireland are also useful, in particular W. G. Hoskins, *Trade, industry and people in Exeter 1688–1800* (1936), C. N. Parkinson, *Rise of the port of Liverpool* (1952), P. McGrath, *Merchants and merchandise in seventeenth century Bristol* (1955), and A. P. Wadsworth and J. de Lacy Mann, *The cotton trade and industrial Lancashire* (1931). The trade of Chester during this period still awaits satisfactory historical treatment.

Finally, attention must be turned to economic policy. Wentworth's economic policy was not something conceived in the abstract but an attempt to find a solution to certain specific problems. The nearest he got to a full discussion of these was in a report made to the English privy council in 1636 (Knowler, *Strafford's letters*, ii. 18–19). In other letters he expressed his views on Spanish trade with Ireland, the Irish wool and linen trade with England and the manufacture of iron. These letters, however, should not be treated in isolation from the general background of English commercial policy, as found illustrated in State Papers, domestic, and Acts of the Privy Council. The letters of Secretary Coke (*H.M.C. Cowper MSS.*) are also relevant in this connection. A full discussion of English commercial policy in the period immediately preceding Wentworth's deputyship is to be found in A. Friis, *Alderman*

Cockayne's project and the cloth trade: the commercial policy of England, 1603–25 (1927). Mercantilism in general is discussed by E. H. Heckscher, *Mercantilism* (1934). There are a number of useful articles on related topics: A. V. Judges, 'The idea of a mercantile state' in *R. Hist. Soc. Trans.* (1939), B. E. Supple, 'Thomas Mun and the commerical crisis, 1623' in *Bull. Inst. Hist. Research*, xxviii (1954) and R. W. K. Hinton, 'The mercantile system in the time of Thomas Mun' in *Econ. Hist. Rev.*, vii, no. 3 (1955). W. R. Scott, *The constitution and finance of English, Scottish and Irish joint stock companies to 1720* (1910–12), is in many ways the best introduction to the economic history of the period.

BIBLIOGRAPHY

	page
A. Guides to Sources	277
B. Original Sources	278
(i) Manuscript material	278
(ii) Printed and Calendared Material	280
C. Contemporary and Nearly Contemporary Chronicles, etc.	281
(i) Manuscript material	281
(ii) Printed Material	281
D. Modern Works	282

A. GUIDES TO SOURCES

Abbott (T. K.). *Catalogue of the manuscripts in the library of Trinity College, Dublin* (Dublin, 1900). Addenda in *Bull. Inst. Hist Research*, iii (1925).

British Museum. Catalogues of Harleian, Stowe, Sloane and Lansdowne collections and of Additions to the Manuscripts.

Davies (Godfrey). *Bibliography of British history, Stuart period* (Oxford, 1928).

Dunlop (R.) 'Bibliography of Irish history from the Ulster plantation to the Cromwellian settlement' in *Cambridge Modern History*, iv.

Edwards (R. D.) (contains an extensive bibliography). *Church and State in Tudor Ireland* (Dublin, 1935).

Hardy (T. D.) & Brewer (J. S.). *Report . . . upon the Carte and Carew papers* (London, 1864).

Hayes (R. J.). *Report of the Council of Trustees of the National Library of Ireland, 1949–50, 1950–1* (Dublin, 1950, 1952).

Hunt (R. W.). *A summary catalogue of western manuscripts in the Bodleian Library at Oxford which have not hitherto been catalogued in the Quarto Series* (7 vols., Oxford, 1922–53) (with index volume 1953).

Madan (Falconer). *Summary catalogue of western manuscripts in the Bodleian Library.*

Murray (R. H.). *Ireland, 1603–1714* (London, 1920).

National Library of Ireland. 'Hand List of MSS. in the Library' in *Report of the Council of Trustees* (1932–3).

Prendeville (P.L.). 'A select bibliography of Irish economic history'. *Econ. Hist. Rev.*, iii (1932).

Public Record Office of Ireland. *Reports of the Deputy-Keeper of the Public Record office of Ireland.* Reports I– (Dublin, 1869–).

Royal Irish Academy. 'Catalogue of Haliday Pamphlets and Tracts' (Manuscript).

Russell (C. W.) & Prendergast (J. P.). *Report on the Carte manuscripts in the Bodleian Library, Oxford* (London, 1871).

Scott (J. R.) & White (N. J. D.). *Catalogue of the manuscripts remaining in Marsh's Library, Dublin* (Dublin, 1913).

Wall (M.) A handlist of Irish county and town histories. (Irish Catholic Historical committee, 1955).

Wood (Herbert). *Guide to the records deposited in the Public Record Office of Ireland* (Dublin, 1919).

B. ORIGINAL SOURCES

(i) Manuscript Material

Ireland

DUBLIN

Public Record Office of Ireland

MS. 2445. Falkland Letter Book, 1629–33.
MS. 2448. Volume of petitions to Wentworth—June–Nov. 1638.
la. 53. 67–8. Transcripts of Court of Wards records. 2 vols.

Trinity College Library

F.3.22. Leases made by Court of Wards, July 1626–Feb. 1627/8.
F.1.12. Leases made by Court of Wards, Feb. 1627/8–July 1634.
F.3.29
F.3.30
F.1.3. } Wardships and alienations, 1630–8.
F.1.9
E.3.7.   Lease of Irish customs to Sir James Hay.
F.3.17. 'Thomas Cave's instructions for customs officers', c. 1630.

National Library of Ireland

MS. 3111. Clanrickarde MSS.
Drogheda MSS. (contain material relating to Viscount Loftus).
Lismore MSS.
MSS. 2301–7. Ormonde MSS.
MSS. 8013–14. Rich MSS.

Marsh's Library

Z.4.2.1. 'Notes of proceedings in the High Commission Court' by Thomas Howel, Registrar.

Royal Irish Academy

Books of Survey and Distribution.

Dublin City Library

Gilbert collection.

BELFAST

Public Record Office of Northern Ireland

Berwick Letters. Transcript no. 415.
Report made by Charles Monck on the Irish customs. Transcript no. 615
from B. M., Harleian MS. 2138, no. 47.

England

LONDON

British Museum

Egerton MS. 2541 (Papers of Sir Edward Nicholas, secretary of state,
1593–1669).
Egerton MSS. 2592–7 (Correspondence of James Hay, earl of Carlisle, d.
1636).
Egerton MSS. 2645–6 (Papers of Sir Thomas Barrington, *c.* 1589–1644).
Harleian MS. 4297 (Wentworth—Council Order Book, 1633–5).
Add. MS. 19832 (Letters of Richard Boyle, earl of Cork, covering period
1598–1640).
Add. MSS. 29974–5 (Correspondence of Pitt family, including an estimate
of Falkland's estate 1630 and instructions concerning 'the Graces'—
24 May 1628).
Add. MS. 44919 (Buckingham to Falkland).
Add. MS. 45498 (Buckingham to Grandison).
Add. MSS. 46920–47213 (Egmont Papers).

Public Record Office

Acts of the privy council (P.C./2).
Port Books (E/190) (Chester, Bristol, Liverpool, Lancaster, Barnstaple,
Bideford, Minehead).
State papers, domestic (S.P./16).
State papers, Ireland (S.P./63).
State papers, Ireland, supplementary (S.P./46) (contain papers of Sir
Matthew Derenzy).
1615 Wine list (E 122/196/14).

ISLE OF ANGLESEY

Anglesey MSS. (Plas Newydd), Box 12 (Correspondence general—
1634–8, Henry Rich, 1st earl of Holland).

LEEDS

City Library

Temple Newsam MSS. (Papers of Sir Arthur Ingram).

SHEFFIELD

City Library

Strafford MSS
T*

MANCHESTER

Chetham Library

    Mun. A.6.77. Commission by Loftus and Cork, lords justices, to George Downham, bishop of Derry.

OXFORD

Bodleian Library

    Carte MSS.
    Add. MSS. *c.* 286. Letters of Christopher Wandesford.

BASLOW, DERBYSHIRE

Chatsworth House

    Letter book of Richard Boyle, 1629–31.

(ii) Printed and Calendared Material

Archivium Hibernicum (1912–).

Berwick (E.), ed. *The Rawdon papers, consisting of letters . . . to and from J. Bramhall, primate of Ireland* (London, 1819).

Calendar of the Carew manuscripts preserved in the archiepiscopal library at Lambeth (6 vols., London, 1867–73).

Calendar of documents relating to Ireland (5 vols. London, 1875–86).

Calendar of State Papers, colonial (vols. i–ix, London, 1860–94).

Calendar of State Papers, domestic series, 1547– (London, 1856).

Calendar of State Papers relating to Ireland, 1509–1670 (24 vols., London, 1860–1911).

Calendar of State Papers, Venetian (vols. x–xxv, London, 1900–25).

Camden Miscellany, vols. viii–ix (London, 1883 & 1895) containing a few letters of Strafford, edited by S. R. Gardiner and C. H. Firth.

Elrington (C.), ed. *Ussher, works* (Dublin, 1864).

Erck (J. C.), ed. *Repertory of patent rolls, Ireland, James I* (Dublin, 1846).

Carte (T.). *Life of James duke of Ormonde* (Oxford, 1851).

Grosart (A. B.), ed. *Lismore papers* (10 vols., London, 1886–8).

Hickson (Mary). *Ireland in the seventeenth century* (London, 1884).

Hill (J.), ed. *The Montgomery Manuscripts* (Belfast, 1869).

Historical Manuscripts Commission

    1st Report. Corporations of Cork, Dublin, Kilkenny, Limerick and Waterford. Earl of Rosse (Parsons).

    2nd Report. Chetham Library, Manchester. Earl of Rosse (Parsons).

    Series 14. Tenth Report. Appendix V. Corporations of Galway and Waterford.

    Egmont MSS.
    Ormonde MSS.
    Cowper MSS.
    Various Collections, viii.
    Hastings MSS.
    Sackville MSS.

Franciscan MSS.
Drogheda MSS.
Ireland: Statutes at large, vol. i (Dublin, 1786).

Irish Manuscripts Commission
  Freeman (A.M.), ed. *The Compossicion Booke of Conought* (Dublin, 1936).
  Simington (R. C.), ed. *Civil Survey* (9 vols. Dublin, 1931–53).
  Hogan (J), ed. *Letters and papers relating to the Irish rebellion 1642–6*
    (Dublin, 1936).
  Jennings (Brendan), O.F.M., ed. *Wadding Papers,* (Dublin, 1954).
  O'Sullivan (W.) ed., *The Strafford Inquisition of County Mayo.* (Dublin, 1958).
Journal of the Irish house of commons, vol. i (Dublin, 1796–1800).
Journal of the Irish house of lords, vol. i (Dublin, 1779–1800).
Knowler (W.), ed. *Letters and dispatches of the earl of Strafforde* (2 vols., London,
    1739).
Lascelles (R.), ed. *Liber munerum publicorum Hiberniae ab an. 1152 usque ad
    1827* (London, 1824–30).
Lodge (J.), ed. *Desiderata curiosa Hiberniae* (2 vols., Dublin, 1772).
Lowry (T. K.), ed. *The Hamilton manuscripts* (Belfast, 1867).
Lyle (J. V.). *Acts of the privy council of England,* xxxi–xliii (1600–28) (London,
    1905–49).
Moran (P. F.), ed. *Spicilegium Ossoriense* (3 vols., Dublin, 1874–84).
Morrin (J.), ed. *Calendar of patent and close rolls, Ireland, Charles I* (London,
    1863).
O'Brien (G.), ed. *Advertisements for Ireland* (Extra volume of R.S.A.I.,
    Dublin, 1923).
Pender (S.), ed. *A Census of Ireland, c. 1659* (Dublin, 1939).
Rushworth (J.). *The tryal of Thomas, earl of Strafford . . .* (London, 1680).
Rushworth (J.). *Historical collections* (7 vols., London, 1659–1701).
Scott (W.) and Bliss (J.), eds. *The works of William Laud* (7 in 9 vols., Oxford,
    1847–60).
Scrope, (R.) and Monkhouse (T.), ed. *State papers collected by Edward, earl of
    Clarendon* (3 vols., Oxford, 1767–86).
Shuckburgh (E. S.). *Two biographies of William Bedell, bishop of Kilmore*
    (London, 1902).
Steele (R.). *Tudor and Stuart proclamations 1485–1714* (2 vols. Oxford, 1910.).

C. CONTEMPORARY AND NEARLY CONTEMPORARY CHRONICLES ETC.

(i) *Manuscript Material*

Anon. 'A discourse between two Counsellors of State, the one of England,
  the other of Ireland' [1] (B. M., Egerton MSS. 917).

(ii) Printed Material

Boate (G.). 'Ireland's natural history' in *Tracts and treatises, Ireland* (2 vols.,
  Dublin, 1860).

---

[1] Printed at Kilkenny in 1642, but I have been unable to locate a copy.

Darcy (Patrick). *An argument . . . by the expresse order of the House of Commons in the parliament of Ireland* (Dublin, 1764).

Gilbert (J. T.), ed. *History of the Irish confederation and war in Ireland* (7 vols., Dublin, 1882–91).

Gilbert (J. T.). *A contemporary history of affairs in Ireland* (3 vols., Dublin, 1879).

Hawkins (E.), ed. *Brereton's Travels in Holland, the United Provinces, England, Scotland and Ireland* (Chetham Society, Manchester, 1844).

Hogan (Edmund), S. J., ed. *Description of Ireland, 1598* (Dublin, 1898).

Hyde (Edward, earl of Clarendon). *History of the rebellion and civil wars in England* (ed. W. D. Macray) (6 vols., Oxford, 1888).

The government of Ireland under the honourable, just and wise governor Sir John Perrott, knight, 1626 (Philip Mainwaring's own copy in Chetham Library Manchester).

Ley (Sir James). *A learned treatise concerning wards and liveries* (London, 1642).

Morley (Henry), ed. *Ireland under Elizabeth and James I* (London, 1890).

Notestein (W.), ed. *D'Ewes Journal,* vol. i (New Haven, 1923).

Roberts (Lewes). *Merchant's Map of Commerce* (London, 1638).

Temple (Sir John). *The Irish Rebellion . . .* (London, 1646).

Ussher (J.). A speech delivered in the Castle Chamber at Dublin 22 Nov. 1622 at the censuring of certain officers who refused to take the oath of supremacy by James, bishop of Meath. Printed 1631. (Copy in Rylands Library, Manchester.)

D. MODERN WORKS

Bagwell (R). *Ireland under the Stuarts* (3 vols., London, 1909–16).

Ball (F. E.). *The judges in Ireland, 1221–1921* (2 vols., London, 1926).

Bell (H. E.). *The court of wards and liveries* (Cambridge, 1953).

Belmore, earl of (S. R. Lowry-Corry). *Parliamentary memoirs of Fermanagh and Tyrone, 1613–1885* (Dublin, 1887).

Bonn (M. J.). *Die englische Kolonisation in Irland* (Stuttgart and Berlin, 1906).

Brunton (D.) and Pennington (D. H.). *Members of the Long Parliament* (London, 1954).

Burghclere (Lady Winifred). *Strafford* (London, 1931).

Burtchaell (G. D.). *Members of parliament for the county and city of Kilkenny* (Dublin, 1888).

Burtchaell (G. D.), and Sadleir (T. U.). *Alumni Dublinenses; a register of students, graduates, professors and provosts of Trinity College in the University of Dublin* (2nd. ed., Dublin, 1935).

Butler (W. F. T.). *Confiscation in Irish history* (Dublin, 1917).

Butler (W. F. T.). *Gleanings from Irish history.* (London, 1925).

Caulfield (R.), ed. *Council book of the corporation of Cork* (Guildford, Surrey, 1876).

Caulfield (R.), ed. *Council book of the corporation of Kinsale* (Guildford, Surrey, 1879).

Caulfield (R.). *The Council book of the corporation of Youghal* (Guildford, Surrey, 1878).

Chart (D. A.). 'The break-up of the estate of Con O'Neill'. *R.I.A. Proc.*, xlviii, sect. C (1942).

Clark (G. N.). *Guide to English commercial statistics 1696–1782* (London, 1938).

Corish (P. J.). 'Two contemporary historians of the confederation of Kilkenny: John Lynch and Richard O'Ferrall'. *I.H.S.*, viii (1953).

Cox (R.). *Hibernia Anglicana* (2 vols., London, 1689).

Dictionary of National Biography.

Dietz (F. C.). *English public finance, 1558–1641* (Philadelphia, 1932).

Dunlop (R.). 'The plantation of Leix and Offaly'. *E.H.R.*, vi (1891).

Dunlop (R.). 'A note on the export trade of Ireland in 1641, 1665 and 1669'. *E.H.R.*, xxii (1907).

Dunlop (R.). *Ireland under the commonwealth* introduction (Manchester, 1913).

Edwards (R. Dudley). 'Church and state in the Ireland of Michel O Clerigh' in Fr. Sylvester O'Brien (ed.), *Miscellany . . . in honour of Michael O Clerigh* (Dublin, 1944).

Edwards (R. D.), and Moody (T. W.). 'The history of Poynings' Law; part I, 1494–1615'. *I.H.S.*, ii (1941).

Evans (E. Estyn). *Mourne country* (Dundalk, 1951).

Evans (F. M. G.). *The principal secretary of state* (Manchester, 1923).

Fisher (F. J.). 'London's export trade in the early seventeenth century'. *Econ. Hist. Rev.*, 2nd ser., iii (1950).

Friis (A.). *Alderman Cockayne's project and the cloth trade: the commercial policy of England, 1603–25* (Copenhagen and London, 1927).

Gardiner (S. R.). *History of England, 1603–42* (London, 1883–4).

Gill (W. C.). *The Irish linen industry* (Oxford, 1925).

Gogarty (T), ed. 'County Louth depositions, 1641'. *Louth Arch. Soc. Jn.*, iii (1913).

Gras (N. S. B.). 'The Tudor Book of Rates'. *Quar. Journ. Econ.*, xxvi (1912).

Green (E. R. R.). *The Lagan valley* (London, 1949).

Gwynn (A). 'The Irish in the west Indies'. *Analecta Hibernica*, iv (Dublin, 1932).

Hall (H.). *History of the customs revenue* (2 vols., London, 1885).

Harvey (M.). *Life of Thomas Howard, earl of Arundel*, (Cambridge, 1921).

Healy (W.). *History and antiquities of Kilkenny* (Kilkenny, 1893).

Heaton (H.). *The Yorkshire woollen industry* (Oxford, 1920).

Heckscher (Eli. F.). *Mercantilism* (2 vols., London, 1934).

Hexter (J. H.). *Reign of King Pym* (Cambridge, Mass., 1941).

Hickson (M. A.). *Old Kerry records* (2 vols., London, 1872–4).

Hill (G.). *The plantation in Ulster* (Belfast, 1877).

Hore (P. H.). *History of the county of Wexford* (6 vols., 1900–11).

Hoskins (W. G.). *Trade, industry and people in Exeter 1688–1800* (Manchester, 1936).

Hoskins (W. G.). *Devon* (London, 1954).

Hughes (J.). 'The fall of the clan Kavanagh'. *J.R.S.A.I.*, 4th ser. ii (1873).

Hurstfield (J.). 'The revival of feudalism in early Tudor England'. *History*, xxxvii (June, 1952).

Hutchinson, (W. R.). *Tyrone precinct* (Belfast, 1952).

Judges (A. V.). 'The idea of a mercantile state'. *Trans. R. Hist. Soc.*, 4th ser., xxi (1939).

Kearney (H. F.). 'Richard Boyle, Ironmaster'. *J.R.S.A.I.*, lxxxiii (1953).

Kearney (H. F.). 'The Court of Wards and Liveries in Ireland'. *R.I.A. Proc.*, lvii, sect. C, no. 2.

Kearney (H. F.), ed. 'The Irish Wine Trade 1614–15'. *I.H.S.*, ix, (1955).

Keeler (Mary Frear). *The Long Parliament* (Philadelphia, 1954).

Keith (T.). *Commercial relations of England and Scotland 1603–1707* (Cambridge, 1910).

Kiernan (T. J.). *History of the financial administration of Ireland* (London, 1930).

Lipson (E.). *History of the woollen and worsted industries* (London, 1921).

Longfield (A.). *Anglo-Irish trade in the sixteenth century* (London, 1929).

MacCormack (J. R.). 'The Irish adventurers and the English civil war'. *I.H.S.*, x (1956).

Mahaffy (J. P.). *An epoch in Irish history* (London, 1903).

Malcolmson (R.). *The Carlow parliamentary roll* (Dublin, 1872).

Mant (R.). *History of the Church of Ireland* (London, 1840).

McGrath (P. V.). 'The merchant venturers and Bristol shipping'. (*Mariners' Mirror*, xxxvi. (1950).

McGrath (P.). *Merchants and merchandise in seventeenth century Bristol* (Bristol Record Society, vol. xix, 1955).

Moody (T. W.). *The Londonderry plantation* (Belfast, 1939).

Moody (T. W.). 'The treatment of the native population under the scheme for the plantation in Ulster'. *I.H.S.*, ii (1938–9).

Moody (T. W.). 'The Irish parliament under Elizabeth and James I'. *R.I.A. Proc.*, xlv, sect. C, no. 6.

Morris (W. A., and Strayer (J. R.). *The English government at work 1327–36.* ii. *Fiscal administration* (Cambridge, Mass., 1947).

Murray, (A. E.). *A history of the commercial and financial relations between England and Ireland from the period of the Restoration* (London, 1907).

Newton (A. P.). 'The establishment of the Great Farm of the English customs'. *Trans. R. Hist. Soc.* 4th ser., i (1918).

Notestein (W.) and Relf (F.). *Commons debates for 1629* (Minneapolis, 1921).

O'Brien (G.). *Economic history of Ireland in the seventeenth century* (Dublin, 1919).

O'Brien (R. Barry). *Studies in Irish history, 1603–29* (Dublin, 1906).

O'Donovan (J.). *Economic history of live stock in Ireland* (Cork, 1940).

O'Hanlon (J.) and O'Leary (E.). *History of Queen's County* (Dublin, 1907).

O'Grady (H.). *Strafford and Ireland* (2 vols., Dublin, 1923).

O'Sullivan (M. D.). *Old Galway* (Cambridge, 1942).

O'Sullivan (W.). *Economic history of Cork city* (Cork, 1937).

Parkinson (C. N.). *Rise of the port of Liverpool* (London, 1952).

Parry (R.). 'The Gloucestershire woollen industry 1100–1690'. *Trans. Bristol and Glouc. Arch. Soc.* lxvi (1945).

Phillips (W. A.), ed. *History of the church of Ireland* (3 vols., London, 1933).

Pilgrim (J. E.). 'The cloth industry in Essex and Suffolk'. *Bull. Inst. Hist. Research*, xvii (1949).

Posthumus (N. W.). *Bronnon tot de Geschiedenis van de Leidsche Textielnykerheid 1611–50.* iv.

Quinn (D. B.). 'The Irish parliamentary subsidy in the fifteenth and sixteenth centuries'. *R.I.A.*, *Proc.* sect. C., xlii, no. 11 (1935).

Reid (J. S.). *History of the Presbyterian Church in Ireland* (3 vols. Belfast, 1834).

Ramsay (G. D.). *The Wiltshire cloth industry in the sixteenth and seventeenth centuries* (Oxford, 1943).

Ranger (T. O.) 'Richard Boyle and the making of an Irish fortune', *I.H.S.*, x (1957).

Ranke (L. von). *History of England chiefly in the seventeenth century* (Oxford, 1859–69).

Rowe (V. A.). 'Influence of the earls of Pembroke on parliamentary elections'. *E.H.R.*, l. (1935).

Sadleir (T. U.). *Kildare members of parliament 1559–1800* (Kildare Arch. Jn., vi–x, 1909–28).

Scott (W. R.) *The constitution and finance of English, Scottish and Irish joint stock companies to 1720* (3 vols., Cambridge, 1910–12).

Smith (J.). *Chronicon rusticum-commerciale or Memoirs of wool* (London, 1747).

Stubbs (J. W.). *History of the university of Dublin* (Dublin, 1889).

Supple (B. E.). 'Thomas Mun and the commercial crisis, 1623.' *Bull. Inst. Hist. Research*, xxvii (1954).

Tawney (R. H.). 'Rise of the Gentry'. *Econ. Hist. Rev.* xi (1941).

Tawney (R. H.). 'The rise of the Gentry: a postcript'. *Econ. Hist. Rev.*, vii (1954).

Trevor-Roper (H.). *Archbishop Laud 1573–1645* (London, 1940).

Trevor-Roper (H.). 'The Gentry 1540–1640'. *Econ. Hist. Rev.*, supplement no. 1 (Cambridge, 1953).

Unwin (G.). *Industrial organisation in the sixteenth and seventeenth centuries* (Oxford, 1904).

Wadsworth (A. P.) and Mann (Julia de Lacy). *The cotton trade and industrial Lancashire* (Manchester, 1931).

Wedgwood (C. V.). *Strafford* (London, 1935).

Wedgwood (C. V.). *The King's peace* (London, 1955).

Whitaker (T. D.). *Life and original correspondence of Sir George Radcliffe* (London, 1810).

Willson (D. H.). *The privy councillors in the house of commons 1604–29* (Minnesota, 1940).

Wood (H.). 'The Court of Castle Chamber'. *R.I.A. Proc.*, 32, c.

Wood-Martin (W. G.). *History of Sligo from the accession of James I to the revolution of 1688* (Dublin, 1889).

Young (R. M.), ed. *Town book of Belfast 1613–1816* (Belfast, 1892).

ADDENDA

Cooper (J. P.). 'The Fortune of Thomas Wentworth, Earl of Strafford'. *Econ. Hist. Rev.*, 2nd ser., xi (1958–9).

Kearney (H.). 'Ecclesiastical Politics and the Counter-Reformation in Ireland'. *Jn. of Eccl. Hist.*, xi (1960).

Supple (B. E.). *Commercial Crisis and Change in England 1600-42*, (Cambridge, 1949).

Treadwell (V.). 'The Irish Court of Wards under James I'. *I.H.S.*, xii (1960).

INDEX

Note. This index does not include the lists of names given in Appendices II and III.

Abbot, George, abp. of Canterbury, 27
Acts of Parliament (Ireland), confirming defective titles, 54; against unnatural vice, 54; of uses, 58; for church reform, 65; setting up houses of correction, 65; voting subsidies, 54, 65, 189
Alexander, Jerome, 255–6
Allen, Hugh, bp. of Ferns, 121
Anderson, Sir William, 247
Andrews, George, bp. of Ferns, 114, 115
Antrim, Randal MacDonnell, 1st earl of, 49; 2nd earl of, 188–9
Archbold, William, 229–30
Argyll, Archibald Campbell, 8th earl of, 187–8
Armagh, abps. of, *see* Hampton, Lombard, MacCaughwell, O'Reilly, Ussher
Army, Irish: under Falkland, 33; Strafford's army, 187; the 'new' army, 188–9
Articles of 1634, *see* Church of Ireland
Arundel, Thomas Howard, 14th earl of, 29–31
Atherton, John, bp. of Waterford, 114

Bagshawe, Sir Edward, 163, 232–3
Baltimore, George Calvert, 1st baron, 27, 49
Bannister, Archibald, 212
Barnewall, Nicholas, 193, 204–6, 214, 229
Barnewall, Richard, 193, 197, 212, 214, 229
Barron, Geoffrey, 59, 242–3
Barry, James, 244–5
Barry, John, 189, 204
Barry, Richard, 46, 229

Bassett, Sir Arthur, 251
Bath, Sir John, 21
Bathe, James, 214
Bedell, William, bp. of Kilmore, 105
Bellew, Christopher, 193, 212, 225
Bellew, John, 214
Bellings, Richard, 176, 214
Beresford, Tristram, 186, 203, 258
Betsworth, Thomas, 239–40
Billingsley, William, 173, 251–2
Bingham, Sir Henry, 247–9
Birley, Robert, 230
Birne's Country, *see* O'Byrne's Country
Blacknall, Richard, 233
Blaghan, Edward, 233
Blake, Richard, 193, 210, 212
Blake, Sir Valentine, 247
Blayney, Arthur, 252–3
Blayney, Richard, 252–3
Blennerhasset, Robert, 245–6
Blount, Edward, 229–30
Blount, George, 258
Blundell, Sir Arthur, 257–8
Bolton, Sir Richard, political associates, 11, 39; and Castle Chamber, 72; and the Commission for Defective Titles, 81–3; impeached, 197, 211
Borlase, Captain John, 195, 253
Borlase, Sir John, and Wentworth, 195; lord justice, 197–8, 204
Bourke, David, 247, 249
Bourke of Brittas, Theobald Bourke, 1st baron, 49
Bourke, Sir Thomas, 193, 214, 247, 249
Boyle, Michael, abp. of Armagh, 129
Boyle, Michael, bp. of Waterford, 114, 121, 126
Boyle, Richard, bp. of Cork, 126
Boyle, Richard, earl of Cork, *see* Cork

287

Brabazon, Edward Brabazon, lord 230–1
Brabazon, Matthew, 251–2
Bramhall, John, bp. of Derry, his religious policy, 113–26, 183, 187; impeached, 211
Brereton, Robert, 197
Brereton, Sir William, 47
Brian, James, 234
Brice, Richard, 225–6
Bristol, John Digby, 1st earl of, 194
Brown, Sir Valentine, 245
Browne, Dominick, 247
Browne, Geoffrey, 190 n., 193, 207
Browne, Richard, 227
Buckingham, George Villiers, 1st duke of, 8, 27–9, 162–3
Buckingham, duchess of, 163–7, 180
Bulkeley, Lancelot, abp. of Dublin, 104
Butler, Edward, 228
Butler, James, 236–8
Butler, Sir Stephen, 257–8
Butler, Sir Thomas, 236–7
Bysse, John, 190 n., 256–7

Cahir, James Butler, 5th baron, 16
Carlingford, 132
Carlisle, James Hay, 1st earl of, 166, 176–7
Carlisle, Lady, 167, 178
Carpenter, Joshua, 173, 181, 196, 225–6
Carr, George, 247–8
Carrickfergus, trade of, 134–5, 144, 157
Cary, George, 258–9
Cashell, Oliver, 47 n., 225
Castle Chamber, Court of, 69–74
Castlehaven, James Touchet, 3rd earl of, 49, 194
Catelin, Nathaniel, 46, 229
Catholicism, see Counter-Reformation
Caulfield, Sir Toby, 163
Cave, Thomas, 247–8
Cavenagh, Daniel, bp. of Leighlin, 121
Chappell, William, bp. of Cork, and Trinity College, 114–15, 118
Charles I, 35, 76, 96, 185, 205, and passim
Cheevers, Garrett, 193, 212

Cheevers, Marcus, 234–5
Cheevers, Richard, 234–5
Chichester, Arthur Chichester, 1st baron, 140–1, 153, 161, 163, 171
Christabel, James, 230–1
Church of Ireland, condition of, 104–5; endowments of, 107–8; alienation of church lands in, 121, 126–9; doctrine of, 105–6; changes of episcopate, in, 113–14; Laudian policy in, 113–26; raising church revenues in 119–29; Puritanism in, 105–6; articles of, 115–16
Clancy, Boethius, 246–7
Claneboye, James Hamilton, 1st viscount, 50, 108, 163
Clanmalier, Terence O'Dempsey, 1st viscount, 49
Clanrickarde, Richard Burke, 4th earl of, 1, 15, 21, 49, 52, 68, 107; resistance to Connacht plantation, 87–93
Clanrickarde, Ulick Burke, 5th earl of, 97, 101, 185
Clifford, Henry Clifford, lord, 35
Clinton, Peter, 47 n., 225–6
Clotworthy, Sir Hugh, 145
Clotworthy, Sir John, 159, 187, 194, 196, 199, 203, 205, 206
Cockayne, Alderman, 142–4
Cogan, Robert, 37, 161–3
Coghlan, Terence, 232
Coke, John, secretary of state, his correspondence with Wentworth, passim
Colbert, 137, 184
Cole, Sir William, 40, 193, 203, 253
Coleraine, trade of, 132, 135–6, 157–8
Colley, Sir William, 232
Coman, James, 230
Comerford, Edward, 228
Comerford, Patrick, bp. of Waterford, 110, 122
Commons, house of (Ireland), elections to, 45–8; officeholders in, 45; committees in, 58, 193–4; membership in 1634, 223–59; agents of in 1640, 203; membership in 1640, 260–3
Connacht, plantation of, see Plantations
Conry, Florence, abp. of Tuam, 111
Cook, Allen, 257–8

Coote, Sir Charles, 10, 12, 39, 83, 88, 94, 247–8
Coppinger, Sir Dominick, 239
Cork, Richard Boyle, 1st earl of, 8, 9, 14, 45, 62, 73, 171, 173; his political associates, 10–11; lord justice, 13–14, 24–6, 34–41; and the 1634 elections, 47; opposition to Wentworth, 70; economic activities, 134; compared with Wentworth, 171, 173, 184–5; and the Connacht plantation, 87, 90; and the Church of Ireland, 107–8, 118–19, 121, 126–8; and Wentworth's impeachment, 200, 206
Cork, trade of, 131, 134, 137, 152
Cottington, Francis Cottington, 1st baron, 26–31, 35, 40, 186, 204
Counter-Reformation in Ireland, 15, 17, 108–12, 122; religious orders in, 109–10; politics of, 110–11; spread of, 111
Crofton, Edward, 101
Crofton, Henry, 247–8
Crofton, Richard, 101
Crofton, William, 255–6
Crosby, David, 245–6
Crosby, Sir Piers, 62, 185, 194, 233
Crosby, Sir Walter, 233
Crowe, Stephen, 244–5
Crown, expanding power of, 2
Croxton, James, 115
Cullen, John, 234
Cusack, James, 190 n., 214, 236–7
Cusacke, Adam, 227
Customs Farm, 37, 71, 159–68, 180–1

Danby, Henry Danvers, earl of, 26, 93
Darcy, Nicholas, 214
Darcy, Patrick, 63, 92–4, 127, 193, 212, 214, 227
Davis, Paul, 253
Deane, Edward, 247–8
Defective Titles, Commission for, 54, 56, 81–4, 201
Derenzi Matthew, 83, 212
Digby, George, 194
Digby, Simon, 193–4, 207, 212
Dillon, Sir James, 88–9, 189
Dillon, Sir James, the elder, 230–1
Dillon, Sir Lucas, 88, 90, 195, 247–8
Dillon, Lucas, 257–8

Dillon of Costello-Gallen, Thomas Dillon, 4th viscount, 50
Dobbins, William, 244
Docwra, Sir Henry, 11
Domvill, Gilbert, 255–6
Dongan, Sir John, 193, 212, 229
Donnellan, James, 46, 229
Donnellan, John, 97
Dormer, Nicholas, 234–5
Dowdall, Christopher, 225
Dowdall, John, 225–6
Dowdall, Lawrence, 227
Down, William Pope, earl of, 49
Downing, George, 258–9
Drogheda, trade of, 134, 135–7, 152, 157–8
Dublin, trade of, 131, 136, 152, 157
Dulan, James, 228
Dundalk, trade of, 154, 157–9
Dungarvan, Richard Boyle, 2nd viscount, 35, 127
Dunsany, Patrick Plunkett, 9th baron, 214

Edmonds, Thomas, 247
Elwall, Thomas, 244–5
Erle, Sir Walter, 205
Erskine, Sir James, 254
Erskine Richard, 254
Esmond, William, 234
Eustace, Maurice, 229–30
Everard, Sir John, 18, 58
Everard, Thomas, 242–3
Evers, Walter, 227

Falkland, Henry Cary, 1st viscount, 11, 21, 24–7, 35, 70, 88–9, 116, 153, 163, 171, 179
Farrell, Faigney, 233
Farrell, Roger, 233
Fenton, Sir William, 47, 244
Fermoy, David Roche, 7th viscount 16, 49
Fermoy, Maurice Roche, 8th viscount, 206
Ferries, Robert, 258
Finance, 32–41; see also Customs Farm; Court of Wards and Liveries; Commission for Defective Titles; Subsidies; Licences; Taxation
Fingall, Luke Plunkett, 1st earl of, 15–16, 21, 44, 49, 52, 55–6, 121

Fingall, Christopher, 2nd earl of, 210, 214
FitzGerald, John, 245–6
FitzGerald, Sir Lucas, 230–1
FitzGerald, Maurice, 193, 212, 229
FitzGerald, Richard, 159, 193, 203–4, 254–5
FitzHarris, Sir Edward, 16, 58, 201, 241
FitzMaurice, James, 1, 108
FitzWilliam of Merrion, Thomas FitzWilliam, 1st viscount, 49
Fortescue, Chichester, 256–7
Fortescue, Sir Faithful, 47
Fox, John, 241
Fullerton, James, 106
Furlong, Walter, 234

Galbreth, James, 255
Galway, Sir Geoffrey, 241
Galway, jury, 90, 95, 202; trade of, 131, 132–3
Galway, William, 239
Gilbert, Sir William, 233
Goodwin, Robert, 258–9
Gookin, Vincent, 65, 73
Gormanston, Nicholas Preston, 6th viscount, 15, 21, 38, 49, 210, 214
Gough, Edward, 239–40
Gough, Patrick, 206
Gough, Sir Thomas, 242
Grace, Robert, 228
Graces, The, 20–3, 33, 44, 53–64, 146
Graham, Sir Richard, 175
Graham, William, 175–6
Grandison, Oliver St. John, 1st viscount, 25, 33, 153, 171–2

Hadsor, Richard, 144
Haley, John, 242
Haley, Simon, 241
Hamilton, Archibald, 212
Hamilton, James, 106, 251
Hampton, Christopher, abp. of Armagh, 112
Harrington, Sir Henry, 176
Haynes, Thomas, 242–3
Henry VIII, and Ireland, 3
High Commission, Court of, 69, 116–17, 207
Hilton, William, 256–7
Hore, David, 234
Hore, John FitzMahowgue, 244

Hopwood, Michael, 38
Howth, Nicholas St. Lawrence, 1st lord, 214
Hoye, John, 237–8
Huckett, John, 228
Hume, Sir John, 253
Hussey, Patrick, 227

Ikerrin, Pierce Butler, 1st viscount, 49
Ingersoll, John, 233
Ingram, Sir Arthur, 27, 37, 161–5, 180

Jackson, John, 247–8
Jephson, Sir John, 107
Jigginstown House, 172–3, 178–9
Jones, Arthur, 247–8
Jones, Oliver, 194, 212
Jones, Sir Roger, 101, 148, 247
Juxon, William, bp. of London, 91

Kavanagh, Morgan, 236–7
Keating, Edward, 230, 232
Keely, James, 228
Kildare, George FitzGerald, 1st earl of, 49, 52
Kilkenny West, Robert Dillon, lord of, later earl of Roscommon, 72, 88, 195, 204, 207, 227
Kinaston, Edward, 252–3
King, Sir Robert, 101, 206, 247–8
Kingsmill, William, 239–40
Kippoke, Thomas, 225–6
Knox, Andrew, bp. of Raphoe, 105–6

Lambart, Charles Lambart, 2nd baron, 211
Lancaster, John, bp. of Lismore, 126
Laud, William, abp. of Canterbury, 29–31, 93, 112, 115, 118–19, 185, 186
Leake, Thomas, 255–6
Leicester, Robert, 232
Leslie, Henry, bp. of Down, 114, 116–17
Ley, Sir James, 28, 144
Licences, 62–3; for wool, 140, 146, 148–9; for tobacco, 182–3
Little, Thomas, 47, 196, 242–3
Livingston, John, 105–6
Loftus, Adam Loftus, 1st viscount, 44, 70; his political associates, 11–14; links with Wentworth, 27, 42,

50; fall from power, 72; and the Church of Ireland, 108, 121; acquisition of land, 174, 236; and Wentworth's impeachment, 200

Loftus, Sir Adam, 136, 150, 157; links with Wentworth, 42, 195; rise to power, 71-2; and the Commission for Defective Titles, 81; and the Customs Farm, 164; and the tobacco monopoly, 182; political influence, 234-6

Loftus, Sir Arthur, 234, 236

Loftus, Nicholas, 234, 236

Loftus, Sir Robert, 251-2

Lombard, Peter, abp. of Armagh, 110-11

Long John, abp. of Armagh, 121

Lords, House of (Ireland), composition of, in 1634, 48-52; nonresident peers in, 51

Lort, Roger, 234

Lowther, Sir Gerald, 71-2, 197; and the Commission for Defective Titles, 81-3; impeached, 211

Luttrell, Sir Thomas, 229

Lynch, Sir Henry, 87, 247

Lynch, Sir Nicholas, 247

Lynch, Sir Roebuck, 193, 206

MacCarty, Sir Donough, 193, 206, 239

MacCaughwell, Hugh, abp. of Armagh, 111

MacDonnell, see Antrim

MacMahon, Art Oge, 252

MacMahon, Coll Brian, 252

Maguire, Rory, 189, 194

Mainwaring, Philip, 47, 195, 239-40

Mainwaring, Roger, 47, 195, 255-6

Maltravers, Lord Henry, 228

Mansell, Thomas, 247

Martin, Richard, 92-4, 127, 247

Maude, Robert, 196

Maxwell, John, bp. of Killala, 114

Meath, William Brabazon, 1st earl of, 176

Melville, Andrew, 106

Meredith, Sir Robert, 73, 83, 254-255

Meredith, Sir Thomas, 251

Mervin, Audley, 194, 197, 211-12

Middlesex, Lionel Cranfield, ear of, 27, 141, 145, 163

Mockler, Geoffrey, 242-3

Monck, Charles, 165-6, 254-5

Montgomery, Hugh, 251

Montgomery, Hugh Montgomery, 1st viscount, 50

Montgomery, Sir James, 193, 203

Moore, Arthur, 256-7

Moore, Thomas, 232

Mountgarret, Richard Butler, 3rd viscount, 16, 49

Mountnorris, Francis Annesley, 1st baron, 8, 9, 27, 42, 49, 90, 93, 159, 180, 185; his rise to power, 11-14; alliance with Wentworth, 35-41; and the Customs Farm, 163-5; his fall from power, 70-2; and Wentworth's impeachment, 200, 206

Mun, Thomas, 138

Murphy, Griffin, 228

Muskerry, Charles MacCarthy, 1st viscount, 16, 49

Netterville, Lucas, 229

Netterville, Nicholas Netterville, 1st viscount, 38, 49, 107, 121, 214

Nevill, Pierce, 234-5

Newcomen, Arthur, 258

Newcomen, Sir Beverley, 245-6

Newcomen, Thomas, 234, 236

Nugent, Francis, 17, 110

Nugent, Sir Thomas, 101

Nugent, Thomas, 230-1

O'Brien, Sir Barnaby, 236-7, 247

O'Brien, Sir Daniel, 246-7

O'Byrne, Feagh MacHugh, 175

O'Byrne, Phelim MacFeagh, 175

O'Byrne's Country, plantation of, 173-8

O'Connor, Tadgh, 247, 249

O'Donnell, Hugh, 3-6, 85

O'Gara, Farrell, 247, 249

'Old English' interest, 15-23; leaders, 15-17; economic power, 17, 137; excluded from political power, 17-18; and the agitation for the Graces, 20-3; and Poynings' Law, 22; role in parliament in 1634, 53 ff; in the 1640 parliament, 192-3, 197, 210-13; and Wentworth's impeachment, 200-8; and the rising of 1641, 214

O'Neale, Brian, 193, 212

O'Neill, Hugh, earl of Tyrone, 1, 3–6, 85, 108, 175
O'Neill, Sir Phelim, 188, 198
O'Reilly, Hugh, abp. of Armagh, 111
Ormonde, James Butler, 12th earl of, 38, 49, 52, 105, 211
O'Shaghness, Sir Robert, 247
O'Shaghnessy, Sir Roger, 92–4

Parkhurst, Alderman Robert, 101
Parliament (Ireland), in sixteenth century, 2, 22; in 1615, 19, 33; see also Commons and Lords
Parsons, Richard, 234, 236
Parsons, Sir William, political associates, 10, 11, 39, 55; and the Court of Wards, 71, 75, 81; and the Commission for Defective Titles, 81–4; stays in power under Wentworth, 72, 195; and the Wicklow plantation, 174, 175–6; estates elsewhere, 256–7; as lord justice, 212
Peere, Lott, 239–40
Peppard, Thomas, 225–6
Percival, Philip, 100, 176, 204
Percival, Richard, 75
Pesely, Bartholomew, 47, 173
Petition of Remonstrance (1640), 201–6
Pettit, Edward, 230–1
Pierce, Pierce FitzJames, 245–6
Pigott, John, 233
Pigott, Richard, 232
Pilsworth, Philip, 229–30
Plantations of Leitrim, 86–7; of Longford, 86–7; of Ulster, 3, 33; of Connacht, 55–6, 80, 85–103; reversal of 190–1, 201, 202, 205, 207; of Wicklow, 174–8
Plunkett, Sir Christopher, 145
Plunkett, Nicholas, 190 n., 193, 204–206, 214, 227
Porter, Endymion, 166
Portland, Richard Weston, 1st earl of, 13, 25, 29–31, 88–90, 95, 118, 130, 148, 163, 169
Power, John, 244
Powerscourt, Richard Wingfield, 1st viscount, 49
Poynings' Law, 22, 55–7, 206, 211
Privy Council (England), 7, 33, 39
Privy Council (Ireland), 8, 45; political groups in 8–14, 25–6; opposition to Wentworth in, 42, 45, 48
Purcell, Theobald, 242
Puritanism, 105–6
Pym, John, 192, 201, 205

Queries, The, 210–13

Radcliffe, Sir George, 36, 83, 101, 135, 163, 165, 173–4, 180, 195, 256–7; impeached, 211
Radcliffe, Thomas, 195
Raleigh, Sir Walter, 126
Ranelagh, Roger Jones, 1st viscount, political associates, 11; alliance with Fingall, 52, 55–6; and the plantation of Connacht, 94; and Wentworth's impeachment, 159, 195–6, 206; and the Wicklow plantation, 174; and the Customs Farm, 163
Recusancy fines, 39
Reformation in Ireland, 3, 104–8
Religion, 80; see also Church of Ireland; Counter-Reformation; Puritanism; Reformation
Revenue, rise in, 169–70; see also Finance
Reynolds, Charles, 247–8
Reynolds, Paul, 251–2
Rice, Dominick, 245–6
Richelieu, 74
Rinuccini, Jean Baptist, abp. of Fermo, 109
Roche, Jacob, 239
Rochfort, Hugh, 197, 214
Rockingham, Charles Watson-Wentworth, 2nd marquis of, 171
Ronane, Theobald, 239–40
Rooth, David, 228
Rooth, Peter, 234–5
Rothe, David, bp. of Ossory, 112
Rothe, Thomas, 234
Rotherham, Sir Thomas, 247–9
Rowley, Edward, 193, 203, 258–9
Ryves, Sir William, 257–8

St. Leger, Sir William, 46, 197, 239
St. Patrick's Cathedral, Dublin, 118
Sambach, William, 190, 196
Sandys, Sir Edward, 145
Sarsfield, Sir William, 239
Scott, Richard, 247

Shee, Robert, 228
Sherlock, Christopher, 229–30
Sherlock, Patrick, 228
Sibthorp, Robert, bp. of Kilfenora, 114
Skipwith, Edward, 239–40
Slane, William Fleming, 14th lord, 210
Slingsby, Gerard, 237–8
Smith, Sir Pierce, 244
Southwell, Sir Richard, 246–7
Spottiswood, Sir Henry, 254
Spottiswood, James, abp. of St. Andrews, 105
Stanhope, Sir Edward, 30, 37
Stanhope, Michael, 255–6
Staple towns, 149–53
Stewart, Sir William, 253
Strabane, James Hamilton, 1st baron of, 49
Strafford, Thomas Wentworth, 1st earl of, personality, 6, 32; policy towards the Catholics, 23, 43–4; appointment as lord deputy, 27–31; views on foreign policy, 27–8, 100; financial policy, 33–41; and the Irish Privy Council, 42–3; and the elections of 1634, 45–8; and the Irish House of Lords, 50; his parliamentary policy, 53–68; and the Graces, 57–64; struggle with Mountnorris, 70–2; and Castle Chamber, 69–74; and the Court of Wards, 74–81; and the Commission for Defective Titles, 81–4; and the Connacht plantation, 88–103; his religious policy, 109, 113–29; and the tobacco monopoly, 137; and the Irish wool trade, 147–53; and the Irish linen trade, 154–9; and the Customs Farm, 159–68; personal gains in Ireland, 171–84; expenditure, 179; income, 179–83
Strange, Richard, 244
Subsidies, 33–4, 42–3

Taaffe, John Taaffe, 1st viscount, 49
Taaffe, Theobald, 189, 214
Talbot, Sir Robert, 237–8
Talles, Thomas, 255–6
Taxation, 33–4, 42–3
Taylor, Brockhall, 257–8
Taylor, John, 193, 212

Terringham, Sir Arthur, 47, 251–2
Thomond, Henry O'Brien, 5th earl of, 49, 52, 105, 107
Tichbourne, Sir Henry, 254
Tilson, Henry, bp. of Elphin, 114
Trade, Irish, with Europe, 131–4; with Scotland, 135; with England, 135–7; old English share in, 137; improvement of 167–8; in linen, 135, 154–6; in wool, 135–6, 137–153; in wine, 131–2, in cattle, 136; in tobacco, 137, 182–3
Travers, John, 225
Travers, Sir Robert, 239–40
Trevor, Sir Edward, 251–2
Trinity College, Dublin, 46–7, 114–115, 118
Tristeene, Sir John, 145
Turner, Patrick, 234–5
Tyrrell, Peter, 227

Ulster, plantation of see Plantations
Ulster Irish, 1, 3–6
Unwin, George, 137
Usher, William, 237–8
Ussher, James, abp. of Armagh, 105–106, 108, 112, 114, 117–19, 124; see also Chapter 10 passim
Ussher, Robert, bp. of Kildare, 115

Vaughan, Sir John, 255

Wadding, Luke, 16, 110–11
Waller, Sir Hardress, 193, 201, 241
Walsh, Jacob, 1, 244
Walsh, James, 228
Walsh, John, 193, 206
Wandesford, Sir Christopher, Master of the Rolls, 71; lord deputy, 189–192, 201; in 1634 parliament, 229
Wards and Liveries, Commission for, 75
Wards and Liveries, Court of ('England), 75
Wards and Liveries, Court of (Ireland), 69, 74–81
Ware, Sir James, 46, 83, 197, 229
Ware, John, 233–4
Waterford, trade of, 131, 136
Weasley, Valerian, 227
Webb, George, bp. of Limerick, 114
Wentworth, George, 47, 148, 239–40
West, John, 166–7

Westmeath, Richard Nugent, 1st earl of, leader of the 'old English' party 15–16; and the Graces, 21; and Wentworth, 38–41; a new peerage, 49; and the Connacht plantation, 89, 101; and the Church of Ireland, 107, 123; opposition to Wentworth, 185, 214

Wharton, Sir Thomas, 195

White, Dominick, 241

White, Sir Nicholas, 229

White, Henry, 242

White, Walter, 251–2

Williams, John, bp. of Lincoln, 27–8

Williams, Maurice, 47, 196, 241

Wilmot, Charles Wilmot, 1st viscount, 11, 73, 206

Windebank, Francis, 188

Wingfield, Edward, 176

Wiseman, William, 239–40

Wolverston, John, 176

Youghal, trade of, 136, 152–3